Flexible Input, Dazzling Output with IBM i

Rafael Victória-Pereira

MC Press Online, LLC
Boise, ID 83703 USA

Flexible Input, Dazzling Output with IBM i

Rafael Victória-Pereira

First Edition

MC Press Online, LLC

Corporate Offices: 3695 W. Quail Heights Court, Boise, ID 83703-3861 USA
Sales and Customer Service: (208) 629-7275 ext. 500; service@mcpressonline.com
Permissions and Bulk/Special Orders: mcbooks@mcpressonline.com
www.mcpressonline.com • www.mc-store.com

ISBN: 978-1-58347-832-5 WB201409

To my wife, Ana

And my sons, David and Lucas—never give up on your dreams,
work hard and make them come true. . . .

Acknowledgments

Ex nihilo omnia — From a blank page, a book

First of all, I'd like to thank you, dear reader, for investing your time in this book.

I'd like to thank Victoria Mack, long-time editor of my TechTips, for believing in my ability to write; Katie Tipton, book editor; Marianne Krcma, editor of this work; and the rest of the dedicated staff at MC Press who made it happen.

A big, big thanks to David Shirey of Shirey LLC and Scott Palma of Arbor Solutions. Without their help, this book simply wouldn't be. Thanks for showing me that there are still good Samaritans out there!

I also would like to thank Paulo Xarez, for helping me (in a very unique way) find the time to write this book. No hard feelings!

Finally, a special word for those who helped with the code, ideas, and general mayhem throughout the years: Paulo Ferreira, Rui Oliveira, David Pereira, and João Roque of LeasePlan Portugal.

If I forgot someone, which is highly likely, and you are that someone, please find it in your heart to forgive my lapse! ☺

Contents

Introduction

In the old days, our beloved server was, in many cases, the only one used by the company to perform its business. That's no longer true.

IBM i is no longer an island.

This book is about building bridges that link your IBM® i system to the modern business server world. It will show you easier and more flexible ways to get data into IBM i, along with rather surprising methods to export and present the vital business data it contains. It will help you automate file transfers, seamlessly connect PC applications with your RPG programs, and much more.

Your input operations will become more flexible and user-proof (even though, of course, a totally user-proof system is just a myth), with self-correcting import processes and direct file transfers that work a minimum of user intervention. Your DB2® data will look great on program-generated Microsoft® Excel® spreadsheets and browser-based, interactive charts, ranging from simple bar charts to complex charts with data tables.

All the solutions presented here are either based on existing open source tools or created from scratch by the author. The full source code is included (via download from the book's page at *http://www.mc-store.com*), along with sample programs that are easy to understand and adapt. This will help you integrate these input/output methods into your own applications, providing flexible, integrated, and modern solutions. All of this is done with RPG Integrated Language Environment® (ILE) programs, avoiding the increased complexity of new servers and programming languages.

Upon completing this book, you will:

- Have new ways to link your IBM i system to the outside world
- Have learned how to automate boring tasks, like file transfers
- Be able to create, read, and write files on the IFS from an RPG program
- Know how to prevent and correct user errors on CSV import files
- Be able to create beautiful interactive charts directly from your RPG code, without having to learn a new programming language
- Be able to easily integrate Microsoft Windows®-based applications with your IBM i programs
- Have your RPG programs produce professional-looking spreadsheets instead of ugly printouts
- Have gained a set of open source, free tools that will help you solve everyday problems with ease and style
- Be inspired to expand what you've learned, creating your own solutions for better output

Book Structure and Organization

This book is divided into two parts: "Flexible Input" and "Dazzling Output." The first part explains how to automate data transfers and make text file uploading to your DB2 database more user-friendly and less IT-dependent, thus making your inputs more flexible. "Dazzling Output" might seem an overstatement, but the second part of the book contains ideas that will surprise you. Hopefully, it will have you thinking, "Wow, I never thought I could do that with only RPG!" It includes Excel file creation as a way to (easily) replace those ugly printer files that still lurk around your application (yes, we all have some), among other things.

This book also includes a bonus part, "Going Global." It includes two chapters about geo-referencing entities in your database and collecting geo-related information for your company and its clients' benefit.

Each chapter is divided into several parts, but should be read as a whole. It's also important to mention that some chapters are linked, because they use what was discussed before as a basis for something new. Each chapter begins with an introduction, which includes its highlights and what you should know to fully enjoy it (knowledge of a certain technology/language, familiarity with material in other chapters, and so on).

Naming Conventions

The source code contained in this book follows a few naming conventions:

- File names:
  - All the physical file names start with *PF*.
  - All logical file names start with *LF*.
- Variables:
  - *W_* identifies a work variable.
  - *P_* identifies a parameter variable (usually a parameter of a procedure or function).
  - *K_* indicates that the variable is part of a key list.
  - *I_* indicates that the variable is an indicator (Boolean) variable, usually containing **On* or **Off*.
  - *C_* is used for constants.

Generic Compilation Instructions

The source code presented in this book is composed mostly of procedures, neatly contained in modules, which in turn are part of service programs. In order to get the sample programs to work, you might have to recompile some or all of the source code.

To compile RPGLE modules, use this command:

```
CRTRPGMOD MODULE(<MODULE_LIB>/<MODULE_NAME>) SRCFILE(<MODULE_LIB>/QRPGLESRC)
DBGVIEW(*SOURCE)
```

To compile SQLRPGLE modules, the following command should be used:

```
CRTSQLRPGI OBJ(<MODULE_LIB>/<MODULE_NAME>) SRCFILE(<MODULE_LIB>/QRPGLESRC)
SRCMBR(*OBJ) COMMIT(*NONE) OBJTYPE(*MODULE) DBGVIEW(*SOURCE)
USRPRF(*OWNER) DYNUSRPRF(*OWNER)
```

To compile service programs, this is the appropriate command:

```
CRTSRVPGM SRVPGM(<SRVPGM_LIB>/<SRVPGM_NAME>) EXPORT(*ALL)
TEXT(<SRVPGM_TEXT>) BNDDIR(<SRVPGM_LIB>/<SRVPGM_NAME>) ACTGRP(<SRVPGM_LIB>)
OPTION(*DUPPROC *DUPVAR) ALWLIBUPD(*YES) USRPRF(*OWNER)
```

To compile programs, use this command:

```
CRTPGM PGM(<PGM_LIB>/<PGM_NAME>) BNDDIR(<PGM_LIB>/<PGM_NAME>) ACTGRP(<PGM_LIB>)
OPTION(*DUPVAR *DUPPROC) ALWLIBUPD(*YES) USRPRF(*OWNER)
```

Open Source Tools Used in This Book

This book includes a lot of code that was created from scratch, but there are some cases in which it didn't make sense to reinvent the wheel, so to speak. In those instances, I resorted to a handful of open source software and expanded upon its functionality. Here's a list of what is used throughout the book:

- *Mime and Mail (MMail)*—This open source utility (library MMAIL) for IBM i allows you to create, send, and receive MIME (Multipurpose Internet Mail Extensions) files. It is authored by Giovanni B. Perotti, a brilliant Italian programmer. The software is frequently updated, so I recommend that you download the latest release and read the documentation from the tool's Web page:

  http://mmail.easy400.net
- *CGIDEV2*—Another of Giovanni's great tools, CGIDEV2 was actually created by Rochester IBMer Mel Rothman back in 1996. Giovanni took over a few years later and has maintained the tool ever since. This tool facilitates the communication between a Web page and your IBM i system. In several chapters, it's used to invoke REST (Representational State Transfer) Web services, so it's a good idea to download the latest version and read the documentation. You can find it here:

  http://cgidev2.easy400.net
- *POI-HSSF*—This pure Java® open source implementation of Excel file creation is used extensively in chapter 6. Don't be scared by the "pure Java open source implementation" bit. Scott Klement, another of the people I look up

to in the IBM i world, wrote a set of procedures that facilitate the use of this tool without knowing the least bit of Java. Be sure to read the documentation from Apache's POI Web site and any articles that you might find online about POI, because this is a very powerful and useful tool. You can download the necessary source code from Scott's POI page:

http://www.scottklement.com/poi

- *IFS tool*—Scott also wrote a nice little tool that makes reading and writing IFS text files from RPG much easier. I use it in chapter 5 to fix some common user errors found in CSV files. This is also a free tool, which you can download here:

  http://www.scottklement.com/rpg/ifs.html

PART ONE

Flexible Input

1

Automate Data Transfers Using FTP

> This chapter addresses ways to automate FTP data transfers, by showing you how to create batch files and FTP scripts. These files and scripts were designed to work on a Windows client, but should be adaptable to any other platform that supports FTP and some sort of command-line script files. Because FTP raises security issues, the concept of authorization lists is explained, with a practical example and the main advantages of using them.

Back in the old days, when our beloved server was called AS/400®, there were few, if any, "satellite systems" like PC servers that needed to pass data to it or receive data from it. Today, it's a totally different landscape: IBM i sits together with a broad range of servers and devices with which it has to communicate, sending and receiving data. These interfaces are, at times, manual data imports or exports, performed by operators via boring and repetitive procedures.

Let's start with the basics. One of the most commonly used procedures to transfer data from/to IBM i is FTP.

There are a few things that you need to make sure of before you start. First, the IBM i FTP server must be started. Ideally, it should be in "auto-start mode"—starting automatically when the *STRTCP* command is issued. You can check that by typing ***CHGFTPA*** and pressing F4. You should get a screen similar to the one shown in Figure 1.1.

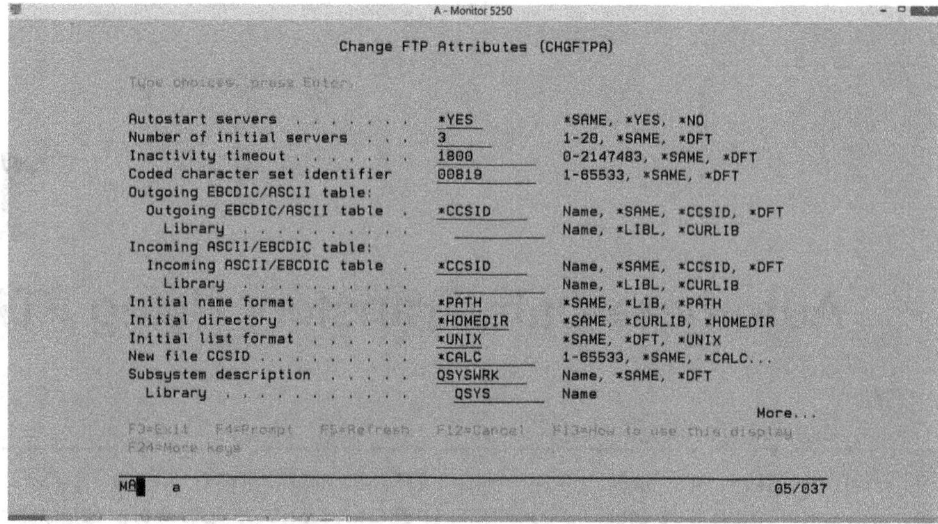

Figure 1.1: Starting the IBM i FTP server.

The first parameter, "Autostart servers" should be set to ****YES***, as it is in Figure 1.1. However, having FTP servers running automatically can be a security issue. Make sure that your data libraries have the correct authority using authorization lists to keep them under control, for instance, to prevent data-related issues. (Later in this chapter you'll learn what authorization lists are and how to set them up.)

If you prefer (or have to) keep the FTP servers off, then all you need to do is issue the following command to start them:

```
STRTCPSVR SERVER(*FTP)
```

Once you're done transferring data, use this command to stop the FTP servers:

```
ENDTCPSVR SERVER(*FTP)
```

Finally, test your connection by opening a command line and typing this:

```
ftp <system_name>
```

If the FTP server is active on your IBM i system, you will be asked to enter user name and password before you're granted access. It's possible that even though the FTP server is running and the user and password are correct, you won't be able to use FTP. This might happen due to authority limitations on your user profile (specifically the "Limit capabilities" parameter, if set to **YES*), or some security limitations enforced by third-party tools (such as PowerLock from PowerTech, for instance). If you run into these kind of problems, I'd recommend that you check with your systems administrator.

Now that you have your FTP up and running on IBM i, we can begin. Throughout this chapter, I'll be referring to FTP started on a Windows PC. This might sound strange, but since Windows is (still) one of the most used file servers and desktop software out there, I think it makes sense.

You can start an FTP session via a command line and use it interactively to transfer data—that's part of the boring procedure mentioned earlier. So, let's automate the data transfer. Using a batch file to invoke the FTP command and a script file to perform the data transfer actions, you avoid typing the same thing over and over.

FTP has some options to perform "batch transfers." Let's start with option ***–n***. This option tells the FTP command not to ask for the username and password when the FTP session is initiated. Then, in order to run the transfer, you need to use a script file (which will contain the commands to perform) and tell the FTP where it's located. This is done using the option ***–s:<script file name>***. Finally, you have to indicate the target system name. So, your batch file should look a bit like this, where *U:\Scripts\MyScript.scp* indicates the name and location of the script and *MyIBMi* indicates the target system name:

```
@echo Transferring file
@echo Off
```

```
ftp -n -s:U:\Scripts\MyScript.scp MYIBMi
```

Of course, this is usually not that simple. You will probably need to change to the proper folder or rename the file to be transferred (or perform some other actions, using DOS commands). You can add entry parameters to your batch file to achieve that. Here's another example:

```
@echo Transferring file %1
@echo Off
H:
CD\
rename %1 myfile.txt
```

```
ftp -n -s:U:\Scripts\MyScript.scp MYIBMi
```

This batch file will change to path *H:*, rename the entry parameter (%1) file name to *myfile.txt*, and execute *myscript.scp*, which resides on *U:\Scripts* on system *MyIBMi*.

The use of entry parameters on the batch file is especially useful because you cannot pass parameters into the script file—it's a kind of black box of commands to execute, without any flexibility. Of course, there are many ways to circumvent this lack of flexibility. Later in this book, when the import of CSV files is discussed, I'll show you a way to rewrite the import script right before the transfer!

Finally, let's see how the script file is composed. Since we're using the *–n* option, which removes the prompt for username and password, the first command of any script should always be the login:

```
User username password logs you into your system.
```

Keep in mind that this is a security risk—you're storing a username and password in a text file, somewhere on a file system! You might want to create a user who cannot sign on interactively to your IBM i system and has very basic authorities. For instance, the user might only have access to the IFS folder or library where it gets or puts the files to be transferred. Also, make sure you have your data libraries properly secured with an authorization list.

After the login, you'll have to indicate the commands to be executed. These are standard FTP commands, like *cd, lcd, put, get*, and so on. Again, keep in mind that the script doesn't have any flexibility, so you have to use fixed directories and IFS folders/libraries on the data transfers.

Here's an example of a complete script file:

```
user myuser mypassword
cd /textfiledir
put myfile.txt
quit
```

Note that FTP is case-sensitive, so be sure to type all commands in lower case. This script, together with the batch file mentioned before, transfers the file indicated when you invoke the batch file to the IFS folder */textfiledir*, under the name *myfile.txt*. Suppose your batch file is named *mybatch.bat*. If you type the following on a command line, you'll be transferring file *h:\inventory.txt* to the IFS folder *\textfiledir*, under the name *myfile.txt*:

```
Mybatch.bat inventory.txt
```

If you're familiar with the concept of authorization lists and how to use them, move on to the next chapter. Otherwise, keep reading.

Authorization Lists

Do you really understand what authorization lists are and what they do? Securing a file, program, or other object with an authorization list is the same as granting access to each user profile on the authorization list. To help understand the concept, think of an authorization as two sub-lists.

The first sub-list holds a register of users (or groups) and their authorities. Each user on the authorization list can have a different authority level. You can add a group profile to an authorization list, which in practical terms means the same thing as putting each member of the group on the authorization list.

The second sub-list enumerates the objects secured by the authorization list. Authorization lists can secure any object type except a user profile or another authorization list. Different types of objects can be mixed on the same list. Each user's access from the first list applies to the objects on the second list. (Actually, this is not exactly how the authorization list is implemented in the system, but it gives you an idea of how it works, for now.)

Each authority level grants different accesses to IBM i objects:

- **ALL* is fairly obvious. A user or group profile with **ALL* authority for an object can do anything with that object, such as change the attributes, change ownership, or delete it. You should be careful, of course, when granting **ALL* authority. You'll understand why when your main accounting history file (or something worse) mysteriously disappears.
- **CHANGE* lets the user or group profile change the object, but this authority means slightly different things for different types of objects. For example, the user can clear, read, or change the records in a database file. With a program or command object, however, the user can only use the object. **CHANGE* authority does not allow users to delete an object or change any of its security attributes (such as the object's owner).
- **USE* also has slightly different effects on different object types. For a database file, it means users get read-only access. For a program or command object, users can only call (execute) it.
- **EXCLUDE*, the fourth specific authority, isn't really an authority at all. It means that users don't have any access to the object. You might call this setting the anti-authority.

In other words, an authorization list contains user (or group) names and their respective authority levels. Changing an object's security attributes to use a certain authorization list is like putting a bouncer at a club's entrance: anytime someone tries to access the object, that user's authority over the object is checked, and the access is granted or not.

The Authority-Checking Process for Objects Using Authorization Lists

When a user tries to access an object that is secured by an authorization list, the system performs authority checks, as discussed in the following list (previously published at *http://www.mcpressonline.com/security/ibm-i-os400-i5os/authorization-list-internals.html* in the article "Authorization List Internals"):

1. *The system determines if there is any private authority to the object. If there aren't any, the system jumps to step 3.*
2. *The user profile is searched for the virtual address of the object (specific authority). If the user is the owner of the object, access is determined directly from the object header, without any profile search. If the*

profile contains the address of the object, the authority to the object is retrieved from the user profile.

3. *If the user does not have private authority over the object, the system replaces the virtual address of the object with the virtual address of the authorization list. The user profile is searched for the virtual address of the authorization list. If the profile contains the address of the authorization list, the authority to the object is retrieved from the user profile. (This is actually the user's authority to the authorization list, but this authority will be used for the object access).*
4. *If no authority is found, steps 1-3 are repeated for the group profile.*
5. *If no authority is found, the *PUBLIC authority is retrieved from the object header.*
6. *If the *PUBLIC authority of the object indicates *AUTL, the system uses the *PUBLIC authority from the authorization list header rather than the object header.*

Now, let's consolidate all that information with an example.

Company X has a human resources application running on its system. Several users from different departments need to access the application for various purposes:

- John and Mary, from the HR department, must be able to use the application in their daily work, managing the HR.
- Steve, from accounting, only needs to read the HR records to process the salaries of the staff.
- Bruce, the internal auditor, wants to run some queries over the HR application's database to ensure consistency and compliance with the internal procedures.
- Tommy, the new programmer, is a nosy kid who wants to know how much money everyone else makes . . . and he shouldn't be allowed to!

Assume that the application has only one library, called HR_APP, where all its objects (programs and files) reside. With this information, we're ready to create our first authorization list, using this command:

```
CRTAUTL AUTL(P_HR_AUTL) TEXT('Production HR App Authorization List') AUT(*EXCLUDE)
```

Now, let's add the users, according to their access requirements.

John and Mary (from HR) need sufficient access to change and delete records. We might be tempted to give them **ALL* authority, but keep in mind that they might accidentally delete a program or file. **CHANGE* should be enough for their needs:

```
ADDAUTLE AUTL(P_HR_AUTL) USER(JOHN MARY) AUT(*CHANGE)
```

Steve and Bruce, from accounting and internal audit, respectively, need the same type of access, read-only. This is implemented as **USE*, because (as mentioned before) this authority corresponds to different behaviors, depending on the object type: they should be able to execute programs, but be unable to change data. Here's how to grant them the necessary authority:

```
ADDAUTLE AUTL(P_HR_AUTL) USER(STEVE BRUCE) AUT(*USE)
```

Finally, we need to do something about Tommy! There are at least two ways to solve the problem: deny him access explicitly (by adding him to the authorization list with **EXCLUDE*) or implicitly (by setting the **PUBLIC* authority of the authorization list to **EXCLUDE*). I recommend you use the **PUBLIC* authority, because you never know how many "Tommies" (and I'm not talking about programmers or IT staff only!) you might have in your organization.

Note that the last parameter (*AUT*) of the authorization list creation command was set to **EXCLUDE* in the beginning of this example. This will be the authority given to all the users and groups not mentioned in the authorization list. Although the *AUT* parameter contains **CHANGE* by default, always setting it to **EXCLUDE* is considered good practice. Of course, you can always change the **PUBLIC* authority after creating the authorization list.

Next, we should change the security attributes of all the objects in library HR_APP in order to have them under our authorization list control:

```
GRTOBJAUT OBJ(HR_APP/*ALL) OBJTYPE(*ALL) AUTL(P_HR_AUTL)
```

Finally, to ensure that the objects don't have any private authorities (defined directly on the object) and that the **PUBLIC* authority won't compromise your security scheme, make sure that all the objects are under full authorization list control with the following two commands:

```
RVKOBJAUT OBJ(HR_APP/*ALL) OBJTYPE(*ALL) USER(*ALL) AUT(*ALL)
GRTOBJAUT OBJ(HR_APP/*ALL) OBJTYPE(*ALL) USER(*PUBLIC) AUT(*AUTL)
```

The first command revokes (removes) any private authorities that might exist on HR_APP's objects. The second command changes the **PUBLIC* authority of all the objects in HR_APP library to use the authorization list's **PUBLIC* authority.

You should submit these commands to batch and schedule them for a date and time when the application is not being used (in other words, the library and its objects are not locked by interactive or batch jobs).

To complete our little example, note that the Work with Authorization Lists (*WRKAUTL*) command enables you to easily manage the authorization lists, as shown in Figure 1.2.

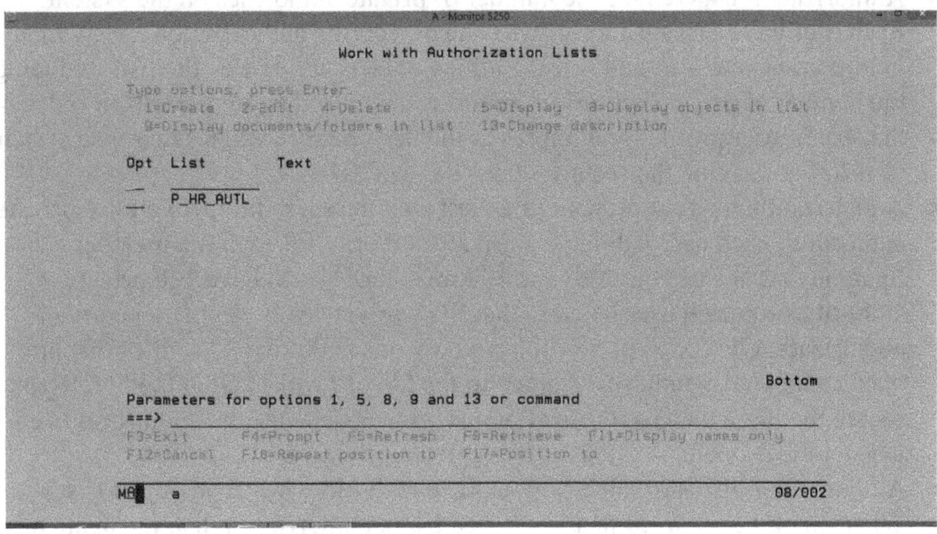

Figure 1.2: With WRKAUTL, you can easily manage your authorization lists.

You could improve this authorization list by creating a group for the HR users and replacing their individual authorities on the authorization list by the group.

This is just an example, a starting point. You should analyze and plan carefully each authorization list that you create on your system.

Selling It to Your SysAdmin

Using authorization lists offers many advantages for those people charged with maintaining system and data security. A well-structured authorization scheme that includes both user groups and authorization lists by application or library type allows for better control over the whole system, thus preventing unpleasant surprises and reducing the risk of unauthorized access. Here's a brief list of advantages of using authorization lists:

- User authority is defined for the authorization list, not for the individual objects on the list. This means that if a new object is secured by the authorization list, the users on the list automatically gain authority to the object, even if the object is being used by another process.
- One operation can be used to give a user authority to all the objects on the list, thus simplifying the security officer's work.
- Authorization lists reduce the number of private authorities on the system. Each user has a private authority to one object (the authorization list), which in turn grants the user authority to all the objects secured by the list. Reducing the number of private authorities in the system also has advantages: it reduces the size of user profiles and improves the performance when saving the system (*SAVSYS*) or saving the security data (*SAVSECDTA*).
- Authorization lists are probably the best way to secure files. If you use private authorities, each user will have a private authority for each file member. Imagine that one of your files has 100 members; you'll have 100 private authorities for each user listed in that file's private authority! If you use an authorization list, each user will have only one authority. Also, files that are open cannot have authority granted to the file or revoked from the file. If you secure the file with an authorization list, you can change the authorities even when a file is open.
- Authorization lists provide a way to keep authorities when an object is saved. When an object is saved that is secured by an authorization list, the name of the authorization list is saved with the object. If the object is deleted and restored to the same system, it is automatically linked to the authorization list again. If the object is restored on a different system, the authorization list is not linked, unless *ALWOBJDIF(*ALL)* or *ALWOBJDIF(*AUTL)* is specified on the restore command.

In conclusion, authorization lists are extremely useful and easy to manage, if well-planned and well-implemented. And they're an all-time favorite with auditors!

2

Automate FTP in "Real Life" via LotusScript

This chapter presents a way to seamlessly integrate data arriving at your organization via email. This "real-life" example assumes that a Lotus® Domino® mail server is used by the organization. It works by creating an agent that is triggered by a specific email subject. This agent uses the method described in the previous chapter to send a data file to IBM i and call an RPG program to process it. The *RMTCMD* and *REXEC* commands are also discussed.

Consider the following scenario: Your company has several branches throughout the country, each with its own server, and you need to get their orders into your core business system (which is IBM i). From this point on, I'll be referring to Lotus Domino because that's the mail server used at the company this "real-life" example comes from and because Lotus Domino is IBM software. It's fair to assume that there's a way to do the same on an Exchange server or some other mail server, but that's outside our scope here.

You have a Lotus Domino mail server running within the same network as your IBM i server. Currently, an operator checks the orders mailbox, saves the order files to a folder on the file server, transfers them to IBM i, and runs a program to integrate them into the "Orders" physical file. If your organization has 100 branches (let's assume business is going well), this means repeating these steps 100 times. A bit boring, to say the least.

What if you could automate the whole procedure? The previous chapter describes how to automate data transfers using plain and simple FTP. Using that, together with a Lotus Domino agent triggered by an email's arrival to the Orders mailbox, you can transfer the file to IBM i and run the appropriate program to integrate it on your database. There are a couple of ways to write an agent. You can either use the Lotus Formula Language, which is vaguely similar to Excel's more complex formulas, or you can use LotusScript®.

LotusScript is the language I'll use in this chapter for Lotus Domino agents. There's plenty of information about it on online—just Google "Learn LotusScript"—but let me quickly address the basics. According to the Wikipedia® entry:

> *LotusScript is very similar to Visual Basic. Code can often be copied without modification from one to the other, and programmers familiar with one can easily understand the syntax and structure of code in the other. The major differences between the two are in their respective Integrated Development Environments and in the product-specific object classes provided in each language that are included. VB includes a richer set of classes for UI manipulation, whereas LotusScript includes a richer set of application-specific classes for Lotus Notes, Lotus Word Pro and Lotus 1-2-3. In the case of Lotus Notes, there are classes to work with Notes databases, documents (records) in those databases, etc. These classes can also be used as OLE Automation objects outside of the Lotus Notes environment, from Visual Basic.*

This web site gives you a crash course in LotusScript that takes you through the basics of creating a back-end agent:

http://www-01.ibm.com/support/docview.wss?uid=swg27010431

The example used at this site is similar to the one I'll be showing here. It also provides the necessary background information about Lotus Notes' application structure and inner workings, so you might want to take a moment to study it before continuing.

The Lotus Domino Agent

I'll start by creating a new agent within the Orders mailbox. This agent will be triggered on the "After new mail has arrived" event, as shown in Figure 2.1.

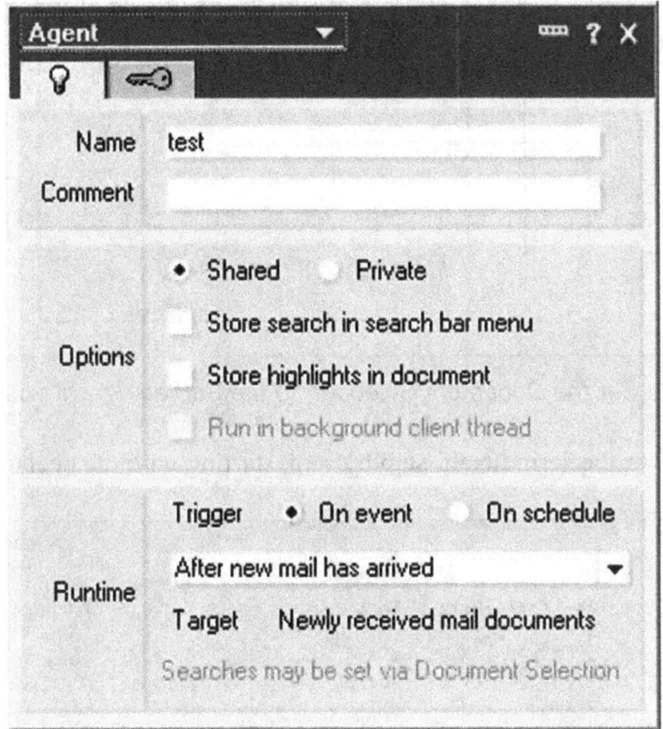

Figure 2.1: Create the agent with an "After new mail has arrived" trigger.

Since this agent will act upon all messages arriving at that mailbox, it's a good idea to arrange a fixed Subject line with your branches (to avoid processing messages that do not contain order files) and set the Document Selection to that subject, as shown in Figure 2.2.

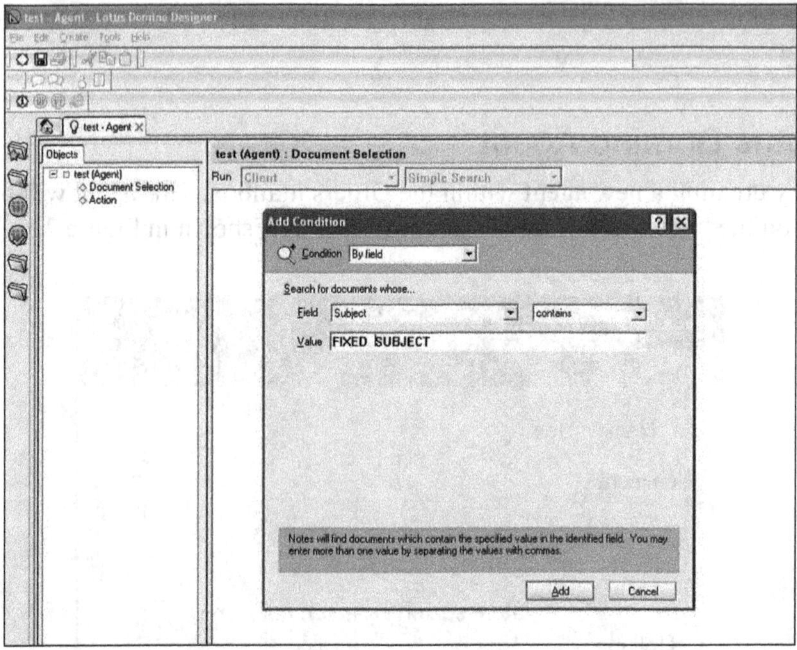

Figure 2.2: Set the Document Selection to the Subject line of your choice.

Now, let's go over the script itself, step by step, starting with the declarations section:

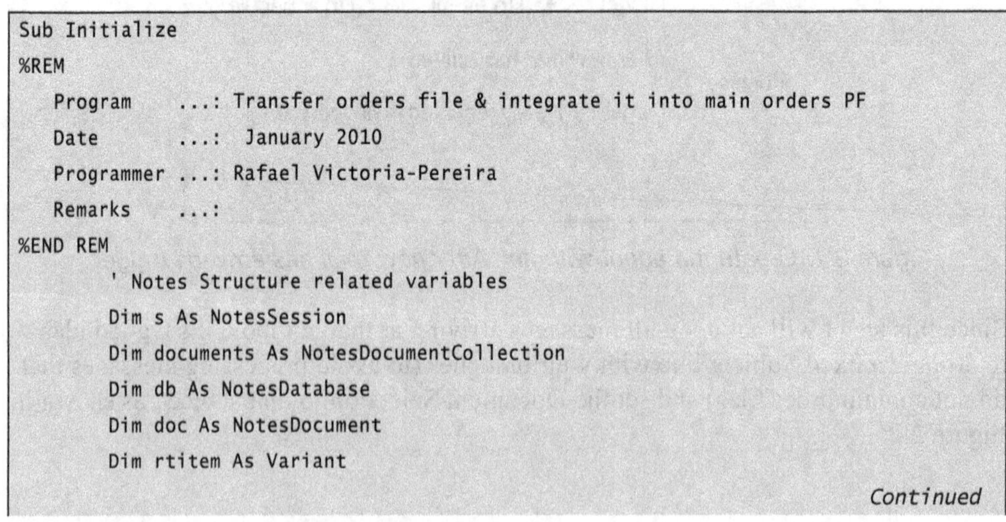

```
Sub Initialize
%REM
   Program    ...: Transfer orders file & integrate it into main orders PF
   Date       ...:  January 2010
   Programmer ...: Rafael Victoria-Pereira
   Remarks    ...:
%END REM
        ' Notes Structure related variables
        Dim s As NotesSession
        Dim documents As NotesDocumentCollection
        Dim db As NotesDatabase
        Dim doc As NotesDocument
        Dim rtitem As Variant
```

Continued

```
        'File transfer related variables
        Dim TransfPath As String
        Dim fileName As String
        Dim cmd As String
        Dim taskId As Integer
        Dim NumDocs As Integer
        Dim SysName As String
```

We're going to have to identify and open the newly arrived message (represented as a document in a Notes database), starting from the top of the Domino structure. For that, we need to define a new Notes Session, Notes Database, Notes Document Collection, Notes Document, and Rich Text Item (shown here as variant data type) to receive the attachment. This structure will allow us to manipulate the contents of the message (subject, body, and attachment).

The next group of variables will be used to transfer the attachment to IBM i and run a program to process it. First, there's the temporary folder in which to store the attachment, then the file's name, and finally, two variables that will be used to execute the DOS commands—in this case, the batch file that transfers the attachment and the program execution to integrate it into the order's main file.

Next, there are some initialization procedures:

```
'=====================================================================

'Indicate to which temporary folder the attachment should be saved
        TransfPath = "C:\\TEMP\\ "

'Indicate the name of the system
        SysName = "MyIBMi"

'Access the Notes structure right down to the document
        Set s = New NotesSession
        Set db = s.CurrentDatabase
        Set documents = db.UnprocessedDocuments
```

The first thing to do is to establish the *NotesSession* (kind of opening a connection) and, since the agent is on the same database as the documents it will work with, set the database object *s* as *CurrentDatabase*. Bear in mind that keeping the agent on the database it is acting upon is good practice, not only for the practical reason that you only need one line of code to set the database object, but also from an organizational point of view—having the agent in the database makes it easier to find and maintain.

Then, from all the documents within the database, we will create a subset with the ones that haven't been processed yet—our new mails, in this particular case.

Next, the script will process all the newly arrived email (documents) using a *FOR* cycle:

```
NumDocs = documents.count
Print ("Num docs - " + Str(NumDocs))
For n = 1 To NumDocs
        Set doc = documents.GetNthDocument(n)
        Set rtitem = doc.GetFirstItem( "Body" )

        notesEmbeddedObject = rtitem.EmbeddedObjects
        If ( rtitem.Type = RICHTEXT ) Then
                Forall o In rtitem.EmbeddedObjects
                   objectName = o.Name

                   'Save the attachment to disk
                   Call o.ExtractFile(TransfPath + objectName)

                   ' Transfer it to IBM i using ftp
                   cmd= "C:\Scripts\\ORDERS_IN\Prc_Order.bat " + _
                        + SysName + " " + objectName"
                   taskId% = Shell(cmd)

                   ' Wait 10 seconds, to ensure the transfer is finished
                   Sleep(10)
```

Continued

```
            ' Command to execute on IBM i
            cmd= "RMTCMD SBMJOB  CMD(CALL CORE_OBJ/PRCORD PARM('M' '" + _
                + objectName+ "')) " + " JOB(ORDERS_IN)"  + _
                + " JOBD(CORE_OBJ/ORDJOBD) JOBQ(QGPL/XML_JOBQ)" +_
                + " INLLIBL(*JOBD)  //" + SysName

            ' Execute the command
            taskId% = Shell(cmd)

            ' Wait 20 seconds before processing the next email
            Sleep(20)

        End Forall
```

It saves the attachment to disk, transfers it to IBM i (putting the teachings from the previous chapter to good use), and ends by running a program via *RMTCMD* (discussed in more detail later in this chapter). To make sure that the program has enough time to process the file, the agent waits 20 seconds before continuing to the next email. Just follow the comments above the lines of code to better understand each step.

Finally, the agent marks the document as processed, transfers it to another folder in the Orders mailbox called "Orders Archive," and loops to process the next document:

```
                ' Archive the email
                Call s.UpdateProcessedDoc( doc )
                Call doc.PutInFolder( "Orders Archive" )
                Call doc.RemoveFromFolder( "($Inbox)" )

        End If

    Next n
End Sub
```

Here's the complete agent:

```
Sub Initialize
%REM
   Program    ...: Transfer orders file & integrate it into main orders PF
   Date       ...:  January 2010
   Programmer ...: Rafael Victoria-Pereira
   Remarks    ...:
%END REM
        ' Notes Structure related variables
        Dim s As NotesSession
        Dim documents As NotesDocumentCollection
        Dim db As NotesDatabase
        Dim doc As NotesDocument
        Dim rtitem As Variant

        'File transfer related variables
        Dim TransfPath As String
        Dim fileName As String
        Dim cmd As String
        Dim taskId As Integer
        Dim NumDocs As Integer
        Dim SysName As String

'=======================================================================

'Indicate to which temporary folder the attachment should be saved
        TransfPath = "C:\\TEMP\\ "

'Indicate the name of the system
        SysName = "MyIBMi"

'Access the Notes structure right down to the document
        Set s = New NotesSession
        Set db = s.CurrentDatabase
        Set documents = db.UnprocessedDocuments
```

Continued

```
    NumDocs = documents.count
    Print ("Num docs - " + Str(NumDocs))
    For n = 1 To NumDocs
        Set doc = documents.GetNthDocument(n)
        Set rtitem = doc.GetFirstItem( "Body" )

        notesEmbeddedObject = rtitem.EmbeddedObjects
        If ( rtitem.Type = RICHTEXT ) Then
           Forall o In rtitem.EmbeddedObjects
              objectName = o.Name

              'Save the attachment to disk
              Call o.ExtractFile(TransfPath + objectName)

              ' Transfer it to IBM i using ftp
              cmd= "C:\Scripts\\ORDERS_IN\Prc_Order.bat " + _
                   + SysName + " " + objectName"
              taskId% = Shell(cmd)

              ' Wait 10 seconds, to ensure the transfer is finished
              Sleep(10)

              ' Command to execute on IBM i
              cmd= "RMTCMD SBMJOB  CMD(CALL CORE_OBJ/PRCORD PARM('M' '"  + _
                   + objectName+ "')) " + " JOB(ORDERS_IN)"  + _
                   + " JOBD(CORE_OBJ/ORDJOBD) JOBQ(QGPL/XML_JOBQ)" +_
                   + " INLLIBL(*JOBD)  //" + SysName

              ' Execute the command
              taskId% = Shell(cmd)

              ' Wait 20 seconds before processing the next email
              Sleep(20)

           End Forall
```

Continued

```
                    ' Archive the email
                    Call s.UpdateProcessedDoc( doc )
                    Call doc.PutInFolder( "Orders Archive" )
                    Call doc.RemoveFromFolder( "($Inbox)" )

            End If

    Next n
End Sub
```

Please note that the *RMTCMD* command is part of the IBM i Access Client installation, so if you use other emulation software, you'll have to replace it with the proper command or use *REXEC*.

Also, keep in mind that this type of agent requires a full text index on the mailbox. This takes up some disk space, especially if there's a high volume of emails arriving at this mailbox. If you have many of these agents running at the same time, they might affect the server's performance.

RMTCMD and REXEC

The *RMTCMD* command is used to send a command to IBM i. It assumes that a connection between the machine invoking the command and the target IBM i system is established. You might get a popup window asking for the user and password, if there's no connection. A nice workaround is to leave a 5250 emulation window open, with the sign-on screen.

RMTCMD used to be an SNA-only command, but now it runs over TCP/IP as well and goes through the Remote Command host server. To use it, you need to start the server first. Do that by typing the following command (on your IBM i system):

```
STRHOSTSRV SERVER(*RMTCMD)
```

Here's a complete description from an (old) IBM manual:

Remote Command (RMTCMD)

You can use the RMTCMD command from PCs running Client Access Express for Windows to send an AS/400 command or group of commands to an AS/400 system. The commands are sent to the default system, unless otherwise specified. The RMTCMD command is useful for running batch jobs on the AS/400 system and other commands that do not produce any output on an AS/400 display. For example, you can use the command to create a file on the AS/400 system, but not to display the contents of a file.

Client Access Express for Windows provides the same Remote Command API that is available with DOS clients. This is the program that you have to run. The syntax of the RMTCMD command and an example of how it can be used are shown here:

Syntax

RMTCMD command [//remotesystem] [/Z]

RMTCMD /I [drive] [path] filename [/Q] [//remotesystem] [/Z]

Parameters

The AS/400 CL command with parameters to send to the AS/400 system.

/I specifies that the commands to be sent are found in the filename specified after the /I parameter. There must be a blank space after the /I.

drive specifies the drive to use.

path specifies the name of the directory path to use on the drive.

filename specifies the name of the file containing the AS/400 CL commands.

The file must have one command (with the necessary parameters) per line.

/Q specifies that no prompts should be displayed when an error is detected by one of the commands.

//remotesystem specifies the name of the system to receive and run the commands.

/Z specifies to only display the required messages on your workstation.

Example:

To issue a series of AS/400 CL commands, on the default system, that are in a file named command.lst on the same drive and path from which the RMTCMD command is being executed, issue the following command:

RMTCMD /I COMMANDS.LST

As an alternative, you can use *REXEC*. *REXEC* is a TCP/IP remote command execution protocol. If you want IBM i to be a *REXEC* server, you must start the **REXEC* TCP/IP server via this command (again, on IBM i):

```
STRTCPSVR *REXEC
```

Once that server is started, type the following command on the remote machine (a PC or any other server running TCP/IP):

```
REXEC [systeminame] -l [userid] [systemi command]
```

Keep in mind that IBM i commands must be *non-interactive*. You'll find more information about REXEC here:

http://publib.boulder.ibm.com/iseries/v5r2/ic2924/info/rzal7/rzal7.pdf

3

Transfer a PC Text File to an IBM i Physical File in One or Two Easy Steps

> In chapter 1, you learned how to automate an FTP transfer. In chapter 2, you saw how to use the procedure from chapter 1 in a real-life situation. This chapter focuses on how to import a text file into a physical file. This is achieved using the Copy From Import File (*CPYFRMIMPF*) command. The chapter ends with some remarks about the potential drawbacks and limitations of the methods described in these three chapters.

The way to import a PC-based text file all depends on how the input file is formatted. Basically, it all comes down to a very simple thing: the file either has fields with fixed lengths or uses some sort of character to separate the values. For example, a CSV file uses the comma character.

In One Step . . .

My approach to importing a fixed-length file would be first to create a physical file with the same field structure as your text file (i.e., the same field lengths and types). Then, I'd transfer the text file directly into the physical file using FTP. This doesn't require any programming, just the steps described in chapter 1, with a little twist: instead of changing the directory to an IFS folder, you'll need to change to the library where your physical file resides. For instance, suppose you want to transfer a text file named "orders.txt" to a physical file called "ORDER_TMP" that resides in library "CORE_DB." The FTP script would look something like this:

```
user myuser mypassword
cd /qsys.lib/core_db.lib
put orders.txt order_tmp.file
quit
```

Note that the *cd* and *put* commands shown here are assuming that the FTP attribute "Initial name format" is set to **PATH*. This is the equivalent to the following command on an FTP command line:

```
quote site namefmt 1
```

Otherwise, the script would look slightly different:

```
user myuser mypassword
cd core_db
put orders.txt order_tmp
quit
```

Personally, I prefer the first format because it's more explicit and less prone to error. It's also clearer for people who are not familiar with the names of things. By enforcing the use of extensions (.lib, .file, and so on), the code is clearly identifying the nature of each name.

Or Two

To import the delimited type of text file, two steps are required:

1. The text file is sent to an IFS folder (via FTP, for instance).
2. The text file is copied to the receiving physical file via the *CPYFRMIMPF* command.

Let's assume that you want to transfer a file called "myfile.txt" to a physical file called "IMPORTFILE." Let's further assume that the text file uses the semicolon (;) as the field separator. The command to import the file would be this:

```
CPYFRMIMPF FROMSTMF('/textfiledir/myfile.txt') TOFILE(IMPORTFILE) MBROPT(*REPLACE)
RCDDLM(*CRLF) FLDDLM(';') RPLNULLVAL(*FLDDFT)
```

Since IMPORTFILE is a temporary input file, I'm using *MBROPT(*REPLACE)*, which will clear the first member of the file (the default value of the *TOFILE* parameter for the file's member) before copying the data. However, if you have multiple files to import that can be processed together (for instance, multiple order files from several branches, as in the previous chapter's example), you can copy them all to IMPORTFILE using *MBROPT(*ADD)* and call the program to process the data just once.

Then, *RCDDLM(*CRLF)* means that each line, terminated by a hard return plus a line feed or [ENTER] character, represents a record. If the input file is generated by a program, this is the most usual record-delimiter character.

Next, the most important parameter: *FLDDLM(';')* indicates that the field-delimiter character is the semicolon. This is the parameter that varies from one file format to another. In some cases, it might be a comma; in others, it might be the semicolon or some other character. It doesn't matter, as long as you change the *FLDDLM* parameter to the appropriate value.

Last, but not least, *RPLNULLVAL(*FLDDFT)* tells the system to replace the NULL values of the input file's fields with the temporary physical file's fields' default value. For instance, if there's no value for an integer field on the physical file, it will be replaced by (or converted to) zero.

Now, how to avoid the repetitive task of copying the text file into the physical file?

The objective is to get the data into the database. Obviously, there will be some sort of field validation, as well as business rules checks. For that, there will be an RPG program. We can use the same program to transfer the data, validate it, and import it to the database. There's a catch, however: once you declare the import file and the program starts running, the file will be locked and the *CPYFRMIMPF* command will not run. The trick is declaring the file as user-open (*USROPN* keyword in the file declaration line):

```
FIMPORTFILEIF   E              Disk    UsrOpn
```

Then, *before* opening the file, copy the data using *CPYFRMIMPF* as shown below:

```
...
  //Prepare the data copy command
   P_Cmdlin = 'CPYFRMIMPF FROMSTMF(' + '''' + '//textfiledir/myfile.txt' +
              '''' + ') TOFILE(IMPORTFILE) MBROPT(*REPLACE) ' +
              'RCDDLM(*CRLF) FLDDLM(' + '''' + ';' + '''' + ') ' +
              'DECPNT(*COMMA) RPLNULLVAL(*FLDDFT)';

  //Execute the data copy command
  ExecCmd(P_CmdLin);
//Open the file to process the data
Open IMPORTFILE;
...
```

This example uses the *ExecCmd* procedure, but you can also use *QCMDEXC* to execute the command. Just remember to close the file before the end of the program!

Drawbacks to FTP

Note that all of the procedures described in the chapters you've read so far have some drawbacks. The first is that storing a user's password in a text file (meaning the FTP script file) is a security risk. This risk can be mitigated in several ways:

- Use adequate file access authorities (such as authorization lists, as suggested in chapter 1).
- Conceal the file using tricks, like hiding it with an inconspicuous name among other files (hiding a tree in a forest, so to speak).
- Change the file's extension to .nfo, .dll, or whatever you prefer. It's not required to be .scp.

Other alternatives for transferring files are available, such as dedicated FTP and SFTP software. If it can be invoked via a command line, it can be used in a batch file, like the plain and simple FTP used in chapter 1.

Another drawback is that email is not 100 percent reliable. Therefore, weigh carefully the pros and cons of the solution proposed in chapter 2.

The bottom line, though, is that you can automate those tedious file-transfer-run-program tasks. Simply use any kind of FTP data transfer that can be invoked via the command line and *RMTCMD* (or its equivalent on non-IBM i Access software).

4

Get Real-Time Integration Between Your PC Application and IBM i

This chapter shows you how to build a simple yet flexible interface between a PC application and an IBM i application. The interface is built using VB, but it could be done with any other language that handles ODBC. Then, ADO DB invokes an RPG program that manages the connection with the business application.

Sometimes you need real-time integration between a PC application and an IBM i application. It might be something simple, like accessing a file and getting a value back. Of course, that's not rocket science: an ODBC connection and a few lines of code on the PC application will do. But what if you need more complex information, something along the lines of a business rule validation that already exists on an RPG program or a comprehensive data set? For example, suppose you need a client's debt report divided by debt age (30, 60, and 90 days), or a query to find out if a certain item exists in stock and how long retrieving it would take.

As always, there are several possibilities to tackle problems like this. You can replicate the business logic on your PC application, create a complex view on your

IBM i database, or simply reuse existing programs and invoke them from your PC application. The first two options, however, can be time-consuming and prone to error. The third one—relying on the existing business rules and the programs that enforce them—seems both simpler and quicker. All you need is an ODBC connection and a few tricks!

This is much easier to explain with an example. Consider the previously mentioned client's debt report, but with a tweak: the PC application also needs to know if the client can increase its debt. In this scenario, that is not a simple check, and the business rules are already implemented in an RPG program. We'd have to reproduce the business rules on the PC application, with all the data requirements associated with it, which is not a cost-effective solution. One workaround is to invoke an RPG program that retrieves the debt aging and also the approval or rejection for additional debt, by calling the existing program that does that validation.

So what do we need? As input, we'd require the system (test or production), the client ID, and a reference date (to calculate the debt aging). As output, we'd have the total debt, the debt aging, a flag for "additional debt allowed, Y/N," and a return code. Table 4.1 gives a quick rundown of these parameters.

The return code, in addition to being a good practice, can provide error handling on the PC side. For example, if the user and password used for the connection are not working, perhaps an email to the sysadmin is in order. Of course, basic validations, such as the client ID's existence, reference date validity, and system type, can also trigger a predefined return code, thus helping both sides (PC application developers and IBM i developers) figure out where the problem is and solve it quickly.

Table 4.1: RPG Interface Input and Output Parameters

Input	
Parameter	***Description***
Client ID	Client ID (shared key between the PC application and the main database)
System Type	Test or Production
Reference Date	Used to calculate the debt age

Table 4.1: RPG Interface Input and Output Parameters (continued)	
Output	
Parameter	*Description*
Total Debt	Client's total debt
Debt 30 Days	Invoices outstanding up to 30 days
Debt 60 Days	Invoices outstanding up to 60 days
Debt 90 Days	Invoices outstanding 90 days or more
Additional Debt Allowed	Yes/No flag indicating whether additional debt is allowed for this client
Return Code	Flag to indicate whether the call was successful, and if not, what the error was

Note that the system type is purely optional. I'm mentioning it because most shops have a dedicated test system or at least a separate test library list. (I'll get back to this later in this chapter.)

This example uses VB and an ADO DB connection, but you can easily use other programming languages to do the same thing. There's an IBM Redbook® entitled *A Fast Path to AS/400 Client/Server Using AS/400 OLE DB Support* that covers this subject in depth. It's available here:

http://www.redbooks.ibm.com/abstracts/sg245183.html

The VB Side of the Interface

Some basic knowledge of Visual Basic is advised, even though the code is quite simple. Now, let's go over the code, step by step, starting with the declarations section:

```
Dim sCall As String
    'Connect to the IBM i
    Set oCmd = New ADODB.Command
```

It starts by declaring a string variable, *sCall*, that will contain the program's name and full path, as well as its parameters. Then, it creates a new ADO command, which will be the support structure for the invocation.

Next, the previously mentioned parameters are added:

```
'set input params
Set oParam = oCmd.CreateParameter("inSystem", adChar, adParamInput, 1, mvarInSystem)
oCmd.Parameters.Append oParam

Set oParam =
        oCmd.CreateParameter("inClientID", adChar, adParamInput, 2, mvarClientID)
oCmd.Parameters.Append oParam

.....

Set oParam = oCmd.CreateParameter("outReturnCode", adChar, adParamOutput, 255)
oCmd.Parameters.Append oParam

sCall = sNrParams(oCmd.Parameters.Count)
```

Only the first two parameters (system type and client ID) and the last one (the return code) are presented here. I'm not mentioning all of them because it's basically the same code, over and over, with the necessary parameter name changes.

After all the parameters are added, the structure is placed upon its final destination: the *sCall* string. By now, *sCall* contains a data structure with our parameters. The next step is to set up the call to the IBM i program. This call will occur without a library list, so the called IBM i program needs to set it up. For that, the system type parameter is relevant. If the test and production environments are in separate servers, the connection string will differ. If they're on the same server, they'll use different library lists. The following lines of code are required to take care of that:

```
' Compose the program invocation command, taking into account the system type
' (Production or Test)
If (mvarInSystem = "P") Then
sCall = "{{CALL " & URL_LIBRARY_PROD & URL_ProgName & "(" & sCall & ")}}"
ElseIf (mvarInSystem = "T") Then
sCall = "{{CALL " & URL_LIBRARY_TEST & URL_ProgName & "(" & sCall & ")}}"
End If
```

URL_LIBRARY_PROD contains the name of the production library where the called program resides; *URL_LIBRARY_TEST* is the same for the test library; *URL_ProgName* contains the name of the program to be called. Now that the call string is complete, let's prepare the command accordingly and get the data:

```
'Prepare command string
 oCmd.CommandType = adCmdText
 oCmd.CommandText = sCall

 'Get data
 subConnAS400 "AS400", oCmd
```

This operation will fill the output parameters with the values returned by the RPG program. If everything goes well, we'll get four amounts, a yes/no flag, and a success return code. A return code of zero means success; anything other than zero means failure. As stated before, multiple return codes can be set up to help fix issues that might occur with the interface.

To finalize our little example, we'll check for the return code and proceed accordingly:

```
mvarOutSuccess = IIf(Trim(oCmd.Parameters("outReturnCode").Value) = "0", True, False)
 If mvarOutSuccess Then
   'If the program ended normally, process the output parameters
.....
Else
   'Handle the error code
.....
End If
```

To wrap it up, here's the complete code for this example:

```
Dim sCall As String

    'Connect to the IBM i
    Set oCmd = New ADODB.Command

    'set input params
    Set oParam =
            oCmd.CreateParameter("inSystem", adChar, adParamInput, 1, mvarInSystem)
oCmd.Parameters.Append oParam

    Set oParam =
            oCmd.CreateParameter("inClientID", adChar, adParamInput, 2, mvarClientID)
oCmd.Parameters.Append oParam

    .....

    Set oParam = oCmd.CreateParameter("outReturnCode", adChar, adParamOutput, 255)
oCmd.Parameters.Append oParam

sCall = sNrParams(oCmd.Parameters.Count)

' Compose the program invocation command,
' taking into account the system type (Production or Test)
    If (mvarInSystem = "P") Then
sCall = "{{CALL " & URL_LIBRARY_PROD & URL_ProgName & "(" & sCall & ")}}"
    ElseIf (mvarInSystem = "T") Then
sCall = "{{CALL " & URL_LIBRARY_TEST & URL_ProgName & "(" & sCall & ")}}"
    End If

    'Prepare command string
    oCmd.CommandType = adCmdText
    oCmd.CommandText = sCall

    'Get data
    subConnAS400 "AS400", oCmd
```

Continued

```
mvarOutSuccess = IIf(Trim(oCmd.Parameters("outReturnCode").Value) = "0", True, False)
    If mvarOutSuccess Then

      'If the program ended normally, process the output parameters
         .....
    Else
      'Handle the error code
         .....
    End If
```

A final note about the ODBC connection: I've assumed that this part should be easy, especially if you've read the IBM documentation. But here's a small piece of code that might help:

```
' Make an ADO connection to the database
' ================================================================
Public Function InitEnvironment(ByVal iDBType As DBType, ByVal sAppName As String,
ByVal sUserID As String, ByVal sPassw As String, ByVal sServer As String, ByVal
sDatabase As String, ByVal CursorLocation As DBCursorLocation) As ADODB.Connection
On Error GoTo errHandler

   Dim ConnectStr As String
   Dim oConn As New ADODB.Connection

   Set InitEnvironment = Nothing

   oConn.CursorLocation = CursorLocation

   Select Case iDBType
   'SQL SERVER
   Case dbSQLServer
      oConn.Provider = "SQLOLEDB"
      oConn.Open "Data Source=" & sServer & ";Initial Catalog=" & sDatabase &
                 ";Application Name=" & sAppName, sUserID, sPassw
      Set InitEnvironment = oConn
```

Continued

```
   'ORACLE
   Case dbOracle
      oConn.Provider = "MSDAORA.1"
      oConn.CursorLocation = adUseClient
sServer = sDatabase
      oConn.Open "Data Source=" & sServer & ";Application Name=" &
                 sAppName, sUserID, sPassw

      Set InitEnvironment = oConn

   'IBM i
   Case dbAS400
      oConn.Provider = "IBMDA400"
      oConn.CursorLocation = adUseClient
      oConn.Open "Data Source=" & sServer & ";User Id=" & sUserID & " ;Password=" &
                 sPassw & ";"

      Set InitEnvironment = oConn

   Case Else
      Set oConn = Nothing

   End Select

   Exit Function
errHandler:
   SetError Err.Number, Err.Description & vbNewLine & "(Data Source: " & sServer &
                       " User: " & sUserID & ")", "(InitEnvironment)"
   Set oConn = Nothing
   Set InitEnvironment = oConn
   Exit Function
   Resume
End Function
```

This function allows connections to multiple databases (DB2/400®, Oracle®, and Microsoft SQL Server®) using a simple variable, *IDBType*, that detects the database type. Using this, everything that was written before becomes equally applicable to a program or stored procedure written on any of the platforms mentioned in the code.

And the RPG Side

It's now time to focus on the RPG program that is called by the VB code. The objective of the program is to get the debt data from the database and call an existing program to determine if the client can increase its debt. Let's go through an overview of the program's structure.

First, the files used by the program have to be defined with the *USROPN* keyword:

```
...
 *------------------------------------------------------------------------*
 *   File Descriptions                                                    *
 *------------------------------------------------------------------------*
FCLIENTF   IF   E           K Disk    Prefix(CLI_) UsrOpn
FCLIINVF   IF   E           K Disk    Prefix(INV_) UsrOpn
....
```

This is mandatory because the program is called without a library list. Its first task will be to compose the proper one, based on the system type parameter.

Then, we'll need to declare the variables required for the input/output parameter of the program and define the prototype for a CL program that sets the proper library list (explained later):

```
...
 *------------------------------------------------------------------------*
 *   Variables                                                            *
 *------------------------------------------------------------------------*
 * Parameter Fields
D P_SysType       S              1A
D P_ClientID      S                   Like(CLI_ID)
D P_TotalDebt     S             21  2
D P_Debt30        S                   Like(Inv_InvTot)
```

Continued

```
D P_Debt60          S                   Like(Inv_InvTot)
D P_Debt90Plus      S                   Like(Inv_InvTot)
D P_DebtAllowed     S              1A
D P_RetCode         S              1A

...

 * Prototype for the SETLIBL CL
D SETLIBL          PR                   ExtPgm('SETLIBLCL')
```

The next detail is the program interface, i.e., the entry parameters:

```
...
 *------------------------------------------------------------------*
 *   Parameters                                                     *
 *------------------------------------------------------------------*
 * Entry parameters
C     *Entry        PList
C                   Parm                    P_SysType
C                   Parm                    P_ClientID
C                   Parm                    P_TotalDebt
C                   Parm                    P_Debt30
C                   Parm                    P_Debt60
C                   Parm                    P_Debt90Plus
C                   Parm                    P_DebtAllowed
C                   Parm                    P_RetCode

...
```

Now, for the program itself! As mentioned previously, the first task is to set up the proper library. This can be achieved using a CL program that contains *CHGLIBL* commands contained within IF statements. These IF statements check the value of the system type parameter and set the library list accordingly. Here's the code for the *SETLIBL* CL program:

```
             PGM         PARM(&P_SYSTYPE)

             DCL         VAR(&P_SYSTYPE) TYPE(*CHAR) LEN(1)

/* Test Library list */
             IF          COND(&P_SYSTYPE = 'T') THEN(CHGLIBL LIBL(TSTFILES +
                           TSTOBJS TSTXXXXLIB))

/* Production library list */
             IF          COND(&P_SYSTYPE = 'P') THEN(CHGLIBL LIBL(PRDFILES +
                           PRDOBJS PRDXXXXLIB))

             ENDPGM
```

Of course, you can make it more dynamic if you create two data areas with the library lists and use their values in the *CHGLIBL* command:

```
             PGM         PARM(&P_SYSTYPE)

             DCL         VAR(&P_SYSTYPE) TYPE(*CHAR) LEN(1)
             DCL         VAR(&PRDLIB) TYPE(*CHAR) LEN(255)
             DCL         VAR(&TSTLIB) TYPE(*CHAR) LEN(255)

/* Retrieve the library lists */
RTVDTAARA   DTAARA(PRDLIBDA) RTNVAR(&PRDLIB)
RTVDTAARA   DTAARA(TSTLIBDA) RTNVAR(&TSTLIB)

 /* Set Test library list */
             IF          COND(&P_SYSTYPE = 'T') THEN(CHGLIBL LIBL(&TSTLIB))

 /* Set Production library list */
             IF          COND(&P_SYSTYPE = 'P') THEN(CHGLIBL LIBL(&PRDLIB))

             ENDPGM
```

You can go even further and skip the CL program. Implement its logic directly in your RPG program, and use *QCMDEXC* to issue the appropriate *CHGLIBL* command!

Back to our program. If setting the library list is the first task, the second is to open the files and clear any "trash" that the output variables might contain. I've created an initialization routine for that:

```
//------------------------------------------------------------------*
//    Initialization                                                *
//------------------------------------------------------------------*
/FREE
  BegSr Init;

 // Set the library list
  CallP SetLibL (P_SysType);

 // Open all files
    Open CLIENTF;
    Open CLIINVF;

 // Other initialization code goes here...

 // Initialize output parms
    P_TotalDebt   = *Zeros;
    P_Debt30      = *Zeros;
    P_Debt60      = *Zeros;
    P_Debt90Plus  = *Zeros;
    P_DebtAllowed = *Blanks;
    P_RetCode     = '0';
  EndSr;
```

Now, it's time to validate the input parameters. In this case, there's only one (the client ID), so a simple chain to the *CLIENTF* file will suffice. In a real-life situation, you would probably have a lot more to validate. Needless to say, an error during the validations should set the return code to failure (one, in this case) and end the program. Creating a validation routine is a good practice and, as you'll see later this chapter, makes the flow of the program logical and easy to understand.

Next, the program will retrieve the necessary data to fill the output parameters via business logic and a call to an existing program that returns the go/no-go for additional debt. This will be done in the "Process" routine. This might be a challenge, because the existing program can be an old-style interactive program with loads and loads of business rules built in. Instead of rewriting it, you can reuse it with a few well-directed changes:

- Add new parameters. The information that is now inputted on the screen can be transformed into entry parameters. I'm talking about the client ID (input), the "interactive mode Y/N" (also input), and the go/no-go for additional debt (obviously output).
- Change the display file definition, adding the *USROPN* keyword, and open the file as indicated by the "interactive mode Y/N" parameter.
- To get the response back to the calling program, pass the value from the screen field (the go/no-go for additional debt) to the last of the entry parameters. Be sure to control all the screen-related operations (*WRITE*, *UPDATE*, *EXFMT* and so on to display file formats) with IF statements that check the "interactive mode Y/N" parameter.

Having said that, let's go back to our interface program. The final step is to close all the files and end the program. This will be performed in the *EndProg* subroutine.

Here's an overview of the code:

```
...
 *-------------------------------------------------------------------------*
 *   File Descriptions                                                     *
 *-------------------------------------------------------------------------*
FCLIENTF   IF   E           K Disk    Prefix(CLI_) UsrOpn
FCLIINVF   IF   E           K Disk    Prefix(INV_) UsrOpn

....

 *-------------------------------------------------------------------------*
 *   Variables                                                             *
 *-------------------------------------------------------------------------*
 * Parameter Fields
                                                                  Continued
```

```
D P_SysType       S             1A
D P_ClientID      S                    Like(CLI_ID)
D P_TotalDebt     S            21  2
D P_Debt30        S                    Like(Inv_InvTot)
D P_Debt60        S                    Like(Inv_InvTot)
D P_Debt90Plus    S                    Like(Inv_InvTot)
D P_DebtAllowed   S             1A
D P_RetCode       S             1A

...

 * Prototype for the SETLIBL CL
D SETLIBL         PR                   ExtPgm('SETLIBLCL')

 /FREE
  //-----------------------------------------------------------------------*
  //   Main Code                                                           *
  //-----------------------------------------------------------------------*

  ExSr Init;

  ExSr Valid;

  ExSr Process;

  ExSr EndProg;

  //-----------------------------------------------------------------------*
  //    Initialization                                                     *
  //-----------------------------------------------------------------------*

  BegSr Init;

 // Set the library list
    CallP SetLibL (P_SysType);
```

Continued

```
// Open all files
   Open CLIENTF;
   Open CLIINVF;

// ...Other initialization code goes here...

// Initialize output parms
   P_TotalDebt   = *Zeros;
   P_Debt30      = *Zeros;
   P_Debt60      = *Zeros;
   P_Debt90Plus  = *Zeros;
   P_DebtAllowed = *Blanks;
   P_RetCode     = '1';

 EndSr;

 //-----------------------------------------------------------------------*
 //    Validate                                                           *
 //-----------------------------------------------------------------------*

 BegSr Valid;

        // Run validations on the input parms
        // ...VALIDATION CODE GOES HERE...

    // In case of error:
        If W_Error = *On;
      P_RetCode = '1';
      Return;
    EndIf;

 EndSr;

 //-----------------------------------------------------------------------*
 //    Process Request                                                    *
 //-----------------------------------------------------------------------*
```

Continued

```
BegSr Process;

        // ...RETRIEVE DATA WITH BUSINESS LOGIC...
        // ...FILL OUTPUT PARMS...

EndSr;

//------------------------------------------------------------------*
//    End program                                                   *
//------------------------------------------------------------------*

BegSr EndProg;

  Close CLIENTF;
  Close CLIINVF;

  *InLr = *On;

EndSr;
```

Because this is meant to be a simple and straightforward example, this is a rather crude interface program. You can (and should) enhance it in a number of ways. For instance, instead of a success/failure code, you might want to build in something more complex, such as an error code (001 meaning "client not found," 002 meaning "debt information not available," and so on). You might implement error-handling to prevent the program from "hanging" your VB application. Or add whatever else is your cup of tea . . . the sky is the limit! I've just presented the basic functionality required to get the interface working.

This is a stripped-down, simplified version of an interface that has been running between a VB application (now converted to .NET) and an IBM i application for almost 10 years. It has changed very little over time, and the main structure still is the one described in this chapter.

5

Import CSV Files with File Correcting

This chapter presents a user-friendly CSV file upload program. While the program itself is simple, it uses some interesting procedures to recover records with the most common user errors in a CSV file. In chapter 6, this program is used to send (via email) a Microsoft Excel file with the records that couldn't be recovered, among other things. MS Excel file creation is explained in chapter 7, and the FTP transfer that puts the CSV file in the IFS is in chapter 1. It's advisable to read chapters 1, 2, and 3 before continuing.

In chapters 1 and 2, you learned how to automate file upload to your IBM i system using FTP. However, if the file doesn't arrive via email, someone from the IT department will still have to upload the file to the IFS, because the end-user won't do it or might delete something that shouldn't be deleted.

The program presented here provides you with a template, which will enable you to build your own user-friendly CSV file-upload programs. The program itself is simple, but it establishes some good practices that I really recommend that you follow.

Imagine the following scenario: your company receives a shipment of items, to be logged in your inventory. Along with the shipment comes a CSV file that the end-user checks and, if necessary, changes by adding or removing records, changing item quantities, and so on. When the CSV and the shipment are in sync, it's time to log the items into the inventory. To do that, the user calls the *INVIMP* sample program, as shown in Figure 5.1.

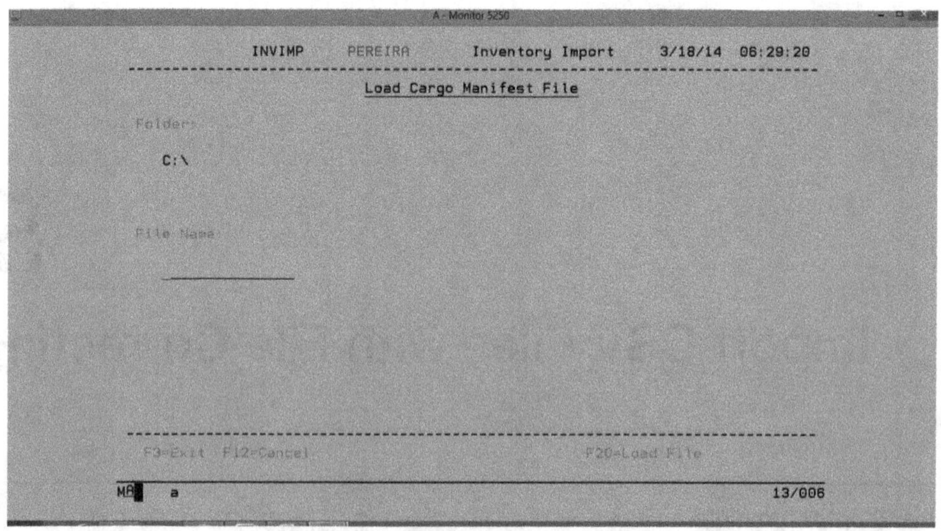

Figure 5.1: The main screen of the INVIMP program for logging inventory.

The user needs to put the CSV file in the folder indicated on the screen (*C:*, in the example in Figure 5.1) and fill the File Name field with the CSV file name. Then, by pressing F20, the CSV file is transferred to the IFS, checked for errors, copied to a temporary physical file, and has its valid records logged into the company's inventory. The invalid records are written to an MS Excel file, with the same structure as the input CSV file and sent, via email, to the user who ran the program. This allows the user to correct the errors, save the file as CSV, and upload it again.

Let's analyze the upload functionality step by step, starting with the program's user interaction. (The email functionality is discussed in the next chapter.)

Main Program Analysis

When the program is called, a few "behind the scenes" things happen. The folder where the CSV file is expected to be placed is dynamic, stored in a data area, and needs to be shown on screen. The folder where the FTP script that will run a bit later on is also dynamic and—you guessed it—also stored in a data area. So, the first thing to do is to read those data areas and put the CSV file folder on screen. Even though the program is able to handle a long path, up to 207 characters, I advise you to keep it as short as possible. Otherwise, you might have problems with the FTP transfer (more on this later). After this, the program's main cycle can begin and follow its course until the user presses F3 to leave.

Here's the code for data area loading and preparing, and for the main cycle:

```
// Load the folder paths
ExSR Load_Paths;

// Main Loop
DoW *InKC <> *On;

  // Show Main screen
  ExFmt INVIMP01;

  // Initialize Indicators/Messages
  ExSR Init_Ind_Msg;

  // Main process
  Select;
  When *InKC = *On;
    // Dummy - Exit Program

  When *InKL = *On;
    // Cancel user input (clear screen fields)
    ExSR Cancel_Input;

  When *InKU = *On;
    // Validate user input
    ExSr Vld_Screen;
    If (W_Screen = *Off);
      // Validate and Load file
      ExSr Vld_Load_File;
    EndIf;
```

Continued

```
  Other;
    // Initialize Indicators/Messages
    ExSR Init_Ind_Msg;
    // Validate user input
    ExSr Vld_Screen;
  EndSL;

EndDo;

// End Program
*InLR = *On;
```

Don't worry, I'll explain all the subroutines mentioned here as we follow the program's cycle. Before the cycle begins, the aforementioned data area reading and preparing takes place in subroutine *Load_Paths*:

```
// ---------------------------------------------------------------------
// Subroutine: Load the folder paths
// ---------------------------------------------------------------------
BegSR Load_Paths;

  // Load Data Area CSV Path Data Area
  IN *LOCK W_DAInvFld;
  W_LoadPath = W_DAInvFld;
  OUT W_DAInvFld;

  // Load FTP Scripts Path Data Area
  IN *LOCK W_DAScpFld;
  W_ScriptFolder = W_DAScpFld;
  OUT W_DAScpFld;

  // Process Data Area to show on screen
  ExSR Process_Path;

EndSR;
```

I'm using data areas to store configuration data simply because it's easier from a programming point of view. However, it's not always the best solution. From a maintenance and user-friendliness point of view, a flexible configurations file is more advisable. (Feel free to change the code and adapt it to whatever your company's best practice is for configuration data.) This subroutine then calls *Process_Path* to transform the big string with the CSV file folder into the screen fields:

```
// ---------------------------------------------------------------------
// Subroutine: Process Data Area to show on screen
// ---------------------------------------------------------------------
BegSR Process_Path;

  // Load long variable used to process the transfer path
  W_PathScript = W_LoadPath;

  // Path size
  W_SizPath = %Len(%Trim(W_LoadPath));

  // Screen's folder path first line (PathFile1) size
  W_SizPathF1 = %Len(PathFile1);
  // Screen's folder path second line (PathFile2) size
  W_SizPathF2 = %Len(PathFile2);
  // Screen's folder path third line (PathFile3) size
  W_SizPathF3 = %Len(PathFile3);

  // Fill first line on screen (field PathFile1)
  If W_SizPath > W_SizPathF1;

    PathFile1 = %Subst(%Trim(W_LoadPath): 1: W_SizPathF1);
    W_SizPath = W_SizPath - W_SizPathF1;

    // Fill second line on screen (field PathFile2)
    If W_SizPath > W_SizPathF1;
      PathFile2 = %SubSt(%Trim(W_LoadPath):
                         W_SizPathF1 + 1  :
                         W_SizPathF2      );
      W_SizPath = W_SizPath - W_SizPathF2;
```

Continued

```
      // Fill third line on screen (field PathFile3)
      PathFile3 = %SubSt(%Trim(W_LoadPath)                :
                         W_SizPathF1 + W_SizPathF2 + 1 :
                         W_SizPath                     );

    Else;
      PathFile2 = %SubSt(%Trim(W_LoadPath) :
                         W_SizPathF1 + 1   :
                         W_SizPath         );
    EndIf;

  Else;
    PathFile1 = %SubSt(%Trim(W_LoadPath): 1: W_SizPath);
  EndIf;

EndSR;
```

The code is dynamic enough to handle any path length, filling the necessary screen fields. After this, the screen is shown and the user can interact with the program. When F20 is pressed, subroutine *Vld_Screen* is invoked:

```
// ----------------------------------------------------------------------
// Subroutine: Validate user input
// ----------------------------------------------------------------------
BegSR Vld_Screen;

  W_Screen = *Off;

  // If the file name has been filled, show F20 function key
  If FileName = *Blanks;
    W_Screen = *On;
    *In21 = *On;
  Else;
    *In21 = *Off;
  EndIf;
```

Continued

```
  // The file extension must be .CSV
  If %Scan('.CSV' : FileName) = *Zeros;
    W_Screen = *On;
    *In23 = *On;
  Else;
    *In23 = *Off;
  EndIf;

EndSR;
```

This subroutine checks if the file name was in fact filled in and if it ends with .CSV, because the file name length is important for the FTP transfer. The errors are handled "old school" with indicators that are linked to error messages on the display file. If everything is OK, subroutine *Vld_Load_File* is called to handle the CSV file's validation and transfer to the IFS:

```
// ------------------------------------------------------------------
// Subroutine: Validate and Load file
// ------------------------------------------------------------------
BegSR Vld_Load_File;

  // Check if the process can continue
  If W_Load_File = *On;
    // Retrieve the file load delay
    ExSr Rtv_Delay;

    If W_Load_File = *On;
      // Transfer the file for the CSV input folder to the IFS
      ExSr Transfer_File;

      If W_Load_File = *On;
        // Wait for the FTP transfer to end before trying to process
        ExSr Delay_FTP;

        // The delay required this workaround to prevent the screen
        // from going black until the end of the process
        WRITE INVIMPW04;
```

Continued

```
// Copy the data from the CSV to the temporary physical file
ExSR COPY_CSV_PF;

IF W_Load_File = *On;
// The delay required this workaround to prevent the screen
// from going black until the end of the process
  WRITE INVIMPW05;

  // Load data to the inventory file
  ExSr Load_Inv_PF;

  If W_Load_File = *On;
    // Delete the CSV file from the IFS
    ExSr Del_CSV;
    // Show success screen
    // with a warning note in case one or more records couldn't
    // be processed
    If W_TotErr > *Zeros;
      TotErrMsg1 = 'However, ' + %Char(W_TotErr) + ' errors ' +
                   'were found.';
      TotErrMsg2 = 'Check the log file sent to your mailbox.';
      TotErrMsg3 = *Blanks;

    Else;
      TotErrMsg1 = *Blanks;
      TotErrMsg2 = *Blanks;
      TotErrMsg3 = *Blanks;
    EndIf;
    ExFmt INVIMPW02;
    // Initialize screen fields
    ExSr Init_Scrn_Fields;
  EndIf;

Else;
  // Process screen errors
  ExSr Prc_Scrn_Errors;
EndIf;
```

Continued

```
    Else;
      // Process screen errors
      ExSr Prc_Scrn_Errors;
    EndIf;

  Else;
    // Process screen errors
    ExSr Prc_Scrn_Errors;
  EndIf;
EndIf;

EndSR;
```

The first task it performs is transferring the file to the IFS, using FTP. Subroutine *Transfer_File* takes care of that:

```
// ----------------------------------------------------------------------
// Subroutine: Transfer the file for the CSV input folder to the IFS
// ----------------------------------------------------------------------
BegSR Transfer_File;

  // Compose transfer path
  W_PathScript = %Trim(PathFile1) + %Trim(PathFile2) + %Trim(PathFile3);


  // Determine the system type (UAT or PRD) in order to set the correct
  // transfer details
  If ProductionSys;
    P_Cmdlin = 'STRPCCMD PCCMD(' + '''' +  %Trim(W_ScriptFolder) +
               '\INVIMP\PRD_Transf_INV.BAT ' + %TRIM(FileName) +
               ' ' + '"' + %TRIM(W_PathScript) + '"' + '''' + ') +
               PAUSE(*NO)';
                                                              Continued
```

```
  Else;
  P_Cmdlin = 'STRPCCMD PCCMD(' + '''' + %Trim(W_ScriptFolder) +
             '\INVIMP\UAT_Transf_INV.BAT '  + %TRIM(FileName) +
             ' ' + '"' + %TRIM(W_PathScript) + '"' + '''' + ') +
             PAUSE(*NO)';
EndIf;
  P_Cmdlen = %LEN(%TRIM(P_CmdLin));

  // Run the FTP transfer
  CALLP(E) $QCMDEXC(P_Cmdlin: P_Cmdlen);

  IF %Error;
    // Show the error on screen
    W_Error_Nbr = 1;
    W_Load_File = *Off;
  EndIf;

EndSR;
```

The subroutine uses function *ProductionSys* to determine if the program is running on a production system or a UAT (user acceptance test) system. Basically, it does this by reading a data area named *DASYSTYPE* and returning **On* if its value is *P*. This is important, because if you have more than one IBM i system, each one will have its own system names, users, and passwords. That's why there are two batch files—you must customize each of them with your production and test credentials.

Finally, the FTP transfer takes place. This is achieved by opening a command line window with the *STRPCCMD* command. The problem is that the window is open, and the program resumes execution. Since the CSV file can take anywhere from a few seconds to a few minutes to transfer, it's necessary to wait for the transfer to complete before continuing. In other words, you need to delay the program's execution. That's what subroutines *RTV_Delay* and *Delay_FTP* do. I won't show every single subroutine here, so please check the downloadable source code (available from this book's page at *http://www.mc-store.com*) if you're curious about how this delay is done. While the delay is running, an empty, not-very-user-friendly screen would be shown. To avoid this, the nice window (*INVIMPW04*) shown in Figure 5.2 is displayed.

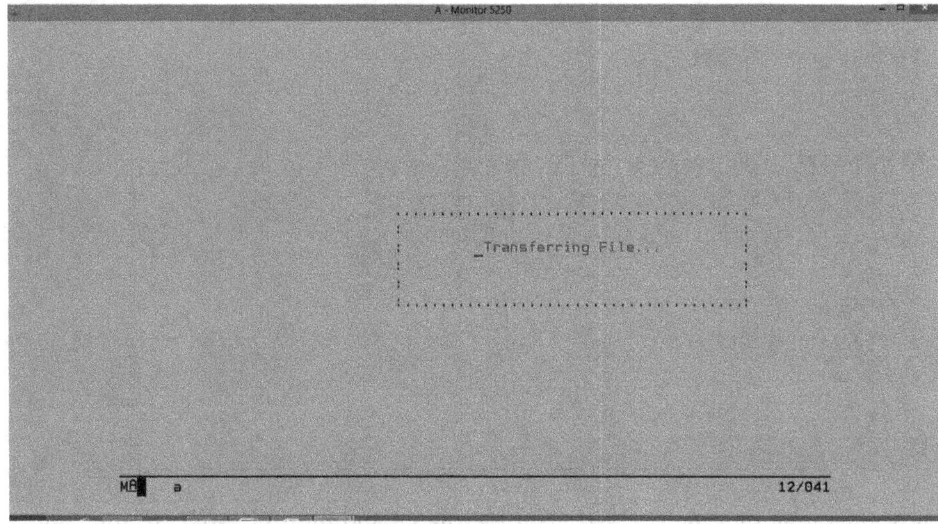

Figure 5.2: The window shown while the FTP transfer is running.

Once the delay ends, the FTP transfer has (hopefully) ended, and the CSV file is now in the IFS. You might need to adjust the *DADLYTIM* data area to match the average size of your CSV files. It contains the number of seconds that the program will wait before resuming execution.

The next steps are checking the CSV file, correcting whatever errors are possible to correct, and copying it to a temporary physical file. Subroutine *COPY_CSV_PF* takes care of that, using the *CSV2PF* procedure that I'll explain later:

```
// -----------------------------------------------------------------
// Subroutine: Copy the data from the CSV to the temporary physical file
// -----------------------------------------------------------------
BegSR Copy_CSV_PF;


  // Set Csv2PF Parameters
  P_InputCSV = '/CSVFILES/INVIMP.CSV';
  P_OutputPF = 'PFIN_INV';
  P_OutputCSV = '/CSVFILES/TEMP_INVIMP.CSV';
```

Continued

```
  P_FieldSep  = ';';
  P_DecimalSep = '*COMMA';
  P_RunCopy = 'Y';

  // Run Csv2PF, thus copying the CSV to the temporary PF
  If  Csv2PF(P_InputCSV : P_OutputPF    : P_OutputCSV :
             P_FieldSep : P_DecimalSep : P_RunCopy) = *On;
    // In case of error, show it on screen
    W_Error_Nbr = 1;
    W_Load_File = *Off;
  EndIf;

EndSR;
```

For now, just note that the *CSVFILES* folder name and the *INVIMP.CSV* file name are hardcoded. This is connected with the lack of flexibility of the FTP script files, as mentioned in chapter 1.

This procedure might take a while to run, depending on the size of the CSV file, and the user would be stuck with another empty screen, if it weren't for the nice window named *INVIMPW05*, shown in Figure 5.3.

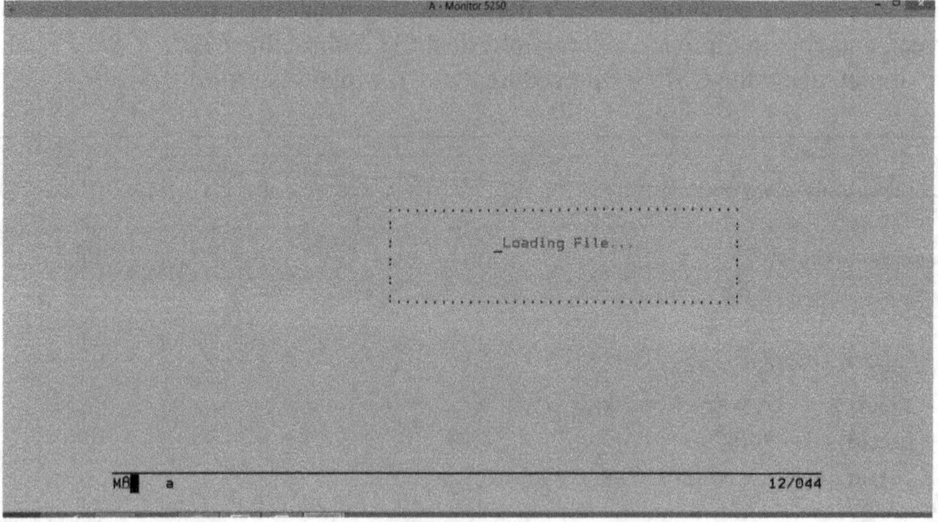

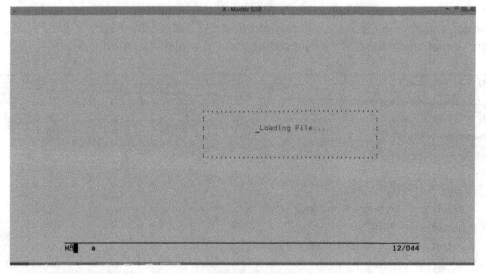

Figure 5.3: The window displayed while the CSV file is being checked.

If the copy from the CSV file to the *PFIN_INV* temporary file is successful, the valid records are processed. The invalid records are placed in a separate file that will be sent to the user later. This happens in subroutine *Load_Inv_PF*:

```
// -----------------------------------------------------------------
// Subroutine: Load data to the inventory file
// -----------------------------------------------------------------
BegSR Load_Inv_PF;

  // Clear the error log file that will be sent to the user
  P_Cmdlin = 'CLRPFM PFOUT_IE';
  P_Cmdlen = %LEN(%TRIM(P_CmdLin));
  CALLP $QCMDEXC(P_Cmdlin: P_Cmdlen);

  // Open files
  Open PFIN_INV;
  Open PFOUT_IE;

  W_Error_Nbr = *Zeros;
  W_TotErr    = *Zeros;

  // Read input file's first record
  Read PFIN_INV;

  DoW Not %Eof(PFIN_INV);
    // Initialize fields
    ExSr Init_Load_Fields;

    // Convert field values
    ExSr Convert_Fields;

    // Validate fields
    ExSr Vld_Fields;

    If W_Error = *Off;
      // If no errors were found, write the record to the application PF
```

Continued

```
        ExSr Wrt_Record;
      EndIf;

      // Read input file's next record
      Read PFIN_INV;
    EndDo;

    // Close files
    Close PFIN_INV;
    Close PFOUT_IE;

EndSR;
```

Notice the *PFOUT_IE* file, being cleared right at the beginning of the subroutine. The file is declared with the *UsrOpn* keyword; otherwise, it would be locked by the program, and the *CLRPFM* command would fail. The *PFIN_INV* file is also defined with *UsrOpn* for the same reason—the file is cleared when the data is copied from the CSV file.

The next step is opening both files and processing the *PFIN_INV* records in a loop. For each record, four operations will be performed:

1. Initialize the process-related fields.
2. Convert IDs and other codes. (In this particular case, the external item ID is converted into the internal item ID.)
3. Validate the record (with the converted data).
4. Write the information to the application (if all the previous steps were successful).

These operations correspond to subroutines *Init_Load_Fields*, *Convert_Fields*, *Vld_Fields*, and *Wrt_Record*. While the first is simply the initialization of the *W_Error_Nbr* variable, the others are more interesting. Let's start with *Convert_Fields*:

```
// ----------------------------------------------------------------------
// Subroutine: Convert field values (temp PF to application's PF)
// ----------------------------------------------------------------------
BegSr Convert_Fields;

  // Business rules related conversions and
  // DB field value code conversions happen here

  // Convert the external Item ID into the company's Item ID
  W_ID = CvtItmID(In_ID);
  // If the function returns *Zeros, the conversion failed
  If W_ID = *Zeros;
    // Step 1: Mark this record as unusable
    W_Error = *On;
    // Step 2: Write it to the error log file
    ExSr Wrt_ErrorLog;
    // Step 3: Increase the records with errors counter
    W_TotErr = W_TotErr + 1;
    // Step 4: Leave the subroutine
    LeaveSr;
  EndIf;

  // Repeat the steps above for each of the fields to convert

  // If the conversion was successful,
  // pass the original record to a temporary data structure
  TempInRec = InRec;
  // And copy all the converted fields
  Tmp_ID = W_Id;

EndSR;
```

As I said before, in this case only one conversion is necessary: the external item ID is converted into the internal item ID. This is done by procedure *CvtItmID*, which is explained in detail later, in the discussion of the *DBH_INV* service program. For the moment, just note the flow of the subroutine:

- Every field that needs conversion is (ideally) handled by a function.
- The result of the conversion is checked.
- In case of error, the whole record is marked as unusable (by setting the *W_Error* variable to **On*) and written to the error log file (by invoking the *Wrt_ErrorLog* subroutine).
- The user can later analyze the error log, correct the record, and try again.

This implies that the records can be processed individually. There are some situations, however, in which this is simply not possible. To handle those situations, some changes to this subroutine and *Load_Inv_PF* would be necessary (addressed later). If everything went smoothly, the data is copied to a temporary data structure named *TempInRec* (similar to the *PFIN_INV* record format), and the converted fields are also copied to this data structure. Although using a temporary data structure is not essential, it can be useful to have the "before" and "after" conversion records when you are debugging the program.

This ends the subroutine. If the *W_Error* indicator is **Off*, the next step can be performed—the validation of the record, which takes place in subroutine *Vld_Fields*:

```
// ----------------------------------------------------------------------
// Subroutine: Validate input file fields
// ----------------------------------------------------------------------
BegSR Vld_Fields;

  If W_Error = *On;
    LeaveSr;
  EndIf;

  // Business rules and data validity checks happen here

                                                            Continued
```

```
  // If an error occurred,
  If ChkInInvRec(TempInRec) = *On;
    // Step 1: Mark this record as unusable
    W_Error = *On;
    // Step 2: Write it to the error log file
    ExSr Wrt_ErrorLog;
    // Step 3: Increase the records-with-errors counter
    W_TotErr = W_TotErr + 1;
  EndIf;

EndSR;
```

The validation itself is performed by function *ChkInInvRec*, explained in depth later, during the discussion of the *DBH_INV* service program. For now, all you need to know is that the function returns **On* if the validation of the record fails. In that case, the flow is similar to the previous subroutine: the record is marked unusable and the error is logged.

There's another step that I neglected to mention before—a counter, named *W_TotErr*, is designed to store the total number of records that were not successfully processed. Even though the user will receive a file with those records, this allows the program to show a nice message at the end of the process, stating that *xx* records couldn't be processed and reminding the user to check his or her mailbox for the details. On the other hand, if the validation was successful, the record is ready to be written to the respective application file, the inventory master file, in this case. This happens in the *Wrt_Record* subroutine:

```
// ----------------------------------------------------------------------
// Subroutine: Write the record to the application PF
// ----------------------------------------------------------------------
BegSR Wrt_Record;

  WrtUpdInvRec(TempInRec);

EndSR;
```

You might ask why I created a subroutine with only one line of code in it. Well, in this simple example, I'm only writing one application file, but in a real-life situation, one input record might correspond to records in several different files. Having a subroutine to concentrate all those write operations in one place is a good practice. Using a procedure to handle the write operation is also a good practice because you can enforce any business rules, additional validations, operations triggered by the write, and so on, in a single place. This way, you don't have to maintain the same code in several programs. Anyway, we'll examine the *WrtUpdInvRec* procedure in depth in the *DBH_INV* section.

These four big operations are performed for each record of the *PFIN_INV* file. When the file ends, the CSV file is removed from the IFS using subroutine *DEL_CSV*. The user is shown a completion screen, which may contain a message stating that *xx* records couldn't be processed, so an error log file should be in the user's mailbox. What the user doesn't see is subroutine *Snd_Errors_EMail*, which produces that MS Excel file:

```
// -----------------------------------------------------------------
// Subroutine: Send the error log file in xls format to the user
// -----------------------------------------------------------------
BegSR Snd_Errors_EMail;

  If FileToXls('PFOUT_IE'
              :'Xls/Templates'
              :'INVIMP_Error_Log.xls'
              :'INVIMP'
              :1
              :8
              :''
              :'Xls'
              :'Inv_Import_Errors.xls'
              ) = *Off;

   //Send to the user who called the program
   W_SName        = UsNm;
   W_SEmail       = 'noreply@yourcompany.com';
   W_MailTo       = UsNm;
```

Continued

```
    W_MailCC       = *Blanks;
    W_MailBCC      = *Blanks;
    W_PathFile(1) = '/Xls/Inv_Import_Errors.xls';
    W_Subject      = 'Inventory import error log';
    W_Body         = 'Please find attached the Inventory import ' +
                     'error log.';


    CallP SndMulFiles(W_SName
                     :W_SEmail
                     :W_MailTo
                     :W_MailCc
                     :W_MailBcc
                     :W_Spool
                     :W_ImbAtt
                     :W_File
                     :W_Lib
                     :W_FmtFich
                     :W_NameFich
                     :W_IncFlds
                     :W_Zip
                     :W_Subject
                     :W_Body
                     :W_PathFile
                     );
  EndIf;

EndSR;
```

This subroutine uses two procedures—*FileToXls*, explained in chapter 7, and *SndMulFiles*, explained in chapter 6. In short, the first procedure transforms the *PFOUT_IE* physical file into an MS Excel file and the second emails that file to the user who called the program.

The main screen is reset and the program is ready to process another file, thus completing the main cycle. It's now time to analyze the service programs that support the functionality described so far.

The DBH_INV Service Program

The *DBH_INV* service program handles the database operations for the inventory master file, *PFINV*, hence its name. Typically, I like to build these service programs with a minimum of two procedures/functions. The first one checks if the record to be written is according to all business rules and data validity checks, such as mandatory fields and valid dates. The other one writes the record itself. Naturally, if some sort of data conversion is necessary, it's also a good idea to write a function for that. Ideally, you'll write one function for each field to convert, so that reusing functions later gets easier.

In this particular case, I have three procedures/functions in the *DBH_INV* service program. Let's start with the simplest, *CvtItmID*, or "Convert external item ID into the company's item ID":

```
 *-------------------------------------------------------------------------
 * Procedure: Convert external item ID into the company's item ID
 *-------------------------------------------------------------------------
P CvtItmID          B                   EXPORT
D CvtItmID          PI                  Like(Inv_Item_ID)
D  P_Ext_ID                             Like(InInvRec.ID) Value

D  W_ID             S                   Like(InInvRec.ID)
 /FREE

   If P_Ext_Id = *Zeros;
     Return *Zeros;
   EndIf;

   If Not %Open(LFIDCNV01);
     Open LFIDCNV01;
   EndIf;

   K_ID = P_Ext_ID;
   Chain K_ID LFIDCNV01;

                                                              Continued
```

```
   If Not %Found(LFIDCNV01);
     W_ID = *Zeros;
   Else;
     W_ID = Id_Int_ID;
   EndIf;

   If %Open(LFIDCNV01);
     Close LFIDCNV01;
   EndIf;

   Return W_Id;

 /END-FREE

P CvtItmID         E
```

This function receives the external item ID (from the cargo manifest CSV file) and converts it to the company's item ID, using the *LFIDCNV01* logical file to find the correct internal ID. If no match is found, the function returns **ZEROS*. Obviously, this is a very basic example of a data conversion function, but it gives you an example of how you can do it.

If you remember the *INVIMP* flow, after the conversions are performed, the next step is validating the record. Procedure *ChkInInvRec* takes care of that:

```
 *-----------------------------------------------------------------
 * Procedure: Check inventory input record fields
 *-----------------------------------------------------------------
P ChkInInvRec      B                   EXPORT
D ChkInInvRec      PI             N
D  P_InInvRec                          LikeDS(InInvRec) Value

 /FREE

                                                       Continued
```

```
// Check the input record fields
// Stop when the first error is found

// ID
// NAME
If P_InInvRec.Name = *Blanks;
  Return *On;
EndIf;

// DESCRIPT
If P_InInvRec.Descript = *Blanks;
  Return *On;
EndIf;

// PRICE
If P_InInvRec.Price <= *Zeros;
  Return *On;
EndIf;

// QTY
If P_InInvRec.Qty <= *Zeros;
  Return *On;
EndIf;

// REMARKS
// The remarks are optional, no validation is required

// ORD_NBR
If P_InInvRec.Ord_Nbr = *Zeros;
  Return *On;
Else;
  // In a real life situation, the order number would be checked
  // in the application's order file...
EndIf;
```

Continued

```
    // IVC_NBR
    If P_InInvRec.Ivc_Nbr = *Zeros;
      Return *On;
    Else;
      // In a real life situation, the supplier's invoice number would
      // be checked in the application's suppliers invoice file...
    EndIf;

  /END-FREE

P ChkInInvRec      E
```

Note that in this case, I'm not validating the inventory master file record (which would be the most natural thing to do), but the input record from *PFIN_INV*. Since this record format contains more information than the inventory master file, but the relevant data is the same in both record formats, I chose to validate this record format instead of *PFINV*. Ideally, in a situation like the one presented here, you should create functions to validate both record formats, because other programs might write data directly to your application physical file, and it's a good practice to check the data before writing it to the database.

Now, let's review the code. To avoid forgetting a field, I always start by copying all the field names from the physical file and pasting them in comment lines, like this:

```
// ID
// NAME
// DESCRIPT
// PRICE
// QTY
// REMARKS
// ORD_NBR
// IVC_NBR
```

Then I write the validation code for each field or a note stating that no validation is required (see the *REMARKS* field, for instance). Some validations are simple, such as the *NAME* and *DESCRIPT* fields. Some others might be more complex, like *ORD_NBR* and *IVC_NBR*.

This form of validation is simple, but it has its shortcomings—it's designed to stop when it encounters the first error, and it doesn't indicate where that error was found. I tried to create a simplistic validation function, but feel free to enhance it with these or other features.

Finally, the function that writes the record has an implicit business rule: if the item's ID and price are the same as those of an existing record, the quantity of that record is updated instead of writing a new one. Here, those lines are bolded in the function's code for your convenience:

```
 *-----------------------------------------------------------------------
 *Procedure: Write or update a record in PFINV
 *-----------------------------------------------------------------------
P WrtUpdInvRec    B                   EXPORT
D WrtUpdInvRec    PI             N
D  P_InInvRec                         LikeDS(InInvRec) Value

 /FREE

   If Not %Open(LFINV01);
     Open LFINV01;
   EndIf;

   // Using the item id and unit price, check if a record already exists
   K_ID    = P_InInvRec.ID;
   K_Price = P_InInvRec.Price;

   Chain K_Inv01 LFINV01;
   If %Found(LFINV01);
     // If it does, update the quantity by adding the input record's
     // quantity to the inventory
     Inv_Qty = Inv_Qty + P_InInvRec.Qty;
     Update(E) INVR;
   Else;
```

Continued

```
    // Otherwise, write a new record
    Inv_Item_Id     = P_InInvRec.Id;
    Inv_Unit_Price = P_InInvRec.Price;
    Inv_Qty         = P_InInvRec.Qty;
    Inv_Upd_Date    = %Date();
    Inv_Upd_User    = User;
    Write(E) INVR;
  EndIf;

  If %Open(LFINV01);
    Close LFINV01;
  EndIf;

  If %Error = *On;
    Return *On;
  Else;
    Return *Off;
  EndIf;

 /END-FREE

P WrtUpdInvRec    E
```

This might not be the most common scenario, but it illustrates the possibility of having business rules enforced when the record is written. Typically, there would be four functions: a read, a write, an update, and a delete function that would handle of the database operations separately. While the need for a read function is arguable, the use of the others is a good practice to enforce database consistency and (when applicable) business rules.

One final note regarding the compilation: I've created a binding directory for this service program, even though it doesn't use any external procedures. I consider it a good practice to always create a binding directory because you can compile all the service programs the same way. (See the "Generic Compilation Instructions" of this book's introduction.) That's all for *DBH_INV*!

The CSVPRC Service Program

The *CSVPRC* service program performs the geekiest and perhaps the most important operation of this chapter: it analyzes the CSV file records and tries to fix all those annoying little errors that users tend to make when creating or modifying CSV files. It contains only one function, named *CSV2PF*, but it's a big and somewhat complex piece of code. Let's go over it, step by step.

CSV2PF's objective is to receive a CSV file as input, analyze it, fix whatever can be fixed, and copy the CSV file data to a physical file. The function's parameters reflect its objective:

```
P CSV2PF            B                     EXPORT
D CSV2PF            PI              N
D  P_InputCSV                    255A
D  P_OutputPF                     10A
D  P_OutputCSV                   255A
D  P_FieldSep                      4A
D  P_DecimalSep                    7A
D  P_RunCopy                       1A
```

The objective of parameters *P_InputCSV* and *P_OutputPF* should be pretty obvious, as it is directly linked to *CSV2PF*'s goal (and name). The other ones, however, are related to the function's inner workings.

To produce a "fixed" CSV file, I chose to write a new file and preserve the original. That's what parameter *P_OutputCSV* is for. If you fill the parameter with a path and file name, it will be used to create the output CSV file with the corrected data. This was done this way to add flexibility to the function; you may use it just to check and correct a CSV file without copying the data to a physical file. To do that, you'd need to pass *N* in the *P_RunCopy* parameter, because it controls the execution of the *CPYFRMIMPF* command. (See chapter 3 for details about that.) Finally, *P_FieldSep* and *P_DecimalSep* are used to determine the field separation character and the decimal point character, respectively.

This might all seem a bit confusing, but it will (hopefully) get clearer with the explanation of the function's source code. Let's start with the main flow and examine the subroutines as we go along:

```
// Initialization procedures
ExSr Init;

// Retrieve destination file field descriptions
ExSr Rtv_FFD;

// Open the CSV file
// and process each record: validate and write to output CSV file
ExSr Prc_CSV;

// Check the P_RunCopy parameter and run CPYFRMIMPF, if needed
ExSr Run_Copy;

// End the procedure by closing everything and return status indicator
ExSr End_Of_Program;
```

The first thing to do is initialize what needs to be initialized. That's the goal of the *Init* subroutine:

```
//--------------------------------------------------------------------*
// Initialization                                                     *
//--------------------------------------------------------------------*
  BegSr  Init;

    // Initialize the arrays
    Clear W_FieldDef;
    Clear W_InFieldVal;
    Clear W_OutFieldVal;

    // Initialize work variables
    W_OutputCSVCreated = 'N';
    W_Idx = *Zeros;
    W_LastField = *Zeros;
    W_Error = *Off;
```

Continued

```
    If P_OutputCSV = *Blanks;
      P_OutputCSV = '/tmp/tempcsv2pf.csv';
    EndIf;

    // Remove the thousands separator from the search string
    Select;
      When P_DecimalSep = '*COMMA';
        W_SearchString = %ScanRpl(',' : 'A' : W_NonNumeric);
      When P_DecimalSep = '*PERIOD';
        W_SearchString = %ScanRpl('.' : 'A' : W_NonNumeric);
      Other;
        W_SearchString = %ScanRpl(',' : 'A' : W_NonNumeric);
      EndSl;

  EndSr;
```

It starts by clearing three arrays, *W_FieldDef*, *W_InFieldVal*, and *W_OutFieldVal*. The first will contain the field definitions (more on this in the *RTV_FFD* subroutine explanation), while the other two will hold the input and output "records." (I'll explain this in the discussion of the *Prc_CSV* subroutine.) Then, it initializes some work variables and fills the *P_OutputCSV* parameter, if no value was passed. Finally, it uses the *%ScanRpl* built-in function (which stands for Scan and Replace, if you're not familiar with it) to remove the thousands separator from a string named *W_NonNumeric*. I'll explain what this string is used for later.

To check and possibly fix each field's value, the next step is to determine that field's type. The way to do that is by determining the corresponding field in the output physical file. This requires a little trick, performed in the *RTV_FFD* subroutine:

```
//---------------------------------------------------------------*
//Retrieve destination file field                                *
//---------------------------------------------------------------*
  BegSr  Rtv_FFD;

    If W_Error = *On;
      LeaveSR;
    EndIf;
```

Continued

```
Monitor;
  P_CmdLin = 'DSPFFD FILE(' + %Trim(P_OutputPF) +
             ') OUTPUT(*OUTFILE) OUTFILE(QTEMP/TEMPFFD) ' +
             'OUTMBR(*FIRST *REPLACE)';
  CallP(E) $QCMDEXC(P_CmdLin : P_CmdLen);
  If %Error;
    W_Error = *On;
    LeaveSR;
  EndIf;

  // Read the field descriptions into an array
  If Not %Open(TEMPFFD);
    Open TEMPFFD;
  EndIf;

  For W_Idx = 1 to C_MaxArraySize;
    Read QWHDRFFD;
    If %EoF(TEMPFFD);
      Leave;
    EndIf;
    W_FieldDef(W_Idx).FieldName     = Fd_WHFLDI;
    W_FieldDef(W_Idx).FieldType     = Fd_WHFLDT;
    // The field size is stored in different columns for Type='A'
    If W_FieldDef(W_Idx).FieldType = 'A';
      W_FieldDef(W_Idx).FieldSize     = Fd_WHFLDB;
      W_FieldDef(W_Idx).FieldDecimals = *Zeros;
    Else;
      W_FieldDef(W_Idx).FieldSize     = Fd_WHFLDD;
      W_FieldDef(W_Idx).FieldDecimals = Fd_WHFLDP;
    EndIf;
  EndFor;

  If %Open(TEMPFFD);
    Close TEMPFFD;
  EndIf;
```

Continued

```
    On-Error;
      W_Error = *On;
      LeaveSR;
    EndMon;

  EndSr;
```

One way to retrieve the output physical file field definition is by using the *DSPFFD* (Display File Field Description) command, with its output directed to a physical file. You can also use a system API named *QUSLFLD*, but I like to keep things simple. Anyway, the command is issued using the physical file name that was passed in the *P_OutputPF* parameter and a hardcoded physical file name, *TEMPFFD*, in the *OUTFILE* parameter. This file is defined in the beginning of the code (not shown here) as *UsrOpn*. Otherwise, this operation would fail, because the file would be locked by the program. The next step is to put the aforementioned *W_FieldDef* array to good use: in a loop, all the field definitions are copied to this array; each line of *TEMPFFD* contains the definitions of one of the output physical file fields.

With these definitions stored in the array, it's time to start the actual processing of the CSV file. That's the mission of the *Prc_CSV* subroutine:

```
//----------------------------------------------------------------------*
//Process each record: validate and write to output CSV file          *
//----------------------------------------------------------------------*
  BegSr  Prc_CSV;

    If W_Error = *On;
      LeaveSR;
    EndIf;

    // Open the CSV file (read only, text mode)
    W_InputCSVFile = Open( %Trim(P_InputCSV) : O_RDONLY+O_TEXTDATA );
    If W_InputCSVFile < *Zeros;
      W_Error = *On;
     LeaveSR;
    EndIf;
```
Continued

```
   // Read and process each line
   Dow ReadLine(W_InputCSVFile : %Addr(W_Line) :
              %Size(W_Line)) >= *Zeros;

     // Check if the line is ok to import:
     // Header line and blank lines are not imported
     ExSr Chk_InputLine;
     If W_LineOK = 'Y';
       // Split the line into fields and store them in an array
       ExSr Prc_InputLine;
       // Check each field against the definition
       // and try to correct its value
       ExSr Prc_Flds;
       // Write the processed line to the output CSV
       ExSr Wrt_OutputLine;
     EndIf;
  EndDo;

   // Close the CSV file
   CallP Close(W_InputCSVFile);

 EndSr;
```

This subroutine will read the CSV file as if it were a database file, with a little help from Scott Klement's IFS tool, mentioned in the introduction to this book. The *Open* and *Close* functions are actually C APIs. They are defined for "RPG usage" in the *IFSIO_H* copy member. The *ReadLine* and *WriteLine* functions (the latter is used in subroutine *Wrt_OutputLine)* are Scott's code, also based on C functions. If you want to know what makes them tick, read the great (and free) e-book that Scott put together to explain the IFS tool, available here:

http://www.scottklement.com/rpg/ifs_ebook

Having said that, let's go back to the code. The CSV file name that was indicated in the *P_InputCSV* parameter is opened in read-only mode with the *Open* function. Then, the lines are read with the *ReadLine* function—imagine this to be the equivalent of a standard RPG *Read* opcode. Just like its RPG equivalent, this function lets the program know when the end of file is reached; when that happens, the return value becomes a negative number.

OK, so we've managed to open the CSV file as if it were a normal database file and we know how to read its lines. The next step is to see if the line is usable.

Two of the most common mistakes users make when saving a CSV file is forgetting to delete the header row (sounds familiar, right?) and leaving blank lines, either in the middle or the end of the file. Subroutine *Chk_InputLine* deals with these two situations:

```
//---------------------------------------------------------------*
//Process each line: split the line into array entries          *
//---------------------------------------------------------------*
 BegSr  Chk_InputLine;

   If W_Error = *On;
     LeaveSR;
   EndIf;

   // The only "safe" way to find and remove a header/blank line is
   // checking if the output PF has numeric fields
   W_Stmt = 'SELECT COUNT(*) FROM TEMPFFD WHERE WHFLDT IN (' +
            W_Ivc + 'B' + W_Ivc + ', ' + W_Ivc + 'F' + W_Ivc + ', ' +
            W_Ivc + 'I' + W_Ivc + ', ' + W_Ivc + 'P' + W_Ivc + ', ' +
            W_Ivc + 'S' + W_Ivc + ', ' + W_Ivc + 'U' + W_Ivc + ')';
   If RecCount(W_Stmt) > *Zeros;
     // Remove all non-numeric characters
     // (including the separator char) from the W_Line string.
     W_TempString = %Trim(%XLate(W_NonNumeric : W_AllStars :
                                 %Trim(W_Line)));
     // Special handling for the euro symbol
     W_TempString = %Trim(%XLate(X'20' : W_AllStars :
                                 %Trim(W_TempString)));
     W_TempString = %Trim(%ScanRpl('*' : '' : W_TempString));
```

Continued

```
      // If nothing is left, then it's either a header/blank line.
      If W_TempString = *Blanks;
        W_LineOK = 'N';
      Else;
        W_LineOK = 'Y';
      EndIf;
    EndIf;

  EndSr;
```

Usually, an application's physical file has, at least, one numeric field. It might be an ID, or a code of some sort, or an amount. I'm using that here to determine if the line that *ReadLine* placed in the *W_Line* variable is a header or a blank line. First, I'm checking if at least one of the *P_OutputFile* fields is numeric, using the *RecCount* function, explained later in the *SQLPRC* service program section. If there's at least one numeric field, I can proceed and remove all non-numeric characters from the *W_Line* variable, using the *%Xlate* BIF, the aforementioned *W_NonNumeric*, and the *W_AllStars* strings. By the way, *W_NonNumeric* and *W_AllStars* are defined in the *QRPGLESRC/CSVPRC* source member. You should review them carefully, because they contain special characters that might not be properly converted when you restore the source code. *W_NonNumeric* is supposed to contain, among other things, special characters that are not used in the English language, such as "Ã" and "Ô". When this *%Xlate* operation runs, all the non-numeric characters that are part of the *W_NonNumeric* string are replaced with the asterisk (*) character.

There's an additional step for the euro symbol—important for European companies, probably irrelevant for most American companies. However, it can serve as an example for you to replace other special characters that might cause problems when you are importing a CSV file. It's just a matter of replacing it with the "offending character" code, and copying and pasting these three lines:

```
// Special handling for the euro symbol
W_TempString = %Trim(%XLate(X'20' : W_AllStars :
%Trim(W_TempString)));
```

X'20' is the hexadecimal code for the euro symbol.

The next step is replacing the asterisk character with a blank space. If the whole *W_Line* string is composed of blank spaces, then it is either a header or a blank line, and it must be ignored. Otherwise, the *W_LineOK* variable is set to *Y* and the line will be checked, corrected, and written in the output CSV file by subroutines *Prc_InputLine*, *Prc_Flds*, and *Wrt_OutputLine*, respectively. The first of these three subroutines takes the *W_Line* variable, which is a huge string that contains the complete CSV file line, and splits it into usable fields:

```
//--------------------------------------------------------------------*
//Process each line: split the line into array entries               *
//--------------------------------------------------------------------*
  BegSr  Prc_InputLine;

    If W_Error = *On;
      LeaveSR;
    EndIf;

    // If the line is not empty, look for the separator character
    // and store each field into an array entry
    // Store the first field
    W_StrPos = %Scan(%Trim(P_FieldSep) : W_Line : 1);
    If W_StrPos = *Zeros;
      W_Error = *On;
      LeaveSR;
    EndIf;
    W_Idx = 1;
    W_InFieldVal(W_Idx).FieldValue = %SubSt(W_Line : 1 : W_StrPos - 1);

    // Then use W_StrPos and W_EndPos to "navigate" within the line
    // and store all the other fields
    W_EndPos = -1;
    DoW W_EndPos <> *Zeros;
      W_EndPos = %Scan(%Trim(P_FieldSep) : W_Line : W_StrPos + 1);
      If W_EndPos <> *Zeros;
        W_Idx += 1;
        W_InFieldVal(W_Idx).FieldValue = %Trim(
           %SubSt(W_Line :  W_StrPos + 1 : W_EndPos - W_StrPos-1));
```

Continued

```
        W_StrPos = W_EndPos;
      Else;
        // Process the last field of the line, in case there's
        // no separator character after it
        W_EndPos = %Scan('          ' : W_Line : W_StrPos + 1);
        W_Idx += 1;
        W_InFieldVal(W_Idx).FieldValue = %Trim(
           %SubSt(W_Line :  W_StrPos + 1 : W_EndPos - W_StrPos - 1));
        // After processing the last field, set W_EndPos to zero,
        // in order to leave the cycle
        W_EndPos = *Zeros;
      EndIf;
    EndDo;

EndSr;
```

It does that by using the field separator character that was passed in *P_FieldSep* to determine where each field's value begins and ends, just like Excel does when you open a CSV file to display each value in a separate column.

The code might seem a little daunting, but it's actually quite simple once you understand the mechanics: the *%Scan* BIF is used to determine where the field separator character is; then the part of the string that lies between the position of the last field separator and the next field separator is the field value.

Perhaps it will get clearer with an example. Suppose we want to process this line:

```
123;AAA;BBBBBBBBB
```

The subroutine will start by looking for the first semicolon character. It's in position 4 of the string, so *W_StrPos* will be filled with 4; then the first field of the *W_InFieldVal* array will get everything between 0 and (4 – 1), because we don't want the separator character ("123" in this case). Then we enter a loop and the search for the separator character begins in position 5 (*W_StrPos + 1*); that search will return position 8, and the 3 characters (that's *W_EndPos – W_StrPos* or 8 – 5) starting in position 5 will be stored in the second field of the *W_InFieldVal* array (that's "AAA").

The loop begins again with the search, starting in position 9 (again, *W_StrPos + 1*). This time, it won't find the separator character because this is the last field, but we still need to know where the content ends, so we search for a few blank spaces. This gives use the first position after the content—17, in this case. With that, we use the *%SubStr* BIF again to extract the content of the third and last field, starting in position 9 (or *W_StrPos*)and composed of the characters between that position and the first blank space minus 1 (or *W_StrPos – 1*), because we don't want the blank space, just the content before it. This translates to *%SubSt(W_Line : W_StrPos + 1 : W_EndPos – W_StrPos – 1)*.

When the subroutine ends, all the fields are stored in *W_FieldVal* and can now be checked and corrected individually. That's what happens in the next subroutine to be executed, *Prc_Flds*:

```
//---------------------------------------------------------------*
//Process each field: compare with the definition and try to correct  *
//---------------------------------------------------------------*
  BegSr  Prc_Flds;

    If W_Error = *On;
      LeaveSR;
    EndIf;

    // Use the W_Idx value to identify how many entries the arrays have
    W_Line = *Blanks;
    W_LastField = W_Idx;
    For W_Idx = 1 to W_LastField;
      Select;
      // Check numeric fields
      When W_FieldDef(W_Idx).FieldType = 'B'
           Or W_FieldDef(W_Idx).FieldType = 'F'
           Or W_FieldDef(W_Idx).FieldType = 'I'
           Or W_FieldDef(W_Idx).FieldType = 'P'
           Or W_FieldDef(W_Idx).FieldType = 'S'
           Or W_FieldDef(W_Idx).FieldType = 'U';
```

Continued

```
// Remove non-numeric characters
// Replace all non-numeric characters with '*'
W_TempString = %Trim(%XLate(W_SearchString :
                            W_AllStars      :
                            W_InFieldVal(W_Idx).FieldValue));
// Special handling for the euro symbol
W_TempString = %Trim(%XLate(X'20' : W_AllStars :
                            %Trim(W_TempString)));
// Remove all '*' from the field
W_OutFieldVal(W_Idx).FieldValue =
    %Trim(%ScanRpl('*' : '' : W_TempString));

 // Remove whatever is left after a blank space
 W_EndPos = %Scan(' ' : W_OutFieldVal(W_Idx).FieldValue : 1);
 If W_EndPos <> *Zeros;
   W_OutFieldVal(W_Idx).FieldValue =
     %SubSt(W_OutFieldVal(W_Idx).FieldValue : 1: W_EndPos - 1);
 EndIf;

// Special checks for (numeric) date fields (8,0)
If W_FieldDef(W_Idx).FieldSize = 8
   And W_FieldDef(W_Idx).FieldDecimals = 0;

  W_Len = %Len(%Trim(W_OutFieldVal(W_Idx).FieldValue));
  Select;
    // If the data length is 6, assume the zeros before the day
    // and month are missing.
     When W_Len = 6;
     // Transform 1-1-2013 into 01-01-2013
     If %SubSt(W_OutFieldVal(W_Idx).FieldValue : 3: 2) = '20'
        Or %SubSt(W_OutFieldVal(W_Idx).FieldValue : 3: 2) = '21';
       W_TempString = '0'
                    + %SubSt(W_OutFieldVal(W_Idx).FieldValue :
                             1 : 1) + '0'
                    + %SubSt(W_OutFieldVal(W_Idx).FieldValue :
                             2 : 5);
```

Continued

```
          Else;
          // Transform 2013-1-1 into 2013-01-01
            W_TempString = %SubSt(W_OutFieldVal(W_Idx).FieldValue :
                                   1 : 4) + '0'
                         + %SubSt(W_OutFieldVal(W_Idx).FieldValue :
                                     5 : 1) + '0'
                         + %SubSt(W_OutFieldVal(W_Idx).FieldValue :
                                     6 : 1);
          EndIf;
          W_OutFieldVal(W_Idx).FieldValue = %Trim(W_TempString);
       EndSl;

     EndIf;
     // For the moment, just pass the other type of fields
     // to the output array
     Other;
       W_OutFieldVal(W_Idx).FieldValue =
           %Trim(W_InFieldVal(W_Idx).FieldValue);
     EndSl;
     If W_Idx = 1;
       W_Line =  %Trim(W_OutFieldVal(W_Idx).FieldValue);
     Else;
       W_Line = %Trim(W_line) + %Trim(P_FieldSep)
              + %Trim(W_OutFieldVal(W_Idx).FieldValue);
     EndIf;
   EndFor;

 EndSr;
```

Other than the header and blank lines, the formatting of numeric values is, in my experience, one of the most common mistakes end-users make when creating a CSV file. It's normal to finding thousand separators or currency symbols where they shouldn't exist. The result is an undecipherable error produced by the *CPYFRMIMPF* command that IT spends quite some time figuring out.

To prevent this type of error, I've used a similar solution to the one used in subroutine *Chk_InputLine*, but this time applied to a single numeric field instead of the complete line. Naturally, this solution is only applicable to numeric fields, so the first step is determining if the corresponding output file field is numeric. That's done by checking the *W_FieldDef.FieldType* field of the output file field. If it contains one of the many possible types for numeric fields, then all non-numeric characters are removed. After this, there's a piece of code related to "fake" date fields—numeric fields with eight positions and no decimals. In many applications, these fields are used to store dates, not in the date format but in a numeric format. If your application doesn't use these "fake" date fields, just remove that piece of code. I couldn't find a generic way to check and correct other types of field, so feel free to create other *When* statements in the *Select* statement just below the *For* cycle to handle those. For now, the *Other* opcode just copies the field value from the *W_InFieldVal* to the *W_OutFieldVal* arrays.

After each field is processed, its value is placed in the *W_Line* variable, along with a separator character. When all fields are processed, *W_Line* will contain a "fixed" version of the input line that can be written to the output CSV file. This happens in subroutine *Wrt_OutputLine*:

```
//-------------------------------------------------------------------*
//Write the processed line to the output CSV file
//-------------------------------------------------------------------*
  BegSr  Wrt_OutputLine;

    ExSR Crt_OutputCSV;

    // Write the processed line
    W_Len = %Len(%TrimR(W_Line));
    WriteLine(W_OutputCSVFile: %addr(W_Line): W_Len);

  EndSr;
```

Even though the subroutine is short and simple, there's a detail worth mentioning. if the CSV file doesn't exist in the IFS, it will be created by subroutine *Crt_OutputCSV*, which I'll explain next. Other than that, the *WriteLine* function, similar to the previously mentioned *ReadLine* function, is used to write the *W_Line* variable content to the output CSV file. But this can only happen if that file already exists! That's where *Crt_OutputCSV* comes in:

```
//---------------------------------------------------------------------*
//Create the output CSV file
//---------------------------------------------------------------------*
  BegSr  Crt_OutputCSV;

    If W_OutputCSVCreated = 'Y' Or W_Error = *On;
      LeaveSR;
    EndIf;

    // Remove the output file, in case it exists
    Unlink(%Trim(P_OutputCSV));

    // Create the output csv file with code page 819
    W_OutputCSVFile = Open(%Trim(P_OutputCSV):
                           O_CREAT + O_WRONLY + O_CODEPAGE :
                           S_IWUSR + S_IRUSR + S_IRGRP + S_IROTH :
                           819);
    If W_OutputCSVFile < *Zeros;
      W_Error = *On;
      LeaveSR;
    EndIf;

    // Close the output csv file
    CallP Close(W_OutputCSVFile);

    // Re-open it in write-only, text mode
    W_OutputCSVFile = Open(%Trim(P_OutputCSV):
                     O_WRONLY + O_TEXTDATA);
    If W_OutputCSVFile < *Zeros;
      W_Error = *On;
      LeaveSR;
    EndIf;


    // Set the flag that controls the output file creation
    W_OutputCSVCreated = 'Y';

  EndSr;
```

Keep in mind that the output CSV file is supposed to be a temporary file used to store the "enhanced" version of the original CSV file. I'm saying this because this subroutine will delete it if it exists, using Scott's *Unlink* function, and re-create it with the *Open* function mentioned earlier, but using different parameters.

There's a little something I've neglected to mention and this is as good time as any: a variable named *W_Error* is checked in the beginning of almost all the subroutines. It's a fast way to skip the subroutine if an error has occurred in the previous piece of code. Of course, I could condition the execution of each subroutine with an *If W_Error = *On* statement, but this seems more neat and tidy.

When the last line is written in the output CSV file, *Prc_CSV*'s *Do* loop ends. That means the temporary file is now ready. The next step, copying it to the physical file, depends on the *P_RunCopy* input parameter. The copy is performed using *CPYFRMIMPF*, as mentioned before and explained in chapter 3, but there are a few details worth mentioning. Let's review subroutine *Run_Copy*, where it all happens:

```
//-------------------------------------------------------------------*
//  Check the P_RunCopy parameter and run CPYFRMIMPF, if needed
//-------------------------------------------------------------------*
   BegSr  Run_Copy;

     If W_OutputCSVCreated = 'N' Or W_Error = *On;
       LeaveSR;
     Else;
       CallP Close(W_OutputCSVFile);
     EndIf;

     // Check if the file should be copied
     If P_RunCopy = 'N';
       LeaveSR;
     EndIf;

     // Set up the command parameters
     P_Cmdlin = 'CPYFRMIMPF' +
                ' FROMSTMF(' + W_IVC + %Trim(P_OutputCSV) + W_IVC + ')' +
                ' TOFILE(' + %Trim(P_OutputPF) + ')' +
```

Continued

```
                  ' MBROPT(*REPLACE) RCDDLM(*CRLF)' +
                  ' FLDDLM(' + W_IVC + %Trim(P_FieldSep) + W_IVC + ')' +
                  ' DECPNT(' + W_IVC + %Trim(P_DecimalSep) +  W_IVC + ')' +
                  ' RPLNULLVAL(*FLDDFT)';

    // Run the copy
    CallP(E) $QCMDEXC(P_Cmdlin: P_Cmdlen);

    // Report back the error, if the transfer failed
    If %Error;
      W_Error = *On;
    Else;
      // If the copy was successful, delete the temp csv
      Unlink(%Trim(P_OutputCSV));
    EndIf;

  EndSr;
```

This subroutine, like many others, starts by checking *W_Error*, but it also checks if the output CSV file was created (that's the *If W_OutputCSVCreated = 'N'* . . . piece of code). I've added this because it wouldn't make any sense to try and copy a non-existing file or, even worse, old data, to the output physical file. If everything went according to plan, there's actual data to be copied, and the *CPYFRMIMPF* command will take care of that. But first, it's necessary to check if the copy was requested (that's the *If P_RunCopy = 'N'* . . . piece of code) and, if so, set the command's parameters.

The *P_FieldSep* and *P_DecimalSep* parameters have been used throughout the *CSV2PF* function to perform many operations, and they are needed once more. This time, they are used to make sure the CSV file is correctly mapped to the output physical file. There's just one more thing: *W_IVC* contains the inverted comma character, needed to specify a path in the copy command.

All that is left to do is "close and clean up," because the function has performed its duty. A subroutine named *End_Of_Program* (OK, it should be *End_Of_Function*, but I prefer more generic names that I can use everywhere) is the last to run:

```
//------------------------------------------------------------------*
//End of the program                                                *
//------------------------------------------------------------------*
  BegSr  End_Of_Program;

    If W_OutputCSVCreated = 'Y' And P_RunCopy = 'N';
      CallP Close(W_OutputCSVFile);
    EndIf;

    Return W_Error;

  EndSr;
```

This subroutine simply closes the file if it was created and the copy to the physical file was not requested, and ends the function by returning the value of the *W_Error* variable.

That concludes the *CSVPRC* service program analysis. Along the way, I mentioned function *RecCount*. That function is part of the *SQLPRC* service program, explained next.

The SQLPRC Service Program

The *SQLPRC* service program has only one function, the aforementioned *RecCount*. This function executes an SQL statement and returns the number of records found. It assumes that the input statement is a *Select Count(*)* or a *Select Count(<field_name>)*. Here's the function's source code:

```
HDatEdit(*YMD) NoMain   ExprOpts(*MaxDigits)
 **************************************************************************
 *                                                                        *
 *š =====================================================================*
 *   Program .... :'SQLPRC                                                *
 *   Description  :'SQL Procedures                                        *
 *   Author ..... :'Rafael Victória-Pereira                               *
 *   Date ....... :'February 2014                                         *
 *š =====================================================================*
                                                                 Continued
```

```
 *--------------------------------------------------------------------------
 *   Prototypes
 *--------------------------------------------------------------------------
 * Prototype definition for SQL Procedures
 /COPY QCPYLESRC,SQLPRC_PR

 *--------------------------------------------------------------------------
 *š  Procedure RecCount - return a record count from a select statement
 *--------------------------------------------------------------------------
PRecCount         B                   EXPORT
D                 PI                  Like(W_Out)
 * Input Parms
DW_Stm                        1000     Value

 * Work variables
DW_Out            S             12  0
D STMT            S           1000

 /FREE
  //-------------------------------------------------------------------*
  // Main Code                                                         *
  //-------------------------------------------------------------------*

    // Initialization
    ExSr Init;

    // Run SQL statement to return a record count
    ExSr RunSQL;

    // Termination
    ExSr Term;

  //-------------------------------------------------------------------*
  // Program Initialization
  //-------------------------------------------------------------------*
```

Continued

```
  BegSr Init;

  EndSr;
 //----------------------------------------------------------------------*
 // Program Termination
 //----------------------------------------------------------------------*
  BegSr Term;

    Return W_Out;

  EndSr;
 //----------------------------------------------------------------------
 // Run SQL statements
 //----------------------------------------------------------------------
  BegSr RunSQL;

    EXEC SQL
      PREPARE S1 FROM :W_Stm;

    EXEC SQL
      DECLARE C1 CURSOR FOR S1;

    EXEC SQL
      OPEN C1;

    EXEC SQL
      FETCH C1 INTO :W_Out;

    EXEC SQL
      CLOSE C1;

  EndSr;
 /END-FREE
PRecCount         E
```

The trick here that allows you to use **any** *Select Count* statement is in the beginning of the *RunSQL* subroutine. The *Prepare* statement creates a dynamic SQL instruction from the *P_Stm* input parameter that cursor *C1* will use. It's a simple procedure designed for a very specific goal, but it serves to show that it's possible to execute SQL statements in a "normal" RPGLE program without all the fuss of creating a SQLRPGLE module/program.

The service program discussed in the next chapter is not so simple, but it provides great functionality: sending email from an RPG program.

6

Send Email from an RPG Program

> This chapter continues the example from the previous chapter, presenting a service program that emails an MS Excel file with the records that couldn't be recovered by the CSV file-upload program.

The *INVIMP* program in chapter 5 uses a function named *SndMulFiles* (short for *Send Multiple Files via Email*) to provide basic functionality. The *Email* service program in this chapter, however, has more to offer.

The four email-sending procedures presented here were created over a couple of years, according to a company's needs. I'll start with the simplest solution—sending short, text-only email—and move up to the most complex—sending formatted text and several types of attachments (text files, Excel spreadsheets, and Adobe® PDF files) to multiple addresses.

The *SndEmail* procedure allows you to send an email message to a maximum of three addresses. Here's the procedure's code:

```
 *-----------------------------------------------------------------------------
 *   Send Email Message
 *-----------------------------------------------------------------------------
PSndEMail          B                    EXPORT
D                  PI
 * Input Parms
DP_SendTo                       75    Value
DP_CopyTo                       75    Value
DP_BlindCopyTo                  75    Value
DP_Subject                      30    Value
DP_Body                        200    Value

 /FREE

 // Set the email destination string
 // (A)
SetDestStr(P_SendTo : P_CopyTo : P_BlindCopyTo : P_DestStr);

  // Send message
  // (B)
P_Cmdlin = 'SNDDST TYPE(*LMSG)'
             + ' TOINTNET(' + %Trim(P_DestStr) + ')'
             + ' DSTD(' + '''' + %Trim(P_Subject) + '''' + ')'
             + ' LONGMSG(' + '''' + %Trim(P_Body) + '''' + ')'
             + ' PTY(*HIGH)';
// (C)
  W_ErrorDS = ExecCmd (%Trim(P_CmdLin));

  // If the mail was sent (no error message id), return *Off
  If W_ErrorDS.APIMsgId = *Blanks;
     Return *Off;
  Else;
     Return *On;
  Endif;

 /END-FREE

PSndEMail          E
```

The message is constrained by the subject and body lengths (30 and 200 characters, respectively) and doesn't allow any attachments. This might suffice if all you need is to alert a user with a short and simple message.

How does it work? Well, this procedure is actually a programmer-friendly mask to the *SNDDST* CL command. The procedure's parameters are transformed to fit the command's keywords. The *P_SendTo*, *P_CopyTo*, and *P_BlindCopyTo* parameters are rearranged by the *SetDestStr* procedure into the destination string that will fit the command's *TOINTNET* keyword (see *A* in the code). The *P_Subject* and *P_Body* parameters are used in the *DSTD* and *LMSG* keywords, respectively (*B*). When the CL command is built, the *ExecCmd* procedure is used to execute it (*C*).

Sounds simple, doesn't it? Too simple? You need to send a message and an output file? Use *SndFileByMail* instead:

```
 *-------------------------------------------------------------------------
 *   Send File By Mail
 *-------------------------------------------------------------------------
PSndFileByMail    B                   EXPORT
D                 PI              N
 * Input Parms
DP_SendTo                       75    Value
DP_CopyTo                       75    Value
DP_BlindCopyTo                  75    Value
DP_Body                        200    Value
DP_FileName                     10    Value
DP_DocName                      12    Value
DP_FolderName                   10    Value
DP_Format                       10    Value

 /FREE

  // Set the email destination string
  // (A)
  SetDestStr(P_SendTo : P_CopyTo : P_BlindCopyTo : P_DestStr);

                                                                 Continued
```

```
// Retrieve the field separator for CSV format
// (B)
  In DaFldSep;
  W_FldSep = DaFldSep;

// Set attachment (either copy PF to folder, or use existing doc in folder)
// (C)
If P_DocName = *Blanks;
    P_DocName = %Trim(P_FileName) + '.' + %Trim(P_Format);
EndIf;
If P_FileName <> *Blanks;
    Select;
      When P_Format = 'TXT';
          P_Cmdlin = 'CPYTOPCD FROMFILE(' + %Trim(P_FileName) + ')'
                     + ' TOFLR(' + %Trim(P_FolderName) + ')'
                     + ' TODOC(' + '''' + %Trim(P_DocName) + '''' + ')'
                     + ' REPLACE(*YES)';

      When P_Format = 'CSV';
          P_Cmdlin = 'CPYTOIMPF FROMFILE(' + %Trim(P_FileName) + ')'
                     + ' TOSTMF(' + '''' + 'QDLS/'
                     + %Trim(P_FolderName) + '/' + %Trim(P_DocName) + ''''
                     + ') MBROPT(*REPLACE) STMFCODPAG(437)'
                     + ' RCDDLM(*CRLF) STRDLM(' + '''' + ' ' + '''' + ')'
                     + ' FLDDLM(' + '''' + W_FldSep + '''' + ')';
      Other;
         Return *On;
    EndSl;
    W_ErrorDS = ExecCmd (%Trim(P_CmdLin));

// If an error occurred (error message id is not blank), return *On
// (D)
    If W_ErrorDS.APIMsgId <> *Blanks;
      Return *On;
   EndIf;

                                                              Continued
```

```
    // Send message
    // (E)
       P_Cmdlin = 'SNDDST TYPE(*DOC)' +
                 ' TOINTNET(' + %Trim(P_DestStr) + ')'
                 + ' DSTD(' + '''' + 'DESC' + '''' + ')'
                 + ' MSG(' + '''' + %Trim(P_Body) + '''' + ')'
                 + ' DOC(' + '''' + %Trim(P_DocName) + '''' + ')'
                 + ' FLR(' + %Trim(P_FolderName) + ') PTY(*HIGH)';
       W_ErrorDS = ExecCmd (%Trim(P_CmdLin));

    // If the mail was sent (no error message id), return *Off
       If W_ErrorDS.APIMsgId = *Blanks;
         Return *Off;
       Else;
         Return *On;
       Endif;
    Endif;

/END-FREE

PSndFileByMail   E
```

This procedure can be used to send an output file generated by your program in text or CSV format to the same three addresses as the previous procedure. Again, the procedure is a mask to the *SNDDST* CL command. The destination addresses are treated the same way as previously (see *A* in the code), but the similarity to the first procedure ends here. The CSV conversion functionality requires a separator, usually a comma. Since this separator can vary in different countries or Excel versions, it's stored in a data area named *DAFLDSEP*. Because of this, the procedure's next step is retrieving the separator character (*B*).

The attachment type, passed in parameter *P_Format*, determines the type of conversion that will be performed. For the text format, the procedure uses the *CPYTOPCD* CL command, while the *CPYTOIMPF* command is used to generate the CSV format (*C*). If the conversion fails, the procedure ends, returning **On*. This is the way to tell the calling program that something went wrong, and the email was not sent (*D*). Finally, the CL command string is formed and executed (*E*).

Notice that the *P_Body* is now placed in the *MSG* keyword, and there is no *P_Subject* parameter. This happens because we are now using a different type of distribution that forces us to do these changes. For more detail, see the explanation of the *SNDDST* command in IBM's iSeries Information Center:

http://publib.boulder.ibm.com/iseries/v5r2/ic2924/info/cl/snddst.htm

What if all you really need is to send a spool file (some sort of business report or purchase order) via email to a supplier or client, without any need for fancy subject or message text because the attachment says it all? In that case, use *SndSplfByMail*:

```
 *-------------------------------------------------------------------------*
 *   Send Spoolfile By Mail
 *-------------------------------------------------------------------------*
PSndSplfByMail    B                   EXPORT
D                  PI             N
 * Input Parms
DP_SplfName                     10    Value
DP_SendTo                       75    Value

DI_ProdSys        S               N   Inz(*Off)

 /FREE

  // (A)
  // Check if this is the production system.
  // If it's not, emails won't be sent out of the company
  I_ProdSys = ProductionSys;

  // Retrieve the PDF transform printer name
  In DaPdfPrt;
  W_PdfPrt = DaPdfPrt;

  // * Get the user's email address (if internal)
  // (B)
  P_SendTo = RtvEmailAddr(P_SendTo);
```

Continued

```
  // If this is not the production system
  // and the destination mail is not from the company, send it.
  // (C)
  If Not I_ProdSys And Not InternalAddr(P_SendTo);
     Return *On;
  EndIf;

  // Change spoolfile attributes and redirect to PDF transform printer
  // (D)
  P_Cmdlin = 'CHGSPLFA FILE(' + %Trim(P_SplfName) + ') SPLNBR(*LAST)'
           + ' OUTQ(*LIBL/' + %Trim(W_PdfPrt) + ')'
           + ' USRDFNDTA(' + ''''
           + 'MAILTAG(' + %Trim(P_SendTo) + ')' + '''' + ')';
  W_ErrorDS = ExecCmd (%Trim(P_CmdLin));

  // If the mail was sent (no error message id), return *Off
  If W_ErrorDS.APIMsgId = *Blanks;
     Return *Off;
  Else;
     Return *On;
  Endif;

 /END-FREE

PSndSplfByMail    E
```

This very simple procedure takes advantage of the PDF conversion functionality provided by the InfoPrint Server licensed program. IBM's Printing Redbook (*http://www.redbooks.ibm.com/abstracts/sg246250.html*) explains how to install and configure this functionality, so I won't waste your time with that here; I'll just explain how it works. The conversion is performed by a virtual printer that also sends the generated PDF file via email to the address you specify in the *USRDFNDTA* keyword of the *CHGSPLFA* CL command.

Let's go over the code. In the beginning of the procedure (labeled *A* in the code), the necessary data is gathered; the system type (development, test, or production) and PDF conversion printer are retrieved. In the next step (*B*), the *P_SendTo* parameter is checked and converted to an Internet email address if necessary. (You'll learn more about procedure *RtvEmailAddr* in the "Other Procedures" section later in this chapter.)

In *C*, the address is checked to prevent sending test data to the "outside world," using the system type information and the destination address. (The procedure *InternalAddr* is also explained in "Other Procedures.") Next, in *D*, the conversion and distribution are performed in one single step: the spool file name (*P_SplfName*), PDF conversion printer (*W_PdfPrtf*), and destination address (*P_SendTo*) are used in the *CHGSPLFA* CL command to send the spool file to the "printer" that sends it to its destination.

Be aware that there are some factors to take into account. Complex printer files (with lines, boxes, or extensive formatting) might not be properly converted. Even worse, they might not be converted at all. Generate the spool file and use the *CHGSPLFA* command or option 2 in the *WRKSPLF* command to test it before you use this procedure.

The procedure requires the InfoPrint Server licensed program to work. Without it, it's useless. Although the conversion is performed by a virtual printer, it might be waiting for a reply to a message or stopped.

Finally, it's time for the procedure *SndMulFiles* used in *INVIMP*. It provides a programmer-friendly interface to the "Mime & Mail" procedures. As mentioned earlier, Mime & Mail was created by Giovanni B. Perotti, a brilliant IBMer from Italy. The current version is available here:

http://mmail.easy400.net

Procedure *SndMulFiles* accepts as parameters spool files that can be converted to text or PDF format, physical files that can be transformed into text or Excel files, other files that already exist in your IFS, and a wide range of destinations (internal user IDs, mailing groups, and individual email addresses retrieved from a sort of address book or from the production data).

Let's begin with the procedure's parameters and work variables definition:

```
 *------------------------------------------------------------------------*
 *   Send Multiple files in an Email Message
 *------------------------------------------------------------------------*
PSndMulFiles      B                   EXPORT
DSndMulFiles      PI               1
 * Input Parms
D P_SName                        50a   Value
D P_SEmail                       50a   Value
D P_MailTo                      200    Value
D P_MailCC                      200    Value
D P_MailBcc                     200    Value
D P_Spool                        10    Value
D                                      Dim(50)
D P_ImbAtt                        1    Value
D                                      Dim(50)
D P_File                         10    Value
D                                      Dim(50)
D P_Lib                          10    Value
D                                      Dim(50)
D P_FmtFile                       1    Value
D                                      Dim(50)
D P_NameFile                     12    Value                    File Name
D                                      Dim(50)
D P_IncFlds                       1    Value                    Include field names
D*                                                              0 - Don't include
D*                                                              1 - Include
D                                      Dim(50)
D P_Zip                          12    Value                    Zipped file name
D                                      Dim(50)
D P_MailSubject                  70a   Value
D P_MailBody                    500    Value
D P_PathFile                     60    Value Options(*NoPass)
D                                      Dim(20)
```

Continued

```
D P_ImbAtt1       S              10i 0 Dim(51) Inz

D FromFName       S             512    Inz(*Blanks)
D FromFNameA      S             512    Dim(200) Inz
D SplName         S              10    Inz(*Blanks)
D ImbAtt          S              10i 0 Inz(*Zeros)
D ToAddrArr       S             256    Dim(1000) Inz
D ToDistArr       S              10i 0 Dim(1000) Inz
D ToNameArr       S              50    Dim(1000) Inz
D ReplyTo         S              50    Inz(*Blanks)

D W_Order         S               3 0  Inz(*Zeros)
D W_ToDist        S               1 0  Inz(*Zeros)
D W_Zip           S              12    Inz(*Blanks)
D W_File          S              10    Inz(*Blanks)
D W_FileSav       S              10    Inz(*Blanks)
D W_Lib           S              10    Inz(*Blanks)
D W_FromMember    S              10    Inz(*Blanks)
D W_ToFile        S              64    Inz(*Blanks)
D W_ToDir         S             128    Inz(*Blanks)
D W_To            S               1    Inz(*Blanks)

D W_Len50         S               5 0  Inz(*Zeros)
D W_Len51         S               5 0  Inz(*Zeros)
D W_Len           S               5 0  Inz(*Zeros)
D W_Len1          S               5 0  Inz(*Zeros)
D W_Len2          S               5 0  Inz(*Zeros)
D W_Res           S              50    Inz(*Blanks)
D Wx              S               5 0  Inz(*Zeros)
D Wy              S               5 0  Inz(*Zeros)
D WxSav           S               5 0  Inz(*Zeros)
D Wn              S               5 0  Inz(*Zeros)
D W_LibSav        S              10    Inz(*Blanks)
D W_LibAux        S              10    Inz(*Blanks)
D W_String        S            1000    Inz(*Blanks)
D W_Pos           S               9 0  Inz(*Zeros)
```

Continued

```
D W_MbrOpt          S           11    Inz(*Blanks)
D W_LenT            S            4 0  Inz(*Zeros)
D W_LenTSav         S            4 0  Inz(*Zeros)
D W_CtlPdf          S            1    Inz(*Blanks)
D W_LstEMail        S           50    Inz(*Blanks)
```

Here's a quick rundown of the parameters:

- *P_SName* is the sender's name. You might use this to enable your program to send emails under a department's name, such as accounting, or customer service.
- *P_SEmail* is the sender's address. This will be the "Reply To" address.
- *P_MailTo* is the "To" field, where you can specify user IDs, groups, and names (from the address group) or Internet email addresses.
- *P_MailCC* is the same as *P_MailTo* for the "Cc" field.
- *P_MailBcc* is the same as *P_MailTo* for the "Bcc" field.
- *P_Spool* is an array that can contain up to 50 spool files to convert and attach to the email message.
- *P_ImbAtt* specifies the conversion to perform in each of the spool files; *1* means embed in the body, *2* means attach to the body, and *3* means convert to PDF and attach to the body.
- *P_File* is an array that can contain up to 10 physical file names to convert and attach to the email message.
- *P_Lib* is an array that contains the library of each physical file mentioned in the previous parameter.
- *P_FmtFile* specifies the conversion to perform in each of the physical files contained in the *P_File* array; *X* means Excel, *T* means text format.
- *P_NameFile* is an array that contains the name of each of the converted physical files
- *P_IncFlds* is an array that indicates whether the column names should be included in each of the converted files; *0* means don't include, *1* means include.
- *P_Zip* is an array that contains the zipped file name of each of the converted files. If an array position is not blank, the corresponding file in array *P_File* will be zipped and attached to the message with the name specified in the *P_Zip* array position.
- *P_MailSubject* is the "Subject" field.
- *P_MailBody* is the "Body" field.

- *P_PathFile* is an optional parameter to specify additional files to attach that already exist in the IFS.

This procedure is divided into four parts: initialization, preparation, execution, and cleanup. The initialization is the smallest part. It includes only the subroutine *Init*:

```
//-----------------------------------------------------------------------*
// Initialization
//-----------------------------------------------------------------------*
  BegSr Init;

// Retrieve the field separator for XLS format
  In DaFldSep;
  W_FldSep = DaFldSep;

// Read the Address of the mail log
// (Used to check if the mail is being correctly sent)
  In DaMailLog;
  W_MailLog = DaMailLog;

// Retrieve the path for file conversion (pdf, xls, etc.)
  In DaCnvPath;
  W_ToDir = DaCnvPath;

// Check if this is the production system.
// If it's not, emails won't be sent out of the company
 I_ProdSys = ProductionSys;

// Set the priority to HIGH
  P_Prio = 2;

// Set the importance to MEDIUM
  P_Impo = 1;

  EndSr;
```

This subroutine retrieves information from several data areas. It also fills the *I_ProdSys* variable using the *ProductionSys* function, which I'll explain later.

The next part, preparation, is the largest of the four. Here's the source code for the preparation:

```
// ***************
// PREPARE TO SEND
// ***************

// Prepare email destinations array
  ExSr DstMails;

// Import message body
  ExSr ImpBody;

// Process spool files to be sent
  ExSr TrSpool;

// Process files to be sent
  ExSr ProccFiles;

// Add the files to the IFS
  ExSr AddIfsFiles;
```

It begins with the setup of the email destinations array (in subroutine *DstMails*, which uses parameters *P_MailTo*, *P_MailCC*, and *P_MailBcc* parameters to fill the *ToAddrArr*, *ToNameArr*, and *ToDistArr* arrays):

```
//-----------------------------------------------------------------------*
// Prepare email destinations array
//-----------------------------------------------------------------------*
  BegSr DstMails;

    Wx = 1;


// To
    Dow P_MailTo <> *Blanks;
       W_ToDist = *Zero;
        W_Len = %Scan(',' : P_MailTo : 1);
```

Continued

```
        If W_Len = *Zeros;
          ToAddrArr(Wx)= %Trim(P_MailTo);

// Retrieve mail address (internet email or internal user)
          ExSr RtvMail;
          Wx = Wx + 1;

// Don't send emails to the outside world from the test system
          If Not I_ProdSys And Not InternalAddr (P_MailTo);
              Wx = Wx - 1;
              ToAddrArr(Wx)= *Blanks;
              ToNameArr(Wx)= *Blanks;
          EndIf;
          Leave;
        EndIf;
        ToAddrArr(Wx)= %Trim(%Subst(P_MailTo : 1 : W_Len-1));

// Remove the address added to the array from the string
       P_MailTo = %Replace(' ' : P_Mailto : 1 : W_Len);

// Retrieve mail address (internet email or internal user)
        ExSr RtvMail;
        Wx = Wx + 1;

// If this is not the production system
// and the destination mail is not from the company, don't send it
        If Not I_ProdSys And Not InternalAddr (P_MailTo);
          Wx = Wx - 1;
          ToAddrArr(Wx)= *Blanks;
          ToNameArr(Wx)= *Blanks;
        EndIf;
  EndDo;

// Cc
    Dow P_MailCc <> *Blanks;
       W_ToDist = 1;
       W_Len = %Scan(',':P_MailCc:1);
```

Continued

```
       If W_Len = *Zeros;
         ToAddrArr(Wx)= %Trim(P_MailCc);

// Retrieve mail address (internet email or internal user)
         ExSr RtvMail;
         Wx = Wx + 1;

// If this is not the production system
// and the destination mail is not from the company, don't send it
         If Not I_ProdSys And Not InternalAddr (P_MailCc);
             Wx = Wx - 1;
             ToAddrArr(Wx)= *Blanks;
             ToNameArr(Wx)= *Blanks;
         EndIf;
         Leave;
       EndIf;
       ToAddrArr(Wx)= %Trim(%Subst(P_MailCc : 1 : W_Len-1));

// Remove the address added to the array from the string
       P_MailCc = %Replace(' ':P_MailCc:1:W_Len);

// Retrieve mail address (internet email or internal user)
       ExSr RtvMail;

// If this is not the production system
// and the destination mail is not from the company, don't send it
       If Not I_ProdSys And Not InternalAddr (P_MailCc);
         Wx = Wx - 1;
         ToAddrArr(Wx)= *Blanks;
         ToNameArr(Wx)= *Blanks;
       EndIf;
       Wx = Wx + 1;
   EndDo;

// Bcc
// BlindCopy - Send to the Mail Log mailbox
```

Continued

```
    If W_MailLog <> *Blanks;
        W_ToDist = 2;
        If P_MailBcc <> *Blanks;
          P_MailBcc = %Trim(P_MailBcc) + ', ' + %Trim(W_MailLog);
        Else;
          P_MailBcc = %Trim(P_MailBcc) + %Trim(W_MailLog);
        EndIf;
    EndIf;

    Dow P_MailBcc <> *Blanks;
        W_ToDist = 2;
        W_Len = %Scan(',' : P_MailBcc : 1);
        If W_Len = *Zeros;
          ToAddrArr(Wx)= %Trim(P_MailBcc);

// Retrieve mail address (internet email or internal user)
          ExSr RtvMail;
          Wx = Wx + 1;

// If this is not the production system
// and the destination mail is not from the company, don't send it
          If Not I_ProdSys And Not InternalAddr (P_MailBcc);
              Wx = Wx - 1;
              ToAddrArr(Wx)= *Blanks;
              ToNameArr(Wx)= *Blanks;
          EndIf;
          Leave;
        EndIf;
        ToAddrArr(Wx)= %Trim(%Subst(P_MailBcc : 1 : W_Len-1));

// Remove the address added to the array from the string
        P_MailBcc = %Replace(' ' : P_MailBcc : 1 : W_Len);

// Retrieve mail address (internet email or internal user)
        ExSr RtvMail;
```

Continued

```
// If this is not the production system
// and the destination mail is not from the company, don't send it
       If Not I_ProdSys And Not InternalAddr (P_MailBcc);
         Wx = Wx - 1;
         ToAddrArr(Wx)= *Blanks;
         ToNameArr(Wx)= *Blanks;
       EndIf;
       Wx = Wx + 1;
   EndDo;

  EndSr;
```

Note that the distribution type (*To*, *Cc*, or *Bcc*) is set in variable *W_ToDist* and passed to the *ToDistArray* in subroutine *RtvMail*:

```
//-----------------------------------------------------------------------*
// Retrieve the user's email address
// look it up in the group and user tables
//-----------------------------------------------------------------------*
  BegSr RtvMail;

// If it's a group
    If %Scan('@':ToAddrArr(Wx)) = *Zero;
       P_Group = ToAddrArr(Wx);
     ToAddrArr(Wx) = *Blanks;
       P_Email = *Blanks;
       P_Eof = *Off;
       Dow P_Eof = *Off;
         RtvGrpAddrs(P_Group : P_Email : P_Emails : P_Names : P_Eof);
// Move the email names and addresses fields to the proper arrays
         Wn = 1;
         Dow Wn < 11;
             If P_Emails(Wn) = *Blanks;
               Leave;
             EndIf;
```

Continued

```
            ToAddrArr(Wx) = P_Emails(Wn);
            ToNameArr(Wx) = P_Names(Wn);
            ToDistArr(Wx) = W_ToDist;
            W_LstEmail = P_Emails(Wn);
            Wn = Wn + 1;
            Wx = Wx + 1;
        EndDo;
// Re-call the Retrieve address procedure from the last address used,
// because the procedure returns blocks of 10 addresses
        P_Email = W_LstEmail;
      EndDo;
        Wx = Wx - 1;

// If it's not a group, check the address associated to the user
      Else;
        P_Email = ToAddrArr(Wx);
        P_Name = ToNameArr(Wx);
        RtvEmailName(P_Email);
      EndIf;

  EndSr;
```

This subroutine retrieves the address or addresses (in case of a group) from the content of each of the *ToDistArr* array entries. Since the entry parameters mentioned before can contain an Internet email address, a group name, a user name, or a system user ID, two conversions are necessary to ensure that the name and address arrays are properly filled. These procedures, *RtvGrpAddr* and *RtvEmailName*, are explained in the "Other Procedures" section later in this chapter.

The next step is moving the *P_Body* parameter to the appropriate place within the email message. Subroutine *ImpBody* prints the *P_Body* parameter to a spool file:

```
//------------------------------------------------------------------------*
// Add the body to the message
//------------------------------------------------------------------------*
  BegSr ImpBody;

// If the message has a body, print it to a spool file and add it
// as an embedded attachment
    If P_MailBody = *Blanks;
        LeaveSr;
    EndIf;

    Open MailBodySp;

    W_Len = 1;
    W_Len2 = 1;
    Dow W_Len > *Zero;
        W_Len = %Scan(':/P' : P_MailBody : W_Len+1);
        If W_Len = *Zero;
          Body1 = %Trim(%Subst(P_MailBody : W_Len2 : 500 - W_Len2));
          Write Body;
          Leave;
        EndIf;
        If W_Len2 > 1;
          Body1 = %Subst(P_MailBody : W_Len2 : W_Len - W_Len2);
        Else;
          Body1 = %Subst(P_MailBody : W_Len2 : W_Len - 1);
        EndIf;
        W_Len2 = W_Len + 3;
       Write Body;
    EndDo;

    Close MailBodySp;

  EndSr;
```

And subroutine *TrSpool* converts it into the message body:

```
//---------------------------------------------------------------------*
// Process spool files to be sent
//---------------------------------------------------------------------*
  BegSr TrSpool;

    Wx = 1;
// Fill the spool file array (used by the mail sending program)
    Dow P_Spool(Wx) <> *Blanks Or %Elem(P_Spool) = Wx;
// If the format is PDF, copy file to the IFS
        If P_ImbAtt(Wx) = '3';
// Retrieve the PDF file name (Sequence Number) to be used
          ExSr RtvSeqNbr;
// Perform PDF conversion
          P_Cmdlin = 'MMAIL/CVTSPLFPDF SPLF(' + %Trim(P_Spool(WX)) + ')'
                  + ' TOPDF(' + '''' + %Trim(P_Path) +''''+ ')';
          W_ErrorDS = ExecCmd (%Trim(P_CmdLin));
// If an error occurred, return *ON. Continue otherwise
          If W_ErrorDS.APIMsgId <> *Blanks;
              Return *On;
          Endif;

// Add the file to the Files To Sent array
// Save the index
          WxSav = Wx;
// Look up the last array entry
          Wx = 1;
          Dow FromFNameA(Wx) <> *Blanks;
              Wx = Wx + 1;
          EndDo;
          FromFNameA(Wx) = %Trim(P_Path);
          Wx = WxSav;
           Wx = Wx + 1;
          Iter;
        EndIf;
```

Continued

```
        P_SplName(Wx) = P_Spool(Wx);
        P_ImbAtt1(Wx) = %Int(P_ImbAtt(Wx));
        Wx = Wx + 1;
    EndDo;

// Look up the last array entry, to add the body
    Wx = 1;
    Dow P_SplName(Wx) <> *Blanks;
        Wx = Wx + 1;
    EndDo;
// Add the body
    If P_MailBody <> *Blanks;
        P_SplName(Wx) = 'MAILBODYSP';
    EndIf;

  EndSr;
```

Note that before the PDF conversion takes place, the subroutine *RtvSeqNbr* is executed. This is necessary because the conversion to PDF can't handle duplicate file names. This subroutine simply ensures that the PDF file name is unique:

```
//---------------------------------------------------------------------*
// Retrieve the PDF file name (Sequence Number) to be used
//---------------------------------------------------------------------*
  BegSr RtvSeqNbr;

// Use the Pdf Lock Data Area to prevent document number duplication
    If W_CtlPdf <> '1';
        In(E) *Lock DaPdfLck;
        Dow %Error = *On;
          In(E) *Lock DaPdfLck;
        EndDo;
    EndIf;
```

Continued

```
// Retrieve the sequence number to be used
    W_CtlPdf = '1';
    W_Order = 1;
    Dow W_Order < 999;
        P_Path = %Trim(W_ToDir) + 'PDF' + %Char(W_Order) + '.pdf';
        W_Order = W_Order + 1;
        ChkObjInIFS (P_Path : P_Response);
        If P_Response = C_NotExists;
          Leave;
        EndIf;
    EndDo;

  EndSr;
```

After all the attachments have been added, the body is also added via the converted spool file *MMailBodySP*. This conversion is necessary because in Mime & Mail, the body might contain formatting. I don't actually use it, except for the new line, ":/P" special notation that you'll find in the *ImpBody* subroutine:

```
//------------------------------------------------------------------------*
// Add the body to the message
//------------------------------------------------------------------------*
  BegSr ImpBody;

// If the message has a body, print it to a spool file and add it
// as an embedded attachment
    If P_MailBody = *Blanks;
        LeaveSr;
    EndIf;

    Open MailBodySp;

    W_Len = 1;
    W_Len2 = 1;
    Dow W_Len > *Zero;
        W_Len = %Scan(':/P' : P_MailBody : W_Len+1);
```

Continued

```
        If W_Len = *Zero;
          Body1 = %Trim(%Subst(P_MailBody : W_Len2 : 500 - W_Len2));
          Write Body;
          Leave;
        EndIf;
        If W_Len2 > 1;
          Body1 = %Subst(P_MailBody : W_Len2 : W_Len - W_Len2);
        Else;
          Body1 = %Subst(P_MailBody : W_Len2 : W_Len - 1);
        EndIf;
        W_Len2 = W_Len + 3;
      Write Body;
    EndDo;

    Close MailBodySp;

  EndSr;
```

This is the easiest way to ensure that nothing gets lost. The aforementioned *TrSpool* subroutine not only embeds the body in the message, but also treats any spool files indicated in the *P_Spool* parameter. This operation consists of converting the spool file to PDF (when indicated in the respective array entry of parameter *P_ImbAtt*) via the *CVTSPLFPDF* command provided by Mime & Mail and filling the *FromFNameA*, *P_SplName*, and *P_ImbAtt1* arrays with the IFS file name, spool file name, and attachment type information, respectively.

The next step is attaching any physical files specified in parameter *P_File* in subroutine *ProccFiles*:

```
//-------------------------------------------------------------------*
// Process files to be sent
// ------------------------------------------------------------------*
  BegSr ProccFiles;

    Wx = 1;
   Dow P_FmtFile(Wx) <> *Blanks;
       Select;
```

Continued

```
// If the format is XLS
          When P_FmtFile(Wx) = 'X' Or P_FmtFile(Wx) = 'T';
             W_To = P_FmtFile(Wx);
// Prepare the parameters for the conversion procedure
             W_File = P_File(Wx);
             W_Lib = P_Lib(Wx);
             W_FromMember = '*FIRST';
// If the file name is not filled, use the physical file name
             If P_NameFile(Wx) = *Blanks;
               W_ToFile = P_File(Wx);
             Else;
               W_ToFile = %Trim(P_NameFile(Wx));
             EndIf;

             If P_FmtFile(Wx) = 'X';
// If the field names should be included in the output file
                 If P_IncFlds(Wx) = '1';
// Write the field names as the file's first record
                 ExSr RtvFlds;
// Copy the physical file to the IFS as XLS file
// Copy the field names from the file in QTEMP
                 W_MbrOpt = '*REPLACE';
                 W_LibSav = W_Lib;
                 W_FileSav = W_File;
                 W_Lib = 'QTEMP';
                 W_File = 'PFFFD';
// Convert files to XLS format
                 CopyToXls(W_File : W_Lib : W_FromMember :
                          W_ToFile : W_ToDir : W_To : W_MbrOpt);
// Duplicate the file to QTEMP, to put the field names in
                 P_Cmdlin = 'DLTF (QTEMP/PFFFD)';
                 W_ErrorDS = ExecCmd (%Trim(P_CmdLin));
// Add the file with the field names to the previous file
                 W_MbrOpt = '*ADD';
                 W_Lib = W_LibSav;
                 W_File = W_FileSav;
```

Continued

```
              Else;
                  W_LibSav = W_Lib;
                  W_FileSav = W_File;
                  W_MbrOpt = '*REPLACE';
              EndIf;
            Else;
              W_MbrOpt = '*REPLACE';
            EndIf;

// Convert files to XLS format
            CopyToXls(W_File : W_Lib : W_FromMember :
                      W_ToFile : W_ToDir : W_To : W_MbrOpt);

// If the output file should be zipped
            If P_Zip(Wx) <> *Blanks;
               ExSr TrZip;
            Else;
// Otherwise attach it as it is
                FromFNameA(Wx) = %Trim(W_ToDir) + '/' + %Trim(W_ToFile);
            EndIf;
          Other;
            Return *On;
       EndSl;
        Wx = Wx + 1;
    EndDo;

  EndSr;
```

The resulting output files are then placed in array *FromFNameA*. There are several options that are driven by *P_FmtFile* (convert to Excel or text format), *P_IncFlds* (include headers in the Excel format), and *P_Zip* (compress the output file). If the headers need to be included, subroutine *RtvFlds* is executed:

```
//------------------------------------------------------------------------*
// Retrieve the field names to include in the IFS file header
//------------------------------------------------------------------------*
  BegSR RtvFlds;

// Initialize fields
    W_LenTSav = *Zeros;
    W_LenT    = *Zeros;
    W_Len50    = *Zeros;
    W_Len51    = *Zeros;

// Create a file in QTEMP with the field definition
    P_Cmdlin = 'DSPFFD FILE(' + %Trim(W_File) + ')'
                + ' OUTPUT(*OUTFILE) '
                + ' OUTFILE(QTEMP/PFEMP) '
                + 'OUTMBR(*FIRST *REPLACE)';
    W_ErrorDS = ExecCmd (%Trim(P_CmdLin));
// Read the field sizes
    Open PfEmp;
    Read QWHDRFFD;

// Add the field sizes and for each field add 1, because of the comma
    W_Pos = *Zeros;
    Dow Not %Eof(PfEmp);
     W_Pos = 1;
      If W_LenTSav <> *Zeros;
          W_LenTSav = W_LenT;
      Else;
          W_LenTSav = 1;
        EndIf;
       If WHFLDD = *Zeros;
          W_LenT = W_LenT + W_Pos + WHFLDB;
        Else;
          W_LenT = W_LenT + W_Pos + WHFLDD;
        EndIf;
```

Continued

```
      If W_LenTSav <> 1;
        W_Len50 = W_LenTSav + 1;
       Else;
        W_Len50 = 1;
       EndIf;
       W_Len51 = W_LenT - W_LenTSav - 1;
       If W_Len51 > 10;
         W_Len51 = 10;
      EndIf;
       W_String = %Replace(%Subst(WHFLDI : 1 : W_Len51) :
                           W_String : W_Len50 : W_Len51);
// If the format is XLS, use the user-defined field separator
       If P_FmtFile(Wx) = 'X';
         W_String = %Replace(W_FldSep : W_String : W_LenT : 1);
       Else;
         W_String = %Replace(' ' : W_String : W_LenT : 1);
       EndIf;
       Read QWHDRFFD;
    EndDo;
    Close PfEmp;

// Duplicate the file to QTEMP to add the field names
    P_Cmdlin = 'CRTPF (QTEMP/PFFFD) RCDLEN(1000)';
    W_ErrorDS = ExecCmd (%Trim(P_CmdLin));

// Put QTEMP at the beginning of the library list
  P_CmdLin = 'ADDLIBLE (QTEMP)';
  W_ErrorDS = ExecCmd(P_CmdLin);

// Write the records to the file in QTEMP
    Open Pfffd;
    FD_Pfffd = %Trim(W_String);
    Write PfffdR;
    Close Pfffd;

  EndSr;
```

This subroutine uses a variant of the *DSPFFD* "trick" that you've seen in the *CSV2PF* function to retrieve the field names. If *P_Zip* indicates that a file needs to be compressed, subroutine *TrZip* is called:

```
//-----------------------------------------------------------------------*
// Zip files
//-----------------------------------------------------------------------*
  BegSr TrZip;

    If P_Zip(Wx) = *Blanks;
        LeaveSr;
    EndIf;

// Replace the file extension with ".zip"
    W_Len = *Zeros;
    W_Len = %Scan('.':P_NameFile(Wx));
    If W_Len > *Zero;
        W_Zip = %SubSt(P_NameFile(Wx):1:W_Len);
    Else;
        W_Zip = P_NameFile(Wx);
        W_Len = 8;
    EndIf;
    W_Zip = %Replace('zip' : W_Zip : W_Len + 1 : 3);
    P_Cmdlin = 'PAEZIP/PAEZIP OPTION(*ZIP)'
               + ' ZIPFILE(' + ''''+ %Trim(W_ToDir) + '/'
               + %Trim(W_Zip) + '''' + ')'
               + ' FILE(' + '''' + %Trim(W_ToDir) + '/'
               + %Trim(P_NameFile(Wx)) + '''' + ')';
    W_ErrorDS = ExecCmd (%Trim(P_CmdLin));

// Add the zip file to the Files to be Sent array
    FromFNameA(Wx) = %Trim(W_ToDir) + '/' + %Trim(W_Zip);

  EndSr;
```

Bear in mind that this subroutine only works if you have PAEZIP installed. If you don't, simply remove the subroutine or replace it with whatever compression tool you use.

The preparation stage ends with the *AddIFSFiles* subroutine:

```
//--------------------------------------------------------------------*
// Add the files to the IFS
//--------------------------------------------------------------------*
  BegSr AddIfsFiles;

    Wx = 1;
    Wy = 1;

// Look up the last filled array position
    Dow FromFNameA(Wx) <> *Blanks And %Elem(FromFNameA) < Wx;
        Wx = Wx + 1;
    EndDo;

// Add the files to be sent to the IFS to the proper array
    Dow P_PathFile(Wy) <> *Blanks And %Elem(FromFNameA) > Wx
        And %Elem(P_PathFile) > Wy And %Parms >= 16;

         FromFNameA(Wx) = P_PathFile(Wy);
        Wx = Wx + 1;
        Wy = Wy + 1;

    EndDo;

    EndSr;
```

This subroutine adds to the *FromFNameA* array any other files (specified in the optional parameter *P_PathFile*) that already exist in the IFS.

The execution stage is simply the invocation of the Mime & Mail procedure wrapper (*MMailSender*) that sends the message:

```
// ***********
// SEND EMAIL
// ***********
// Invoke the MMailSender procedure to send email
  ExSr SendMMAIL;
(...)
//-------------------------------------------------------------------*
// Invoke the MMAILSND procedure to send email
//-------------------------------------------------------------------*
  BegSr SendMMail;
  // Add the mail processing library
    P_CmdLin = 'ADDLIBLE (MMAIL)';
    W_ErrorDS = ExecCmd(P_CmdLin);


  // Call the mail sending program
    MMailSender(P_Error : P_SName : P_SEmail : ToNameArr : ToAddrArr :
                ToDistArr : ReplyTo : P_MailSubject : P_Impo :
                P_Prio : FromFNameA : P_SplName : P_ImbAtt1);

 // Remove the mail processing library
    P_CmdLin = 'RMVLIBLE (MMAIL)';
    W_ErrorDS = ExecCmd(P_CmdLin);

  EndSr;
```

The *MMailSender* procedure is explained in the “Other Procedures” section later in this chapter.

Finally, the cleanup consists of two subroutines that remove the spool and PDF files (*RmvSpl* and *RmvPDFs*, respectively) generated by the *SndMulFiles* procedure:

```
// ********
// CLEAN UP
// ********

// Remove the PDF files created for the message and unlock PDF creation
  ExSr RmvPdfs;

// Remove the spool file generated for the message body
  ExSr RmvSpl;



// *************
// RETURN STATUS
// *************

// Return: *On means error
  If P_Error = '2';
    Return *On;
  Else;
    Return *Off;
  EndIf;
(...)

//-----------------------------------------------------------------------*
// Remove the spool file created for the body
//-----------------------------------------------------------------------*
  BegSr RmvSpl;

// Delete the body spool file
    If P_MailBody = *Blanks;
        LeaveSr;
    EndIf;
    P_Cmdlin = 'DLTSPLF FILE(MAILBODYSP) SPLNBR(*LAST)';
    W_ErrorDS = ExecCmd (%Trim(P_CmdLin));
```

Continued

```
// Clear the spool file array
    P_SplName = *Blanks;

  EndSr;
(...)
  //-----------------------------------------------------------------------*
  // Remove the PDF files created for the message and unlock PDF creation
  //-----------------------------------------------------------------------*
    BegSr RmvPdfs;

      If W_CtlPdf = '1';
          P_CmdLin = 'RMVLNK OBJLNK('
                      + '''' + %Trim(W_ToDir) + 'PDF*.pdf' + '''' + ')';
          W_ErrorDs = ExecCmd(P_CmdLin);
          Out DAPdfLck;
          W_CtlPdf = *Blanks;
      EndIf;

    EndSr;
/END-FREE
PSndMulFiles     E
```

Requirements

To take full advantage of the procedures discussed so far in this chapter, you need to have several programs installed. Table 6.1 lists the required software for each procedure.

Table 6.1: Required Programs	
Procedure	**Additional Software Required**
SndEmail	None
SndSplfByMail	InfoPrint Server Licensed Program
SndFileByMail	None
SndMulFiles	Mime & Mail and PAEZIP (SndMulFiles will work without PAEZIP if you always leave parameter *P_Zip* blank.)

Keep in mind that you also need to configure your IBM i system to be able to send email. For more on this topic, see the "Configuration" section at the end of this chapter. Also, note that *SndMulFiles* was built using Mime & Mail's version dated April 26, 2005. You might have to perform minor adjustments to parameter sizes and such when you download and install the current version of the application.

Other Procedures

For the email sending to work, quite a few other procedures are necessary. They are presented here, divided into three groups: email address-related procedures (service program *ADDRESS*), Mime & Mail sending procedures (service program *MMAILSND*), and miscellaneous procedures (service program *MISC*).

Email Address-Related Procedures

The following procedures are used to handle email addresses and groups. If you decide not to use the PFEMAIL file, you can always store the email address directly in the user's directory entry and use the *RtvSmtpAddr* procedure:

- *RtvGrpAddrs*—This procedure retrieves the email addresses that belong to the group specified in parameter *P_Group*. It can return up to 10 email addresses and email names in parameters *P_Emails* and *P_Names*, respectively. The addresses are retrieved from file *LFEGRP01*, a logical file over *PFEGRP* (Email Groups file). The names are retrieved via procedure *RtvEMailName*, explained next. Although the procedure's arrays return only 10 addresses at a time, there is a way to read a group with more than 10 members: if parameter *P_Email* is filled, the group's file will be read from that address on.
- *RtvEMailName*—This procedure returns the name associated with the email address passed in parameter *P_Email*. It can be either the name found for the email address in the *LFEMAIL02* file or a logical file over *PFEMAIL* (the Email Addresses file), or it can be composed from the left part of the *P_Email* parameter (before the @ sign).
- *RtvEMailAddr*—This procedure retrieves the email address associated with the name passed in parameter *P_Name*. If the parameter does not contain an Internet email address already, it is looked up in the email addresses file via *P_Name*. If it is not found, the *RtvSmtpAddr* procedure (explained next) is used to find it in the system's directory.

- *InternalAddr*—This is a rather useful yet simple procedure. It returns **On* if the email address passed in the *P_Address* parameter belongs to the company and **Off* otherwise. The check is performed based on the email domain name of the company, defined in data area *DaMailDmn*. Function *ScanForString* is used to search for the domain in the *P_Address* parameter.
- *RtvSmtpAddr*—This procedure retrieves the email address from the system directory for the specified user ID.

The *RtvSmtpAddr* procedure was created by Carsten Flensburg and published here:

http://iprodeveloper.com/rpg-programming/apis-example-office-apis-search-system-directory

I've converted it to free-format and performed minor changes. The author's description of the procedure (used with permission) follows.

> *Searches system directory based directory on input search criteria(s) and returns the requested user information for the found entries.*
>
> *Sequence of events:*
>
> 1. *The API input parameters are initialized*
> 2. *The search directory API is called*
> 3. *If an error occurs while calling the API or no entry is found blanks are returned to the caller*
> 4. *If an entry is found the requested SMTP-address is retrieved, formatted and returned to the caller*
>
> *Parameters:*
>
> - *P_User (INPUT)—User-id of the directory entry searched. Determined by the presence of the second parameter this can be both a user profile name and the first part of the system directory entry user identifier. The special value *CURRENT will be replaced by the job's current user profile name.*
> - *P_Addr (INPUT)—The address qualifier of the directory entry searched.*

- *Return-value (OUTPUT)—The formatted SMTP-address of the system directory entry specified by the input parameter(s). If no matching entry was found or an error occurred blanks are returned to the caller.*

Mime & Mail Sending Procedures

The *MMailSender* procedure invokes all the necessary Mime & Mail APIs to create and send an email message, based on the following input parameters:

- *P_Error*—An error indicator; 2 means error
- *P_SName*—The sender's name
- *P_SEmail*—The sender's email address
- *ToNameArr*—An array containing the email names of the message's destinations
- *ToAddrArr*— An array containing the email addresses of the message's destinations
- *ToDistArr*— An array containing the type of destination ("To," "Cc," or "Bcc") for each entry of the previous arrays
- *P_ReplyTo*—The "Reply To" address
- *P_MailSubject*—The subject
- *P_Impo*—The importance
- *P_Prio*—The priority
- *FromFNameA*—An array containing IFS file names to attach (spool files, physical files, and other IFS files)
- *P_SplName*—An array containing the names of the spool files to be sent as attachments to the message
- *P_ImbAtt*—An array containing the treatment of each of the previous array's entries

Since this procedure uses Mime & Mail APIs, please refer to the application's documentation for more information:

http://mmail.easy400.net

There are some details worth mentioning. The *DaMimeLck* data area is used to prevent a problem with the sending process—some sort of temporary file duplication that causes messages to get mixed up. It's possible that the current Mime & Mail version no longer requires this "trick" to work properly, but the one that I have installed does. It is assumed, in this procedure, that the spool file that is supposed to be attached to the message is the last generated.

Miscellaneous Procedures

The following set of procedures includes a *QCMDEXC* replacement, a couple of string-handling tools, and a handy tool to determine the type of system (test or production):

- *ExecCmd*—This very handy procedure is used to replace the call to the *QCMDEXC* API. It was created by the bright guys of the Free RPG Tools Web site (*http://www.freerpgtools.com*), and it consists of the invocation of the *QCAPCMD* API with a programmer-friendly interface. The main advantage over *QCMDEXC* is that the command is validated before execution, thus ensuring the call won't end in error. If there is an error (usually CPF something), it is returned in *ApiError.ApiMsgID*. I've initialized some variables early in the code to prevent a bug that occurred when the procedure was invoked multiple times within the same program.
- *ScanForString*—This simple yet extremely useful procedure returns **On* if the value passed in the *ScanString* parameter is found in the *Text* parameter. It can also convert both parameters to upper case (a kind of "ignore case search" if the *CvtUpC* parameter contains *Y)* and return the position in the *Text* parameter, where the *ScanString* parameter begins, if a receiving variable is provided for the fourth parameter (*P_Position*).
- *CvtLwcUpc*—This is another simple yet extremely useful procedure. Using the *%XLATE* BIF and the *W_Up* and *W_Lo* work variables, it converts the *TextLower* parameter to upper case. Note that the content of these variables must be adjusted to use your language's special characters in upper case and lower case, respectively.
- *ProductionSys*—If you have more than one IBM i system, you're probably familiar with those annoying situations in which, for some reason, someone does something in the production system, mistakenly thinking it's the development or test system. This procedure returns **On* if the data area *DASYSTYPE* is set to *P* (production). I use it in the email procedures to avoid having test messages sent outside the company.

These are minor procedures, but they are very effective and time-saving tools. I recommend that you use them.

How to Configure Your IBM i to Send Email

*The following explanation was adapted from an article written by Steve Miall from Genesisv (*www.genesisv.com*) on October 4, 2000.*

To configure email sending from your IBM i system, you need to have OS/400® release 4.2 or higher and an SMTP gateway somewhere in your network. The setup is a bit tricky, so be sure to follow the steps in this section carefully.

First, you need to get the IP address of the email (SMTP) gateway. This is either a PC or network server on your network, or it is the server at your local ISP. Then, make sure this SMTP gateway is in your IBM i hosts table by entering the following command:

```
ADDTCPHTE INTNETADR('192.168.1.50') HOSTNAME('SMTP')
```

If the Internet address is already in the table, make a note of its host table name and use it from here on instead of "SMTP." The next step is changing the SMTP attributes, to get the SMTP server starting automatically when the *STRTCP* command is issued:

```
CHGSMTPA AUTOSTART(*YES) MAILROUTER('SMTP') FIREWALL(*YES)
```

These steps enable the email sending. However, you must perform some additional configuration steps for the users that will use this functionality. Add your email users to the SMTP alias names system table via *CFGTCPSMTP* and option 1. This is necessary for the email to have a decent-looking "from" name and for the email replies to get to a real email account. If you don't add an alias table, your email will be sent from "USER@ADDR.DOMAIN.COM," where "USER" and "ADDR" correspond to your user ID and address, and "DOMAIN.COM" is the domain name of your IBM i system. It might be easier to use *WRKDIRE *ALL* to see the user names registered in the directory and then use F19 to specify the SMTP user ID and domain to use. I highly recommend that you fill these parameters for all your users, since procedure *RtvSmtpAddr* will use this information.

To review or change the domain name of the system, use the *CHGTCPDMN* command (prompt command with F4). The alias table consists of the user ID, address, SMTP user ID, and SMTP domain. Here is an example entry:

```
USERID MYUSER
ADDRESS GVUK
SMTP user name support
SMTP Domain GENESISV.COM
```

With this entry, email is sent from "support@GENESISV.COM." Without it, it is sent from "MYUSER@GVUK.GVUK.GENESISV.COM."

Just a few more steps to go! Add a generic user in the directory to route email. Either use *WRKDIRE* and take the add option, or use the following:

```
ADDDIRE (INTERNET SMTPRTE) USRD('Internet generic user') +
  SYSNAME(TCPIP) NETUSRID(*USRID)                        +
  MSFSRVLVL(*USRIDX) PREFADR(NETUSRID *IBM ATCONTXT)
```

Then add a distribution queue:

```
ADDDSTQ DSTQ(QSMTPQ) RMTLOCNAME(TCPIP) DSTQTYPE(*RPDS)
```

Add a routing table entry, via *CFGDSTSRV* and option 2, as shown in Figure 6.1.

```
A - Monitor 5250
                          Add Routing Table Entry

Type choices, press Enter. (At least one queue name is required.)

  System name/Group . .   ________  ________
  Description . . . . .   TCP/IP
  Service level:
    Fast:
      Queue name . . . .  QSMTP              Distribution queue name
      Maximum hops . . .  *DFT               Number of hops, *DFT
    Status:
      Queue name . . . .  QSMTP
      Maximum hops . . .  *DFT
    Data high:
      Queue name . . . .  QSMTP
      Maximum hops . . .  *DFT
    Data low:
      Queue name . . . .  QSMTP
      Maximum hops . . .  *DFT

F3=Exit    F12=Cancel
MA    a                                                          19/029
```

Figure 6.1: Adding a routing table entry for SMTP.

Finally, change the distribution attributes:

```
CHGDSTA KEEPRCP(*BCC) USEMSFLCL(*NO) SMTPRTE(INTERNET SMTPRTE)
```

That's it! There can be an authority problem, which can cause the MSF facility to die. This will cause all emailing and all QSNADS message-sending to stop until MSF is restarted (*ENDMSF* and *STRMSF*). To get around it, grant the following authorities:

```
GRTOBJAUT OBJ(QSYS/QZMFARSV) OBJTYPE(*PGM) USER(QTCP) AUT(*USE)
GRTOBJAUT OBJ(QSYS/QZMFARSV) OBJTYPE(*PGM) USER(QMSF) AUT(*USE)
GRTOBJAUT OBJ(QSYS/QZMFASCR) OBJTYPE(*PGM) USER(QTCP) AUT(*USE)
GRTOBJAUT OBJ(QSYS/QZMFASCR) OBJTYPE(*PGM) USER(QMSF) AUT(*USE)
GRTOBJAUT OBJ(QSYS/QZMFACHG) OBJTYPE(*PGM) USER(QTCP) AUT(*USE)
GRTOBJAUT OBJ(QSYS/QZMFACHG) OBJTYPE(*PGM) USER(QMSF) AUT(*USE)
GRTOBJAUT OBJ(QSYS/QZMFACRT) OBJTYPE(*PGM) USER(QTCP) AUT(*USE)
GRTOBJAUT OBJ(QSYS/QZMFACRT) OBJTYPE(*PGM) USER(QMSF) AUT(*USE)
```

All the configuration is done, so it's time to start the server:

```
STRTCPSVR *SMTP
```

Next, test to see if it sends:

```
SNDDST TYPE(*LMSG) TOUSRID((INTERNET SMTPRTE)) +
        DSTD('Email')                          +
        TOINTNET((me@mysystem.com'))           +
        SUBJECT('This is the subject')         +
        LONGMSG('This is the message')
```

Then, go to your mailbox and see if you have received the message. You can also use the command below to send a QDLS document:

```
SNDDST TYPE(*FILE) TOUSRID((INTERNET SMTPRTE)) +
      TOINTNET(('me@mysystem.com'))            +
      DSTD('Email')                            +
      MSG('This is a test')                    +
      DOC(document.TXT) FLR(folder)
```

The subject will be the document description; the *SUBJECT* parameter is accepted but ignored. The *MSG* parameter is optional. You cannot have a long message with an attached document, and you cannot attach two documents.

If you have problems and need additional information on setting up TCP/IP and other related issues, try going to *http://www.easy400.net/tcpcfgs*.

Where to Go from Here

As I mentioned in chapter 5, *INVIMP* is an over-simplistic example of a CSV import file, which can be enhanced in a number of ways. It's up to you to decide where to go from here. All the support procedures and functions presented here can (and should, in my humble opinion) be included in your "arsenal of cool things" and used as often as possible. Not only do they simplify some tasks, but they also open new possibilities to your programs.

Let me leave you with a note of caution: the *INVIMP* program uses a lot of different procedures, described in this chapter and in chapter 5. It's probably a good idea to recompile all the modules and service programs before trying to use *INVIMP*. Bear in mind that some of my code is already a few years old and might not match the latest versions of the open source tools that it relies upon to work. You might have to do some (hopefully minor) adjustments. If you get stuck, just send me an email (*books.rafael.vp@gmail.com*) and I'll try to help as best as I can.

PART TWO

Dazzling Output

7

Easily Transform Legacy Printouts into Excel Files

This chapter discusses Apache POI's HSSF, a pure Java implementation capable of creating MS Excel 97-2003 (.xls) files. Procedures that facilitate HSSF's use are also discussed, starting with a section called "The Easy Way." At the end of the chapter, a "cheat sheet" gives the parameters of each procedure and some sample program skeletons.

I'd like to thank Paulo Ferreira, an analyst/developer at LeasePlan Portugal with more than 10 years of experience on IBM i systems, for his invaluable help with the procedures in this chapter, especially with the last one, which he conceived and implemented.

Modernizing applications is a recurring theme these days. Revamping good old green-screen applications with user-friendly screens, Web pages, or some other form of user interaction is widely discussed online and offline. But what about the output produced by your legacy programs? Is it still an ugly printout?

This chapter will help you modernize that output, with a quick and easy approach. You'll learn how to use the POI-HSSF Java APIs to create Excel spreadsheets *directly* from an RPG program. Don't be scared about the "Java APIs" part; they will be hidden "under the hood," and you won't even notice them.

According to the Apache Web site (*http://poi.apache.org/spreadsheet/index.html*), HSSF is "the POI Project's pure Java implementation of the Excel '97(-2007) file format." It's basically a set of APIs that allows you to create a personalized spreadsheet with almost as much detail as Excel itself. (HSSF currently doesn't support the creation of graphs and such.) The problem is that this flexibility comes at a high cost: it's not very easy, especially for an RPG programmer, to use the Java APIs and concepts involved. Also, when the spreadsheet you're building has a lot of columns, it gets tiresome and monotonous to code and maintain.

One of my personal references in the IBM i world, Scott Klement, wrote an RPG-friendly wrapper to these Java APIs that I'll be using from this point on. So, if you don't have HSSF already installed on your IBM i system, you must download and install it. There are two parts:

- The Java binary files at *http://poi.apache.org/download.html*
- Klement's HSSFR4 implementation for RPG at *http://www.scottklement.com/poi*

Klement wrote quite a bit about this subject. I strongly advise you to visit Scott's POI page and read how to install both the Java binary files and Scott's HSSFR4 routines.

Before we continue, the following section explains a bit more about Java. If you're already familiar with the basics of this programming language, just skip ahead to the next section of this chapter.

A Quick Java Rundown

Even though it's not essential to know about Java to understand and use HSSF, it actually helps a lot. I'll try to summarize the basic concepts, but I'd recommend that you read a bit on your own about this extremely useful programming language. Object-oriented languages are based on the concept of an object. The concept of an object comes from the real-world model of an object. If I were at home, I'd see many objects: my chair, my television, my computer, etc. In Java, objects always have a "current state" and "behaviors."

Let's use horses as an example. A horse has a current state:

- Hair is brown.
- Breed is palomino.
- Location is pasture.

A horse also has behaviors:

- A horse can snort.
- A horse can run.

Note that behaviors can change the current state! Running may change the location, for instance.

Software objects are conceptually the same—the state is stored in fields (variables), and the behavior is carried out by calling a method (routine). *Fields* are variables that represent the current state of the object. You can think of these in the same way you think of fields in a data structure in RPG, or fields in a database record. *Methods* are like subprocedures (subroutines with parameters) in RPG. They're little pieces of code that carry out behaviors. In addition to fields and methods, *constructors* are special methods that are called when an object is created. They're a kind of **INZSR* in RPG, but they can receive parameters.

Being class-based and object-oriented means that there's a certain hierarchy, which is crucial for you to understand: you cannot have an object in Java without a class. This class contains the *schematics*, which define the "blueprint" or "DNA" for the object. You cannot use the class itself, as it is just a set of definitions, and you have to define an object based on that class to have something to work with. For example, to have a Horse object in Java, I'd need a class with the schematics of that horse, similar to this:

```
Import java.lang;
Public class Horse {
String color;
String breed;
String location;
```

Continued

```
int gender; // 0=male, 1=female
public Horse(String c, String b,
String l, int g) {
color = c;
breed = b;
location = l;
gender = g;
}
public void snort() {
// insert code to make the horse snort
...
}
public void run() {
// insert code to make the horse run
...
}
public void runTo(String l) {
location = l;
}
public Horse havePony(horse father){
// code to mix attributes of mother and father go here
...
}
}
```

Note that the code defines the fields *color*, *breed*, *location*, and *gender*. The methods *snort*, *run*, *runTo*, and *havePony* are also defined. With this class, you can now create a Horse object in Java. To create a Horse object, you use the keyword *new*:

```
new Jolly_Roger = Horse('Cream', 'Palomino', '0', 'Green pasture');
new Beauty = Horse('Black', 'Andalusian', '1', 'Stables');
```

After this, you can use the object's fields and methods:

```
if ( Jolly_Roger.location == "Green pasture" ) {
Jolly_Roger.run();
}
```

An object can also be created by calling a method from another object. This usually occurs when there's a relationship between the two objects:

```
if ( Jolly_Roger.gender != Beauty.gender ) {
Beauty.snort();
Jolly_Roger.RunTo(Beauty.location);
Horse Binky = Beauty.havePony(Jolly_Roger);
}
```

That's just the very, very basics of it. I'd recommend that you learn a bit more about Java to fully understand and take full advantage of POI. Here are a few Web sites to get you started:

- *http://www.learnjavaonline.org*
- *http://docs.oracle.com/javase/tutorial/java*
- *https://www.udemy.com/blog/learn-java*
- *http://www.tutorialspoint.com/java*

I've been talking about Java, but this book is about RPG, so let's get back to that topic. As I said before, POI is a pure Java implementation, but we need to use it in RPG programs. How do we do that?

RPG Support for Java

Since V5R1, RPG supports calling Java methods, even though it does not have direct support for accessing fields in a Java object or class. You have to call a Java method that returns the field, or call an API to retrieve the field. This isn't actually a problem, because most Java classes do not make fields available, as it's considered a bad practice. (Find out more about this in IBM's *ILE RPG Programmer's Guide* at *http://publib.boulder.ibm.com/iseries/v5r1/ic2924/books/c0925073.pdf.*)

The features added to support Java method calls are as follows:

- *O* data type in the D-spec
- *CLASS(*JAVA : 'class-name')* D-spec keyword (used with the *O* data type)
- *EXTPROC(*JAVA : 'class-name': 'method-name')* on prototypes
- Special value of **CONSTRUCTOR* for *'method-name'*

For example, to create a Java String object (which is how Java stores alphanumeric data), you'd have to create a prototype that calls the constructor for the java.lang.String class:

```
D new_String      PR                    like(jString)
D                                       EXTPROC(*JAVA
D                                       :'java.lang.String'
D                                       :*CONSTRUCTOR)
D value                       32767A    VARYING const
```

This prototype returns a Java object that is to be an instance of the *'java.lang.String'* class. It actually creates an object by calling **CONSTRUCTOR*. Finally, it passes a variable-length string as a parameter to the constructor. Note that Java class names are case-sensitive, which means that "string," "String," and "strING" are different things!

To create a string, you just call the prototype (shown above). You'll need a "type *O*" field to receive the result. Simply declaring the type *O* field does not create a string—only a placeholder for one. The call to the **CONSTRUCTOR* prototype is what actually creates the string:

```
D breed           S              O    CLASS(*Java:'java.lang.String')
...
  breed = new_String('Palomino');
```

Here's a quick tip: Typing *CLASS(*Java:'java.lang.String')* repeatedly can be very tiring. There's an easier way, shown here:

```
D jString         S              O    Class(*Java:'java.lang.String')
...
D color           S                   Like(jString)
D breed           S                   Like(jString)
D location        S                   Like(jString)
```

You can do the same for any Java class name! You'll find this definition and more in the *JNI* member of the *QSYSINC/QRPGLESRC* source file.

Finally, you can also use the keyword *Like* in prototypes:

```
D Horse           S                0   Class(*java:'Horse')

D new_Horse       PR                   Like(Horse)
D                                      ExtProc(*Java:'Horse':*CONSTRUCTOR)
D color                                Like(jString)
D breed                                Like(jString)
D location                             Like(jString)
D gender                        10I 0 Value

D Jolly           S                    Like(Horse)
D color           S                    Like(jString)
D breed           S                    Like(jString)
D location        S                    Like(jString)

 /free

  color = new_String('cream');
  breed = new_String('Palomino');
  location = new_String('stables');
  Jolly = new_Horse(color: breed: location: 0);
 /end-free
```

Anytime you use Java from RPG on IBM i, you need the following licensed programs:

- 57xx-SS1, opt 13 System Openness Includes (library *QSYSINC*)
- 57xx-JV1, *BASE Developer Kit for Java
- 57xx-JV1, opt 7 Java Developer Kit 5.0 (JDK 5.0)
- 57xx-WDS ILE RPG compiler

JDK 5.0 is the minimum version for POI 3.6. Version 1.4 worked fine for older versions. Each version has a different "5722-JV1, opt" number. All of these licensed programs are shipped on the CDs with IBM i. The only one that's an extra charge is the ILE RPG compiler, and you already own that.

Now That You Know a Little About Java, We Can Continue

Let's return to an example from chapter 4, in which a client's debt report is divided by debt age (the total debt at 30, 60, and 90 days). Assume that this program currently generates a printout with six columns:

- Client ID
- Client Name
- Total Debt—The client's total debt
- Debt 30 Days—Invoices outstanding up to 30 days
- Debt 60 Days—Invoices outstanding up to 60 days
- Debt 90 Days—Invoices outstanding up to 90 days or more

It might be a good idea at this point to browse through POI's Web site, as I won't go into details about every single thing. (The explanation would get huge.) I'll try to explain as much as possible without boring you to death.

The following section describes how you can do it with HSSF APIs. If you're familiar with HSSF, just skip to the section titled "The Easy Way" a bit further in the chapter.

The Hard Way

First, you must define the variables required to store and handle the workbook, sheet, rows, and cell styles you'll be working with:

```
 /copy qcpylesrc,hssf_h
D Str              s                   like(jString)
D Book             s                   like(HSSFWorkbook)
D Sheet            s                   like(HSSFSheet)
D row              s                   like(HSSFRow)
D outfile          s                   like(jFileOutputStream)
D ColHeading       s                   like(HSSFCellStyle)
D Dec0             s                   like(HSSFCellStyle)
D Dec2             s                   like(HSSFCellStyle)
D rowcount         s             10I 0 inz(0)
D W_Col            s             10I 0 inz(0)
```

Continued

```
D W_PathFile      s              45
D W_File          s              45
D W_Count         S              10  0 inz(0)
```

As you probably noticed, there are some special types of data here (*HSSFWorkbook*, *HSSFSheet*, and so on). These definitions come from the copy member *hssf_h* and are thoroughly described in the HSSF online documentation.

Most of the names should be self-explanatory, but I'd like to explain a few. *Str* is just a Java string field that will be used to compose the output file IFS path, which will then be stored in *outfile* for the write-to-disk operation. *W_PathFile* and *W_File* are used to receive the file's path and name (as entry parameters or as data being read from a file or data area). I'll explain the rest as we go along.

There's a small but extremely important detail here. The copy member *hssf_h* contains the definition of all the APIs and data types related to HSSF. Be sure that you always include it! If you do so on an *SQLRPGLE* source, use */Include* instead of */Copy*. Otherwise, you'll get a "Nested copy not allowed" error. (For more detail, see *http://publib.boulder.ibm.com/iseries/v5r2/ic2924/books/c092508406.htm#HDRCDINCL.*)

The next step is to create the workbook and sheet to which the data will be written. If you want it to look better than the ugly, old, basic printout, there's work to be done: formatting the columns, creating the necessary style for each type of data (client ID, name, and amounts), and finally writing the header row with the titles to the file. This is performed in the routine *IniXls*:

```
BegSr IniXls;
   hssf_begin_object_group(100);

   book = new_HSSFWorkbook();
   sheet = hssf_newSheet(book: 'MAIN');

   FormatColumns(book:sheet);
   CreateCellStyles(book);

                                                              Continued
```

```
    rowcount = 0;

    // create the header row
    rowcount += 1;
    row = HSSFSheet_createRow(sheet: rowcount);

    // write column A
    W_Col = 0;
    hssf_text(row: W_Col: 'Client ID' : ColHeading);

    // write column B
    W_Col += 1;
    hssf_text(row: W_Col: 'Client Name' : ColHeading);

    // write column C
    W_Col += 1;
    hssf_text(row: W_Col: 'Total Debt' : ColHeading);

    // write column D
    W_Col += 1;
    hssf_text(row: W_Col: 'Debt 30 Days' : ColHeading);
    // write column E
    W_Col += 1;
    hssf_text(row: W_Col: 'Debt 60 Days' : ColHeading);

    // write column F
    W_Col += 1;
    hssf_text(row: W_Col: 'Debt 90 Days' : ColHeading);

Endsr;
```

Let's analyze this routine, beginning with *hssf_begin_object_group(100)*, which creates a group of objects able to handle up to 100 object references. I must create an object group and delete it when the program ends because JVM's garbage collector, the process that frees up memory when an object is no longer being used, cannot recognize that the RPG program is no longer running. Using *hssf_begin_group* and *hssf_end_object_group* tells the JVM to free the memory that was allocated by the objects created while the RPG program was running.

In this example, I'll be creating only one object, so I shouldn't need an object group. However, the Java code that is being called might create other objects, over which I have no control, so it's a good practice to always create an object group in the beginning of your program and always delete it before the program ends. It's also important to choose wisely the size of the object group, because the error that you get when you try to create more objects than you're ready for is not very user-friendly. A value of 100 is a good place to start.

Then, these lines create the workbook and sheet in memory:

```
book = new_HSSFWorkbook();
sheet = hssf_newSheet(book: 'MAIN');
```

These are plain and unformatted, the same as you get when you create a new workbook in Excel. They need to be embellished to make a good impression. That's what the next two lines of code are for:

```
FormatColumns(book:sheet);
CreateCellStyles(book);
```

Procedure *FormatColumns* formats the column's width and some other details, like the rows printed at the top of each new page:

```
 *+++++++++++++++++++++++++++++++++++++++++++++++++++++++++++++
 * FormatColumns():  Set the column widths & merged cells
 *    in a given worksheet.
 *
 *   sheet = (input) sheet to set the column widths in
 *+++++++++++++++++++++++++++++++++++++++++++++++++++++++++++++
P FormatColumns   B
D FormatColumns   PI
D   book                            like(HSSFWorkbook)
D   sheet                           like(HSSFSheet)
```

Continued

```
/free

  // Set repeating rows at top of each page
  HSSFWorkbook_setRepeatingRowsAndColumns(book : 0 : 0 : 5 : 0 : 0);
  //
  // The column width setting is in units that are approx
  //   1/256 of a character.
  //
  //Column A
  HSSFSheet_setColumnWidth( sheet:  0: 10 * 256);

  //Column B
  HSSFSheet_setColumnWidth( sheet:  1: 40 * 256);

  //Column C
  HSSFSheet_setColumnWidth( sheet:  2: 15 * 256);

  //Column D
  HSSFSheet_setColumnWidth( sheet:  3: 15 * 256);

  //Column E
  HSSFSheet_setColumnWidth( sheet:  4: 15 * 256);

  //Column F
  HSSFSheet_setColumnWidth( sheet:  5: 15 * 256);

/end-free
P                E
```

The *HSSFSheet_SetColumnWidth* function does what its name implies: sets the column width. It has three parameters: the sheet name, the column number (*A* is zero, *B* is one, and so on) and the desired width for the column. There's a trick in this last parameter. The units in which the width is defined are about 1/256 of a character. Therefore, if you want to have a column width of 10, you need to enter 2560 (10 * 256) in this parameter.

Next are the cell styles. Since each cell will have a header row and several types of data, you have to create a cell style for each. This is achieved in the procedure *CreateCellStyles*:

```
 *++++++++++++++++++++++++++++++++++++++++++++++++++++++++++++++
 * CreateCellStyles(): Create the different display styles
 *    used for cells in this Excel workbook.
 *
 *++++++++++++++++++++++++++++++++++++++++++++++++++++++++++++++
P CreateCellStyles...
P                B
D CreateCellStyles...
D                PI
D Book                                    like(HSSFWorkBook)
D ChFont         s                        like(HSSFFont)
D TempStr        s                        like(jString)

 /free

    //
    // Create a cell style for the column headings.
    // These are bold and have a border line at the bottom
    //

    ColHeading = HSSFWorkbook_createCellStyle(book);

    ChFont = HSSFWorkbook_createFont(book);
    HSSFFont_setFontHeightInPoints(ChFont: 11);
    TempStr = new_String('Calibri');
    HSSFFont_setFontName(ChFont: TempStr);
    HSSFCellStyle_setFont(ColHeading: ChFont);

    HSSFCellStyle_setFillForegroundColor(ColHeading: COLOR_LIGHT_ORANGE);
    HSSFCellStyle_setFillPattern(ColHeading: SOLID_FOREGROUND);
    HSSFCellStyle_setAlignment(ColHeading: ALIGN_CENTER);
```

Continued

```
HSSFCellStyle_setWrapText(ColHeading: *On);
HSSFCellStyle_setBorderBottom(ColHeading: BORDER_THIN);
HSSFCellStyle_setBorderTop(ColHeading: BORDER_THIN);
HSSFCellStyle_setBorderRight(ColHeading: BORDER_THIN);
HSSFCellStyle_setBorderLeft(ColHeading: BORDER_THIN);

// Create a cell style for numeric 0-dec
// right-aligned and the number formatted nicely
//
Dec0 = HSSFWorkbook_createCellStyle(book);

ChFont = HSSFWorkbook_createFont(book);
TempStr = new_String('Arial');
HSSFFont_setFontName(ChFont: TempStr);
HSSFCellStyle_setFont(Dec0: ChFont);
HSSFCellStyle_setBorderBottom(Dec0: BORDER_THIN);
HSSFCellStyle_setBorderTop(Dec0: BORDER_THIN);
HSSFCellStyle_setBorderRight(Dec0: BORDER_THIN);
HSSFCellStyle_setBorderLeft(Dec0: BORDER_THIN);

HSSFCellStyle_setDataFormat(Dec0: 0);

// Create a cell style for numeric 2-dec
// right-aligned and the number formatted nicely
//
Dec2 = HSSFWorkbook_createCellStyle(book);

ChFont = HSSFWorkbook_createFont(book);
TempStr = new_String('Arial');
HSSFFont_setFontName(ChFont: TempStr);
HSSFCellStyle_setFont(Dec2: ChFont);
HSSFCellStyle_setBorderBottom(Dec2: BORDER_THIN);
HSSFCellStyle_setBorderTop(Dec2: BORDER_THIN);
HSSFCellStyle_setBorderRight(Dec2: BORDER_THIN);
HSSFCellStyle_setBorderLeft(Dec2: BORDER_THIN);
```

Continued

```
      HSSFCellStyle_setDataFormat(Dec2: 2);

      // Create a cell style for text so that it's
      // left-aligned
      //

      Text = HSSFWorkbook_createCellStyle(book);

      ChFont = HSSFWorkbook_createFont(book);
      TempStr = new_String('Arial');
      HSSFFont_setFontName(ChFont: TempStr);
      HSSFCellStyle_setFont(Text: ChFont);
      HSSFCellStyle_setBorderBottom(Text: BORDER_THIN);
      HSSFCellStyle_setBorderTop(Text: BORDER_THIN);
      HSSFCellStyle_setBorderRight(Text: BORDER_THIN);
      HSSFCellStyle_setBorderLeft(Text: BORDER_THIN);

      HSSFCellStyle_setAlignment(Text: ALIGN_LEFT);

    /end-free
P                 E
```

Here, four cell styles are created:

- *ColHeading*—This style is in the Calibri font, size 11, centered text, light orange background, and thin borders. This style will be used for the Header row.
- *Dec0*— This style is in the Arial font with default size and alignment, without a background and with thin borders. The numbers will be displayed without decimals. This style will be applied to the client ID.
- *Dec2*— This style is basically the same as *Dec0*, but it holds two decimals. This style will be used for the debt amounts.
- *Text*—This is a rather simple cell style: Arial font with default size, left-aligned, and thin borders.

Let's review how these styles are created, by analyzing the most complex procedure, *ColHeading*.

We have a variable named *ColHeading* already defined, but it currently means nothing to HSSF; it's simply a placeholder. To create it in memory as a cell style, thus making it useful, a *create* command is necessary:

```
ColHeading = HSSFWorkbook_createCellStyle(book);
```

This creates the *ColHeading* cell style in memory, associated with the *book* workbook that was previously created. The next step is to define the attributes or properties of the cell style, starting with the font:

```
ChFont = HSSFWorkbook_createFont(book);
HSSFFont_setFontHeightInPoints(ChFont: 11);
TempStr = new_String('Calibri');
HSSFFont_setFontName(ChFont: TempStr);
HSSFCellStyle_setFont(ColHeading: ChFont);
```

What was said before regarding the cell style is also applicable to the *ChFont* variable—it's created in memory first, with a *create* command, and then its properties are set. The font size is set to 11 (no special coding here), and the font name is set to *'Calibri'*. Because RPG strings and Java strings are different things, you cannot simply assign *'Calibri'* to a JavaString parameter (the second parameter of *HSSF_Font_setFontName*, in this case); you have to create a new Java string (*TempStr*) with the *'Calibri'* value and then use that JavaString variable in the *HSSF_Font_setFontName*.

So far, we've set the font to Calibri, size 11. That's not very flashy for a column heading, right? It needs a little more, something to make it stand out. Let's "paint" the cell orange, center its text, and create a thin border around it:

```
HSSFCellStyle_setFillForegroundColor(ColHeading: COLOR_LIGHT_ORANGE);
HSSFCellStyle_setFillPattern(ColHeading: SOLID_FOREGROUND);
HSSFCellStyle_setAlignment(ColHeading: ALIGN_CENTER);
HSSFCellStyle_setWrapText(ColHeading: *On);
HSSFCellStyle_setBorderBottom(ColHeading: BORDER_THIN);
HSSFCellStyle_setBorderTop(ColHeading: BORDER_THIN);
HSSFCellStyle_setBorderRight(ColHeading: BORDER_THIN);
HSSFCellStyle_setBorderLeft(ColHeading: BORDER_THIN);
```

Note that the first parameter in all of the functions above is the *ColHeading* cell style. We're simply setting its attributes, one by one, to predefined values; *COLOR_LIGHT_ORANGE*, *SOLID_FOREGROUND*, and so on are actually numeric constants defined in the *hssf_h* copy member.

The same process is then applied to the other three cell styles. I invite you to review it by yourself, spotting and understanding the differences. Quite a few more functions are available to tweak the cell style attributes, so be sure to have a look at the HSSF Cell Style object documentation (*http://poi.apache.org/apidocs/org/apache/poi/hssf/usermodel/HSSFCellStyle.html*).

Going back to the routine *IniXls* where we left off, the book and sheet are created (in memory only), the columns are properly formatted, and the necessary cell styles have been made available. The next step is to write the header row. Here's the first shortcoming of HSSF: you need to write a cell at a time, specifying the row, column, data type, and cell style every time. Since I'm writing the header row (simple text), I'll use the *HSSF_Text* API, which has four parameters: the row number, the column number, the string to put in the previously identified cell, and the cell style. There are other functions to change the content of a cell, named *hssf_num* (for numeric values) and *hssf_formula* (as the name implies, for Excel formulas). They all have the same for parameters and only the third is different, according to the function. Later, you'll see other APIs being used to write other types of data.

The *rowcount* variable indicates the number of the row to create. Be sure to set it to zero when you start to work on a new sheet. If for some reason you forget to increment it, the *HSSFSheet_createRow* will overwrite the last row written, so it's a good practice to have these two lines together at all times:

```
// create the header row
rowcount += 1;
row = HSSFSheet_createRow(sheet: rowcount);
```

The next (tedious) step is to write each column title, one by one:

```
// write column A
W_Col = 0;
hssf_text(row: W_Col: 'Client ID' : ColHeading);

// write column B
W_Col += 1;
hssf_text(row: W_Col: 'Client Name' : ColHeading);

// write column C
W_Col += 1;
hssf_text(row: W_Col: 'Total Debt' : ColHeading);

// write column D
W_Col += 1;
hssf_text(row: W_Col: 'Debt 30 Days' : ColHeading);

// write column E
W_Col += 1;
hssf_text(row: W_Col: 'Debt 60 Days' : ColHeading);

// write column F
W_Col += 1;
hssf_text(row: W_Col: 'Debt 90 Days' : ColHeading);
```

The caution about the *rowcount* variable applies equally to the *W_Col* variable: if you neglect to increment it, you'll be overwriting the same cell over and over again.

Note that I'm using a string directly in the *hssf_text* function. This was not supposed to be possible, right? Well, it's possible because *hssf_text* is one of the many functions that Scott Klement created to simplify and reduce the programmer's work. Otherwise, you'd have to create a new JavaString variable, set its value, and then use it in the *hssf_text* function, making an already tedious task even more annoying.

And with that, the header is done!

Now, let's write some actual data to the spreadsheet. My example program gathers the necessary data from the files/business rules and places it in temporary variables. Then, routine *WrtXls* writes the data to the spreadsheet, again cell by cell:

```
BegSr WrtXls;

  If (W_Count = 0);
    // If this is the first write, initialize the spreadsheet
    ExSr IniXls;
  EndIf;

    W_Count += 1;
    rowcount += 1;
    row = HSSFSheet_createRow(Sheet: rowcount);

    W_Col = 0;

    // Write column A
    hssf_num(row: W_Col: W_ClientID: Dec0);

    // Write column B
    W_Col += 1;
    hssf_text(row: W_Col: %Trim(W_ClientName) : Text);

    // Write column C
    W_Col += 1;
    hssf_text(row: W_Col: W_TotalDebt :Dec2);

    // Write column D
    W_Col += 1;
    hssf_num(row: W_Col: W_Debt30 : Dec2);

    // Write column E
    W_Col += 1;
    hssf_num(row: W_Col: W_Debt60: Dec2);

    // Write column F
    W_Col += 1;
    hssf_num(row: W_Col: W_Debt90 : Dec2);

EndSr;
```

In this routine, I'm determining whether the spreadsheet was already created, via the *W_Count* variable, and creating it if necessary through the routine *IniXls*, described earlier:

```
If (W_Count = 0);
  // If this is the first write, initialize the spreadsheet
  ExSr IniXls;
EndIf;

W_Count += 1;
```

Then, I'm creating a new row using *HSSFSheet_createRow* and writing the data to it. I'm using the *hssf_text* or *hssf_num* APIs, depending on the data type. Also, notice that the last parameter of each API call is the cell style previously defined.

This routine will be called for each client in the database; it writes a new row for each, directly replacing the *WRITE <format name>* of the printer file being replaced.

At the end of the program, you need to actually write the spreadsheet to the IFS. (It only exists in memory, remember?) This is achieved using routine *EndXls*:

```
BegSr EndXls;

 // Prepare output file path
   W_File     = 'Debt_Report.xls';
   W_PathFile = 'AccountReports' + %Trim(W_File);
   Str = new_String(%Trim(W_PathFile));
   outfile = new_FileOutputStream(Str);

 // Write output file

   HSSFWorkbook_write(Book: outfile);
   FileOutputStream_close(outfile);

 // Close object group to free memory
  hssf_end_object_group();

EndSr;
```

This process requires three steps:

1. Prepare the file's name and path on the IFS. (I'm using a fixed name and path, but it could easily have variables instead.) Again, note the detail about the RPG string being converted to a JavaString before being used on a Java function. The file is created on the IFS path by the *new_FileOutputStream* function.
2. Write the file to the IFS by indicating which workbook I want to write to disk (the *book* variable, in this case), and close the output file. This becomes very relevant when you're working on more than one sheet. You can handle multiple *HSSFSheet* variables at the same time and write them all to the same workbook, but I'm trying to keep it simple here.
3. Close the object group to free the allocated memory. As I mentioned before, this is a good practice. It not only frees memory, but also frees the IFS file, so be sure to always include this line!

In short, our legacy program will have a few new routines to handle the spreadsheet output (*IniXls*, *WrtXls*, and *EndXls*) and two new procedures (*FormatColumns* and *CreateCellStyles*). These last two have to be added to the program instead of a service program because they are specific to the spreadsheet (the *book* variable) we're creating in this program.

The routines *IniXls* and *WrtXls* replace the *WRITE* of the print file header and detail record formats, respectively. If you imagine that the printer file would have the *USROPN* keyword (not very common, but possible), routine *EndXls* would hold the *Close* opcode. The two procedures replace the printer file keywords related to the appearance of the fields.

Well, that wraps up "the hard way." As you can see, it's not very hard to create a spreadsheet this way, but it can get rather confusing and tedious when you have a lot of columns.

The Easy Way

Recently, I had to create an Excel file with 70 columns. As you might imagine, I was dreading the task! So, I decided to create an easier way to do it.

The starting point is the fact that there are three basic stages to creating a spreadsheet:

1. Create the workbook and sheet in memory. This includes creating the header and all the formatting.
2. Write records to it.
3. Output it to an IFS folder.

These stages match routines *IniXls*, *WrtXls*, and *EndXls* in "The Hard Way" section (just in case you didn't read that section).

Instead of creating the workbook and sheet within the program, why not use an existing spreadsheet as a starting point? That's much easier (no coding involved) and much, much quicker. Using Excel, you see exactly what the result will be and can quickly adjust any formatting detail. This method also facilitates future maintenance, because the user can change the look of the spreadsheet without the help of a developer.

The template workbook can contain one or more sheets, each with its own set of columns. It's also important to include one row of dummy data, properly formatted (font name, size, color, background, and so on), just after the header row(s) to allow the procedures that use the template to recognize the formatting to use on the real data rows.

I've created procedure *XlsCrtBook*, which creates a workbook in memory and returns a pointer to it, using a template location and name supplied as entry parameters. You might ask, "Why not create the sheet at the same time, as in routine *IniXls*?" It's simple: this way, you can have different template sheets within the same workbook and create only the one(s) you need.

This means that another procedure is required to create the sheet. That's procedure *XlsCrtSheet*. This procedure returns a pointer to the sheet indicated on the entry parameter. (I'll explain the details later on.) This takes care of the first stage.

The second part (writing the actual data rows) is the most tedious part if the spreadsheet has a lot of columns. However, my new approach had to be a bit different, because it had to be flexible and couldn't depend on the type of value (numeric or alphanumeric) of each column to work. So, it uses a string to store the row of data to be written, and a separator character to distinguish the columns, like a CSV file would.

Finally, writing the spreadsheet to the IFS also had to be easy and flexible. All the necessary API calls are condensed into a simple procedure named *XlsWrtBook* that receives the pointers to the workbook and sheet I'm writing to disk, and the name and location of the IFS file.

I know this might sound a bit confusing now, but it will be clearer with an example. Let's use the debt report program again. Instead of routine *IniXls*, assume I've already created a template with the name *DebtRepTpl.XLS* and uploaded it to the IFS folder *XLS*. Here's how the workbook is created:

```
If XlsCrtBook('XLS': 'DebtRepTpl.XLS': P_Book) = *Off;
EndIf;
```

Now, you must indicate which sheet within the template you want to use. Let's use sheet *DebtSummary*:

```
If XlsCrtSheet(P_Book: 'DebtSummary': 1: 6:
            P_Sheet: P_Style: P_Type) = *Off;
EndIf;
```

You probably noticed some additional parameters that were not previously mentioned. After the sheet name, there's a one and a six, and some other values that I'll explain later. These two are the number of rows and columns of the header, respectively. This is used to avoid overwriting the header with data and, most importantly, to find the first row of data. In this case, row 2 is the first row of data. It contains the cell types and styles (equivalent to the formatting that was created in procedure *CreateCellStyles* in the previous section). These cell types and styles are returned in parameters *P_Type* and *P_Style*, respectively, which are arrays with one position for each column used. In this case, only the first six positions will be used, because I've indicated that there are six columns. These parameters will be used to write the data rows with the proper formatting. This is achieved through procedure *XlsWrtLin*:

```
P_Row = '123§Dummy Client§2000§200§800§1000';

If XlsWrtLin(P_Book: P_Sheet: P_Style: P_Type: 2:  P_Row: '§') = *Off;
EndIf;
```

Here, I've hard-coded values to the *P_Row* variable, just to make things clearer. The call to procedure *XlsWrtLin* will write the following information to the second row of the sheet I've previously created:

- The client named "Dummy Client," which has an internal ID of 123
- A total debt of $2,000: $200 of outstanding invoices due in 30 days or less, $800 under 60 days, and $1,000 up to or over 90 days

In a real program, the *P_row* variable would contain the concatenation of database fields, properly transformed into character values (when needed) to form a string.

There's another detail I haven't talked about yet: the separation character. You'll notice that the "§" character (also known as the paragraph symbol) is used in *P_Row* and as a parameter of the *XlsWrtLin* procedure. This is because you might need to choose another separator character if your data contains "§". You can use any character you want, as long as you use it in the composition of the *P_row* variable and the call to *XlsWrtLin*. I strongly recommend defining a constant (*C_Sep*, for instance) and using that instead of repeating the character everywhere.

Finally, I'm ready to output my spreadsheet to disk:

```
If XlsWrtBook('XLS': 'DebtReport.xls': P_Book) = *Off;
EndIf;
```

This call to procedure *XlsWrtBook* writes my *P_Book* spreadsheet to the IFS folder XLS with the name *DebtReport.XLS*.

In short, with four simple calls that you can easily include in any program, you have all the functionality of the HSSF APIs, without the complexity!

Next, I'll go through the inner workings of each procedure.

Wow, That *Was* Easy! But How Does It Work?

The procedure *XlsCrtBook* is quite simple:

```
P XlsCrtBook      B                   EXPORT
D XlsCrtBook      PI              N

 * Input Parms
D P_Folder                     250A   Value
D P_File                        50A   Value

 * Output Parms
D P_Book                              Like(HSSFWorkbook)

 *   Main Code
 /FREE

       // If the folder or file names weren't supplied => error!
        If (P_Folder = *Blanks) or (P_File   = *Blanks);
          Return *On;
        EndIf;

       // create space for 100 object references
       // in the object group.
         Hssf_Begin_Object_Group(100);

       // Read the template file into memory
         P_Book = Hssf_Open('/' + %Trim(P_Folder)
                          + '/' + %Trim(P_File) );

       // If the file was not found => error!
         If P_Book = *Null;
          Return *On;
         EndIf;

    Return    *Off;

 /END-FREE
P XlsCrtBook      E
```

This procedure simply opens an existing file, using the name and location provided as entry parameters, and returns a pointer to the workbook. *Hssf_Open* is usually used to open files for reading, but it can also be used for writing. The procedure returns an indicator (**ON*, in case of error) so that it can be used in an If statement to provide some degree of control over the events.

The next procedure, *XlsCrtSheet*, is slightly more complex:

```
P XlsCrtSheet      B                     EXPORT
D XlsCrtSheet      PI               N

 * Input Parms
D P_Book                                 Like(HSSFWorkbook) Value
D P_SheetName                     50A    Value
D P_CabRow                         3  0 Value
D P_CabCol                         5  0 Value

 * Output Parms
D P_Sheet                                Like(HSSFSheet)
D P_Style                                Like(HSSFCellStyle) Dim(250)
D P_Type                                 Like(jInt) Dim(250)

D Row              S                     Like(HSSFRow)
D Cell             S                     Like(HSSFCell)
D W_Col            S                5I 0

 *   Main Code
 /FREE

    ExSr      IniPgm;
    ExSr      Procc;
    ExSr      EndPgm;
    Return    *Off;

                                                           Continued
```

```
//  Sub Routines

//  Obtain the style and type of each column
  BegSr  Procc;

     W_Col = 1;

     Dow (W_Col <= P_CabCol);
       Cell = HssfRow_GetCell(Row: W_col-1);

       // If the cell is not filled in, set P_Type to *HiVal
       // in order to prevent this column from being written by XlsWrtLin
       If (Cell = *Null);
         P_Type(W_col)  = *HiVal;

// Obtain the style and type of each column from the template's dummy row
       Else;
         P_Style(W_col)   = HssfCell_GetCellStyle(Cell);
         P_Type(W_col)    = HssfCell_GetCellType(Cell);

         // Clear the dummy content
         If P_Type(W_Col) <> CELL_TYPE_FORMULA and
            P_Type(W_Col) <> CELL_TYPE_BOOLEAN and
            P_Type(W_Col) <> CELL_TYPE_ERROR;
           Hssf_Text(Row: W_Col-1: '': P_Style(W_col));
         EndIf;
       EndIf;

       W_Col += 1;
     EndDo;

  EndSr;

//  Initialization
  BegSr  IniPgm;
```

Continued

```
        // If the workbook or sheet are not supplied => Error
         If (P_Book = *Null) or (P_SheetName = *Blanks) or
            (P_CabCol = *Zeros);
           Return *On;
         EndIf;

        // Read sheet from the template
          P_Sheet = Hssf_GetSheet(P_Book: %Trim(P_SheetName));
          If (P_Sheet = *Null);
            Return *On;
          EndIf;

        // Read the first row AFTER the header to get formatting and cell types
          Row = HssfSheet_GetRow(P_Sheet: P_CabRow);
          If (Row = *Null);
            Return *On;
          EndIf;

      EndSr;

    //  End procedure
      BegSr  EndPgm;

      EndSr;

 /END-FREE
P XlsCrtSheet      E
```

The code is divided into three parts: initialization, processing, and termination routines. The initialization simply loads the proper sheet of the template workbook into memory and reads the dummy data row. Next, the processing routine reads one cell at a time and stores its type (see the *CELL_TYPE* constants in the POI-HSSF documentation for the available types) and style (in other words, its formatting) in the *P_Type* and *P_Style* arrays, respectively. I'll get back to these two in the explanation of the next procedure. Finally, the termination procedure is empty (at least for now; it might be necessary in a later version), but it was included for coherence. If everything went OK, an **OFF* indicator is returned. An **ON* is returned if something went wrong reading the template sheet or the dummy data row.

I've mentioned the arrays *P_Type* and *P_Style* several times without a proper explanation for their existence. I hope their purpose is clear after the explanation of the next procedure:

```
P XlsWrtLin        B                   EXPORT
D XlsWrtLin        PI               N

 * Input Parms
D P_Book                               Like(HSSFWorkbook) Value
D P_Sheet                              Like(HSSFSheet) Value
D P_Style                              Like(HSSFCellStyle) Dim(250) Value
D P_Type                               Like(jInt) Dim(250) Value
D P_NumRow                        10  0 Value
D P_Row                        32767    Varying Value
D P_Sep                             1A  Value

D Row              S                   Like(HSSFRow)
D Cell             S                   Like(HSSFCell)
D W_Col            S               5I 0
D W_PosB           S               5I 0
D W_PosE           S               5I 0
D W_Cell           S            5000A   Varying

 *   Main Code
 /FREE

    ExSr      IniPgm;
    ExSr      Procc;
    ExSr      EndPgm;
    Return    *Off;

    //  Sub Routines

    //  Write the data row to the sheet
      BegSr  Procc;

                                                            Continued
```

```
W_Col  = 0;
W_PosB = 1;
W_PosE = %Scan(P_Sep: P_Row);

Dow (W_PosE <> *Zeros);
  W_Col += 1;
  If (W_PosE - W_PosB > *Zeros);
    W_Cell = %SubSt(P_Row: W_PosB: W_PosE - W_PosB);
  Else;
    W_Cell = *Blanks;
  EndIf;

  Select;

  // If the cell is numeric
  When P_Type(W_Col) = CELL_TYPE_NUMERIC;
    If (W_Cell = *Blanks);
      W_Cell = *Zeros;
    EndIf;
    Hssf_Num(Row: W_Col-1: %Dec(W_Cell: 63: 20) : P_Style(W_Col));

  // If the cell is a character
  When P_Type(W_Col) = CELL_TYPE_STRING;
    Hssf_Text(Row: W_Col-1: %Trim(W_Cell) : P_Style(W_Col));

  // If the cell contains a formula
  When P_Type(W_Col) = CELL_TYPE_FORMULA;

  // If the cell is empty
  When P_Type(W_Col) = CELL_TYPE_BLANK;
    Hssf_Text(Row: W_Col-1: %Trim(W_Cell) : P_Style(W_Col));

  // If the cell contains a boolean
  When P_Type(W_Col) = CELL_TYPE_BOOLEAN;

  // If the cell has an error
```

Continued

```
          When P_Type(W_Col) = CELL_TYPE_ERROR;

          EndSL;

          W_PosB = W_PosE + 1;
          W_PosE = %Scan(P_Sep: P_Row: W_PosB);
        EndDo;

     EndSr;

   //  Initialization
     BegSr  IniPgm;

       // If there's a problem with the book, sheet,
       // or separator character => Error
        If (P_Book = *Null) or (P_Sheet = *Null) or
           (P_Sep = *Blanks);
          Return *On;
        EndIf;

       // Retrieve the row in which to write
        Row = HssfSheet_GetRow(P_Sheet: P_NumRow - 1);

       // If it doesn't exist, create it
        If Row = *Null;
          Row = HSSFSheet_createRow(P_Sheet: P_NumRow - 1);
        EndIf;

     EndSr;

   //  End Procedure
     BegSr  EndPgm;

     EndSr;

 /END-FREE
P XlsWrtLin       E
```

Again, the code is divided into three parts: initialization, processing, and termination routines. The first part simply obtains the pointer to the row in which to write data. If I'm writing the first line (the one that contains dummy data on the template) or, for any reason, the template has data in more than one row, it uses the row indicated in the entry parameter. Otherwise, it creates a new row (the most common situation).

Now comes the tricky part: writing the data. Here's where the *P_Type* and *P_Style* arrays are (finally) put to good use. In order to choose which API to use (*hssf_num*, *hssf_text*, or *hssf_formula*), the procedure needs to know which type of data to write. For instance, if you try to write a string variable using *hssf_num*, you'll get a very ugly and non-user-friendly Java error (the type of thing that gives HSSF APIs a bad rep). To circumvent this, *P_Type* is used. It contains the type of cell for the one being currently written. So, if it's a number, *hssf_num* will be used; if it's a string, *hssf_text* will be used; and so on. Whichever API is used to write the cell, it requires a cell style. (If you read "The Hard Way" section earlier in this chapter, you'll remember the cell styles defined in the *CreateCellStyles* procedure.) Now it's array *P_Style*'s turn; it provides the formatting previously defined on the template sheet for the column currently being written.

Let's go back a bit and analyze the *Do* loop that encloses the writing part. The most programmer-friendly way I've found of passing the row to write is by stuffing it into a huge string, using a separator character to segregate the values. The loop is used for reading that string, jumping from separator character to separator character, and writing a cell with each value.

Again, the termination procedure is empty, but included for coherence. (It might be necessary in a later version.) If everything went OK, an **OFF* indicator is returned. An **ON* is returned if something went wrong reading the template sheet or if the separation character was not supplied.

The data writing is done. Let's move on to the file writing to the IFS:

```
P XlsWrtBook      B                   EXPORT
D XlsWrtBook      PI             N

 * Input Parms
D P_Folder                     250A   Value
```

Continued

```
D P_File                          50A    Value
D P_Book                                 Like(HSSFWorkbook)

D Str             S                      Like(jString)
D OutFile         S                      Like(jFileOutputStream)

 *   Main Code
 /FREE

   ExSr      IniPgm;
   ExSr      Procc;
   ExSr      EndPgm;
   Return    *Off;

   //  Sub Routines

   //  Write the file to the IFS
     BegSr  Procc;

        Str = New_String('/' + %Trim(P_Folder) +
                         '/' + %Trim(P_File) );
        OutFile = New_FileOutputStream(Str);
        HssfWorkBook_write(P_Book: OutFile);

        FileOutputStream_Close(OutFile);
        Hssf_End_Object_Group();

     EndSr;

   //  Initialization
     BegSr  IniPgm;

       // If all the necessary information was not supplied => Error
        If (P_Folder = *Blanks) or (P_File   = *Blanks) or
           (P_Book = *Null);
          Return *On;
        EndIf;
```

Continued

```
      EndSr;

    //  End procedure
      BegSr  EndPgm;

      EndSr;

 /END-FREE
P XlsWrtBook        E
```

This procedure is basically the same as routine *EndXls*, handling all the necessary API calls to write the workbook to disk and free the memory.

To finalize, I'll consolidate all of this with a two-sheet example. Assume that I have a template workbook with two sheets, one for the debt summary (as previously explained) and another for the invoice list that details that debt. This sheet has the following columns: invoice number, invoice date, invoice due date, and invoice amount.

I'll write a row on the first sheet with the client's debt, and a few rows on the second sheet with invoice information (just to give you an idea):

```
FINVOICES  IF   E           K Disk

 /copy qcpylesrc,EASYXLS_PR

 *   Variables
 * Work Fields
D P_Book          s                   like(HSSFWorkbook)
D P_Sheet         s                   like(HSSFSheet)
D P_style         s                   like(HSSFCellStyle) dim(250)
D P_Type          s                   Like(jInt) dim(250)
D P_Row           S           5000
D P_Sheet2        s                   like(HSSFSheet)
D P_style2        s                   like(HSSFCellStyle) dim(250)
D P_Type2         s                   Like(jInt) dim(250)
```

Continued

```
*   Main Code

/FREE

    ExSr Init;

  // Create Book
    If XlsCrtBook('XLS': 'DebtRepTpl.xls': P_Book) = *Off;

    // Create first Sheet (summary)
      If XlsCrtSheet(P_Book: 'DebtSummary': 1: 6:
                    P_Sheet: P_Style: P_Type) = *Off;
      EndIf;

    // Create second Sheet (detail)
      If XlsCrtSheet(P_Book: 'DebtDetail': 1: 4:
                    P_Sheet2: P_Style2: P_Type2) = *Off;
      EndIf;

    // Write a line for the client's debt on the first sheet
       P_Row = '555§Another Client§1000§800§200§0';

      If XlsWrtLin(P_Book: P_Sheet: P_Style: P_Type: 2:  P_Row: '§') = *Off;
      EndIf;

    // Write invoice data in sheet "DebtDetail"
      P_Row = 'Inv. Nbr. 12§20010101§20100131§200';

      If XlsWrtLin(P_Book: P_Sheet2: P_Style2: P_Type2: 2:
                                                   P_Row: '§') = *Off;
      EndIf;

    // Write a second invoice to sheet "DebtDetail"
      P_Row = 'Inv. Nbr. 25§20010601§20100630§800';
```

Continued

```
    If XlsWrtLin(P_Book: P_Sheet2: P_Style2: P_Type2: 3:
                                                P_Row: '§') = *Off;
    EndIf;


  // Write Book to IFS
    If XlsWrtBook('XLS': 'DebtReport.xls': P_Book) = *Off;
    EndIf;

  EndIf;

  Exsr End_Of_Program;

//  Sub Routines

//  Initialization
  BegSr  Init;


  EndSr;

//End of the program
  BegSr  End_Of_Program;

  *InLr = *On;

  EndSr;
```

In this program, I'm working with an "Excel file" or workbook, named *P_Book*. This workbook has two sheets, represented by the variables *P_Sheet* and *P_Sheet2*. To provide separate formatting for each sheet, two sets of formatting arrays were also created: *P_Style* and *P_Type* for *P_Book*, and *P_Style2* and *P_Type2* for *P_Book2*. I could have also duplicated the *P_Row* variable, but since I'm always assigning a new value to it before calling the *XlsWrtLin* procedure, I didn't think it was necessary. To keep things simple, only a couple of dummy rows of data are being written to the second sheet. Ideally, you'd have a loop reading the client's invoices and calculating the total debt amount while writing each invoice amount (the detail line) to the second sheet. Once the client changed, it would write the debt total (the summary line) to the first sheet.

What I've discussed so far helps to replace a printout with relative ease, but what if you have an output file instead of a printer file? It's a fairly common technique: write the output data to a temporary physical file, and then transfer the data to an IFS folder (via *CPYTOIMPF*) or to a PC folder (via the IBM i Access Data Transfer program, for instance) in CSV or XLS format afterward. Well, I also have a solution for that. Keep reading . . . .

The Even Easier Way

For situations in which there's already an output file, it makes no sense to develop code to read it again and write it line by line. So, this section provides another procedure to help you. It's quite simple to use, actually. You just add the *USROPN* keyword to the output file, close it once it's ready to transfer, and include these lines of code:

```
// Write physical file to IFS spreadsheet
  If FileToXls('OUTF': 'XLS': 'MyTemplate.xls': 'MySheet': 1: 4: '§':
             'XLS': 'MyOutputFile.xls') = *Off;
  EndIf;
```

Sound simple enough?

Let's look at the parameters:

- *OUTF* is the name of the physical file.
- *XLS*, *MyTemplate.xls*, and *MySheet* indicate the IFS folder, workbook, and sheet to use as templates, respectively.
- *1* indicates that there's only one header row.
- *4* indicates that the template has four columns.
- "§" is the separator character.
- The second *XLS* indicates the output IFS folder.
- *MyOutputFile.xls* indicates the name of the output file.

This procedure relies on the previously described procedures to function, as you might have gathered from the parameters. However, it uses a simple trick devised to provide the necessary flexibility to process almost *any* file, as you'll see next:

```
P FileToXls       B                   EXPORT
D FileToXls       PI              N

 * Input Parms
D P_File                        10A   Value
D P_FolderT                    250A   Value
D P_FileXlsT                    50A   Value
D P_SheetName                   50A   Value
D P_CabRow                       3  0 Value
D P_CabCol                       5  0 Value
D P_Sep                          1A   Value
D P_FolderOut                  250A   Value
D P_FileXlsOut                  50A   Value
D W_Lin           S              5I 0
D W_Book          S                   Like(HSSFWorkbook)
D W_Row           S          32767A
D W_Sheet         S                   Like(HSSFSheet)
D W_Style         S                   Like(HSSFCellStyle) Dim(250)
D W_Type          S                   Like(jInt) Dim(250)
D P_Cmdlin        S            350A
D P_Cmdlen        S             15  5

 * Programs Call
D $QCMDEXC        PR                  ExtPgm('QCMDEXC')
D P_Cmdlin                     350A
D P_Cmdlen                      15  5

 *   Main Code
 /FREE

  ExSr      IniPgm;
  ExSr      Procc;
  ExSr      EndPgm;
```

Continued

```
Return    *Off;

//  Sub Routines

//  Read temporary physical file and write it to IFS
BegSr  Procc;

  // Create Book
  If XlsCrtBook(P_FolderT: P_FileXlsT: W_Book) = *On;
    Return *On;
  EndIf;
  // Create Sheet
  If XlsCrtSheet(W_Book: P_SheetName: P_CabRow: P_CabCol:
                                W_Sheet: W_Style: W_Type) = *On;
    Return *On;
  EndIf;

  // Read intermediate physical file
  Open PFXLS;
  Read PFXLS;
  W_Lin = P_CabRow;

  // Write lines (records) to spreadsheet
  Dow Not %Eof(PFXLS);
    W_Row = %Trim(XlsTxt) + P_Sep;
    W_Lin += 1;

    If XlsWrtLin(W_Book: W_Sheet: W_Style: W_Type: W_Lin:
                                               W_Row: P_Sep) = *On;
      Close PFXLS;
      Return *On;
    EndIf;

    Read PFXLS;
  EndDo;
```

Continued

```
  // Write the workbook to IFS
    If XlsWrtBook(P_FolderOut: P_FileXlsOut: W_Book) = *On;
      Close PFXLS;
      Return *On;
    EndIf;

EndSr;

  //  Initialization
BegSr  IniPgm;

  // If a parameter is blank => Error
  If (P_File = *Blanks) or (P_FolderT = *Blanks) or
     (P_FileXlsT = *Blanks) or (P_SheetName = *Blanks) or
     (P_CabRow = *Zeros) or (P_CabCol = *Zeros) or
     (P_Sep = *Blanks) or (P_FolderOut = *Blanks) or
     (P_FileXlsOut = *Blanks);
    Return *On;
  EndIf;

  // Create the intermediate file in QTEMP
  P_Cmdlin = 'CRTDUPOBJ OBJ(PFXLS) FROMLIB(*LIBL) ' +
             'OBJTYPE(*FILE) TOLIB(QTEMP)';
  P_Cmdlen = %LEN(%TRIM(P_CmdLin));

  CallP(E) $QCMDEXC(P_Cmdlin: P_Cmdlen);

  // If the file already exists, clear it
  If %Error;
    P_Cmdlin = 'CLRPFM FILE(QTEMP/PFXLS)';
    P_Cmdlen = %LEN(%TRIM(P_CmdLin));
    CallP(E) $QCMDEXC(P_Cmdlin: P_Cmdlen);

    If %Error;
      Return *On;
    EndIf;
  EndIf;
```

```
    // Copy the physical file to the intermediate file,
    // using the separator character to segregate fields
    P_Cmdlin = 'CPYTOIMPF FROMFILE(' + %Trim(P_File) +
               ') TOFILE(QTEMP/PFXLS) MBROPT(*REPLACE) RCDDLM(*EOR) ' +
               'STRDLM(*NONE) FLDDLM(''' + %Trim(P_Sep) + ''') ' +
               'DECPNT(*COMMA)';
    P_Cmdlen = %LEN(%TRIM(P_CmdLin));

CallP(E) $QCMDEXC(P_Cmdlin: P_Cmdlen);

    // If the copy ended in error
    If %Error;
      Return *On;
    EndIf;

  EndSr;

  //  End Procedure
  BegSr  EndPgm;

    Close PFXLS;

  EndSr;

 /END-FREE
P FileToXls        E
```

The initialization procedure uses the trick I mentioned before: since *XlsWrtLin* reads a string that contains the cell values segregated by a special character, the first step is to copy the physical file to an intermediate file that has only one field, basically a big string. This is achieved with the *CPYTOIMPF* command, using the separator character to segregate the fields. Once the copy is done, file *PFXLS* will contain records similar to the *P_Row* variable in the previous examples.

From this point on, it's easy! The main processing is just a matter of reading the intermediate file, writing each line to the spreadsheet, closing it, and writing it to the IFS. This time, the termination routine is actually doing something: closing the intermediate file so that no locks occur.

Easy, But . . .

All these procedures designed to build spreadsheets in an easier way have (I hope) advantages, but they also have some limitations worth discussing. Since they're Java-based, speed is not their strongest attribute; if you're transforming a report program that uses a printer file into another that generates an Excel file, you'll notice mild to severe performance degradation. It's hard to predict exactly how slow it will get, but as a rule of thumb, estimate at least twice the time. It depends on a lot of factors, such as the number of columns and the data types.

Another limitation is the usage of date and timestamp fields when using the *FileToXls* procedure. The corresponding spreadsheet column has to be formatted as text, instead of date, because IBM i and Excel have different notions of what a date is! You can change either the physical file field type or the spreadsheet column formatting, but I suppose changing the latter is easier.

It's also really important to choose the right separator character; otherwise, you might get indecipherable errors and odd results. This can lead to a lot of frustration and wasted time.

Easy, Easy, Easy

I hope you find these procedures useful. In addition, I hope the great tool created and maintained by Scott Klement (and my humble procedures with it) are used by programmers to modernize the part of applications that is mostly ignored: the output.

The EasyXLS Cheat Sheet

This "cheat sheet" is designed to be a quick reference guide to the procedures discussed in this chapter. It provides parameter information and examples.

XlsCrtBook

The *XlsCrtBook* procedure creates the workbook in memory.

Input parms:

- *P_Folder*—IFS folder where the template is located
- *P_File*—Template name

Output parms:

- *P_Book*—Pointer to the newly created workbook

XlsCrtSheet

The *XlsCrtSheet* procedure creates the sheet in memory.

Input parms:

- *P_Book*—Pointer to the workbook
- *P_SheetName*—Sheet name in the template
- *P_CabRow*—Number of rows that compose the header in the template
- *P_CabCol*—Number of columns that compose the header in the template

Output parms:

- *P_Sheet*—Pointer to the newly created sheet
- *P_Style*—Array with the style of each column
- *P_Type*—Array with the data type of each column

XlsWrtLin

The *XlsWrtLin* procedure writes a new row to the sheet.

Input parms:

- *P_Book*—Pointer to the workbook
- *P_Sheet*—Pointer to the sheet

Continued

- *P_Style*—Array with the style of each column
- *P_Type*—Array with the data type of each column
- *P_NumRow*—Row number in which to write
- *P_Row*—Data to write, each field separated by *P_Sep*
- *P_Sep*—Separator character

XlsWrtBook

The *XlsWrtBook* procedure writes the workbook to disk.

Input parms:

- *P_Folder*—Output folder for the workbook
- *P_File*—Output file name
- *P_Book*—Pointer to the workbook

FileToXls

The *FileToXls* procedure writes a workbook to disk from a PF.

Input parms:

- *P_File*—Physical file name
- *P_FolderT*—IFS folder where the template is located
- *P_FileXlsT*—Template name
- *P_SheetName*—Sheet name in the template
- *P_CabRow*—Number of rows that compose the header in the template
- *P_CabCol*—Number of columns that compose the header in the template
- *P_Sep*—Separator character
- *P_FolderOut*—Output folder for the workbook
- *P_FileXlsOut*—Output file name

Continued

Code Sample 1

The following code writes one workbook with two sheets:

```
FINVOICES  IF   E           K Disk

 /copy qcpylesrc,EASYXLS_PR

 *   Variables
 * Work Fields
D P_Book          s                    like(HSSFWorkbook)
D P_Sheet         s                    like(HSSFSheet)
D P_style         s                    like(HSSFCellStyle) dim(250)
D P_Type          s                    Like(jInt) dim(250)
D P_Row           S            5000
D P_Sheet2        s                    like(HSSFSheet)
D P_style2        s                    like(HSSFCellStyle) dim(250)
D P_Type2         s                    Like(jInt) dim(250)

*   Main Code

 /FREE

     ExSr Init;

   // Create Book
     If XlsCrtBook('XLS': 'DebtRepTpl.xls': P_Book) = *Off;

     // Create first Sheet (summary)
       If XlsCrtSheet(P_Book: 'DebtSummary': 1: 6:
                     P_Sheet: P_Style: P_Type) = *Off;
       EndIf;
```

Continued

```
// Create second Sheet (detail)
  If XlsCrtSheet(P_Book: 'DebtDetail': 1: 4:
                 P_Sheet2: P_Style2: P_Type2) = *Off;
  EndIf;

// Write a line for the client's debt on the first sheet
   P_Row = '555§Another Client§1000§800§200§0';

  If XlsWrtLin(P_Book: P_Sheet: P_Style: P_Type: 2:  P_Row: '§') = *Off;
  EndIf;

// Write invoice data in sheet "DebtDetail"
  P_Row = 'Inv. Nbr. 12§20010101§20100131§200';

  If XlsWrtLin(P_Book: P_Sheet2: P_Style2: P_Type2: 2:
                                                   P_Row: '§') = *Off;
  EndIf;

// Write a second invoice to sheet "DebtDetail"
  P_Row = 'Inv. Nbr. 25§20010601§20100630§800';

  If XlsWrtLin(P_Book: P_Sheet2: P_Style2: P_Type2: 3:
                                                   P_Row: '§') = *Off;
  EndIf;


// Write Book to IFS
  If XlsWrtBook('XLS': 'DebtReport.xls': P_Book) = *Off;
  EndIf;

EndIf;

Exsr End_Of_Program;
```

Continued

```
    //  Sub Routines

    //  Initialization
      BegSr  Init;

      EndSr;

    //End of the program
      BegSr  End_Of_Program;

      *InLr = *On;

      EndSr;
```

Code Sample 2

The following code writes a physical file to a workbook:

```
FOUTF  O    E           K Disk USROPN

 /copy qcpylesrc,EASYXLS_PR
   // Some code here to produce the output physical file

(...)

   // Always remember to close the output physical file
   // before using FileToXls!!!

   // Write physical file to IFS spreadsheet
     If FileToXls('OUTF': 'XLS': 'MyTemplate.xls': 'MySheet': 1: 4: '§':
                 'XLS': 'MyOutputFile.xls') = *Off;
      EndIf;
```

8

Generate Professional Charts in Real Time

This chapter shows you how to create beautiful, fluid, and interactive charts in real time, from an RPG program, just by pressing a function key. It covers various types of charts, from a simple pie chart to intensity maps and tree charts. CGIDEV2 is used along with several Google® chart APIs to provide professional-grade charts in a browser window. This is a long but interesting chapter, because it discusses more than a dozen different charts. However, each section details a different aspect of the functionality, which is why I recommend reading the complete chapter. (The code in this chapter produces color charts and graphs; the figures shown have been altered slightly to reproduce better on the printed page. To see them in living color, click the **Book Code and Examples** link on the book's page at *http://www.mc-store.com*.)

A picture is worth 1,000 words. In business, a chart is worth 1,000 rows of data—or more! It's common sense that a well-prepared chart can make a difference when you're trying to prove that the numbers are on your side. From the simplest of charts to the most complex, their goal is to provide clarity to the (vast) amount of data behind them.

Numerous business tools are able to generate charts on demand, including MS Excel and SAP's Business Objects, among others. However, you need to set up a connection or extract the data first. Wouldn't it be nice to see the data on your program's screen and then, just by pressing a key, have it displayed as a chart? What I mean is going from Figure 8.1 to Figure 8.2, just by pressing a function key!

First, you have to download the CGIDEV2 freeware tool from *http://www.easy400.net/cgidev2/start*. This is a very powerful tool, which I got to know it as part of the MMAIL program, another great tool from easy400.net. Be sure to read the documentation and examples provided. In this chapter, we'll use it to generate an HTML file in a process vaguely similar to a Microsoft Word® mail merge.

The Pie Chart

Having said that, let's move on to the process of generating the nice-looking, interactive pie chart, as shown in Figure 8.2. I'm going to invoke a Google API by creating an HTML file with some code in it to call the API, thus generating the chart. I advise you to read the API's documentation at *http://code.google.com/apis/chart/interactive/docs/gallery/piechart.html*, because I won't explain every detail of the API here. I will, however, focus on the most relevant aspects of the API and its limitations/drawbacks.

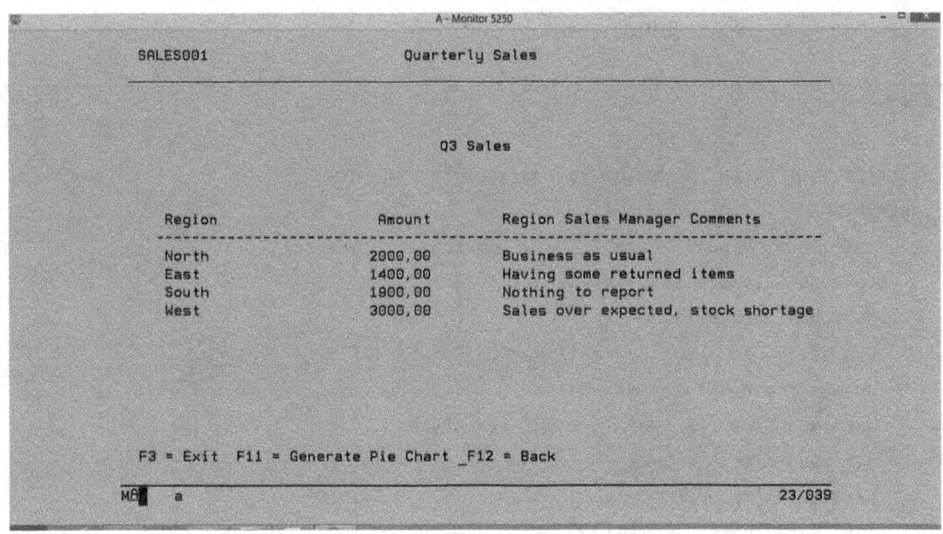

Figure 8.1: Here's your dreary green-screen data.

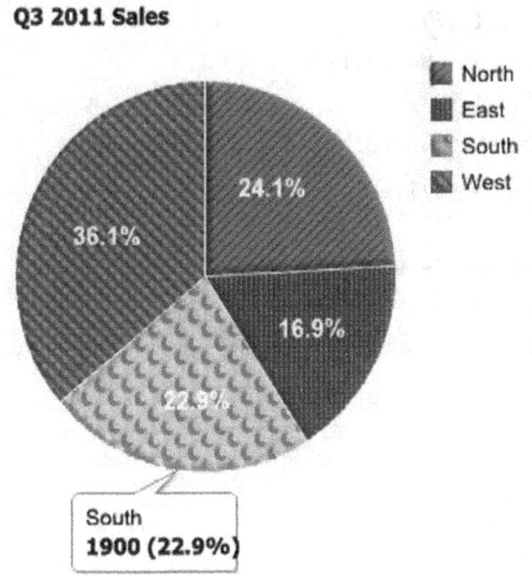

Figure 8.2: The same data looks a lot nicer now!

Let's go over Google's example source code:

```
<html>
  <head>
    <script src="https://www.google.com/jsapi"></script>
    <script>
      google.load("visualization", "1", {packages:["corechart"]});
      google.setOnLoadCallback(drawChart);
      function drawChart() {
        var data = new google.visualization.DataTable();
        data.addColumn('string', 'Task');
        data.addColumn('number', 'Hours per Day');
        data.addRows(5);
        data.setValue(0, 0, 'Work');
        data.setValue(0, 1, 11);
        data.setValue(1, 0, 'Eat');
        data.setValue(1, 1, 2);
        data.setValue(2, 0, 'Commute');
        data.setValue(2, 1, 2);
        data.setValue(3, 0, 'Watch TV');
        data.setValue(3, 1, 2);
        data.setValue(4, 0, 'Sleep');
        data.setValue(4, 1, 7);

        var chart = new google.visualization.PieChart(
            document.getElementById('chart_div'));
        chart.draw(data, {width: 450, height: 300, title: 'My Daily Activities'});
      }
    </script>
  </head>

  <body>
    <div></div>
  </body>
</html>
```

I'm definitely not the world's leading expert in JavaScript® or Google APIs, but I will give a brief explanation of what's going on here, establishing a comparison to an RPG program. The typical HTML document has at least two sections: *<head>* and *<body>*. In this case, the body is just a placeholder with a single *<div>* tag to hold the chart. All the "magic" happens in the *<head>* tag. It starts by indicating that the code will use Google's *jsapi*:

```
<head>
    <script src="https://www.google.com/jsapi"></script>
```

Think of this as something similar to a copy member. (In RPG, it would be something like */COPY QCPYLESRC, JSAPI.*) The next step is to load the necessary "program" into memory:

```
<script>
  google.load("visualization", "1", {packages:["corechart"]});
```

I can't find a direct equivalent for this, but think of it as calling a program that creates a set of data structures in memory, preparing them for use. Then, things start actually happening:

```
google.setOnLoadCallback(drawChart);
```

This line works a bit like an **INZSR* would. It's the first thing that will happen when the HTML file is "executed": it runs the *drawChart* function, detailed below. Let's review it, step by step:

```
function drawChart() {
  var data = new google.visualization.DataTable();
  data.addColumn('string', 'Task');
  data.addColumn('number', 'Hours per Day');
  data.addRows(5);
```

This function starts by defining a *DataTable* (think of it as an array), with the *var data* line. This array has no defined dimensions, however! The next couple of lines define two columns ("Task" and "Hours per Day"), and the *addRows* line defines the number of rows. So far, we have a bidimensional array with two columns and five rows. It doesn't have data yet. The next block of *setValue* lines takes care of that:

```
data.setValue(0, 0, 'Work');
data.setValue(0, 1, 11);
data.setValue(1, 0, 'Eat');
data.setValue(1, 1, 2);
data.setValue(2, 0, 'Commute');
data.setValue(2, 1, 2);
data.setValue(3, 0, 'Watch TV');
data.setValue(3, 1, 2);
data.setValue(4, 0, 'Sleep');
data.setValue(4, 1, 7);
```

The value of each element of the array is set individually, starting with *data(0,0)* all the way to *data(4,1)*. Note that the array's first position is not *(1,1)*, but *(0,0)*. This is important to understand, in order to avoid confusion later, when the values are assigned in the RPG code. The first column, a string called "Task," will be the pie slice label. The second column, a numeric called "Hours per day," will hold the corresponding value. The problem is that we don't have a pie chart yet, just the values that we want on it.

The next line, which defines the *chart* variable, creates the pie chart itself:

```
var chart = new google.visualization.PieChart(document.getElementById('chart_div'));
```

At this moment, there's an object in memory named *chart* that is a Google *PieChart*, but it's an empty shell. So, we need to associate our array, the variable named *data*, to it:

```
chart.draw(data, {width: 450, height: 300, title: 'My Daily Activities'});
```

The *draw* method (think of it as an RPG procedure or function) is responsible for drawing the chart in the browser window. It has two parameters: the data table (or array) that we want to show in *PieChart* and a huge string containing the configuration options, separated by commas. Here, I'm simply defining the chart's width, height, and title, but there are many other things you can tweak. Read the

"Configuration Options" section of the API documentation (*http://code.google.com/apis/chart/interactive/docs/gallery/piechart.html#Configuration_Options*) for more detail. The next charts will explore the different configuration options, most of which are common to almost all the chart APIs.

All that is left to do is end the function (the "*}*" line does that), and then finish the code with the closing *</script>* and *</head>* tags:

```
    }
  </script>
</head>
```

Following CGIDEV2 methodology for HTML creation, I've created a template based on Google's sample HTML file:

```
/$Header
<!DOCTYPE html PUBLIC "-//W3C//DTD XHTML 1.0 Strict//EN" "http://www.w3.org/TR/
xhtml1/DTD/xhtml1-strict.dtd">
<html xmlns="http://www.w3.org/1999/xhtml">
  <head>
    <meta http-equiv="content-type" content="text/html; charset=utf-8"/>
    <title>
      /%PageTitle%/
    </title>
    <script src="http://www.google.com/jsapi"></script>
    <script>
      google.load('visualization', '1', {packages: ['corechart']});
    </script>
    <script>
      function drawVisualization() {
        // Create and populate the data table.
        var data = new google.visualization.DataTable();
        data.addColumn('string', 'Col1');
        data.addColumn('number', 'Col2');
        data.addRows(/%TotalRows%/);
/$Row
```

Continued

```
        data.setValue(/%RowNbr%/, 0, '/%RowTitle%/');
        data.setValue(/%RowNbr%/, 1, /%RowValue%/);
/$Footer
        // Create and draw the visualization.
        new google.visualization.PieChart(
            document.getElementById('visualization'));
            chart.draw(data, {width: /%Width%/,
                              height: /%Height%/,
                              title:"/%ChartTitle%/"
                              });
            }
      google.setOnLoadCallback(drawVisualization);
    </script>
  </head>
  <body style="font-family: Arial;border: 0 none;">
    <div style="width: /%Width%/px; height: /%Height%/px;"></div>
  </body>
</html>
```

Everything you see in the template that starts with /% and ends with %/ is a variable name. For example, */%PageTitle%/* will be linked to a program variable called "PageTitle." The lines starting with */$* mark the beginning of the sections "Header," "Row," and "Footer." The HTML file uses these three sections as building blocks, repeating them as needed. In this case, the Header block is used once, followed by multiple Row blocks for as many slices as are in the pie chart, and ending with a single Footer block.

To dynamically generate the proper HTML page with my data in real time, I created an RPG procedure called *GenPieChart*:

```
 *------------------------------------------------------------------------*
 *   Generate Pie Chart                                                   *
 *------------------------------------------------------------------------*
PGenPieChart      B                   EXPORT
D                 PI            N
 * Input Parms
DP_PageTitle                    50A                 Value
```

Continued

```
DP_ChartTitle                 50A                  Value
DP_RowDS                           LikeDS(RowDS)    Dim(C_MaxRows)
D                                  Value
DP_Width                       4  0 Value
DP_Height                      4  0 Value
DP_FileName                   50A   Value
 * Output Parms
DP_ErrorDesc                  50A

 /FREE

     ExSr Init;

     ExSr Proc;

     ExSr End_Of_Program;

    //  Sub Routines

    //-------------------------------------------------------------------*
    //  Initialization                                                   *
    //-------------------------------------------------------------------*
      BegSr  Init;

      P_ErrorDesc = *Blanks;

      // Check if there is data in the P_RowDS array
      If P_RowDS(1).RowTitle = *Blanks;
        P_ErrorDesc = 'No row data';
        Return *On;
      EndIf;

      // Assume default width, if none was passed
      If P_Width = *Zeros;
        P_Width = C_DftWidth;
      EndIf;
```

Continued

```
    // Assume default height, if none was passed
    If P_Height = *Zeros;
      P_Height = C_DftHeight;
    EndIf;

    // Check if the file name was passed
    If P_FileName = *Blanks;
      P_ErrorDesc = 'No file name';
      Return *On;
    EndIf;

    EndSr;
  //-------------------------------------------------------------------*
  //End of the program                                                 *
  //-------------------------------------------------------------------*
    BegSr  End_Of_Program;

       Return *Off;

    EndSr;
  //-------------------------------------------------------------------*
  // Process input parms and generate the proper xml file              *
  //-------------------------------------------------------------------*
    BegSr  Proc;


     SetNoDebug(*OFF);
     getHtmlIfsMult(C_PieTmpl);

     // Header Section
     // Update the Header variables
     updHtmlVar('PageTitle' : %Trim(P_PageTitle));

     // Find out how many rows have data
     For W_Idx = 1 to C_MaxRows;
```

Continued

```
      If P_RowDS(W_Idx).RowTitle = *Blanks;
        Leave;
      Else;
        // If this was not the last row containing data, keep the row number
        W_TotalRows = W_Idx;
      EndIf;
    EndFor;
    // Update the TotalRows variables
    updHtmlVar('TotalRows' : %Char(W_TotalRows));
    // Write the Header section
    WrtSection('Header');

    // Row Section
    For W_Idx = 1 to C_MaxRows;
      If P_RowDS(W_Idx).RowTitle = *Blanks;
        Leave;
      EndIf;
    // Update the Row variables
    updHtmlVar('RowNbr'   : %Char(W_Idx-1));
    updHtmlVar('RowTitle' : %Trim(P_RowDS(W_Idx).RowTitle));
    updHtmlVar('RowValue' : %Char(P_RowDS(W_Idx).RowValue));
    // Write the Row section
    WrtSection('Row');
    EndFor;

    // Footer Section
    // Update the Footer variables
    updHtmlVar('ChartTitle' : %Trim(P_ChartTitle));
    updHtmlVar('Width'      : %Char(P_Width));
    updHtmlVar('Height'     : %Char(P_Height));
    // Write the Footer section
    WrtSection('Footer');

    // Set the appropriate file name and path
    W_FileName = %Trim(C_OutputPath) + '/' + %Trim(P_FileName);
```

Continued

```
      // Write the html file to disk
      WrtHtmlToStmf(%Trim(W_FileName): 819);

     EndSr;
 /END-FREE
PGenPieChart      E
```

This procedure receives a few parameters:

- The data in an array
- The page title
- The chart's title, width, and height
- The output file name

It returns a string, which is used to pass back an error description if something goes wrong. The input parms are checked in routine *Init* (nothing out of the ordinary here) and builds the HTML file in routine *Proc*. Here's where all the "magic" happens. I start by indicating which template I want to use by invoking the *getHtmlIfsMult* CGIDEV2 function:

```
BegSr  Proc;

      SetNoDebug(*OFF);
      getHtmlIfsMult(C_PieTmpl);
```

The constant *C_PieTmpl* was previously defined, outside the procedure. It contains the IFS path and the name of the template file shown earlier. Then, the function *updhtmlVar* is used to replace */%<variable_name>%/* with the data from the entry parameters. This composes the proper HTML code required to generate the chart, starting with the page title:

```
// Header Section
// Update the Header variables
updHtmlVar('PageTitle' : %Trim(P_PageTitle));
```

Note that /% and %/ are not used in the RPG code, just the template variable name. The Header section contains another variable: the total number of rows (or pie slices). To fill it, I'll have to find out how many rows of actual data were passed in the *P_RowDS* array. This array can hold up to 20 elements, but that doesn't mean that all the pies will have 20 slices. So, a nice little *For* cycle is used to determine how many valid rows the array actually has:

```
// Find out how many rows have data
For W_Idx = 1 to C_MaxRows;
  If P_RowDS(W_Idx).RowTitle = *Blanks;
    Leave;
  Else;
    // If this was not the last row containing data, keep the row number
    W_TotalRows = W_Idx;
  EndIf;
EndFor;
```

After that, all that is left to do is update the *TotalRows* variable and write the Header section. Again, note that the /$ notation for the section is not used:

```
// Update the TotalRows variables
    updHtmlVar('TotalRows' : %Char(W_TotalRows));
    // Write the Header section
    WrtSection('Header');
```

Naturally, I only need to write the Header and Footer sections once, but I'll have to write a Row section for each slice of the pie, or, in other words, for each line of the *P_RowDS* array. Let's look at the source code for this particular section:

```
// Row Section
     For W_Idx = 1 to C_MaxRows;
       If P_RowDS(W_Idx).RowTitle = *Blanks;
         Leave;
       EndIf;
```

I'm using a *For* cycle, starting at one and ending at 20 (the value of *C_MaxRows*, which you can change in source member *QCPYLESRC/GENCHRT_PR*). I'll leave the cycle whenever the current line doesn't have a title, which indicates there's no more data in the array. Be careful with this, and always clear the array before use!

If there's data, let's update the respective variables and write the section. Here's a small trick: as I mentioned before, Google's API expects the values to start at index 0 instead of 1, so the *RowNbr* variable is getting the array position minus one:

```
// Update the Row variables
updHtmlVar('RowNbr'   : %Char(W_Idx-1));
updHtmlVar('RowTitle' : %Trim(P_RowDS(W_Idx).RowTitle));
updHtmlVar('RowValue' : %Char(P_RowDS(W_Idx).RowValue));
// Write the Row section
WrtSection('Row');
EndFor;
```

Once that is done, the next step is writing the Footer section:

```
// Footer Section
// Update the Footer variables
updHtmlVar('ChartTitle' : %Trim(P_ChartTitle));
updHtmlVar('Width'      : %Char(P_Width));
updHtmlVar('Height'     : %Char(P_Height));
// Write the Footer section
WrtSection('Footer');
```

Because this section also has variables, they must be passed on to the respective template variables before the Footer section is written to memory. And voilá, the HTML file has been created! But only in memory . . . . After this, it's time to write the file to disk, using the *WrtHtmlToStmf(%Trim(W_FileName): 819)* line, which contains the hardcoded path */GCHARTS/OUTPUT/* and the file name from the *P_FileName* entry parameter.

Note that I'm using hardcoded IFS folder names. Be sure to copy the *GCHARTS* folder to your IFS and create a share with the same name. Otherwise, you won't be able to display the chart automatically, as shown in the included sample programs. (See programs *TST_GENPIE* and *TSTGENPIE1* in the downloadable source code for this chapter). You can always change this hardcoding to something a bit more dynamic by using a data area for the Template and Output paths. I decided not to do that to try to keep the code as simple as possible. However, I used a data area to store the system name (*DaSysName*), which you'll need to update to run the sample programs. I'll go through *TSTGENPIE1*, just to give you some pointers on the dos and don'ts of this procedures usage. Here's the complete source code for *TSTGENPIE1*:

```
H DECEDIT(',') DATEDIT(*DMY.)

 * Generate Charts using Google Chart APIs Procedures
 /Copy QCPYLESRC,GENCHRT_PR
 * Misc Procedures
 /Copy QCPYLESRC,MISC_PR

 *Data Areas
D Da_SystemName    S                   Like(W_SysName) DtaAra(DaSysName)
DW_PCCmd           S            200A   Inz(*Blanks)
DW_SysName         S             20A   Inz(*Blanks)
DW_Response        S             52A   Inz(*Blanks)
DW_ErrorDS         DS                  LikeDS(ApiError) Inz

 /FREE
      // Retrieve system name
      In Da_SystemName;
      W_SysName = %Trim(Da_SystemName);
    // First, I'll set up the page and chart titles and the html file name
    //  With a little humor :-)
          P_PageTitle = 'Did you know?';
          P_ChartTitle = 'Most Common Cell Phone uses';
          P_FileName = 'CellPhones.HTML';
    // Then the Rows
          Clear P_RowDS;
          P_RowDS(1).RowTitle = 'Games';
          P_RowDS(1).RowValue = 10;
          P_RowDS(2).RowTitle = 'Making Calls';
          P_RowDS(2).RowValue = 15;
          P_RowDS(3).RowTitle = 'Texting';
          P_RowDS(3).RowValue = 17;
          P_RowDS(4).RowTitle = 'Checking the Time';
          P_RowDS(4).RowValue = 23;
          P_RowDS(5).RowTitle = 'Flashlight';
```

Continued

```
        P_RowDS(5).RowValue = 140;
    // Finally, the Chart size
        P_Width = 600;
        P_Height = 400;
    // Generate the Chart
        If GenPieChart(P_PageTitle : P_ChartTitle : P_RowDS :
                       P_Width     : P_Height     :
                       P_FileName  : P_ErrorDesc  ) = *Off;
     // Display the Chart
     W_PCCmd = '\\' + %Trim(W_SysName) + '\GCHARTS\OUTPUT\'
               + %Trim(P_FileName);
     P_CmdLin = 'STRPCCMD PCCMD(''' + %Trim(W_PCCmd) +
                ''') PAUSE(*NO)';
     W_ErrorDs = ExecCmd(%Trim(P_CmdLin));
        Else;
          // Error occurred in the GenPieChart procedure
           W_Response = 'Error = ' +
                        %Trim(P_ErrorDesc);
           Dsply W_Response;
        EndIf;

    *InLr = *On;
 /END-FREE
```

Let's start with the copy members and variable declaration:

```
 * Generate Charts using Google Chart APIs Procedures
 /Copy QCPYLESRC,GENCHRT_PR
 * Misc Procedures
 /Copy QCPYLESRC,MISC_PR

 *Data Areas
D Da_SystemName   S                    Like(W_SysName) DtaAra(DaSysName)
DW_PCCmd          S            200A    Inz(*Blanks)
DW_SysName        S             20A    Inz(*Blanks)
DW_Response       S             52A    Inz(*Blanks)
DW_ErrorDS        DS                   LikeDS(ApiError) Inz
```

Notice the *GENCHRT_PR* copy member. It contains the prototype for all the procedures discussed in this chapter. It also contains all those procedure's parameter definitions, so you won't need to define them in your program. The other copy member contains a procedure called *EXECCMD*, which replaces *QCMDEXC*.

Next are the variable declarations. Since the procedure's parameters are already defined in *GENCHRT_PR*, all I need are the support variables for this example:

- *Da_SystemName* and *W_SysName* retrieve the IBM i system name from the *DASYSNAME* data area. (I know there are other ways to do this, but I'm trying to keep this code simple!)
- *W_PcCmd* issues the DOS command that will (hopefully) open the browser window and show the pie chart.
- *W_Response* shows the user how the procedure call ended.
- *W_ErrorDS* is part of the *ExecCmd* invocation. It's a general-purpose error data structure.

The code itself begins by assigning values to the page and chart titles, and a name to the HTML output file:

```
// First, I'll set up the page and chart titles and the html file name
//  With a little humor :-)
      P_PageTitle = 'Did you know?';
      P_ChartTitle = 'Most Common Cell Phone uses';
      P_FileName = 'CellPhones.HTML';
```

So far, our chart has a title, but nothing else. The next step is building the data table, by populating the procedure's *P_RowDS* data structure:

```
// Then the Rows
      Clear P_RowDS;
P_RowDS(1).RowTitle = 'Games';
P_RowDS(1).RowValue = 10;
(...)
P_RowDS(5).RowTitle = 'Flashlight';
P_RowDS(5).RowValue = 140;
```

The first thing that happens here is the clearing of the *P_RowDS* array. This is crucial to the correct use of the procedure, because it relies on the array's element values being null to determine if there's more data to process. Then, I'm assigning two values, a string and a numeric, to each position of the array. These will be the slices' title and value. Next, the chart's dimensions are set, and the procedure is called within an IF statement:

```
// Finally, the Chart size
    P_Width = 600;
    P_Height = 400;
// Generate the Chart
    If GenPieChart(P_PageTitle : P_ChartTitle : P_RowDS :
                   P_Width     : P_Height     :
                   P_FileName  : P_ErrorDesc  ) = *Off;
```

If the procedure returned **Off*, the HTML file was successfully generated, and the chart can be displayed:

```
// Display the Chart
W_PCCmd = '\\' + %Trim(W_SysName) + '\GCHARTS\OUTPUT\'
          + %Trim(P_FileName);
P_CmdLin = 'STRPCCMD PCCMD(''' + %Trim(W_PCCmd) +
           ''') PAUSE(*NO)';
W_ErrorDs = ExecCmd(%Trim(P_CmdLin));
```

Opening a DOS command line (here with *ExecCmd*, but you can also use *QCMDEXC*) with the HTML file's name and path, via *STRPCCMD*, will cause a browser window to open and display the file. When that happens, if there's an Internet connection and your browser is recent (in other words, if it can handle Google's APIs JavaScript), the pie chart will be displayed. Otherwise, it's necessary to alert the user that something went wrong:

```
     Else;
       // Error occurred in the GenPieChart procedure
       W_Response = 'Error = ' +
                    %Trim(P_ErrorDesc);
```

Continued

```
Dsply W_Response;
        EndIf;
   *InLr = *On;
/END-FREE
```

This is a very crude example, but it serves the purpose of showing how you can easily integrate this functionality into your programs.

Figure 8.3 is the completed pie chart, which shows, with a little humor, the most common uses of cell phones.

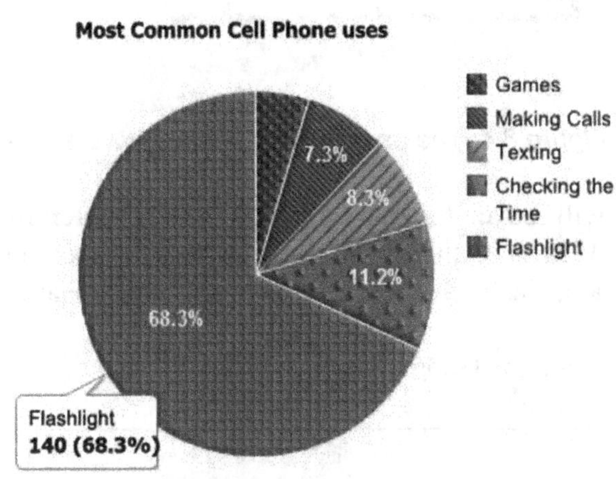

Figure 8.3: This pie chart shows how most people use their cell phones!

The Bar Chart

The pie chart is a useful tool that graphically summarizes data, but it only provides a snapshot of a moment. If I wanted to show how those cell-phone uses evolved through time, it would be impossible to do with only the pie chart. This section focuses on bar charts, which show the data's evolution. The Bar Chart API provides an easy way to graphically summarize period-related sets of values, as shown in Figure 8.4. It's available at *http://code.google.com/apis/chart/interactive/docs/gallery/barchart.html*.

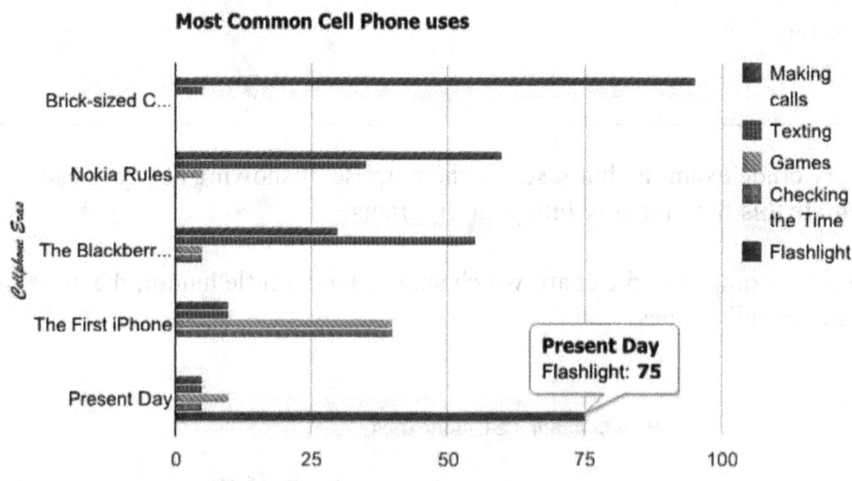

Figure 8.4: The uses for cell phones have evolved!

The method used will remain the same throughout the chapter: first a quick look at Google's sample HTML file, then an analysis of the template, followed by the RPG procedure that creates the final HTML to merge the template and your data.

Let's start by analyzing the Google sample HTML file:

```
<html>
<head>
<script type="text/javascript" src="https://www.google.com/jsapi"></script>
<script type="text/javascript">
      google.load("visualization", "1", {packages:["corechart"]});
      google.setOnLoadCallback(drawChart);
      function drawChart() {
        var data = google.visualization.arrayToDataTable([
          ['Year', 'Sales', 'Expenses'],
          ['2004',  1000,      400],
          ['2005',  1170,      460],
          ['2006',  660,       1120],
```

Continued

```
        ['2007',  1030,      540]
      ]);

      var options = {
        title: 'Company Performance',
        vAxis: {title: 'Year',  titleTextStyle: {color: 'red'}}
      };

      var chart = new google.visualization.BarChart(
                    document.getElementById('chart_div'));
                 chart.draw(data, options);
    }
</script>
</head>
<body>
<div id="chart_div" style="width: 900px; height: 500px;"></div>
</body>
</html>
```

This looks somewhat similar to the pie chart code in the previous section. All the same pieces are there, just presented differently: the data is being loaded all at once into an array that is then converted to a *DataTable*, the chart options are now passed to a variable called *options*, and that variable is used on the *chart.draw* call instead of the direct value. It's just another way of doing the same operations. However, because of the nature of the chart, there's one subtle but important difference: the number of columns. In the pie chart, only two columns were possible—one for the slice title and the other for the respective value. Here, the number of columns is variable. It depends on the number of "records" each set of data has. In this case, the sets of data are the years (2004, 2005, and so on), while the "records" of each year are sales and expenses. To represent the same information in pie charts, you'd need four pies, one for each year, and each of them would have two slices, one for sales and the other for expenses.

As you might imagine, this makes a big difference in terms of data organization. It's like adding a new dimension of data to our set. Naturally, the template needs to accommodate these new requirements, so it's going to be different from the previous one:

```
/$Header
<!DOCTYPE html PUBLIC "-//W3C//DTD XHTML 1.0 Strict//EN" "http://www.w3.org/TR/
xhtml1/DTD/xhtml1-strict.dtd">
<html xmlns="http://www.w3.org/1999/xhtml">
  <head>
    <meta http-equiv="content-type" content="text/html; charset=utf-8"/>
    <title>
      /%PageTitle%/
    </title>
    <script src="https://www.google.com/jsapi"></script>
    <script>
      google.load("visualization", "1", {packages:["corechart"]});
      google.setOnLoadCallback(drawChart);
      function drawChart() {
        var data = new google.visualization.DataTable();
        data.addColumn('string', 'col1');
/$Column
        data.addColumn('/%ColumnType%/', '/%ColumnTitle%/');
/$TotalRows
        data.addRows(/%TotalRows%/);
/$FirstRow
        data.setValue(/%RowNbr%/, 0, '/%RowTitle%/');
/$Row
        data.setValue(/%RowNbr%/, /%ColNbr%/, /%CellValue%/);
/$Footer

        var chart = new google.visualization.BarChart(
                         document.getElementById('chart_div'));
        chart.draw(data, {width: /%width%/,
                          height: /%height%/,
                          title: '/%ChartTitle%/',
                          vAxis: {title: '/%VAxisTitle%/'},
                          hAxis: {title: '/%HAxisTitle%/'}
                         });
      }
    </script>
  </head>
```

Continued

```
  <body>
    <div></div>
  </body>
</html>
```

The Header and Footer sections do basically the same as in the previous chart, but there are a few additional sections. These new sections are directly linked to the way the chart works. While the pie chart needed only two columns (one for the label and the other for the value), here the number of columns must be dynamic, as it depends on the number of different values within each set (the "cell phone uses" in Figure 8.4). However, the first column is still fixed; it's used to store the label of each set. This is why there are new sections named "Column" and "Total Rows":

```
/$Column
        data.addColumn('/%ColumnType%/', '/%ColumnTitle%/');
/$TotalRows
        data.addRows(/%TotalRows%/);
```

Just like before, the number of rows is dynamic, but now there are two types of rows. For each set of data (the "cell phone eras" in Figure 8.4), there's a label (the section "FirstRow," which provides the era's name—"Brick-Sized Cell Phones," for instance) and a dynamic number of values (the "Row" section, which corresponds to each use's percentage during the era):

```
/$FirstRow
        data.setValue(/%RowNbr%/, 0, '/%RowTitle%/');
/$Row
        data.setValue(/%RowNbr%/, /%ColNbr%/, /%CellValue%/);
```

These structural changes also affect procedure *GenBarChart*, making it a different bit from *GenPieChart*:

```
 *-------------------------------------------------------------------
 *   Generate Bar Chart
 *-------------------------------------------------------------------
PGenBarChart       B                    EXPORT
D                  PI             N
```

Continued

```
 * Input Parms
DP_PageTitle                          Like(t_PageTitle)  Value
DP_ChartTitle                         Like(t_ChartTitle) Value
DP_BarColumnDS                        LikeDS(BarColumnDS)
D                                     Dim(C_BarMaxColumns) Value
DP_BarRowDS                           LikeDS(BarRowDS) Dim(C_BarMaxRows)
D                                     Value
DP_Width                              Like(t_Width)    Value
DP_Height                             Like(t_Height)   Value
DP_VAxisTitle                         Like(t_VAxisTitle) Value
DP_HAxisTitle                         Like(t_HAxisTitle) Value
DP_FileName                           Like(t_FileName) Value
* Output Parms
DP_ErrorDesc                          Like(t_ErrorDesc)

 /FREE

     ExSr Init;

     ExSr Proc;

     ExSr End_Of_Program;

    //  Sub Routines

    //-----------------------------------------------------------------
    //  Initialization
    //-----------------------------------------------------------------
      BegSr  Init;

      P_ErrorDesc = *Blanks;

      // Check if there is data in the P_BarColumnDS array
      If P_BarColumnDS(1).ColumnTitle = *Blanks;
        P_ErrorDesc = 'No column data';
        Return *On;
      EndIf;
```

Continued

```
    // Check if there is data in the P_BarRowDS array
    If P_BarRowDS(1).RowTitle = *Blanks;
      P_ErrorDesc = 'No row data';
      Return *On;
    EndIf;

    // Assume default width, if none was passed
    If P_Width = *Zeros;
      P_Width = C_DftWidth;
    EndIf;

    // Assume default height, if none was passed
    If P_Height = *Zeros;
      P_Height = C_DftHeight;
    EndIf;

    // Check if the file name was passed
    If P_FileName = *Blanks;
      P_ErrorDesc = 'No file name';
      Return *On;
    EndIf;

    EndSr;
  //-----------------------------------------------------------------
  //End of the program
  //-----------------------------------------------------------------
    BegSr  End_Of_Program;

       Return *Off;

    EndSr;
  //-----------------------------------------------------------------
  // Process input parms and generate the proper xml file
  //-----------------------------------------------------------------
    BegSr  Proc;
```

Continued

```
SetNoDebug(*OFF);
getHtmlIfsMult(C_BarTmpl);

// Header Section
// Update the Header variables
updHtmlVar('PageTitle' : %Trim(P_PageTitle));
// Write the Header section
WrtSection('Header');

// Column Section
For W_ColIdx = 1 to C_BarMaxColumns;
  If P_BarColumnDS(W_ColIdx).ColumnTitle = *Blanks;
    Leave;
  EndIf;
  updHtmlVar('ColumnType'  :
             %Trim(P_BarColumnDS(W_ColIdx).ColumnType));
  updHtmlVar('ColumnTitle' :
             %Trim(P_BarColumnDS(W_ColIdx).ColumnTitle));
  // Write the Column section
  WrtSection('Column');
EndFor;

// TotalRows Section
// Find out how many rows have data
For W_RowIdx = 1 to C_BarMaxRows;
  If P_BarRowDS(W_RowIdx).RowTitle = *Blanks;
    Leave;
  Else;
    // If this was not the last row containing data, keep the row number
    W_TotalRows = W_RowIdx;
  EndIf;
EndFor;
// Update the TotalRows variables
updHtmlVar('TotalRows' : %Char(W_TotalRows));
// Write the TotalRows section
WrtSection('TotalRows');
```

Continued

```
// FirstRow And Row Sections
For W_RowIdx = 1 to C_BarMaxRows;
  If P_BarRowDS(W_RowIdx).RowTitle = *Blanks;
    Leave;
  EndIf;
  // Update the Row variables
  updHtmlVar('RowNbr'    : %Char(W_RowIdx-1));
  updHtmlVar('RowTitle' : %Trim(P_BarRowDS(W_RowIdx).RowTitle));
  // Write the FirstRow section
  WrtSection('FirstRow');
  For W_ColIdx = 1 to C_BarMaxColumns;
    If P_BarRowDS(W_RowIdx).Cell(W_ColIdx).CellValue= *Zeros;
      Leave;
    EndIf;
    updHtmlVar('ColNbr' : %Char(W_ColIdx));
    updHtmlVar('CellValue' : %Char(
                P_BarRowDS(W_RowIdx).Cell(W_ColIdx).CellValue));
    // Write the Row section
    WrtSection('Row');
  EndFor;
EndFor;

// Footer Section
// Update the Footer variables
updHtmlVar('ChartTitle' : %Trim(P_ChartTitle));
updHtmlVar('Width'       : %Char(P_Width));
updHtmlVar('Height'      : %Char(P_Height));
updHtmlVar('VAxisTitle' : %Trim(P_VAxisTitle));
updHtmlVar('HAxisTitle' : %Trim(P_HAxisTitle));
// Write the Footer section
WrtSection('Footer');

// Set the appropriate file name and path
W_FileName = %Trim(C_OutputPath) + '/' + %Trim(P_FileName);

// Write the html file to disk
WrtHtmlToStmf(%Trim(W_FileName): 819);
```

Continued

```
     EndSr;
 /END-FREE
PGenBarChart       E
```

Note that there are new entry parameters for the column titles and the vertical and horizontal axis titles. All the other parameters are the same as before, but I've changed some of the names to provide independence from the pie chart:

```
 *------------------------------------------------------------------
 *   Generate Bar Chart
 *------------------------------------------------------------------
PGenBarChart       B                   EXPORT
D                  PI          N
 * Input Parms
DP_PageTitle                           Like(t_PageTitle)  Value
DP_ChartTitle                          Like(t_ChartTitle) Value
DP_BarColumnDS                         LikeDS(BarColumnDS)
D                                      Dim(C_BarMaxColumns) Value
DP_BarRowDS                            LikeDS(BarRowDS) Dim(C_BarMaxRows)
D                                      Value
DP_Width                               Like(t_Width)    Value
DP_Height                              Like(t_Height)   Value
DP_VAxisTitle                          Like(t_VAxisTitle) Value
DP_HAxisTitle                          Like(t_HAxisTitle) Value
DP_FileName                            Like(t_FileName) Value
* Output Parms
DP_ErrorDesc                           Like(t_ErrorDesc)
```

The procedure is organized the same way as before, with the "magic" happening in the *Proc* subroutine. The whole Header section is quite similar, so I won't waste time with it. Because the columns are now dynamic, there's a new bit of code, similar to the Row section of the pie chart:

```
// Column Section
For W_ColIdx = 1 to C_BarMaxColumns;
  If P_BarColumnDS(W_ColIdx).ColumnTitle = *Blanks;
    Leave;
  EndIf;
  updHtmlVar('ColumnType'  :
            %Trim(P_BarColumnDS(W_ColIdx).ColumnType));
  updHtmlVar('ColumnTitle' :
            %Trim(P_BarColumnDS(W_ColIdx).ColumnTitle));
  // Write the Column section
  WrtSection('Column');
EndFor;
```

Using a *For* loop, the *P_BarColumnDS* array is read. For each entry that contains data, a new Column section will be written. Keep in mind that the first column, which identifies the data set, was already handled by the Header section. With that, the columns are done!

Moving on to the rows, notice that the total number of rows is also mandatory, just like before. However, it's not part of the Header—it has its own section. This means that an additional piece of code is necessary to handle it:

```
// TotalRows Section
// Find out how many rows have data
For W_RowIdx = 1 to C_BarMaxRows;
  If P_BarRowDS(W_RowIdx).RowTitle = *Blanks;
    Leave;
  Else;
    // If this was not the last row containing data, keep the row number
    W_TotalRows = W_RowIdx;
  EndIf;
EndFor;
// Update the TotalRows variables
updHtmlVar('TotalRows' : %Char(W_TotalRows));
// Write the TotalRows section
WrtSection('TotalRows');
```

It's very similar to the pie chart, just moved a bit down the code. What is not similar to the pie chart is the way the rows are written:

```
// FirstRow And Row Sections
For W_RowIdx = 1 to C_BarMaxRows;
  If P_BarRowDS(W_RowIdx).RowTitle = *Blanks;
    Leave;
  EndIf;
  // Update the Row variables
  updHtmlVar('RowNbr'   : %Char(W_RowIdx-1));
  updHtmlVar('RowTitle' : %Trim(P_BarRowDS(W_RowIdx).RowTitle));
  // Write the FirstRow section
  WrtSection('FirstRow');
  For W_ColIdx = 1 to C_BarMaxColumns;
    If P_BarRowDS(W_RowIdx).Cell(W_ColIdx).CellValue= *Zeros;
      Leave;
    EndIf;
    updHtmlVar('ColNbr' : %Char(W_ColIdx));
    updHtmlVar('CellValue' : %Char(
                P_BarRowDS(W_RowIdx).Cell(W_ColIdx).CellValue));
    // Write the Row section
    WrtSection('Row');
  EndFor;
EndFor;
```

Since the *P_BarRowDS* parameter is now two-dimensional (picture this array as a spreadsheet), I need two cycles to extract all the values from the "cells." The outer cycle checks whether there is data on the row by looking for a title. If a title is found, the section "FirstRow" is written and the processing continues; otherwise, it leaves the outer cycle and continues to the Footer section. The title by itself is not enough, however; I need values. The inner cycle starts by checking whether the "cell" contains a value and leaves the inner cycle if it doesn't, returning control to the outer cycle. If there's a value, a Row section is written.

The Footer section is similar to the one in *GenPieChart*, with the addition of axis titles. I chose to include these as a reminder of the customization allowed by the Google API. However, as you probably gathered from Google's sample HTML file, it's possible to have dynamic options! (We will cover this in the next section. Meanwhile, be sure to read this chart's Configuration Options at *http://code.google.com/apis/chart/interactive/docs/gallery/barchart.html#Configuration_Options* for more details and customization possibilities.)

Finally, let's briefly review the *TSTGENBAR1* sample program. It generates the bar chart depicted in Figure 8.4 by filling the *P_BarColumnDS* and *P_BarRowDS* parameters values, one by one:

```
(...)
Clear P_BarColumnDS;
P_BarColumnDS(1).ColumnType  = 'number';
P_BarColumnDS(1).ColumnTitle = 'Making calls';
(...)
Clear P_BarRowDS;
P_BarRowDS(1).RowTitle = 'Brick-sized Cellphones';
P_BarRowDS(1).Cell(1).CellValue = 95;
P_BarRowDS(1).Cell(2).CellValue = 5;
(...)
```

Note that both arrays are being cleared before usage. This is a good practice, because the *GenBarChart* procedure relies on null values (**Zeros* or **Blanks*) to determine if there's more data.

The next step is invoking the procedure:

```
If GenBarChart(P_PageTitle   : P_ChartTitle :
               P_BarColumnDS : P_BarRowDS   :
               P_Width       : P_Height     :
               P_VAxisTitle  : P_HAxisTitle :
               P_FileName    : P_ErrorDesc  ) = *Off;
```

This is performed with an IF statement to produce the appropriate response: either a Web page with the chart, or a message to the user with a description of the error. As you might remember, *GenBarChart*'s subroutines *Init* and *End_of_Program* handle the return value. The first one checks the parameters and returns **On* if something is not right, and the second one simply returns **Off*. The reasoning here is simple: if the *End_of_Program* routine is being executed, it's because nothing failed so far.

Naturally, there's plenty of room for improvement, both in the *GenBarChart* procedure itself and in the sample programs, but there are many more types of charts to cover in this chapter, so there's no need to provide all the details at once.

The Geo Map Chart (Location Name Mode)

Some of the information stored in our ERPs can be geo-referenced: warehouses, stores, branches, client and supplier addresses. All of that is just sitting there, but unless you can form a coherent map in your head, it's almost impossible to analyze and compare. With the geo map chart, you can analyze this information like never before, in an actual customizable map. Keep reading to find out how!

I'm not going to show you the classic business-type charts that even MS Excel can provide. The Geo Map API (*http://code.google.com/apis/chart/interactive/docs/gallery/geomap.html*) is a totally different chart type, engineered to allow you to display your data in ways the pie and bar charts presented in the previous sections of this chapter could never achieve. As usual, this API is quite simple, but be sure to read all the documentation before continuing, because I won't go over every detail or possible configuration. I'll just show a couple of examples, depicting the practical effect of different configuration options.

The geo map has two distinct ways of working. You can provide a set of strings containing the location name, which can be an address, a country name, a region name, or a U.S. metropolitan area code (more details in the API's documentation). I call this "Location Name Mode." Alternatively, you can provide a set of GPS coordinates that pinpoint your locations, "GPS Mode." The latter way of working has some advantages—like accuracy, for instance—but it also limits the options. I'll get back to the pros and cons of each way of working later on, when I explain the sample programs. Initially, I tried to bundle up these two approaches to the chart in a single procedure, but it lost much of the simplicity and clarity I like my code to have, so I created two separate procedures, *GenMapChart* and *GenMapGPSChart*. I'll focus on "Location Name Mode" in this section, and explain "GPS Mode" in the next.

So, let's get started with "Location Name Mode."

This chart requires only two columns—location name and value—but it allows the customization of the "tooltip text" (or "hover text," as Google calls it) by adding an additional column of data. As you might have guessed, the location names and respective values are going into the chart as rows.

Google's sample HTML, presented below, is a mix between the pie and bar chart samples, in the sense that it has the same two columns as the pie chart sample, but it features the data entry and option configuration of the bar chart:

```
<html>
<head>
<script type='text/javascript' src='https://www.google.com/jsapi'></script>
<script type='text/javascript'>
   google.load('visualization', '1', {'packages': ['geomap']});
   google.setOnLoadCallback(drawMap);

    function drawMap() {
      var data = google.visualization.arrayToDataTable([
        ['Country', 'Popularity'],
        ['Germany', 200],
        ['United States', 300],
        ['Brazil', 400],
        ['Canada', 500],
        ['France', 600],
        ['RU', 700]
      ]);

      var options = {};
      options['dataMode'] = 'regions';

      var container = document.getElementById('map_canvas');
      var geomap = new google.visualization.GeoMap(container);
      geomap.draw(data, options);
  };
</script>
</head>

<body>
<div id='map_canvas'></div>
</body>

</html>
```

Note that the options are specified using a different notation, a bit like an array of options where the option name is the index. In this particular case, the "datamode" option sets the type of map that will be displayed. The option used here, "regions," produces a default world map divided into countries, but there are many other possibilities, explained later. The options are crucial in this type of chart, because they dramatically change what is presented. That, together with the fact that I basically hardcoded options in the previous sections, led me to add a bit of complexity, but also flexibility, to the way options are handled from here on.

Based on this sample, I've created a template for this mode (the *GeoMap.Tmpl* file in the *GCHARTS/Templates* folder of this chapter's downloadable source code):

```
/$Header
<!DOCTYPE html PUBLIC "-//W3C//DTD XHTML 1.0 Strict//EN" "http://www.w3.org/TR/
xhtml1/DTD/xhtml1-strict.dtd">
<html xmlns="http://www.w3.org/1999/xhtml">
<head>
  <meta http-equiv="content-type" content="text/html; charset=utf-8" />
  <title>/%PageTitle%/</title>
  <script src="http://www.google.com/jsapi"></script>
  <script>
    google.load('visualization', '1', {packages: ['geomap']});

    function drawVisualization() {
      var data = new google.visualization.DataTable();
      data.addRows(/%TotalRows%/);
      data.addColumn('string', 'Location');
      data.addColumn('number', '/%ColumnTitle%/');
/$HoverColumn
      data.addColumn('string', 'hovertext');
/$Row
      data.setValue(/%RowNbr%/, 0, '/%RowTitle%/');
      data.setValue(/%RowNbr%/, 1, /%RowValue%/);
/$HoverRow
      data.setValue(/%RowNbr%/, 2, '/%RowHover%/');
/$OptionsBegin
```

Continued

```
      var options = {
/$Option
      '/%OptionTitle%/': /%OptionValue%/
/$OptionsEnd
                    };

/$Footer
      var geomap = new google.visualization.GeoMap(
          document.getElementById('visualization'));
      geomap.draw(data, options);
    }
      google.setOnLoadCallback(drawVisualization);
  </script>
</head>
<body style="font-family: Arial;border: 0 none;">
<div></div>
</body>
</html>
```

The Header, Row, and Footer sections are basically the same as usual. I had to add some new sections to handle the optional hover text functionality. They are HoverColumn and HoverRow. Finally, I'm introducing a new way of handling the chart options, implemented here in the OptionsBegin, Option, and OptionsEnd sections.

It's now time to review the *GenMapChart* procedure itself, which is based on *GenPieChart*:

```
 *-------------------------------------------------------------------------*
 *   Generate GeoMap Chart                                                 *
 *-------------------------------------------------------------------------*
P  GenMapChart     B                     EXPORT
D                  PI               N
 * Input Parms
DP_PageTitle                             Like(t_PageTitle)  Value
```

Continued

```
DP_MapColumnDS                        LikeDS(MapColumnDS)  Value
DP_MapRowDS                           LikeDS(MapRowDS) Dim(C_MapMaxRows)
D                                     Value
DP_OptionDS                           LikeDS(OptionDS) Dim(C_MaxOptions)
D                                     Value
DP_FileName                           Like(t_FileName) Value
 * Output Parms
DP_ErrorDesc                          Like(t_ErrorDesc)

 /FREE

     ExSr Init;

    ExSr Proc;

    ExSr End_Of_Program;

    //  Sub Routines

    //---------------------------------------------------------------*
    //  Initialization                                               *
    //---------------------------------------------------------------*
      BegSr  Init;

      P_ErrorDesc = *Blanks;

      // Check if there is data in the P_MapColumnDS array
      If P_MapColumnDS.ColumnTitle = *Blanks;
        P_ErrorDesc = 'No column data';
        Return *On;
      EndIf;

      // Check if there is data in the P_MapRowDS array
      If P_MapRowDS(1).RowTitle = *Blanks;
        P_ErrorDesc = 'No row data';
        Return *On;
      EndIf;
```

Continued

```
    // Check if the file name was passed
    If P_FileName = *Blanks;
      P_ErrorDesc = 'No file name';
      Return *On;
    EndIf;

    EndSr;
 //-----------------------------------------------------------------*
 //End of the program                                               *
 //-----------------------------------------------------------------*
    BegSr  End_Of_Program;

       Return *Off;

    EndSr;
 //-----------------------------------------------------------------*
 // Process input parms and generate the proper xml file            *
 //-----------------------------------------------------------------*
    BegSr  Proc;


      SetNoDebug(*OFF);
      getHtmlIfsMult(C_MapTmpl);

      // Header Section
      // Update the Header variables
      updHtmlVar('PageTitle' : %Trim(P_PageTitle));
      // Update the Column Title variable
      updHtmlVar('ColumnTitle' : %Trim(P_MapColumnDS.ColumnTitle));
      // Find out how many rows have data
      For W_RowIdx = 1 to C_MapMaxRows;
        If P_MapRowDS(W_RowIdx).RowTitle = *Blanks;
          Leave;
        Else;
          // If this was not the last row containing data, keep the row number
          W_TotalRows = W_RowIdx;
```
Continued

```
  EndIf;
EndFor;
// Update the TotalRows variable
updHtmlVar('TotalRows' : %Char(W_TotalRows));
// Write the Header section
WrtSection('Header');

// HoverColumn Section, if required
If P_MapColumnDs.HoverText <> *Blanks;
  // Update the TotalRows variable
  updHtmlVar('HoverText' : %Trim(P_MapColumnDs.HoverText));
  // Write the HoverColumn section
  WrtSection('HoverColumn');
EndIf;

// Row Section
For W_RowIdx = 1 to C_MapMaxRows;
  If P_MapRowDS(W_RowIdx).RowTitle = *Blanks;
    Leave;
  EndIf;
  // Update the Row variables
  updHtmlVar('RowNbr'   : %Char(W_RowIdx-1));
  updHtmlVar('RowTitle' : %Trim(P_MapRowDS(W_RowIdx).RowTitle));
  updHtmlVar('RowValue' : %Char(P_MapRowDS(W_RowIdx).RowValue));
  // Write the Row section
  WrtSection('Row');
  // HoverRow section, if required
  If P_MapRowDS(W_RowIdx).RowHover <> *Blanks;
    updHtmlVar('RowHover' : %Trim(P_MapRowDS(W_RowIdx).RowHover));
    // Write the HoverRow section
    WrtSection('HoverRow');
  EndIf;
EndFor;
// Options Section
// Define the Options variable
  WrtSection('OptionsBegin');
// Write each option on a separate line
```

Continued

```
      For W_Idx = 1 to C_MaxOptions;
        If P_OptionDS(W_Idx).OptionTitle = *Blanks;
          Leave;
        EndIf;
        // Update the Option variables
        updHtmlVar('OptionTitle' :
                   %Trim(P_OptionDS(W_Idx).OptionTitle));
        // If this is not the last option of the array and the next
        // option was filled in, add a comma after the value
        If (((W_Idx + 1) < C_MaxOptions) And
            (P_OptionDs(W_Idx + 1).OptionTitle <> *Blanks));
          P_OptionDS(W_Idx).OptionValue =
           %Trim(P_OptionDS(W_Idx).OptionValue) + ',';
        EndIf;
        updHtmlVar('OptionValue' :
                   %Trim(P_OptionDS(W_Idx).OptionValue));
        // Write the Option section
        WrtSection('Option');
      EndFor;
      // Close the Options definition
        WrtSection('OptionsEnd');

      // Footer Section
      // Because the options are now an array, this section has no
      // variables, so simply write the section
      // Write the Footer section
      WrtSection('Footer');

      // Set the appropriate file name and path
      W_FileName = %Trim(C_OutputPath) + '/' + %Trim(P_FileName);

      // Write the html file to disk
      WrtHtmlToStmf(%Trim(W_FileName): 819);

     EndSr;
 /END-FREE
PGenMapChart        E
```

Let's review this procedure in detail, starting with the parameters:

```
 *-----------------------------------------------------------------------*
 *   Generate GeoMap Chart                                               *
 *-----------------------------------------------------------------------*
P  GenMapChart     B                    EXPORT
D                  PI           N
 * Input Parms
DP_PageTitle                            Like(t_PageTitle)  Value
DP_MapColumnDS                          LikeDS(MapColumnDS)  Value
DP_MapRowDS                             LikeDS(MapRowDS) Dim(C_MapMaxRows)
D                                       Value
DP_OptionDS                             LikeDS(OptionDS) Dim(C_MaxOptions)
D                                       Value
DP_FileName                             Like(t_FileName) Value
 * Output Parms
DP_ErrorDesc                            Like(t_ErrorDesc)
```

The first thing you might notice is that the parameter list includes a new data structure: *P_OptionDS*. As the name implies, this passes the options to the chart. To keep things simple in the examples in previous sections, I was passing some options as individual parameters (width and height, for instance). Now, you can indicate any parameter you want, just by setting the values of the *OptionTitle* and *OptionValue* fields of the *P_OptionDS* data structure, which is also an array, to handle multiple options. The maximum number of options is currently set to 100, but you can change the *C_MaxOptions* constant in the *QCPYLESRC/GENCHRT_PR* source member to a number that better suits your needs. The maximum number of 100 represents many more options than any of the charts provide, so feel free to customize it. Other than that change, the parameters are the same as before, but I've changed some of the names to provide independence from the pie chart.

The code is structured the same way as the previous examples, with the *Init* routine checking the parameters' values and the *Proc* routine taking care of the main work. There's nothing really special about the first one, so let's skip directly to *Proc*:

```
//------------------------------------------------------------------*
// Process input parms and generate the proper xml file             *
//------------------------------------------------------------------*
 BegSr  Proc;


  SetNoDebug(*OFF);
  getHtmlIfsMult(C_MapTmpl);

  // Header Section
  // Update the Header variables
  updHtmlVar('PageTitle' : %Trim(P_PageTitle));
  // Update the Column Title variable
  updHtmlVar('ColumnTitle' : %Trim(P_MapColumnDS.ColumnTitle));
  // Find out how many rows have data
  For W_RowIdx = 1 to C_MapMaxRows;
    If P_MapRowDS(W_RowIdx).RowTitle = *Blanks;
      Leave;
    Else;
      // If this was not the last row containing data, keep the row number
      W_TotalRows = W_RowIdx;
    EndIf;
  EndFor;
  // Update the TotalRows variable
  updHtmlVar('TotalRows' : %Char(W_TotalRows));
  // Write the Header section
  WrtSection('Header');
```

Following in its predecessor's footsteps, the *Proc* routine starts by opening the proper template (*C_MapTmpl*) and continues by taking care of the Header section—filling the *PageTitle*, *ColumnTitle*, and *TotalRows* variables, and pushing them to the respective placeholders on the template. After these simple operations, the Header section is written.

I mentioned before that a new feature is available to us—the tooltip text that Google calls "hover text." The template includes a few new sections to handle this, the first of which is supported by the following lines of code:

```
// HoverColumn Section, if required
If P_MapColumnDs.HoverText <> *Blanks;
  // Update the TotalRows variable
  updHtmlVar('HoverText' : %Trim(P_MapColumnDs.HoverText));
  // Write the HoverColumn section
WrtSection('HoverColumn');
EndIf;
```

This will only add the necessary hover text column to the DataTable, in order to handle the value for each row, provided later, when the rows are processed. This piece of code was isolated in a section because it's an optional feature. If you decide not to use it, it won't mess up your HTML file with additional, unnecessary lines of code. Speaking of code, the one here is very simple—if you filled the *P_MapColumnDS.HoverText* field, the section will be written to the HTML file, otherwise it won't.

What really needs to be written (otherwise there's no chart) is the next section:

```
// Row Section
For W_RowIdx = 1 to C_MapMaxRows;
  If P_MapRowDS(W_RowIdx).RowTitle = *Blanks;
    Leave;
  EndIf;
  // Update the Row variables
  updHtmlVar('RowNbr'   : %Char(W_RowIdx-1));
  updHtmlVar('RowTitle' : %Trim(P_MapRowDS(W_RowIdx).RowTitle));
  updHtmlVar('RowValue' : %Char(P_MapRowDS(W_RowIdx).RowValue));
  // Write the Row section
  WrtSection('Row');
  // HoverRow section, if required
  If P_MapRowDS(W_RowIdx).RowHover <> *Blanks;
    updHtmlVar('RowHover' : %Trim(P_MapRowDS(W_RowIdx).RowHover));
    // Write the HoverRow section
    WrtSection('HoverRow');
  EndIf;
EndFor;
```

Here, the *P_MapRowDS* data structure is passed to the respective template variables the same way as before. Notice the additional code to handle the *HoverRow* variable; it enables you to provide tooltip text for all or just some of the rows. It might be a way to insert comments or additional information in your chart that will be displayed when the user moves the mouse over that region of the map. I know this might be a bit confusing, but it will get clearer when we analyze an example.

Finally, there's something totally new: the dynamic option handling. To understand this better, let's go back to the template. I've created three new sections, *OptionsBegin*, *Options*, and *OptionsEnd*. The objective was to have something like this as the final result:

```
var options = {
'region': 'world',
'dataMode': 'regions',
'width': '556px',
'height': '347px'
};
```

The first line is provided by the *OptionsBegin* section and the last one (just the "};" characters) comes from *OptionsEnd*. Everything in the middle, ranging from one to 100 options, is stored in the *P_OptionsDS* data structure. Now that we have a clear context for the option handling, the code below should be easier to understand:

```
// Options Section
// Define the Options variable
  WrtSection('OptionsBegin');
// Write each option on a separate line
For W_Idx = 1 to C_MaxOptions;
  If P_OptionDS(W_Idx).OptionTitle = *Blanks;
    Leave;
  EndIf;
  // Update the Option variables
  updHtmlVar('OptionTitle' :
           %Trim(P_OptionDS(W_Idx).OptionTitle));
```

Continued

```
  // If this is not the last option of the array and the next
  // option was filled in, add a comma after the value
  If (((W_Idx + 1) < C_MaxOptions) And
     (P_OptionDs(W_Idx + 1).OptionTitle <> *Blanks));
    P_OptionDS(W_Idx).OptionValue =
     %Trim(P_OptionDS(W_Idx).OptionValue) + ',';
  EndIf;
  updHtmlVar('OptionValue' :
            %Trim(P_OptionDS(W_Idx).OptionValue));
  // Write the Option section
  WrtSection('Option');
EndFor;
// Close the Options definition
  WrtSection('OptionsEnd');
```

Let me just mention another small trick. The *Options* section doesn't include the comma that is mandatory to separate the option. This was done on purpose, because you can decide to use only one option and leave the rest of them at their default values. After passing each option to the respective template variables, the code checks if the end of the array was reached. If it wasn't, it checks whether the next position was filled. In other words, it checks whether there are more options. If it finds something, it assumes that the current option is not the last, which makes the comma after it mandatory.

The *Proc* routine ends with the Footer section, which is a bit different from the previous ones, because it has no variables. Previously, the options were part of the Footer section, in a hardcoded, ugly, quick-and-dirty way. Since they are now dynamic and have their own sections, the code for the Footer section is much simpler:

```
      // Footer Section
      // Because the options are now an array, this section has no
      // variables, so simply write the section
      // Write the Footer section
      WrtSection('Footer');
```

Continued

```
        // Set the appropriate file name and path
        W_FileName = %Trim(C_OutputPath) + '/' + %Trim(P_FileName);

        // Write the html file to disk
        WrtHtmlToStmf(%Trim(W_FileName): 819);

       EndSr;
  /END-FREE
 PGenMapChart       E
```

That concludes the analysis of this procedure. However, the functionality itself is probably not very clear, so let's analyze a couple of examples, starting with *TSTGENMAP1*:

```
 H DECEDIT(',') DATEDIT(*DMY.)

  * Generate Charts using Google Chart APIs Procedures
  /Copy QCPYLESRC,GENCHRT_PR
  * Misc Procedures
  /Copy QCPYLESRC,MISC_PR

  *'Data Areas
 D Da_SystemName    S                        Like(W_SysName) DtaAra(DaSysName)
 DW_PCCmd           S              200A      Inz(*Blanks)
 DW_SysName         S               20A      Inz(*Blanks)
 DW_Response        S               52A      Inz(*Blanks)
 DW_ErrorDS         DS                       LikeDS(ApiError) Inz

  /FREE
       // Retrieve system name
       In Da_SystemName;
       W_SysName = %Trim(Da_SystemName);
     // First, I'll set up the page title and the html file name
           P_PageTitle = 'CellPhone usage per country';
           P_FileName = 'CellPhonesMap.HTML';
                                                                   Continued
```

```
   // Next the Columns
         Clear P_MapColumnDS;
         P_MapColumnDS.ColumnTitle = 'CellPhone usage';
   // Then the Rows
         Clear P_MapRowDS;
         P_MapRowDS(1).RowTitle = 'Germany';
         P_MapRowDS(1).RowValue = 80;
         P_MapRowDS(2).RowTitle = 'France';
         P_MapRowDS(2).RowValue = 95;
         P_MapRowDS(3).RowTitle = 'Netherlands';
         P_MapRowDS(3).RowValue = 90;
         P_MapRowDS(4).RowTitle = 'Austria';
         P_MapRowDS(4).RowValue = 73;
         P_MapRowDS(5).RowTitle = 'Belgium';
         P_MapRowDS(5).RowValue = 86;
   // Generate the Chart
         If GenMapChart(P_PageTitle : P_MapColumnDS : P_MapRowDS :
                        P_OptionDS  :
                        P_FileName  : P_ErrorDesc  ) = *Off;
    // Display the Chart
    W_PCCmd = '\\' + %Trim(W_SysName) + '\GCHARTS\OUTPUT\'
              + %Trim(P_FileName);
    P_CmdLin = 'STRPCCMD PCCMD(''' + %Trim(W_PCCmd) +
               ''') PAUSE(*NO)';
    W_ErrorDs = ExecCmd(%Trim(P_CmdLin));
         Else;
           // Error occurred in the GenMapChart procedure
           W_Response = 'Error = ' +
                         %Trim(P_ErrorDesc);
           Dsply W_Response;
         EndIf;

   *InLr = *On;
/END-FREE
```

The code is divided in two parts: assigning the proper values to the procedure's parameters (some totally fictitious values to a few European countries), and generating the chart by calling the procedure. If everything went according to plan and the system name is set in the *DaSysName* data area, the result should be a browser window popping up and showing Figure 8.5.

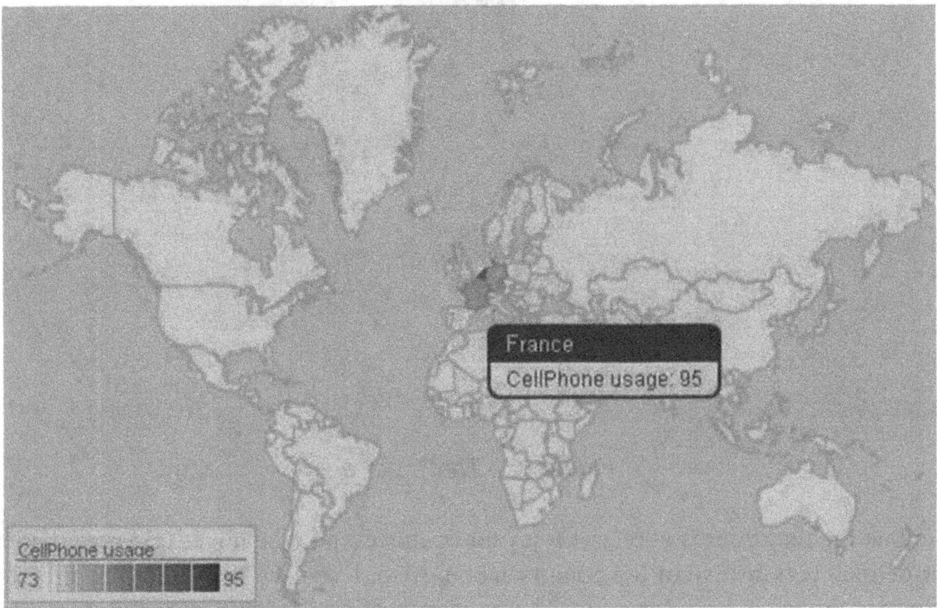

Figure 8.5: This result isn't particularly useful.

Well, it doesn't look great, does it? By default, the geo map chart presents a world map and a green gradient legend. This might be okay for certain situations, but it's clearly not ideal for this one. How can the chart be adapted to better match this situation? By using the configuration options of the API and the *P_OptionDS* array (*http://code.google.com/apis/chart/interactive/docs/gallery/geomap.html#Configuration_Options*). The same data is used in *QRPGLESRC/TSTGENMAP2*, but the options used here make a huge difference, as shown in Figure 8.6.

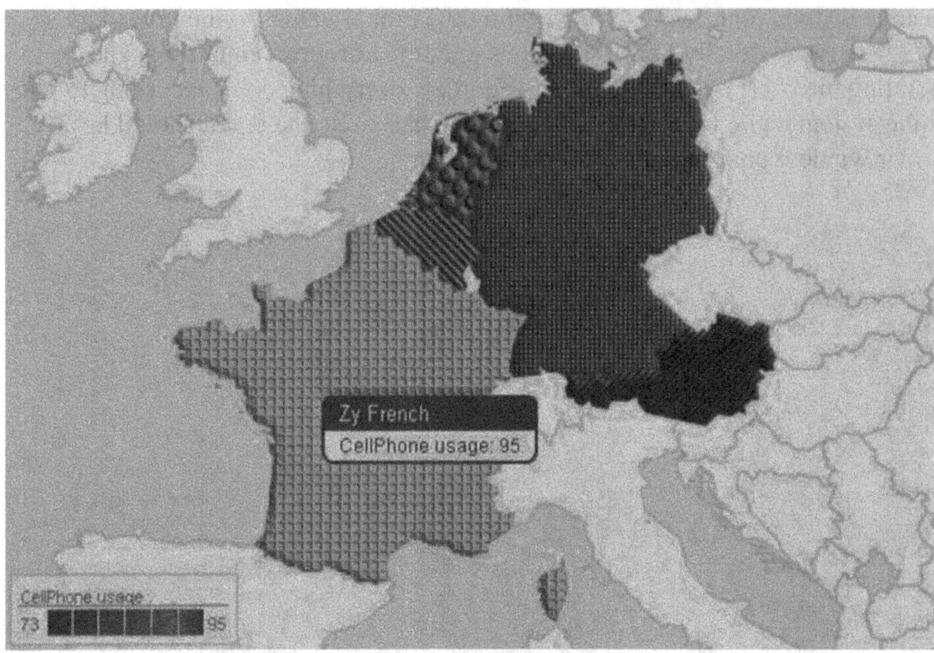

Figure 8.6: That's better!

Note that the map zooms in on the relevant countries, and the hover text now displays user-defined text instead of the country name. Also, I've used the "colors" option to customize the legend's color scale. The patterns that you see in Figure 8.6 were not created by Google's API; they were artificially inserted to improve readability.

This is how I got it (*TSTGENMAP2*'s source code):

```
H DECEDIT(',') DATEDIT(*DMY.)

 * Generate Charts using Google Chart APIs Procedures
 /Copy QCPYLESRC,GENCHRT_PR
 * Misc Procedures
 /Copy QCPYLESRC,MISC_PR

 *'Data Areas
D Da_SystemName   S                  Like(W_SysName) DtaAra(DaSysName)
```

Continued

```
DW_PCCmd          S            200A   Inz(*Blanks)
DW_SysName        S             20A   Inz(*Blanks)
DW_Response       S             52A   Inz(*Blanks)
DW_ErrorDS        DS                  LikeDS(ApiError) Inz

 /FREE
      // Retrieve system name
      In Da_SystemName;
      W_SysName = %Trim(Da_SystemName);
    // First, I'll set up the page title and the html file name
        P_PageTitle = 'CellPhone usage per country';
        P_FileName = 'CellPhonesMap2.HTML';
    // Next the Columns
        Clear P_MapColumnDS;
        P_MapColumnDS.ColumnTitle = 'CellPhone usage';
        P_MapColumnDS.HoverText  = 'Funny Country Names';
    // Then the Rows
        Clear P_MapRowDS;
        P_MapRowDS(1).RowTitle = 'Germany';
        P_MapRowDS(1).RowValue = 80;
        P_MapRowDS(1).RowHover= 'The Gerrmans';
        P_MapRowDS(2).RowTitle = 'France';
        P_MapRowDS(2).RowValue = 95;
        P_MapRowDS(2).RowHover= 'Zy French';
        P_MapRowDS(3).RowTitle = 'Netherlands';
        P_MapRowDS(3).RowValue = 90;
        P_MapRowDS(3).RowHover= 'The Orange Kingdom';
        P_MapRowDS(4).RowTitle = 'Austria';
        P_MapRowDS(4).RowValue = 73;
        P_MapRowDS(4).RowHover= 'Walse Country';
        P_MapRowDS(5).RowTitle = 'Belgium';
        P_MapRowDS(5).RowValue = 86;
        P_MapRowDS(5).RowHover= '1000s of different beers!';
    // Finally, the options
        P_OptionDS(1).OptionTitle = 'width';
        P_OptionDS(1).OptionValue = '600';
```

Continued

```
        P_OptionDS(2).OptionTitle = 'height';
        P_OptionDS(2).OptionValue = '400';
        P_OptionDS(3).OptionTitle = 'region';
        P_OptionDS(3).OptionValue = '''155''';//Western Europe Map
        P_OptionDS(4).OptionTitle = 'colors';
        P_OptionDS(4).OptionValue = '[0x9400D3, 0xFF2400]';
  // Generate the Chart
        If GenMapChart(P_PageTitle : P_MapColumnDS : P_MapRowDS :
                       P_OptionDS  :
                       P_FileName  : P_ErrorDesc  ) = *Off;
   // Display the Chart
   W_PCCmd = '\\' + %Trim(W_SysName) + '\GCHARTS\OUTPUT\'
             + %Trim(P_FileName);
   P_CmdLin = 'STRPCCMD PCCMD(''' + %Trim(W_PCCmd) +
              ''') PAUSE(*NO)';
   W_ErrorDs = ExecCmd(%Trim(P_CmdLin));
        Else;
          // Error occurred in the GenMapChart procedure
          W_Response = 'Error = ' +
                       %Trim(P_ErrorDesc);
          Dsply W_Response;
        EndIf;

  *InLr = *On;
/END-FREE
```

If you compare this code with *TSTGENMAP1*'s, you'll notice two big differences. First, the hover text is now being used:

```
(...)
P_MapColumnDS.HoverText  = 'Funny Country Names';
(...)
P_MapRowDS(1).RowHover= 'The Gerrmans';
(...)
```

Second, *P_OptionsDS* holds a few options:

```
// Finally, the options
P_OptionDS(1).OptionTitle = 'width';
P_OptionDS(1).OptionValue = '600';
P_OptionDS(2).OptionTitle = 'height';
P_OptionDS(2).OptionValue = '400';
P_OptionDS(3).OptionTitle = 'region';
P_OptionDS(3).OptionValue = '''155''';//Western Europe Map
P_OptionDS(4).OptionTitle = 'colors';
P_OptionDS(4).OptionValue = '[0x9400D3, 0xFF2400]';
```

One final note regarding this data structure's use: whenever you specify an option that requires inverted commas (single quotation marks) for delimitation, such as the *'region'*, be sure to enclose the *OptionValue* in triple inverted commas in your code. This will make the variable's value begin and end with the inverted comma character.

Depending of the data, you can tune the options to enhance the final chart, thus achieving a great result that most chart-generating tools can't provide!

The Geo Map (GPS Mode)

The previously presented "Location Name Mode" is very useful when the data being presented refers to countries or parts of a country, because the location is not very accurate (nor does it intend to be). The most accurate way to pinpoint a location using this API is by using GPS coordinates. That's exactly what "GPS Mode" allows.

As briefly mentioned in the previous section, this mode requires you to indicate the GPS coordinates in order to put the location on the map. However, that's not enough; you have to be able to assign a value and a label to that location. For that, the API has two optional columns that, in my opinion, shouldn't be optional, because the chart (working in this mode) simply doesn't make sense without them.

I won't reproduce Google's complete sample HTML here, because it's basically the same as in the previous section, but I'll show you the main differences:

```
(...)
dataTable = new google.visualization.DataTable();
dataTable.addRows(1);
dataTable.addColumn('number', 'LATITUDE', 'Latitude');
dataTable.addColumn('number', 'LONGITUDE', 'Longitude');
dataTable.addColumn('number', 'VALUE', 'Value'); // Won't use this column, but
                                                  // still must define it.
dataTable.addColumn('string', 'HOVER', 'HoverText');
(...)
dataTable.setValue(0,0,47.00);
dataTable.setValue(0,1,-122.00);
dataTable.setValue(0,3,"Hello World!");
(...)
```

So, in total, you have to fill four columns: latitude, longitude, value, and label. Based on this, I've created the template below for this mode (the *GeoMapGPS.Tmpl* file in the *GCHARTS/Templates* folder of this chapter's downloadable source code):

```
/$Header
<!DOCTYPE html PUBLIC "-//W3C//DTD XHTML 1.0 Strict//EN" "http://www.w3.org/TR/
xhtml1/DTD/xhtml1-strict.dtd">
<html xmlns="http://www.w3.org/1999/xhtml">
<head>
  <meta http-equiv="content-type" content="text/html; charset=utf-8" />
  <title>/%PageTitle%/</title>
  <script src="http://www.google.com/jsapi"></script>
  <script>
    google.load('visualization', '1', {packages: ['geomap']});

    function drawVisualization() {
      var data = new google.visualization.DataTable();
      data.addRows(/%TotalRows%/);
      data.addColumn('number', 'Latitude');
      data.addColumn('number', 'Longitude');
      data.addColumn('number', '/%ColumnTitle%/');
      data.addColumn('string', 'hovertext');
```

Continued

```
/$Row
      data.setValue(/%RowNbr%/, 0, /%RowLat%/);
      data.setValue(/%RowNbr%/, 1, /%RowLng%/);
      data.setValue(/%RowNbr%/, 2, /%RowValue%/);
      data.setValue(/%RowNbr%/, 3, '/%RowTitle%/');
/$OptionsBegin

      var options = {
/$Option
      '/%OptionTitle%/': /%OptionValue%/,
/$OptionsEnd
        'dataMode': 'Markers'
                    };

/$Footer
      var geomap = new google.visualization.GeoMap(
          document.getElementById('visualization'));
      geomap.draw(data, options);
    }

    google.setOnLoadCallback(drawVisualization);
  </script>
</head>
<body style="font-family: Arial;border: 0 none;">
<div></div>
</body>
</html>
```

This template is similar to the previous one, even though it's simpler. There are no optional rows or columns, and only the options part is dynamic. Note that the *OptionsEnd* section has a hardcoded option called *'dataMode': 'Markers'*. This is necessary because the GPS mode requires the API to represent the data in markers instead of regions—the only other possibility, and the default value for this option.

To try to keep things as simple as possible, I created a separate procedure for the GPS mode, named *GenMapGPSChart*:

```
 *-----------------------------------------------------------------------*
 *   Generate GeoMap Chart                                                *
 *-----------------------------------------------------------------------*
P GenMapGPSChart  B                   EXPORT
D                 PI              N
 * Input Parms
DP_PageTitle                          Like(t_PageTitle)  Value
DP_MapGPSColumnTitle...
D                                     Like(t_ColumnTitle) Value
DP_MapGPSRowDS                        LikeDS(MapGPSRowDS)
D                                     Dim(C_MapMaxRows) Value
DP_OptionDS                           LikeDS(OptionDS) Dim(C_MaxOptions)
D                                     Value
DP_FileName                           Like(t_FileName) Value
 * Output Parms
DP_ErrorDesc                          Like(t_ErrorDesc)

 /FREE

     ExSr Init;
     ExSr Proc;
     ExSr End_Of_Program;

    //  Sub Routines

    //-------------------------------------------------------------------*
    //  Initialization                                                    *
    //-------------------------------------------------------------------*
      BegSr  Init;

      P_ErrorDesc = *Blanks;

      // Check if there is data in the P_MapGPSColumnTitle variable
      If P_MapGPSColumnTitle = *Blanks;
        P_ErrorDesc = 'No column title';
        Return *On;
      EndIf;
```

Continued

```
    // Check if there is data in the P_MapGPSRowDS array
    If P_MapGPSRowDS(1).RowTitle = *Blanks;
      P_ErrorDesc = 'No row data';
      Return *On;
    EndIf;

    // Check if the file name was passed
    If P_FileName = *Blanks;
      P_ErrorDesc = 'No file name';
      Return *On;
    EndIf;

    EndSr;
  //----------------------------------------------------------------------*
  // End of the program                                                   *
  //----------------------------------------------------------------------*
    BegSr  End_Of_Program;

       Return *Off;

    EndSr;
  //----------------------------------------------------------------------*
  // Process input parms and generate the proper xml file                 *
  //----------------------------------------------------------------------*
    BegSr  Proc;


     SetNoDebug(*OFF);
     getHtmlIfsMult(C_MapGPSTmpl);

     // Header Section
     // Update the Header variables
     updHtmlVar('PageTitle' : %Trim(P_PageTitle));
     // Update the Column Title variable
     updHtmlVar('ColumnTitle' : %Trim(P_MapGPSColumnTitle));
     // Find out how many rows have data
     For W_RowIdx = 1 to C_MapMaxRows;
```

Continued

```
    If P_MapGPSRowDS(W_RowIdx).RowTitle = *Blanks;
      Leave;
    Else;
      // If this was not the last row containing data, keep the row number
      W_TotalRows = W_RowIdx;
    EndIf;
  EndFor;
  // Update the TotalRows variable
  updHtmlVar('TotalRows' : %Char(W_TotalRows));
  // Write the Header section
  WrtSection('Header');

  // Row Section
  For W_RowIdx = 1 to C_MapMaxRows;
    If P_MapGPSRowDS(W_RowIdx).RowTitle = *Blanks;
      Leave;
    EndIf;
    // Update the Row variables
    updHtmlVar('RowNbr'   : %Char(W_RowIdx-1));
    updHtmlVar('Rowlat'   : %Char(P_MapGPSRowDS(W_RowIdx).RowLat));
    updHtmlVar('RowLng'   : %Char(P_MapGPSRowDS(W_RowIdx).RowLng));
    updHtmlVar('RowValue' : %Char(P_MapGPSRowDS(W_RowIdx).RowValue));
    updHtmlVar('RowTitle' : %Trim(P_MapGPSRowDS(W_RowIdx).RowTitle));
    // Write the Row section
    WrtSection('Row');
  EndFor;
  // Options Section
  // Define the Options variable
    WrtSection('OptionsBegin');
  // Write each option on a separate line
  For W_Idx = 1 to C_MaxOptions;
    If P_OptionDS(W_Idx).OptionTitle = *Blanks;
      Leave;
    EndIf;
    // Update the Option variables
    updHtmlVar('OptionTitle' :
               %Trim(P_OptionDS(W_Idx).OptionTitle));
```

Continued

```
        updHtmlVar('OptionValue' :
                   %Trim(P_OptionDS(W_Idx).OptionValue));
        // Write the Option section
        WrtSection('Option');
      EndFor;
      // Close the Options definition
        WrtSection('OptionsEnd');

      // Footer Section
      // Because the options are now an array, this section has no
      // variables, so simply write the section
      // Write the Footer section
      WrtSection('Footer');

      // Set the appropriate file name and path
      W_FileName = %Trim(C_OutputPath) + '/' + %Trim(P_FileName);

      // Write the html file to disk
      WrtHtmlToStmf(%Trim(W_FileName): 819);

     EndSr;
 /END-FREE
PGenMapGPSChart   E
```

The source code follows the same line of *GenMapChart*, but only has a simple string as the column title instead of a data structure. On the other hand, quite a complex data structure is used for the rows:

```
 *----------------------------------------------------------------------*
 *   Generate GeoMap Chart                                              *
 *----------------------------------------------------------------------*
P GenMapGPSChart  B                   EXPORT
D                 PI            N
 * Input Parms
DP_PageTitle                          Like(t_PageTitle)  Value
DP_MapGPSColumnTitle...
D                                     Like(t_ColumnTitle) Value
```

Continued

```
DP_MapGPSRowDS                          LikeDS(MapGPSRowDS)
D                                       Dim(C_MapMaxRows) Value
DP_OptionDS                             LikeDS(OptionDS) Dim(C_MaxOptions)
D                                       Value
DP_FileName                             Like(t_FileName) Value
 * Output Parms
DP_ErrorDesc                            Like(t_ErrorDesc)
```

This data structure, *P_MapGPSRowDS*, will be used to store the previously mentioned four pieces of information for each location (latitude, longitude, value, and label). Naturally, this will have a direct impact on the way the rows are handled:

```
// Row Section
For W_RowIdx = 1 to C_MapMaxRows;
  If P_MapGPSRowDS(W_RowIdx).RowTitle = *Blanks;
    Leave;
  EndIf;
  // Update the Row variables
  updHtmlVar('RowNbr'    : %Char(W_RowIdx-1));
  updHtmlVar('Rowlat'    : %Char(P_MapGPSRowDS(W_RowIdx).RowLat));
  updHtmlVar('RowLng'    : %Char(P_MapGPSRowDS(W_RowIdx).RowLng));
  updHtmlVar('RowValue'  : %Char(P_MapGPSRowDS(W_RowIdx).RowValue));
  updHtmlVar('RowTitle'  : %Trim(P_MapGPSRowDS(W_RowIdx).RowTitle));
  // Write the Row section
  WrtSection('Row');
EndFor;
```

The remainder of the code is similar to *GenMapChart*.

To illustrate the differences between the two modes, I've created the *TSTGENMAP3* sample program, which uses the same data as *TSTGENMAP2* (from the previous section). However, *TSTGENMAP3* uses the capital's GPS coordinates instead of countries:

```
H DECEDIT(',') DATEDIT(*DMY.)

 * Generate Charts using Google Chart APIs Procedures
 /Copy QCPYLESRC,GENCHRT_PR
 * Misc Procedures
 /Copy QCPYLESRC,MISC_PR

 *'Data Areas
D Da_SystemName   S                    Like(W_SysName) DtaAra(DaSysName)
DW_PCCmd          S            200A    Inz(*Blanks)
DW_SysName        S             20A    Inz(*Blanks)
DW_Response       S             52A    Inz(*Blanks)
DW_ErrorDS        DS                   LikeDS(ApiError) Inz

 /FREE
      // Retrieve system name
      In Da_SystemName;
      W_SysName = %Trim(Da_SystemName);
    // First, I'll set up the page title and the html file name
          P_PageTitle = 'CellPhone usage per country';
          P_FileName = 'CellPhonesMap3.HTML';
    // Next the Column title
          P_MapGPSColumnTitle = 'CellPhone usage';
    // Then the Rows
          Clear P_MapGPSRowDS;
          P_MapGPSRowDS(1).RowLat   = 52.516074;
          P_MapGPSRowDS(1).RowLng   = 13.376987;
          P_MapGPSRowDS(1).RowValue = 80;
          P_MapGPSRowDS(1).RowTitle = 'Berlin, Germany';
          P_MapGPSRowDS(2).RowLat   = 48.856930;
          P_MapGPSRowDS(2).RowLng   =  2.341200;
          P_MapGPSRowDS(2).RowValue = 82;
          P_MapGPSRowDS(2).RowTitle = 'Paris, France';
          P_MapGPSRowDS(3).RowLat   = 52.373095;
          P_MapGPSRowDS(3).RowLng   =  4.893305;
          P_MapGPSRowDS(3).RowValue = 90;
```

Continued

```
        P_MapGPSRowDS(3).RowTitle = 'Amsterdam, The Netherlands';
        P_MapGPSRowDS(4).RowLat   = 48.202548;
        P_MapGPSRowDS(4).RowLng   = 16.368805;
        P_MapGPSRowDS(4).RowValue = 73;
        P_MapGPSRowDS(4).RowTitle = 'Vienna, Austria';
        P_MapGPSRowDS(5).RowLat   = 50.848381;
        P_MapGPSRowDS(5).RowLng   =  4.349680;
        P_MapGPSRowDS(5).RowValue = 86;
        P_MapGPSRowDS(5).RowTitle = 'Brussels, Belgium';
  // Finally, the options
        P_OptionDS(1).OptionTitle = 'width';
        P_OptionDS(1).OptionValue = '600';
        P_OptionDS(2).OptionTitle = 'height';
        P_OptionDS(2).OptionValue = '400';
        P_OptionDS(3).OptionTitle = 'region';
        P_OptionDS(3).OptionValue = '''155''';//Western Europe Map
        P_OptionDS(4).OptionTitle = 'colors';
        P_OptionDS(4).OptionValue = '[0x9400D3, 0xFF2400]';
  // Generate the Chart
        If GenMapGPSChart(P_PageTitle   : P_MapGPSColumnTitle :
                          P_MapGPSRowDS : P_OptionDS          :
                          P_FileName    : P_ErrorDesc         ) = *Off;
   // Display the Chart
   W_PCCmd = '\\' + %Trim(W_SysName) + '\GCHARTS\OUTPUT\' + %Trim(P_FileName);
   P_CmdLin = 'STRPCCMD PCCMD(''' + %Trim(W_PCCmd) + ''') PAUSE(*NO)';
   W_ErrorDs = ExecCmd(%Trim(P_CmdLin));
        Else;
          // Error occurred in the GenMapGPSChart procedure
          W_Response = 'Error = ' + %Trim(P_ErrorDesc);
          Dsply W_Response;
        EndIf;

  *InLr = *On;
/END-FREE
```

This produces the chart shown in Figure 8.7 (except for the textures, that were once again artificially inserted to increase readability). Compare this with the result of *TSTGENMAP2*, in Figure 8.6. The lesson here is, if you have just a few values,

"Location Name Mode" will probably produce a more appealing result, but if you have a lot of values to include on the chart, or if the locations are near each other, then go for "GPS Mode."

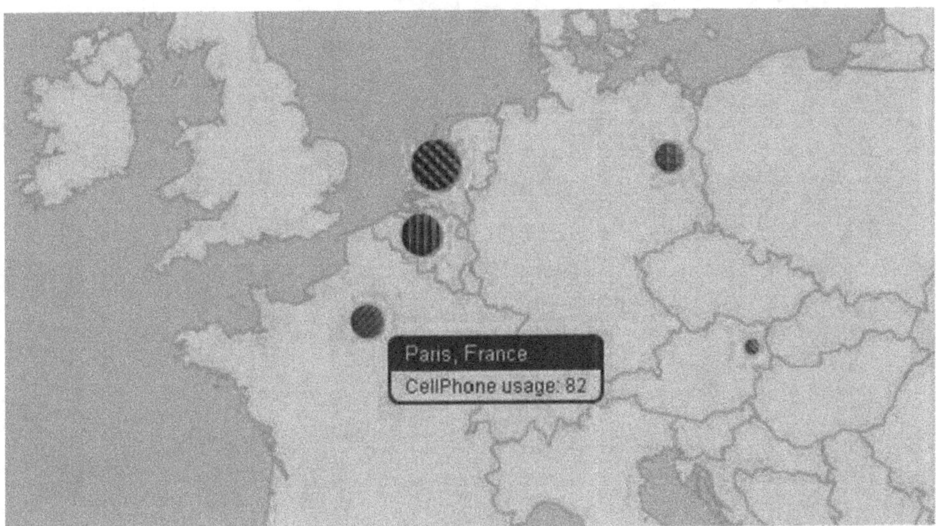

Figure 8.7: Here is the cell phone usage for a few of Europe's capitals, displayed using "GPS Mode."

The *TSTGENMAP4* sample program uses the information contained in a *Los Angeles Times* article entitled "America's 20 most-visited National Monuments," which details the number of visitors to these locations during 2009. As you can see in Figure 8.8, some of the monuments are near each other, and some actually overlap. (There are several in New York City, for instance.) The program is quite long, as it contains four lines of code for each of the monuments, so I'll just show the option setting code:

```
// Finally, the options
P_OptionDS(1).OptionTitle = 'width';
      P_OptionDS(1).OptionValue = '600';
      P_OptionDS(2).OptionTitle = 'height';
      P_OptionDS(2).OptionValue = '400';
      P_OptionDS(3).OptionTitle = 'region';
      P_OptionDS(3).OptionValue = '''US''';//US Map
      P_OptionDS(4).OptionTitle = 'colors';
      P_OptionDS(4).OptionValue = '[0xFF0000, 0xFFFFFF, 0x0000FF]';
```

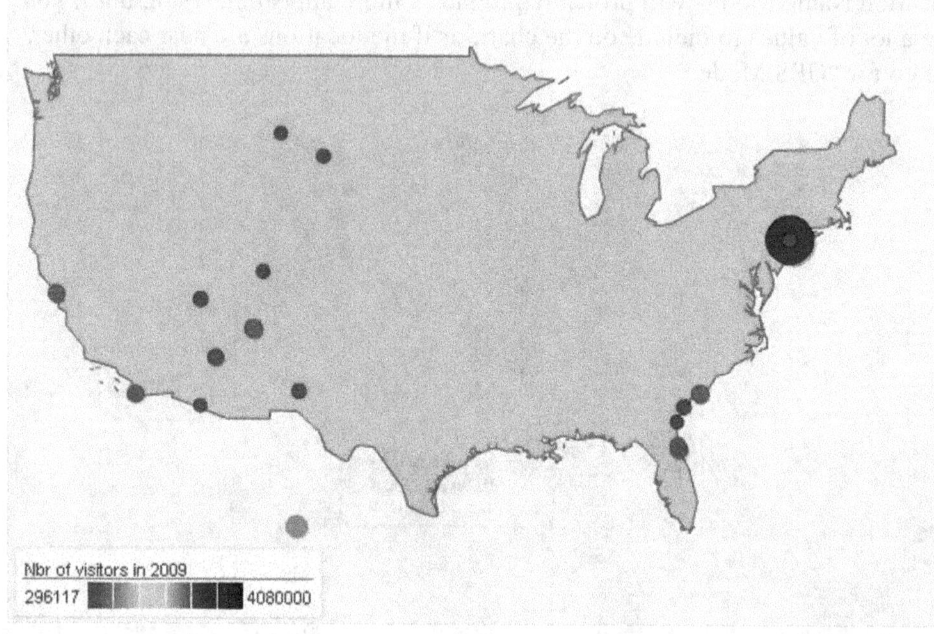

Figure 8.8: The final result of TSTGENMAP4, mapping the number of visitors to U.S. national monuments in 2009.

The legend color gradient presented in the code tried to include the red, white, and blue of the U.S. flag. (Note that the "whitest" on the map is Hawaii, which would have to have a slightly higher value to actually be white.) This was achieved by indicating these three colors in the "colors" option of the code. The hard part is that the colors must be represented in their hexadecimal RGB notation. Well, here's another tip: at *http://web.njit.edu/~kevin/rgb.txt.html*, you will find not only the main colors but also their variations and the respective notation in hexadecimal RGB, courtesy and copyright of Kevin J. Walsh.

The customization that this chart allows goes way beyond changing the legend colors, so be sure to read the documentation at *http://code.google.com/ apis/ chart/interactive/docs/gallery/geomap.html*. Also, experiment at the Visual Playground provided by Google, at *http://code.google.com/apis/ajax/ playground/?type=visualization#geo_map*.

As you might have noticed, Geo Map is an Adobe Flash® chart generator, which brings some limitations, including issues of browser compatibility and performance. Google recently introduced a Geo Chart API, which is SVG-based, thus compatible with more browsers. Geo Chart also has more configuration options, but it lacks a GPS mode. (I'll explain the Geo Chart API later in this chapter.)

The Gauge Chart

This chapter started with rather "normal" charts, but then it jumped to the geo map, which is a bit unusual. The Gauge API (*http://code.google.com/apis/chart/interactive/docs/gallery/gauge.html*) takes it to the next level of strangeness. A gauge chart is not exactly a chart in the traditional sense, like a pie or bar chart, but it is a useful display that enables you to immediately figure out if a given number is within the expected limits.

The downside of the gauge chart is that if you have multiple values to represent, you'll get multiple gauges from the API. This is not really a bad thing, but it can be a constraint if the limits for the values you want to represent are not the same. (This will become clearer in the second example presented in this section.)

The mechanics of this procedure are the same as the previous ones. Google's sample HTML file shows a possible use for a gauge chart—monitoring a computer's CPU, memory, and network traffic:

```
<html>
  <head>
    <scripttype='text/javascript'src='https://www.google.com/jsapi'></script>
    <scripttype='text/javascript'>
      google.load('visualization','1',{packages:['gauge']});
      google.setOnLoadCallback(drawChart);
      function drawChart(){
        var data = google.visualization.arrayToDataTable([
          ['Label','Value'],
          ['Memory',80],
          ['CPU',55],
          ['Network',68]
        ]);
```

Continued

```
      var options ={
        width:400, height:120,
        redFrom:90, redTo:100,
        yellowFrom:75, yellowTo:90,
        minorTicks:5
      };

      var chart = new google.visualization.Gauge(
          document.getElementById('chart_div'));
      chart.draw(data, options);
    }
   </script>
 </head>
 <body>
   <divid='chart_div'></div>
 </body>
</html>
```

The only relevant difference between this chart and the previous charts is in the options, where the green (not used in this example), yellow, and red areas of the gauge are defined. This code produces three gauges and sets each pointer to the value specified in the data table: 80 for the memory, 55 for the CPU, and 68 for the network. All these gauges have a yellow area that ranges from 75 to 90, and a red area that goes from there all the way to 100.

Based on this, I've created a template, *Gauge.tmpl*, somewhat similar to what I've shown you before. (You'll find this template in folder *GCHARTS/Templates* of this chapter's downloadable source code, under the name *Gauge.tmpl*.) I'll start by reviewing it, because it will determine the way the code is written:

```
/$Header
<!DOCTYPE html PUBLIC "-//W3C//DTD XHTML 1.0 Strict//EN" "http://www.w3.org/TR/
xhtml1/DTD/xhtml1-strict.dtd">
<html xmlns="http://www.w3.org/1999/xhtml">
  <head>
    <meta http-equiv="content-type" content="text/html; charset=utf-8"/>
    <title>
      /%PageTitle%/
    </title>
    <script src="http://www.google.com/jsapi"></script>
    <script>
      google.load('visualization', '1', {packages: ['gauge']});
    </script>
    <script>
      function drawVisualization() {
        // Create and populate the data table.
        var data = new google.visualization.DataTable();
        data.addRows(/%TotalRows%/);
        data.addColumn('string', 'Label');
        data.addColumn('number', 'Value');
/$Row
        data.setValue(/%RowNbr%/, 0, '/%RowTitle%/');
        data.setValue(/%RowNbr%/, 1, /%RowValue%/);
/$OptionsBegin

      var options = {
/$Option
      '/%OptionTitle%/': /%OptionValue%/
/$OptionsEnd
                    };

/$Footer
        // Create and draw the visualization.
        new google.visualization.Gauge(document.getElementById('visualization'));
        chart.draw(data, options);
      }
```

Continued

```
      google.setOnLoadCallback(drawVisualization);
    </script>
  </head>
  <body style="font-family: Arial;border: 0 none;">
    <div></div>
  </body>
</html>
```

This is probably the simplest template so far. All the sections are quite straightforward; if you've read the previous examples in this chapter, you'll be familiar with them, as they were used before. Note that this template doesn't have a "Column" section; that fact is directly linked to the data format expected by the Gauge API. (See *http://code.google.com/apis/chart/interactive/docs/gallery/gauge.html#Data_Format* for more information. Actually, I'd recommend reading all the API's documentation carefully before continuing, because I won't explain all the details here.)

The source code of the *GenGaugeChart* procedure is also quite simple:

```
 *-----------------------------------------------------------------------*
 *   Generate Gauge Chart                                                *
 *-----------------------------------------------------------------------*
P GenGaugeChart    B                   EXPORT
D                  PI             N
 * Input Parms
DP_PageTitle                           Like(t_PageTitle)  Value
DP_GaugeRowDS                          LikeDS(GaugeRowDS)
D                                      Dim(C_GaugeMaxRows) Value
DP_OptionDS                            LikeDS(OptionDS) Dim(C_MaxOptions)
D                                      Value
DP_FileName                            Like(t_FileName) Value
 * Output Parms
DP_ErrorDesc                           Like(t_ErrorDesc)

 /FREE

                                                                Continued
```

```
   ExSr Init;

   ExSr Proc;

   ExSr End_Of_Program;

  //  Sub Routines

  //-----------------------------------------------------------------*
  //  Initialization                                                 *
  //-----------------------------------------------------------------*
    BegSr  Init;

    P_ErrorDesc = *Blanks;

    // Check if there is data in the P_GaugeRowDS array
    If P_GaugeRowDS(1).RowTitle = *Blanks;
      P_ErrorDesc = 'No row data';
      Return *On;
    EndIf;

    // Check if the file name was passed
    If P_FileName = *Blanks;
      P_ErrorDesc = 'No file name';
      Return *On;
    EndIf;

    EndSr;
  //-----------------------------------------------------------------*
  //End of the program                                               *
  //-----------------------------------------------------------------*
    BegSr  End_Of_Program;

      Return *Off;

    EndSr;
```

Continued

```
//---------------------------------------------------------------------*
// Process input parms and generate the proper xml file                 *
//---------------------------------------------------------------------*
  BegSr  Proc;

   SetNoDebug(*OFF);
   getHtmlIfsMult(C_GaugeTmpl);

   // Header Section
   // Update the Header variables
   updHtmlVar('PageTitle' : %Trim(P_PageTitle));
   // Find out how many rows have data
   For W_RowIdx = 1 to C_GaugeMaxRows;
     If P_GaugeRowDS(W_RowIdx).RowTitle = *Blanks;
       Leave;
     Else;
       // If this was not the last row containing data, keep the row number
       W_TotalRows = W_RowIdx;
     EndIf;
   EndFor;
   // Update the TotalRows variable
   updHtmlVar('TotalRows' : %Char(W_TotalRows));
   // Write the Header section
   WrtSection('Header');

   // Row Section
   For W_RowIdx = 1 to C_GaugeMaxRows;
     If P_GaugeRowDS(W_RowIdx).RowTitle = *Blanks;
       Leave;
     EndIf;
     // Update the Row variables
     updHtmlVar('RowNbr'   : %Char(W_RowIdx-1));
     updHtmlVar('RowValue' : %Char(P_GaugeRowDS(W_RowIdx).RowValue));
     updHtmlVar('RowTitle' : %Trim(P_GaugeRowDS(W_RowIdx).RowTitle));
     // Write the Row section
     WrtSection('Row');
   EndFor;
```

Continued

```
    // Options Section
    // Define the Options variable
      WrtSection('OptionsBegin');
    // Write each option on a separate line
    For W_Idx = 1 to C_MaxOptions;
      If P_OptionDS(W_Idx).OptionTitle = *Blanks;
        Leave;
      EndIf;
      // Update the Option variables
      updHtmlVar('OptionTitle' :
                 %Trim(P_OptionDS(W_Idx).OptionTitle));
      // If this is not the last option of the array and the next
      // option was filled in, add a comma after the value
      If (((W_Idx + 1) < C_MaxOptions) And
          (P_OptionDs(W_Idx + 1).OptionTitle <> *Blanks));
        P_OptionDS(W_Idx).OptionValue =
         %Trim(P_OptionDS(W_Idx).OptionValue) + ',';
      EndIf;
      updHtmlVar('OptionValue' :
                 %Trim(P_OptionDS(W_Idx).OptionValue));
      // Write the Option section
      WrtSection('Option');
    EndFor;
    // Close the Options definition
      WrtSection('OptionsEnd');

    // Footer Section
    // Because the options are now an array, this section has no
    // variables, so simply write the section
    // Write the Footer section
    WrtSection('Footer');

    // Set the appropriate file name and path
    W_FileName = %Trim(C_OutputPath) + '/' + %Trim(P_FileName);

    // Write the html file to disk
    WrtHtmlToStmf(%Trim(W_FileName): 819);
```

Continued

```
      EndSr;
 /END-FREE
PGenGaugeChart     E
```

This code follows the same logic as the previous procedures, adapted to the API's requirements, so I won't repeat myself. The only thing worth mentioning is the lack of column-handling code. In all the other procedures, there was a section that took care of the columns (sometimes the Header, sometimes a dedicated section). Since this API does not require any column-related information, the RPG code reflects that.

Now, let's get to the fun part: the examples. The first one (*QRPGLESRC/TSTGENGAU1*) is very simple:

```
H DECEDIT(',') DATEDIT(*DMY.)

 * Generate Charts using Google Chart APIs Procedures
 /Copy QCPYLESRC,GENCHRT_PR
 * Misc Procedures
 /Copy QCPYLESRC,MISC_PR

 *'Data Areas
D Da_SystemName   S                   Like(W_SysName) DtaAra(DaSysName)
DW_PCCmd          S            200A   Inz(*Blanks)
DW_SysName        S             20A   Inz(*Blanks)
DW_Response       S             52A   Inz(*Blanks)
DW_ErrorDS        DS                  LikeDS(ApiError) Inz

 /FREE
      // Retrieve system name
      In Da_SystemName;
      W_SysName = %Trim(Da_SystemName);
    // First, I'll set up the page title and the html file name
          P_PageTitle = 'System Status';
          P_FileName = 'SystemStatus.HTML';
                                                               Continued
```

```
    // Then the Rows
          Clear P_GaugeRowDS;
          P_GaugeRowDS(1).RowTitle = 'CPU %';
          P_GaugeRowDS(1).RowValue = 52;
    // Generate the Chart
          If GenGaugeChart(P_PageTitle : P_GaugeRowDS :
                           P_OptionDS  :
                           P_FileName  : P_ErrorDesc  ) = *Off;
     // Display the Chart
     W_PCCmd = '\\' + %Trim(W_SysName) + '\GCHARTS\OUTPUT\'
               + %Trim(P_FileName);
     P_CmdLin = 'STRPCCMD PCCMD(''' + %Trim(W_PCCmd) +
                 ''') PAUSE(*NO)';
     W_ErrorDs = ExecCmd(%Trim(P_CmdLin));
          Else;
            // Error occurred in the GenGaugeChart procedure
            W_Response = 'Error = ' +
                         %Trim(P_ErrorDesc);
            Dsply W_Response;
          EndIf;

    *InLr = *On;
 /END-FREE
```

It adds only one row of data (a label and a value), thus producing the gauge shown in Figure 8.9. It looks nice, but it's very basic. Let's take it a step further. What if the "CPU %" reading was the real CPU percentage of your system? Nice, right? Well, that's what *TSTGENGAU2* does! It uses the Retrieve System Status (*QWCRSSTS*) API, which is the "program-friendly" version of the *WRKSYSSTS* command. You'll find its documentation here for V5R4M0:

http://publib.boulder.ibm.com/infocenter/iseries/v5r4/index.jsp?topic=%2Fapis%2Fqwcrssts.htm

For V7R1M0, the documentation is here:

http://publib.boulder.ibm.com/infocenter/iseries/v7r1m0/index.jsp?topic=%2Fapis%2Fqwcrssts.htm

Figure 8.9: We've created a gauge chart!

Of the many pieces of information the *QWCRSSTS* API returns, I'm only going to use the ASP occupation percentage and the CPU used percentage. If you're curious to know how this was implemented, check out the *MISC_PR* copy member in *QCPYLESRC*. There, you'll find the API declared as a procedure with the *ExtPGM* keyword, and the *SysStsDS* data structure used to store the three bits of information I use in *TSTGENGAU2*.

Here's the program's complete source:

```
H DECEDIT(',') DATEDIT(*DMY.)

 * Generate Charts using Google Chart APIs Procedures
 /Copy QCPYLESRC,GENCHRT_PR
 * Misc Procedures
 /Copy QCPYLESRC,MISC_PR

 *'Data Areas
DW_PCCmd          S            200A   Inz(*Blanks)
DW_SysName        S             20A   Inz(*Blanks)
DW_Response       S             52A   Inz(*Blanks)
DW_AspPerc        S              5  2 Inz(*Zeros)
DW_ErrorDS        DS                  LikeDS(ApiError) Inz
```

Continued

```
/FREE

    // Invoke the Retrieve System Status API
    RtvSysSts(SysStsDS : %Size(SysStsDS) : C_SSTS0200 : '*NO' : ErrorDS);
    // If an error occurred, display the error message code and end program
    If  ErrorDS.Msgid <> *Blanks;
          W_Response = 'Error Message Code = ' +  %Trim(ErrorDS.Msgid);
          Dsply W_Response;
          Return;
    Endif;

    // Retrieve system name
        W_SysName = SysStsDS.SysName;

  // First, I'll set up the page title and the html file name
        P_PageTitle = 'Live ' + %Trim(W_SysName) + ' System Status';
        P_FileName = 'LiveSystemStatus.HTML';
  // Then the Rows
        Clear P_GaugeRowDS;
        P_GaugeRowDS(1).RowTitle = 'ASP %';
        P_GaugeRowDS(1).RowValue = SysStsDS.AspPercUsed / 10000;
        P_GaugeRowDS(2).RowTitle = 'CPU %';
        P_GaugeRowDS(2).RowValue = SysStsDS.CPUPercUsed / 10;
  // and the Options
        P_OptionDS(1).OptionTitle = 'redFrom';
        P_OptionDS(1).OptionValue = '87.5';
        P_OptionDS(2).OptionTitle = 'redTo';
        P_OptionDS(2).OptionValue = '100';
        P_OptionDS(3).OptionTitle = 'yellowFrom';
        P_OptionDS(3).OptionValue = '75';
        P_OptionDS(4).OptionTitle = 'yellowTo';
        P_OptionDS(4).OptionValue = '87.5';
        P_OptionDS(5).OptionTitle = 'greenFrom';
        P_OptionDS(5).OptionValue = '0';
        P_OptionDS(6).OptionTitle = 'greenTo';
        P_OptionDS(6).OptionValue = '75';
```

Continued

```
        P_OptionDS(7).OptionTitle = 'min';
        P_OptionDS(7).OptionValue = '0';
        P_OptionDS(8).OptionTitle = 'max';
        P_OptionDS(8).OptionValue = '100';
        P_OptionDS(9).OptionTitle = 'redColor';
        P_OptionDS(9).OptionValue = '''#EE0000''';
        P_OptionDS(10).OptionTitle = 'yellowColor';
        P_OptionDS(10).OptionValue = '''#FFFF00''';
        P_OptionDS(11).OptionTitle = 'greenColor';
        P_OptionDS(11).OptionValue = '''#32CD32''';
  // Generate the Chart
        If GenGaugeChart(P_PageTitle : P_GaugeRowDS : P_OptionDs :
                         P_FileName  : P_ErrorDesc  ) = *Off;
   // Display the Chart
   W_PCCmd = '\\' + %Trim(W_SysName) + '\GCHARTS\OUTPUT\'
             + %Trim(P_FileName);
   P_CmdLin = 'STRPCCMD PCCMD(''' + %Trim(W_PCCmd) +
              ''') PAUSE(*NO)';
   W_ErrorDs = ExecCmd(%Trim(P_CmdLin));
        Else;
          // Error occurred in the GenGaugeChart procedure
          W_Response = 'Error = ' +
                       %Trim(P_ErrorDesc);
          Dsply W_Response;
        EndIf;

  *InLr = *On;
/END-FREE
```

This sample program is vaguely similar to the previous one, but it has some important differences. So far, I've been using a data area to store the system name. (You'd have to change it to your system name to automatically launch the HTML files.) I chose this way of getting the system name to keep things as simple as possible. Now, however, I'm using this API to retrieve the system name, along with the ASP and CPU percentages. These three values are passed on to *GenGaugeChart* in order to produce two gauges (one for the ASP and another for the CPU) and a nice title for the page.

Go ahead, run the *TSTGENGAU2* program and see for yourself! You'll notice that the gauges now have a colored scale, ranging from green to red. This is achieved by setting the proper options, which determine not only where each colored section begins, but also which number values correspond to green, yellow, and red. I've used the HTML notation for the three colors, obtained from the site mentioned in the previous section. I've also set the minimum and maximum values for the gauge; since both ASP and CPU are represented as percentages, I used zero and 100, but you can set any values you'd like.

As with the previous Google Chart APIs presented in this chapter, this chart offers a lot of customization possibilities, so be sure to read the configuration options section of the documentation (*http://code.google.com/apis/chart/interactive/docs/gallery/gauge.html#Configuration_Options*) and play with them in the Visualization Playground (*http://code.google.com/apis/ajax/playground/?type=visualization#gauge*).

The Column, Line, and Area Charts

When I started my research for this section, I realized that the Column API (*http://code.google.com/apis/chart/interactive/docs/gallery/columnchart.html*) had a very similar structure to the Line API (*http://code.google.com/apis/chart/interactive/docs/gallery/linechart.html*). Curious, I reviewed the Area API (*http://code.google.com/apis/chart/interactive/docs/gallery/areachart.html*), only to find out that its structure was the same as the other two. In the end, what started as a section about only the Column API became a section about the Column, Line, and Area APIs.

The three Google sample HTML files are similar, so I'll just reproduce the column example here:

```
<html>
<head>
<script type="text/javascript" src="https://www.google.com/jsapi"></script>
<script type="text/javascript">
      google.load("visualization", "1", {packages:["corechart"]});
      google.setOnLoadCallback(drawChart);
      function drawChart() {
        var data = google.visualization.arrayToDataTable([
```

Continued

```
        ['Year', 'Sales', 'Expenses'],
        ['2004', 1000,      400],
        ['2005', 1170,      460],
        ['2006', 660,       1120],
        ['2007', 1030,      540]
      ]);

      var options = {
        title: 'Company Performance',
        hAxis: {title: 'Year', titleTextStyle: {color: 'red'}}
      };

      var chart = new google.visualization.ColumnChart(
                    document.getElementById('chart_div'));
      chart.draw(data, options);
    }
</script>
</head>
<body>
<div id="chart_div" style="width: 900px; height: 500px;"></div>
</body>
</html>
```

This should look familiar by now, if you read the previous sections. As I mentioned, the line and area examples are almost exactly the same, "almost" being the important word. I started by creating a column template as I usually do, and then opted to merge the three charts together. This three-in-one approach required some tweaking to the original column template, and to the procedure. Let's start with the template:

```
/$Header
<!DOCTYPE html PUBLIC "-//W3C//DTD XHTML 1.0 Strict//EN" "http://www.w3.org/TR/
xhtml1/DTD/xhtml1-strict.dtd">
<html xmlns="http://www.w3.org/1999/xhtml">
<head>
   <meta http-equiv="content-type" content="text/html; charset=utf-8"/>
                                                                    Continued
```

```
  <title>
    /%PageTitle%/
  </title>
  <script type="text/javascript" src="https://www.google.com/jsapi"></script>
  <script type="text/javascript">
    google.load("visualization", "1", {packages:["corechart"]});
    google.setOnLoadCallback(drawChart);
    function drawChart() {
      var data = new google.visualization.DataTable();
      data.addRows(/%TotalRows%/);
      data.addColumn('string', 'col1');
/$Column
      data.addColumn('/%ColumnType%/', '/%ColumnTitle%/');
/$FirstRow
      data.setValue(/%RowNbr%/, 0, '/%RowTitle%/');
/$Row
      data.setValue(/%RowNbr%/, /%ColNbr%/, /%CellValue%/);
/$OptionsBegin

    var options = {
/$Option
    '/%OptionTitle%/': /%OptionValue%/
/$OptionsEnd
                    };
/$Footer

      var chart = new google.visualization./%ChartType%/Chart(
          document.getElementById('chart_div'));
      chart.draw(data, options);
    }
  </script>
</head>

<body>
  <div id="chart_div"></div>
</body>
</html>
```

The template has the standard Header, Row, and Footer sections, along with the Options sections that I started to include a few pages back. However, it also includes the Column and FirstRow sections that I used in the bar chart example. These last sections are required because the APIs can handle multiple values per row. These values will be grouped in different ways on the three types of chart, but they will be displayed together. (This might sound a bit confusing, but it will be clearer when you see the examples.)

Each value within the row will be a cell, just like on a spreadsheet. The first cell of each row will contain the title of that row. This will be handled by the FirstRow section. After that, multiple Row sections will be written, up to the maximum number of columns defined. This two-dimensional matrix requires some special coding in the *GenCLAChart* procedure:

```
 *-----------------------------------------------------------------------*
 *   Generate Column, Line or Area (CLA) Chart                           *
 *-----------------------------------------------------------------------*
P GenCLAChart     B                   EXPORT
D                 PI              N
 * Input Parms
DP_ChartType                          Like(t_ChartType)  Value
DP_PageTitle                          Like(t_PageTitle)  Value
DP_CLAColumnDS                        LikeDS(CLAColumnDS)
D                                     Dim(C_CLAMaxColumns) Value
DP_CLARowDS                           LikeDS(CLARowDS) Dim(C_CLAMaxRows)
D                                     Value
DP_OptionDS                           LikeDS(OptionDS) Dim(C_MaxOptions)
D                                     Value
DP_FileName                           Like(t_FileName) Value
 * Output Parms
DP_ErrorDesc                          Like(t_ErrorDesc)
 /FREE

     ExSr Init;

     ExSr Proc;

                                                                Continued
```

```
  ExSr End_Of_Program;

 //  Sub Routines

 //------------------------------------------------------------------*
 //  Initialization                                                  *
 //------------------------------------------------------------------*
   BegSr  Init;

   P_ErrorDesc = *Blanks;

   // Check if there is data in the P_ChartType variable
   If P_ChartType = *Blanks;
     P_ErrorDesc = 'No chart type';
     Return *On;
   EndIf;
   // Check if P_ChartType has a valid value
   If ((P_ChartType <> 'C') And (P_ChartType <> 'L') And
       (P_ChartType <> 'A'));
     P_ErrorDesc = 'Chart type is not valid';
     Return *On;
   EndIf;

   // Check if there is data in the P_CLAColumnDS array
   If P_CLAColumnDS(1).ColumnTitle = *Blanks;
     P_ErrorDesc = 'No column data';
     Return *On;
   EndIf;

   // Check if there is data in the P_CLARowDS array
   If P_CLARowDS(1).RowTitle = *Blanks;
     P_ErrorDesc = 'No row data';
     Return *On;
   EndIf;

   // Check if the file name was passed
   If P_FileName = *Blanks;
```

Continued

```
    P_ErrorDesc = 'No file name';
    Return *On;
  EndIf;

  EndSr;
//-----------------------------------------------------------------------*
//End of the program                                                    *
//-----------------------------------------------------------------------*
  BegSr  End_Of_Program;

     Return *Off;

  EndSr;
//-----------------------------------------------------------------------*
// Process input parms and generate the proper xml file                 *
//-----------------------------------------------------------------------*
  BegSr  Proc;


   SetNoDebug(*OFF);
        getHtmlIfsMult(C_CLATmpl);

   // Header Section
   // Update the Header variables
   updHtmlVar('PageTitle' : %Trim(P_PageTitle));
   // Find out how many rows have data
   For W_RowIdx = 1 to C_CLAMaxRows;
     If P_CLARowDS(W_RowIdx).RowTitle = *Blanks;
       Leave;
     Else;
       // If this was not the last row containing data, keep the row number
       W_TotalRows = W_RowIdx;
     EndIf;
   EndFor;
   // Update the TotalRows variable
   updHtmlVar('TotalRows' : %Char(W_TotalRows));
   // Write the Header section
```

Continued

```
WrtSection('Header');

// Column Section
For W_ColIdx = 1 to C_CLAMaxColumns;
  If P_CLAColumnDS(W_ColIdx).ColumnTitle = *Blanks;
    Leave;
  EndIf;
  updHtmlVar('ColumnType'  :
             %Trim(P_CLAColumnDS(W_ColIdx).ColumnType));
  updHtmlVar('ColumnTitle' :
             %Trim(P_CLAColumnDS(W_ColIdx).ColumnTitle));
  // Write the Column section
  WrtSection('Column');
EndFor;


// FirstRow And Row Sections
For W_RowIdx = 1 to C_CLAMaxRows;
  If P_CLARowDS(W_RowIdx).RowTitle = *Blanks;
    Leave;
  EndIf;
  // Update the Row variables
  updHtmlVar('RowNbr'   : %Char(W_RowIdx-1));
  updHtmlVar('RowTitle' : %Trim(P_CLARowDS(W_RowIdx).RowTitle));
  // Write the FirstRow section
  WrtSection('FirstRow');
  For W_ColIdx = 1 to C_CLAMaxColumns;
    If P_CLARowDS(W_RowIdx).Cell(W_ColIdx).CellValue= *Zeros;
      Leave;
    EndIf;
    updHtmlVar('ColNbr' : %Char(W_ColIdx));
    updHtmlVar('CellValue' : %Char(
               P_CLARowDS(W_RowIdx).Cell(W_ColIdx).CellValue));
    // Write the Row section
    WrtSection('Row');
  EndFor;
EndFor;
```

Continued

```
// Options Section
// Define the Options variable
  WrtSection('OptionsBegin');
// Write each option on a separate line
For W_Idx = 1 to C_MaxOptions;
  If P_OptionDS(W_Idx).OptionTitle = *Blanks;
    Leave;
  EndIf;
  // Update the Option variables
  updHtmlVar('OptionTitle' :
             %Trim(P_OptionDS(W_Idx).OptionTitle));
  // If this is not the last option of the array and the next
  // option was filled in, add a comma after the value
  If (((W_Idx + 1) < C_MaxOptions) And
      (P_OptionDs(W_Idx + 1).OptionTitle <> *Blanks));
    P_OptionDS(W_Idx).OptionValue =
     %Trim(P_OptionDS(W_Idx).OptionValue) + ',';
  EndIf;
  updHtmlVar('OptionValue' :
             %Trim(P_OptionDS(W_Idx).OptionValue));
  // Write the Option section
  WrtSection('Option');
EndFor;
// Close the Options definition
  WrtSection('OptionsEnd');

// Footer Section
// Determine the chart type and update the respective variable
Select;
  When P_ChartType = 'C';
    updHtmlVar('ChartType' : 'Column');
  When P_ChartType = 'L';
    updHtmlVar('ChartType' : 'Line');
  When P_ChartType = 'A';
    updHtmlVar('ChartType' : 'Area');
```

Continued

```
      EndSl;
      // Write the Footer section
      WrtSection('Footer');

      // Set the appropriate file name and path
      W_FileName = %Trim(C_OutputPath) + '/' + %Trim(P_FileName);

      // Write the html file to disk
      WrtHtmlToStmf(%Trim(W_FileName): 819);

     EndSr;
 /END-FREE
PGenCLAChart     E
```

Like Google's sample HTML, the procedure should also look familiar by now. However, the "matrix-style" data representation required some additional work. I had to use a cycle within a cycle to loop through the rows and, within each row, through each cell.

Here's how I did it:

```
 // FirstRow And Row Sections
For W_RowIdx = 1 to C_CLAMaxRows;
If P_CLARowDS(W_RowIdx).RowTitle = *Blanks;
   Leave;
EndIf;
// Update the Row variables
updHtmlVar('RowNbr'   : %Char(W_RowIdx-1));
updHtmlVar('RowTitle' : %Trim(P_CLARowDS(W_RowIdx).RowTitle));
// Write the FirstRow section
WrtSection('FirstRow');
For W_ColIdx = 1 to C_CLAMaxColumns;
   If P_CLARowDS(W_RowIdx).Cell(W_ColIdx).CellValue= *Zeros;
     Leave;
   EndIf;
   updHtmlVar('ColNbr' : %Char(W_ColIdx));
```

Continued

```
    updHtmlVar('CellValue' : %Char(
                P_CLARowDS(W_RowIdx).Cell(W_ColIdx).CellValue));
    // Write the Row section
    WrtSection('Row');
    EndFor;
EndFor;
```

The only problem is that you can decide not to provide values for all the cells in each row or for all the rows. (The maximum number of rows is defined in the *C_CLAMaxRows* constant.) This problem was solved by checking whether the data structure fields shown below were filled right in the beginning of each iteration of the respective cycles:

```
P_CLARowDS(W_RowIdx).Cell(W_ColIdx).CellValue
P_CLARowDS(W_RowIdx).RowTitle
```

However, this coding assumes that a missing value indicates that the data for that row is over. If you want to allow missing values in the middle of a row, just change the *Leave* statement to an *Iter* statement.

There's just one more detail: this procedure has a rather unique parameter, called *P_ChartType*. As the name implies, it's used to determine which type of chart (column, line, or area) will be produced. The rest of the procedure's code is quite simple and similar to the previously presented procedures in this chapter.

As you might have guessed by now, this procedure can also be used to produce bar charts, since they are also part of Google's "corechart" package. The bar chart shares the same structure used by the other three types of chart. The procedure needs only a few adjustments related to the *P_ChartType* parameter. If you want to do it, just allow the *B* value in the *Init* routine check, and translate it into *Bar* in the Footer section of the *Proc* routine.

Now, let's see what this piece of code can generate. I created three sample programs (*TSTGENCLA1*, *TSTGENCLA2*, and *TSTGENCLA3*), each producing a different type of chart. Here's the source for the first sample program:

```
H DECEDIT(',') DATEDIT(*DMY.)

 * Generate Charts using Google Chart APIs Procedures
 /Copy QCPYLESRC,GENCHRT_PR
 * Misc Procedures
 /Copy QCPYLESRC,MISC_PR

 *'Data Areas
D Da_SystemName   S                    Like(W_SysName) DtaAra(DaSysName)
DW_PCCmd          S            200A    Inz(*Blanks)
DW_SysName        S             20A    Inz(*Blanks)
DW_Response       S             52A    Inz(*Blanks)
DW_ErrorDS        DS                   LikeDS(ApiError) Inz

 /FREE
      // Retrieve system name
      // Invoke the Retrieve System Status API
      RtvSysSts(SysStsDS : %Size(SysStsDS) : C_SSTS0200 : '*NO' : ErrorDS);
      // If an error occurred, display the error message code and end program
      If  ErrorDS.Msgid <> *Blanks;
            W_Response = 'Error Message Code = ' +  %Trim(ErrorDS.Msgid);
            Dsply W_Response;
            Return;
      Endif;

      // Retrieve system name
          W_SysName = SysStsDS.SysName;

    // First, I'll set up the page title, the chart type (C for Column)
    // and the output file name
          P_ChartType = 'C';
          P_PageTitle = 'Did you know?';
          P_FileName = 'CellPhonesColumn.HTML';
    // Next the Columns
```

Continued

```
      Clear P_CLAColumnDS;
      P_CLAColumnDS(1).ColumnType  = 'number';
      P_CLAColumnDS(1).ColumnTitle = 'Making calls';
      P_CLAColumnDS(2).ColumnType  = 'number';
      P_CLAColumnDS(2).ColumnTitle = 'Texting';
      P_CLAColumnDS(3).ColumnType  = 'number';
      P_CLAColumnDS(3).ColumnTitle = 'Games';
      P_CLAColumnDS(4).ColumnType  = 'number';
      P_CLAColumnDS(4).ColumnTitle = 'Checking the Time';
      P_CLAColumnDS(5).ColumnType  = 'number';
      P_CLAColumnDS(5).ColumnTitle = 'Flashlight';
// Then the Rows
      Clear P_CLARowDS;
      P_CLARowDS(1).RowTitle = 'Brick-sized Cellphones';
      P_CLARowDS(1).Cell(1).CellValue = 95;
      P_CLARowDS(1).Cell(2).CellValue = 5;
      P_CLARowDS(1).Cell(3).CellValue = 0;
      P_CLARowDS(1).Cell(4).CellValue = 0;
      P_CLARowDS(1).Cell(5).CellValue = 0;
      P_CLARowDS(2).RowTitle = 'Nokia Rules';
      P_CLARowDS(2).Cell(1).CellValue = 60;
      P_CLARowDS(2).Cell(2).CellValue = 35;
      P_CLARowDS(2).Cell(3).CellValue = 5;
      P_CLARowDS(2).Cell(4).CellValue = 0;
      P_CLARowDS(2).Cell(5).CellValue = 0;
      P_CLARowDS(3).RowTitle = 'The Blackberry Era';
      P_CLARowDS(3).Cell(1).CellValue = 30;
      P_CLARowDS(3).Cell(2).CellValue = 55;
      P_CLARowDS(3).Cell(3).CellValue = 5;
      P_CLARowDS(3).Cell(4).CellValue = 5;
      P_CLARowDS(3).Cell(5).CellValue = 0;
      P_CLARowDS(4).RowTitle = 'The First iPhone';
      P_CLARowDS(4).Cell(1).CellValue = 10;
      P_CLARowDS(4).Cell(2).CellValue = 10;
      P_CLARowDS(4).Cell(3).CellValue = 40;
      P_CLARowDS(4).Cell(4).CellValue = 40;
```

Continued

```
      P_CLARowDS(4).Cell(5).CellValue = 0;
      P_CLARowDS(5).RowTitle = 'Present Day';
      P_CLARowDS(5).Cell(1).CellValue = 5;
      P_CLARowDS(5).Cell(2).CellValue = 5;
      P_CLARowDS(5).Cell(3).CellValue = 10;
      P_CLARowDS(5).Cell(4).CellValue = 5;
      P_CLARowDS(5).Cell(5).CellValue = 75;
  // Finally, the Options
      P_OptionDS(1).OptionTitle = 'width';
      P_OptionDS(1).OptionValue = '800';
      P_OptionDS(2).OptionTitle = 'height';
      P_OptionDS(2).OptionValue = '400';
      P_OptionDS(3).OptionTitle = 'title';
      P_OptionDS(3).OptionValue = '"Most Common Cell Phone uses"';
      P_OptionDS(4).OptionTitle = 'vAxis';
      P_OptionDS(4).OptionValue = '{title: "Cellphone Eras"}';
      P_OptionDS(5).OptionTitle = 'hAxis';
      P_OptionDS(5).OptionValue = '{title: "Most Common Use", ' +
                                 'titleTextStyle: {color: "blue"}}';
      P_OptionDS(6).OptionTitle = 'legend';
      P_OptionDS(6).OptionValue = '{position: "top"}';
  // Generate the Chart
      If GenCLAChart(P_ChartType   : P_PageTitle :
                     P_CLAColumnDS : P_CLARowDS  :
                     P_OptionDS    :
                     P_FileName    : P_ErrorDesc ) = *Off;
  // Display the Chart
  W_PCCmd = '\\' + %Trim(W_SysName) + '\GCHARTS\OUTPUT\'
          + %Trim(P_FileName);
  P_CmdLin = 'STRPCCMD PCCMD(''' + %Trim(W_PCCmd) +
           ''') PAUSE(*NO)';
  W_ErrorDs = ExecCmd(%Trim(P_CmdLin));
      Else;
        // Error occurred in the GenCLAChart procedure
        W_Response = 'Error = ' +
                     %Trim(P_ErrorDesc);
```

Continued

```
            Dsply W_Response;
          EndIf;

      *InLr = *On;
  /END-FREE
```

It's almost like the *TSTGENBAR1* source, but there are a couple of differences. First, the system name is now obtained using the API I mentioned during the discussion of the Gauge API. Second, there is a single, but extremely important, line of code near the beginning:

```
P_ChartType = 'C';
```

You can transform the chart produced by this sample program just by changing the value assigned to the *P_ChartType* variable to L or A. That will cause Figure 8.10 to become Figure 8.11 (note that the key was artificially inserted next to the lines to improve readability). The values are exactly the same in the two charts, but their graphical representation lost clarity in Figure 8.11. Depending on the number of columns and the distribution of the values, what seemed a perfectly good choice could produce a rather confusing result!

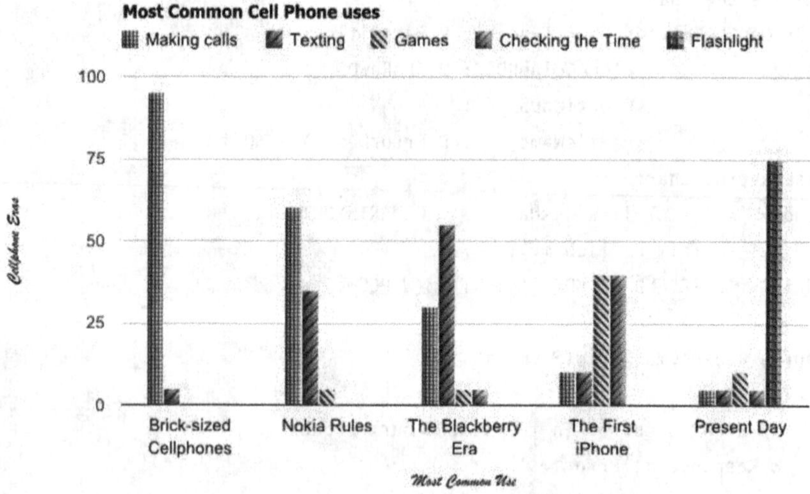

Figure 8.10: You had a column chart.

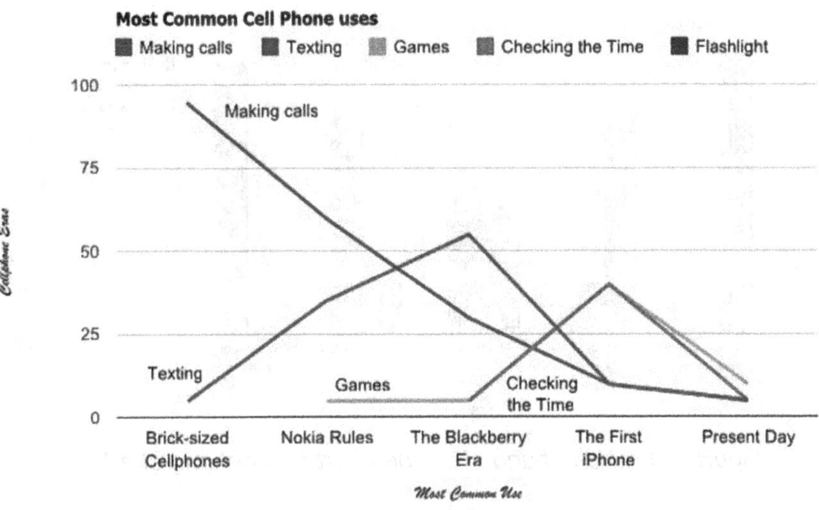

Figure 8.11: Now your column chart is a line chart.

As another example, let's take the line chart produced by *TSTGENCLA2* and change it to a column chart. *TSTGENCLA2* is very similar to the previously presented sample program, so I won't include it here. (You can find all the sample programs in the downloadable source code of this chapter.) We'll go from what's shown in Figure 8.12 to what's shown in Figure 8.13. Again, it loses clarity, and the evolution of the values also loses impact.

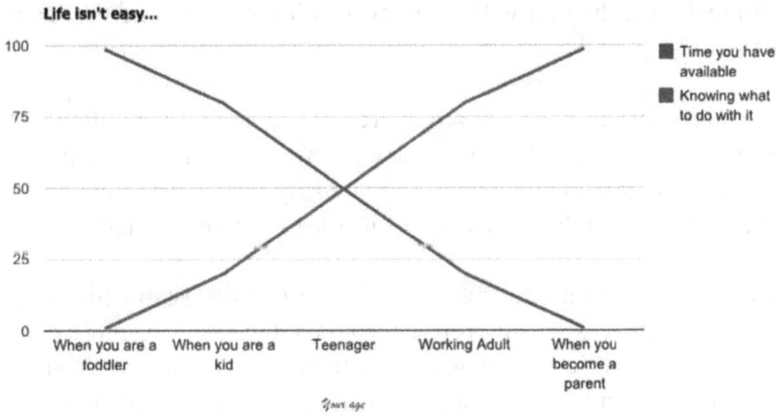

Figure 8.12: You start with a line chart.

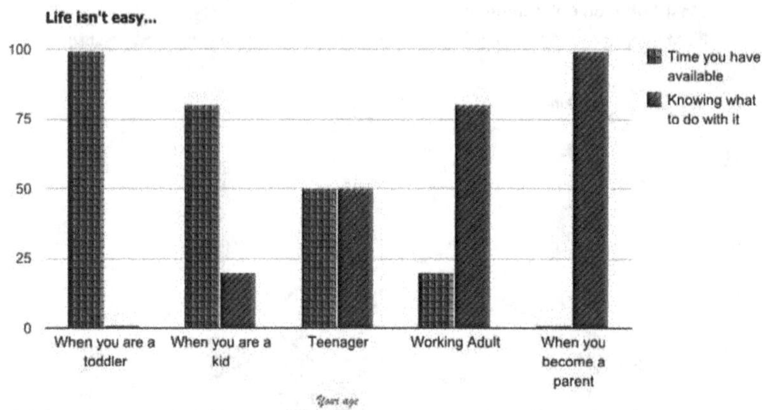

Figure 8.13: You change the line chart to a column chart.

So, what's the lesson here? As a rule of thumb, I would say that line and area charts are better suited for fewer columns and more rows than the column chart. This is just my humble opinion, and I'm definitely not the world's leading chart expert, so feel free to use this procedure in any way that you'd like. If you figure out a way to improve it, be sure to let me know!

The Intensity Map Chart

The intensity map chart has a few of the interesting characteristics of the geo map, and some special features of its own. In this section, I'll present a new API and two examples with real data, the first with international information and the second with U.S. info per state.

While the geo map chart allows a certain degree of interactivity and flexibility, it also has some limitations: it's Flash-based and doesn't allow the simultaneous display of different types of data, just to name two. The intensity map chart overcomes some of these limitations, even though it has some of its own (explained later).

This type of map, also known as a "heat map," is perfect for establishing comparisons between large sets of geographically referenced data. Google's example compares the populations of a few countries in one map with their areas in another. You need to go back and forward between the two maps to do an actual comparison, but it's still a useful tool under the right circumstances.

Here's the sample HTML provided by Google:

```
<html>
  <head>
    <scripttype='text/javascript'src='https://www.google.com/jsapi'></script>
    <scripttype='text/javascript'>
      google.load('visualization','1',{packages:['intensitymap']});
      google.setOnLoadCallback(drawChart);
      function drawChart(){
        var data = google.visualization.arrayToDataTable([
          ['Country','Population (mil)','Area (km2)'],
          ['CN',          1324,          9640821],
          ['IN',          1133,          3287263],
          ['US',          304,           9629091],
          ['ID',          232,           1904569],
          ['BR',          187,           8514877]
        ]);

        var chart =new google.visualization.IntensityMap(
            document.getElementById('chart_div'));
        chart.draw(data,{});
      }
    </script>
  </head>

  <body>
    <divid="chart_div"></div>
  </body>
</html>
```

As you can see, there's nothing really special about the way the maps are built. You get a map for each additional column that you add. The template used to generate the HTML file that, in turn, creates the chart in your browser will be the starting point of the exploration of this API. As usual, I really recommend that you read all the previous sections of this chapter, starting with the first one, as well as the Intensity Map documentation (*http://code.google.com/apis/chart/interactive/docs/gallery/intensitymap.html*), because each section highlights an area or detail of the process of generating the charts, and the API's documentation is usually clear and complete. Even though all the chart types are somewhat similar, each of them has its uniqueness.

Let's start by reviewing the *IntMap.tmpl* template:

```
 /$Header
<!DOCTYPE html PUBLIC "-//W3C//DTD XHTML 1.0 Strict//EN" "http://www.w3.org/TR/
xhtml1/DTD/xhtml1-strict.dtd">
<html xmlns="http://www.w3.org/1999/xhtml">
<head>
   <meta http-equiv="content-type" content="text/html; charset=utf-8"/>
   <title>
     /%PageTitle%/
   </title>
   <script type="text/javascript" src="http://www.google.com/jsapi"></script>
   <script type="text/javascript">
     google.load('visualization', '1', {packages: ['intensitymap']});
   </script>
   <script type="text/javascript">
     function drawVisualization() {
       // Create and populate the data table.
       var data = new google.visualization.DataTable();
       data.addRows(/%TotalRows%/);
       data.addColumn('string', 'Country');
/$Column
       data.addColumn('number', '/%ColumnTitle%/');
/$FirstRow
       data.setValue(/%RowNbr%/, 0, '/%RowTitle%/');
/$Row
       data.setValue(/%RowNbr%/, /%ColNbr%/, /%CellValue%/);
/$OptionsBegin

     var options = {
```

Continued

```
/$Option
      '/%OptionTitle%/': /%OptionValue%/
/$OptionsEnd
                  };

/$Footer
        // Create and draw the visualization.
        new google.visualization.IntensityMap(
            document.getElementById('visualization'));
            chart.draw(data, options);
      }


      google.setOnLoadCallback(drawVisualization);
    </script>
</head>
<body style="font-family: Arial;border: 0 none;">
    <div id="visualization"></div>
</body>
</html>
```

This template has a similar structure to the one presented in the "Column, Line, and Area Charts" section. Of course, some details are specific to this type of chart, such as the package name and the function that creates the chart. However, this similarity allowed me to almost duplicate the previously presented procedure and use it with the new template, so I won't waste your time by repeating myself. I'll go straight to the examples and explain a bit more about this chart along the way.

The first sample program (*TSTGENINM1*) presents some interesting numbers regarding mobile phones and the population of 57 countries. The values are represented using the intensity of the assigned color (hence, the name of the chart): a faint, almost white tone for the lowest values of the interval and an intense tone for the highest values. This is shown in Figure 8.14.

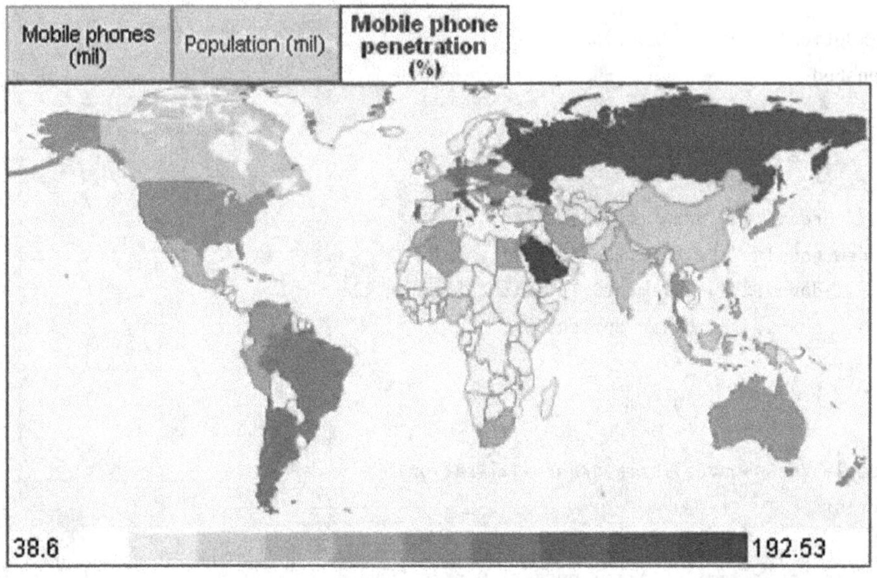

Figure 8.14: In the intensity map, values are represented by the intensity of the colors.

I mentioned earlier that one of the downsides of the geo map is its inability to display multiple values in the same chart. A quick glance at Figure 8.14 shows how this chart overcomes that. It's true that the different value representations are not overlapped, which might be confusing; instead, it presents an elegant tabbed display, using one tab for each set of data. (Speaking of data, the information used on this sample program is real. It can be found at *http://en.wikipedia.org/wiki/List_of_countries_by_number_of_mobile_phones_in_use*.)

Here's the program's source code:

```
H DECEDIT(',') DATEDIT(*DMY.)

FINM1F     IF   E           K DISK

 * Generate Charts using Google Chart APIs Procedures
 /Copy QCPYLESRC,GENCHRT_PR
 * Misc Procedures
 /Copy QCPYLESRC,MISC_PR

 *'Data Areas
D Da_SystemName   S                   Like(W_SysName) DtaAra(DaSysName)
DW_PCCmd          S            200A   Inz(*Blanks)
DW_SysName        S             20A   Inz(*Blanks)
DW_Response       S             52A   Inz(*Blanks)
DW_ErrorDS        DS                  LikeDS(ApiError) Inz
DW_Pos            S              3  0 Inz(*Zeros)

/FREE
      // Retrieve system name
      // Invoke the Retrieve System Status API
      RtvSysSts(SysStsDS : %Size(SysStsDS) : C_SSTS0200 : '*NO' : ErrorDS);
      // If an error occurred, display the error message code and end program
      If  ErrorDS.Msgid <> *Blanks;
            W_Response = 'Error Message Code = ' +  %Trim(ErrorDS.Msgid);
            Dsply W_Response;
            Return;
      Endif;

      // Retrieve system name
          W_SysName = SysStsDS.SysName;

    // First, I'll set up the page title and the html file name
          P_PageTitle = 'Mobile Phones and Population per country';
          P_FileName = 'MobilePhonesIntMap.HTML';
    // Next the Columns
          Clear P_IntMapColumnDS;
```

Continued

```
      P_IntMapColumnDS(1).ColumnTitle = 'Mobile phones (mil)';
      P_IntMapColumnDS(2).ColumnTitle = 'Population (mil)';
      P_IntMapColumnDS(3).ColumnTitle = 'Mobile phone penetration (%)';
  // Then the Rows
      Clear P_IntMapRowDS;
      W_Pos = *Zeros;
      Read Inm1F;
      Dow Not(%Eof(Inm1F));
        W_Pos = W_Pos + 1;
        P_IntMapRowDS(W_Pos).RowTitle = Country;
        P_IntMapRowDS(W_Pos).Cell(1).CellValue = MobPhones / 1000000;
        P_IntMapRowDS(W_Pos).Cell(2).CellValue = Population / 1000000;
        P_IntMapRowDS(W_Pos).Cell(3).CellValue = (MobPhones / Population) * 100;
        Read Inm1F;
      EndDo;
  // Finally, the Options
      P_OptionDS(1).OptionTitle = 'region';
      P_OptionDS(1).OptionValue = '''world''';
      P_OptionDS(2).OptionTitle = 'colors';
      P_OptionDS(2).OptionValue = '["blue", "green", "red"]';
  // Generate the Chart
      If GenIntMapChart(P_PageTitle : P_IntMapColumnDS :
                     P_IntMapRowDS   : P_OptionDS  :
                     P_FileName   : P_ErrorDesc  ) = *Off;
   // Display the Chart
   W_PCCmd = '\\' + %Trim(W_SysName) + '\GCHARTS\OUTPUT\' + %Trim(P_FileName);
   P_CmdLin = 'STRPCCMD PCCMD(''' + %Trim(W_PCCmd) + ''') PAUSE(*NO)';
   W_ErrorDs = ExecCmd(%Trim(P_CmdLin));
      Else;
        // Error occurred in the GenIntMapChart procedure
        W_Response = 'Error = ' + %Trim(P_ErrorDesc);
        Dsply W_Response;
      EndIf;

  *InLr = *On;
/END-FREE
```

If you review this source code, you'll find that the data comes from a physical file, and the *P_IntMapRowDS* array is loaded using a cycle. Since none of my previous sample programs used files, for simplicity's sake, I decided to do so now. It's the only "new" thing about this sample program, as it follows the same line as its predecessors.

You can use this file, or an adaptation of it, to quickly create your own charts. There are only two details you need to watch out for. First, the country or U.S. state (more on this in the second example) has to follow the ISO country two-letter naming convention (*http://en.wikipedia.org/wiki/ISO_3166-2*) or the U.S. state two-letter abbreviation convention (*http://www.stateabbreviations.us*). Otherwise, the chart API won't recognize it. Second, be aware of the size of the numbers you want to represent. I had to reduce the scale of the population to millions in order for it to fit the *CellValue* field size. Of course, you can also go to the *QCPYLESRC/GENCHRT_PR* source member and change the *t_CellValue* definition to a larger number instead. Just be sure to recompile the *GENCHRT* service program afterward.

The second sample program, named *TSTGENINM2* and with the same structure as *TSTGENINM1*, also uses real data, extracted from the Census.gov Web site (more specifically, from *http://quickfacts.census.gov/qfd/download_data.html* and *http://www.census.gov/govs*). It took me a bit to reformat it so that the API could identify all 50 states. You can find the result in the *MobilePhonesIntMap.HTML* file in the downloadable source code. Cool, isn't it? I hope these two examples are enough to convince you to add this chart type to your arsenal!

Unfortunately, this chart type doesn't offer much customization. You're limited to a maximum chart size of 440x220 pixels, and the choice of maps only has *world, africa, asia, europe, middle_east, south_america*, and *usa* as possible values. The one thing you can have a little bit of fun customizing is the color used in each data tab. By setting the *colors* array in the options, you get to choose the best colors for your data. Be careful; lighter colors don't produce very visible color scales. Always try to use intense colors to make the map scale clear.

The Combo Chart

On many occasions, a single way of representing values (such as a set of columns, lines, or bars) is not enough to truly get the right message across. If you want to show the evolution of a certain value and simultaneously compare that value with what was planned, the charts presented in the previous sections just won't do.

That's where the Combo Chart API comes in (*http://code.google.com/apis/chart/interactive/docs/gallery/combochart.html*). The combo chart will allow you to show, for example, those bar/line combination charts that your finance department loves so much. As the name implies, this chart type allows you to combine up to three different types of charts (columns, lines, and areas) into a single chart. You can go so far as to represent each value of your data set with a different type of chart, or at least, represent it with different characteristics.

I advise you to review the API's documentation at *http://code.google.com/apis/chart/interactive/docs/gallery/combochart.html*, because I won't repeat myself by focusing on topics that have been covered in previous sections. Having said that, let's move on to Google's example, which depicts the evolution of coffee production in several countries over a period of five years, and also the average production:

```
<!DOCTYPE html PUBLIC "-//W3C//DTD XHTML 1.0 Strict//EN" "http://www.w3.org/TR/
xhtml1/DTD/xhtml1-strict.dtd">
<htmlxmlns="http://www.w3.org/1999/xhtml">
  <head>
    <metahttp-equiv="content-type"content="text/html; charset=utf-8"/>
    <title>
      Google Visualization API Sample
    </title>
    <scripttype="text/javascript"src="https://www.google.com/jsapi"></script>
    <scripttype="text/javascript">
      google.load('visualization','1',{packages:['corechart']});
    </script>
    <scripttype="text/javascript">
      function drawVisualization(){
        // Some raw data (not necessarily accurate)
        var data = google.visualization.arrayToDataTable([
          ['Month','Bolivia','Ecuador','Madagascar','Papua New Guinea',
           'Rwanda','Average'],
          ['2004/05', 165,     938,       522,          998,          450,      614.6],
```

Continued

```
        ['2005/06',  135,   1120,    599,    1268,    288,   682],
        ['2006/07',  157,   1167,    587,     807,    397,   623],
        ['2007/08',  139,   1110,    615,     968,    215,   609.4],
        ['2008/09',  136,    691,    629,    1026,     66,   569.6]
      ]);

      var options ={
        title :'Monthly Coffee Production by Country',
        vAxis:{title:"Cups"},
        hAxis:{title:"Month"},
        seriesType:"bars",
        series:{5:{type:"line"}}
      };

      var chart =new google.visualization.ComboChart(
          document.getElementById('chart_div'));
      chart.draw(data, options);
    }
    google.setOnLoadCallback(drawVisualization);
  </script>
 </head>
 <body>
   <divid="chart_div"style="width:900px;height:500px;"></div>
 </body>
</html>
```

It looks “normal” enough, right? But pay close attention to the *options* declaration:

```
var options = {
  title : 'Monthly Coffee Production by Country',
  vAxis: {title: "Cups"},
  hAxis: {title: "Month"},
  seriesType: "bars",
  series: {5: {type: "line"}}
};
```

The first three options are pretty standard, but the last two are completely new. They hold the key to the combo chart, as I'll explain later, with a few examples! Anyway, based on this information, I've created the *Combo.tmpl* template:

```
/$Header
<!DOCTYPE html PUBLIC "-//W3C//DTD XHTML 1.0 Strict//EN" "http://www.w3.org/TR/
xhtml1/DTD/xhtml1-strict.dtd">
<html xmlns="http://www.w3.org/1999/xhtml">
<head>
   <meta http-equiv="content-type" content="text/html; charset=utf-8"/>
   <title>
     /%PageTitle%/
   </title>
   <script type="text/javascript" src="http://www.google.com/jsapi"></script>
   <script type="text/javascript">
     google.load('visualization', '1', {packages: ['corechart']});
   </script>
   <script type="text/javascript">
     function drawVisualization() {
       // Create and populate the data table.
       var data = new google.visualization.DataTable();
       data.addRows(/%TotalRows%/);
       data.addColumn('string', 'Col1');
/$Column
       data.addColumn('number', '/%ColumnTitle%/');
/$FirstRow
       data.setValue(/%RowNbr%/, 0, '/%RowTitle%/');
/$Row
       data.setValue(/%RowNbr%/, /%ColNbr%/, /%CellValue%/);
/$OptionsBegin

     var options = {
/$Option
     '/%OptionTitle%/': /%OptionLongValue%/
/$OptionsEnd
                    };
```

Continued

```
/$Footer
        // Create and draw the visualization.
        var ac = new google.visualization.ComboChart(
            document.getElementById('visualization'));
        ac.draw(data, options);
      }

      google.setOnLoadCallback(drawVisualization);
    </script>
</head>
<body style="font-family: Arial;border: 0 none;">
    <div id="visualization"></div>
</body>
</html>
```

It's an almost exact copy of the previous template. However, the Option section is a bit different; the */%OptionValue%/* variable was replaced by an */%OptionLongValue%/* variable. This is not mandatory, but I've done it to keep the template variable names in line with the data structure variable names. To explain why a new variable was necessary, I need to explain a bit more about this chart type. As the template hinted, it's a regular two-dimensional, table-based chart. However, the trick behind the "combo" is the choice of options. Two new keywords—"*seriesType*" and "*series*"— allow you to customize each set of data in multiple ways by specifying attributes that apply only to that subset of values within your set, just like I mentioned when explaining the Options in Google's sample HTML file. The *OptionValue* variable has a length of 100 characters; in some cases, this wouldn't be enough to accommodate the string of attributes for the *seriesType* keyword, so I decided to create the *OptionLongValue* variable, which has a length of 255 characters.

Let me try to make this clearer with a few examples. Imagine that you want the classical column chart with a line indicating the average, like the one in Figure 8.15, which Google presents as the example in the chart's documentation.

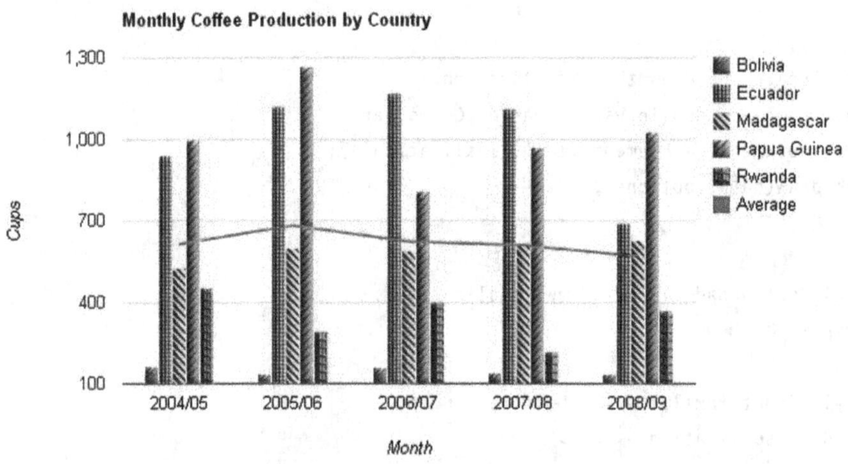

Figure 8.15: Put a line into your column chart.

Here, the primary chart is a column chart, and the secondary chart is a line chart. To achieve this result, you'd need to specify the following *seriesType* and *series* options:

```
(...)
seriesType: "bars", series: {5: {type: "line"}}
(...)
```

As you probably guessed by now, *seriesType* is used to set the type of chart to be used by default. If you don't specify a different type on the *series* keyword, all the data will be represented using the chart type you defined in the *seriesType* keyword. But for that, you wouldn't need the combo chart! The "magic trick" is performed by the *series* keyword. In this example, I'm telling the chart to represent the sixth column of data as a line. Be aware that the count starts at zero instead of one, so column number 6 is actually the fifth for this keyword; also note that the type attribute for columns (used on the *series* keyword) is actually "bars." If I wanted to specify more attributes for column 5, like color, for instance, I'd just have to add a comma and insert the attribute name and value within the inner brackets.

For complete (and a bit more complex) examples, let's review the source code of the *TSTGENCMB1* and *TSTGENCMB2* sample programs. They both use the same data. I'm building charts that depict a company's performance and the shares evolution over the same period. I won't reproduce the entire source here, as it is similar to most sample programs previously presented. Instead, I'll show you just two pieces of code of *TSTGENCMB1*—the column declaration and the options:

```
(...)
    // Next the Columns
        Clear P_ComboColumnDS;
        P_ComboColumnDS(1).ColumnType  = 'number';
        P_ComboColumnDS(1).ColumnTitle = 'Sales (thousands)';
        P_ComboColumnDS(2).ColumnType  = 'number';
        P_ComboColumnDS(2).ColumnTitle = 'Expenses (thousands)';
        P_ComboColumnDS(3).ColumnType  = 'number';
        P_ComboColumnDS(3).ColumnTitle = 'Finantial Performance';
        P_ComboColumnDS(4).ColumnType  = 'number';
        P_ComboColumnDS(4).ColumnTitle =
            'Company Shares Performance (dollars)';
(...)
    // Finally, the Options
        P_LongOptionDS(1).OptionTitle = 'seriesType';
        P_LongOptionDS(1).OptionLongValue = '"bars"';
        P_LongOptionDS(2).OptionTitle = 'series';
        P_LongOptionDS(2).OptionLongValue =
            '{2: {type: "area", color: "green"},' +
            ' 3: {type: "line", color: "orange"}}';
        P_LongOptionDS(3).OptionTitle = 'width';
        P_LongOptionDS(3).OptionLongValue = '800';
        P_LongOptionDS(4).OptionTitle = 'height';
        P_LongOptionDS(4).OptionLongValue = '400';
        P_LongOptionDS(5).OptionTitle = 'title';
        P_LongOptionDS(5).OptionLongValue =
                    '"Performance over the last 5 years"';
```

This produces a very informative chart, combining several types of representation, as you can see in Figure 8.16. A careful analysis of the Options section reveals that this is indeed a bar chart (as defined by the *seriesType* keyword), but some of the columns have a different representation. The "Financial Performance" (column number 2, but actually the third column) will be represented by a green colored area chart. This is achieved by the following string, assigned to the *series* keyword: *{2: {type: "area",* *color: "green"}*. But that's not all – the "Company Shares Performance (dollars)" (column number 3) also needed some sort of distinction from the rest. That's why it is represented as an orange line. That's what the second part of the *series* keyword value means: *3: {type: "line", color: "orange"}}*. Here's the final result:

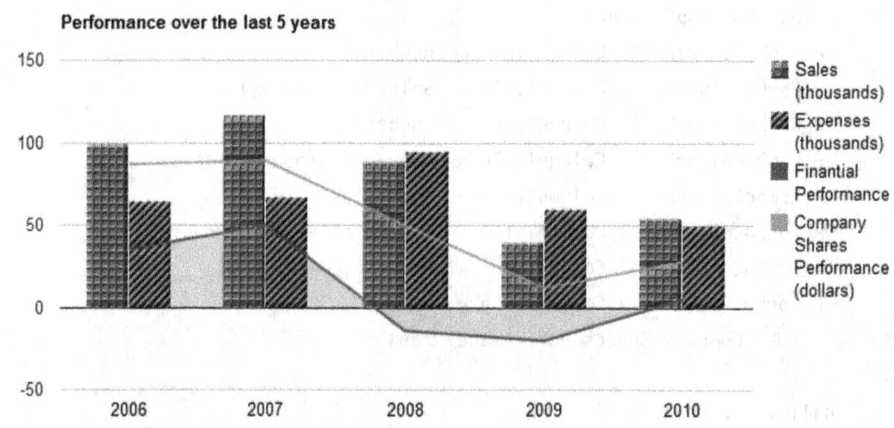

Figure 8.16: TSTGENCMB1 produces this combo chart.

TSTGENCMB2 presents the same information, but using a different combination of chart types and options, as shown in Figure 8.17.

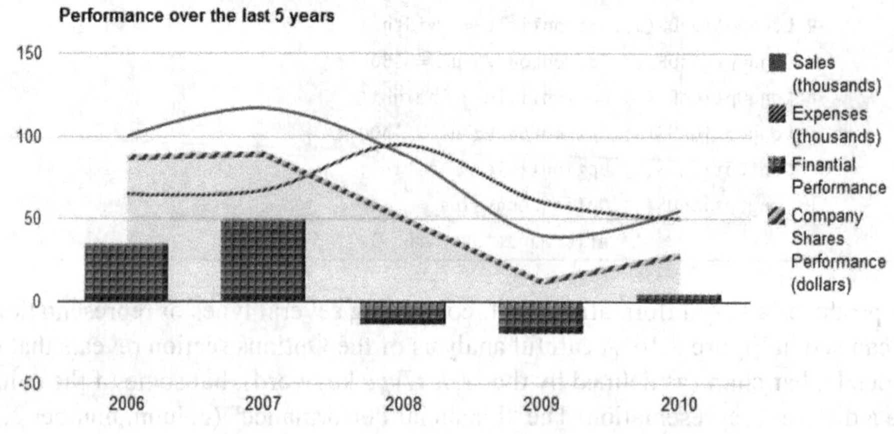

Figure 8.17: Here is the final product of TSTGENCMB2.

In these sample programs, I'm combining the three possible chart types and adding some additional keywords and attributes to embellish the final result. There are numerous possibilities, although not all of them produce good results. My advice is to experiment in the Visualization Playground (*http://code.google.com/apis/ajax/playground/?type=visualization#combo_chart*) before using the attributes in your programs.

The "Bars of Stuff" and "Piles of Money" Charts

After so many pages about serious charts, it's time to have a little fun. Let's start with "bars of stuff." This is basically a bar chart in which the bars are replaced with a cartoon-like object. The image choices include a train (default), chocolate, a rope, a truffle, a worm, and a horse. From a technical point of view, this is a very simple chart: it supports two columns, *label* and *value*, and multiple rows. There's a little trick on the rows, though: instead of showing only the title of the row next to the bar, you can also include a string, defined by you.

Here's the sample code from the API's documentation (*http://visapi-gadgets.googlecode.com/svn/trunk/barsofstuff/doc.html*):

```
<html>
<head>
<link rel="stylesheet" type="text/css" href="http://visapi-gadgets.googlecode.com/
svn/trunk/barsofstuff/bos.css"/>
<script type="text/javascript" src="http://visapi-gadgets.googlecode.com/
svn/trunk/barsofstuff/bos.js"></script>
<script type="text/javascript" src="http://www.google.com/jsapi"></script>
</head>
<body>
<div id="chartdiv" style="width: 500px"></div>
<script type="text/javascript">
      google.load("visualization", "1");
      google.setOnLoadCallback(drawChart);
      var chart;
      function drawChart() {
        var data = new google.visualization.DataTable();
        data.addColumn('string', 'Label');
```

Continued

```
        data.addColumn('number', 'Value');
        data.addRows(4);
        data.setCell(0, 0, 'France');
        data.setCell(1, 0, 'Sweden');
        data.setCell(2, 0, 'USA');
        data.setCell(3, 0, 'Poland');
        data.setCell(0, 1, 10000, '10,000');
        data.setCell(1, 1, 30000, '30,000');
        data.setCell(2, 1, 20000, '20,000');
        data.setCell(3, 1, 7500, '7,500');
        var chartDiv = document.getElementById('chartdiv');
        var options = {title: 'Commuters By Country'};
        chart = new BarsOfStuff(chartDiv);
        chart.draw(data, options);
        //google.visualization.events.addListener(chart, 'select', handleSelect);
    }
</script>
</body>
</html>
```

This is not exactly like the previously shown charts, because it's not a "Google brewed" chart. It's actually a third-party API that conforms to the standards of the Google Chart API. The main differences are bolded. This code produces the chart in Figure 8.18.

Figure 8.18: This example (from the API's documentation page) uses trains to show commuters by country.

The template was easy enough to build. I took one of the existing templates and changed it a bit, to match the sample. Let's have a quick look at it:

```
/$Header
<html>
<head>
   <link rel="stylesheet" type="text/css" href="http://visapi-gadgets.googlecode.com/
svn/trunk/barsofstuff/bos.css"/>
   <title>
     /%PageTitle%/
   </title>
   <script type="text/javascript" src="http://visapi-gadgets.googlecode.com/
svn/trunk/barsofstuff/bos.js"></script>
   <script type="text/javascript" src="http://www.google.com/jsapi"></script>
   <script type="text/javascript">
     google.load("visualization", "1");
   </script>
   <script type="text/javascript">
     function drawChart() {
       var data = new google.visualization.DataTable();
       data.addRows(/%TotalRows%/);
       data.addColumn('string', 'Label');
       data.addColumn('number', 'Value');
/$Row
       data.setCell(/%RowNbr%/, 0, '/%RowTitle%/');
       data.setCell(/%RowNbr%/, 1, /%RowValue%/, '/%RowValueLabel%/');
/$OptionsBegin

     var options = {
/$Option
     '/%OptionTitle%/': /%OptionValue%/
/$OptionsEnd
              };


/$Footer
       var chartDiv = document.getElementById('chartdiv');
```

Continued

```
      var chart = new BarsOfStuff(chartDiv);
      chart.draw(data, options);
    }

    google.setOnLoadCallback(drawChart);
  </script>
</head>
<body>
  <div id="chartdiv"></div>
</body>
</html>
```

The only new thing in this template is the *RowValueLabel* variable, which will store the text that shows under the row title; that's the "10,000" under "France" in the first row of Figure 8.18. There's no Column section, and the Row section is a hybrid between the FirstRow and Row sections of previously presented templates. This was possible because the "bars of stuff" chart supports only one value per row.

The procedure that implements this template is called *GenBOSChart*. It's very similar to the ones you've seen for other chart types; the only difference is the handling of the aforementioned *RowValueLabel* variable, which happens in the Row section:

```
// Row Section
For W_Idx = 1 to C_BOSMaxRows;
  If P_BOSRowDS(W_Idx).RowTitle = *Blanks;
    Leave;
  EndIf;
// Update the Row variables
updHtmlVar('RowNbr'    : %Char(W_Idx-1));
updHtmlVar('RowTitle'  : %Trim(P_BOSRowDS(W_Idx).RowTitle));
updHtmlVar('RowValue'  : %Char(P_BOSRowDS(W_Idx).RowValue));
updHtmlVar('RowValueLabel' :
           %Trim(P_BOSRowDS(W_Idx).RowValueLabel));
// Write the Row section
WrtSection('Row');
EndFor;
```

The sample program *TSTGENBOS1* (boringly similar to the previous examples, so I won't reproduce it here) produces the chart shown in Figure 8.19.

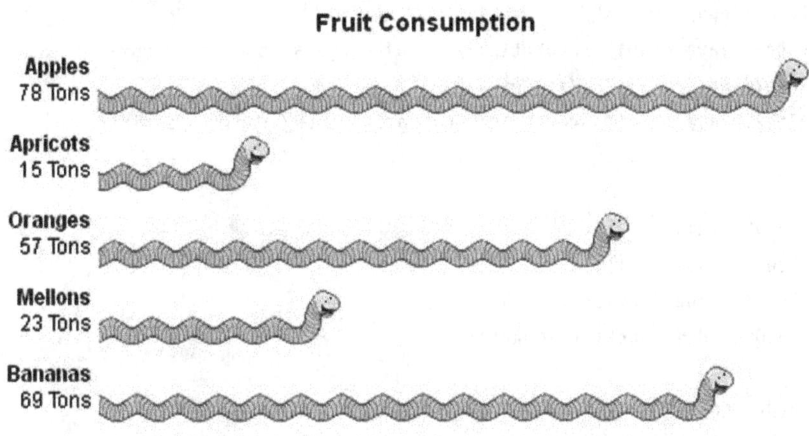

Figure 8.19: Who said a bug was a bad thing?

If you take a look at the source code, you'll find the by-now-familiar filling of the procedure arrays (*P_BOSRowDS* and *P_OptionDS*, in this case), followed by the invocation of the procedure and the showing of the HTML page it generated.

I'd like to take a moment to explain the most important option of this chart: the *type* keyword. This is the way to indicate which object you want to use instead of the traditional bar. In this example, I'm using the *worm* attribute to produce the cute green bugs you see in Figure 8.19. Read the Bars of Stuff API documentation (*http://visapi-gadgets.googlecode.com/svn/trunk/barsofstuff/doc.html*) to find out what else you can customize on this chart. Now it's up to you to choose where and when to use this less serious and more smile-inducing chart type!

The second part of this section focuses on the "piles of money" chart type. As usual, let's start by having a quick look at the sample provided:

```
<html>
<head>
<link rel="stylesheet" type="text/css" href="http://visapi-gadgets.googlecode.com/
svn/trunk/pilesofmoney/pom.css"/>
<script type="text/javascript" src="http://visapi-gadgets.googlecode.com/
svn/trunk/pilesofmoney/pom.js"></script>
<script type="text/javascript" src="http://www.google.com/jsapi"></script>
</head>
<body>
<div id="chartdiv"></div>
<script type="text/javascript">
      google.load("visualization", "1");
      google.setOnLoadCallback(drawChart);
      var chart;
      function drawChart() {
        var data = new google.visualization.DataTable();
        data.addColumn('string', 'Label');
        data.addColumn('number', 'Value');
        data.addRows(4);
        data.setCell(0, 0, 'France');
        data.setCell(1, 0, 'Germany');
        data.setCell(2, 0, 'USA');
        data.setCell(3, 0, 'Poland');
        data.setCell(0, 1, 10, '$10,000');
        data.setCell(1, 1, 30, '$30,000');
        data.setCell(2, 1, 20, '$20,000');
        data.setCell(3, 1, 7.5, '$7,500');
        var chartDiv = document.getElementById('chartdiv');
        var options = {title: 'Reveneues By Country'};
        chart = new PilesOfMoney(chartDiv);
        chart.draw(data, options);
        //google.visualization.events.addListener(chart, 'select', handleSelect);
      }
</script>
</body>
</html>
```

It's very similar to the "bars of stuff." Again, the main differences from Google's original charts are bolded. With this, I've built the template show below:

```
/$Header
<html>
<head>
   <link rel="stylesheet" type="text/css" href="http://visapi-gadgets.googlecode.com/
svn/trunk/pilesofmoney/pom.css"/>
   <title>
     /%PageTitle%/
   </title>
   <script type="text/javascript" src="http://visapi-gadgets.googlecode.com/
svn/trunk/pilesofmoney/pom.js"></script>
   <script type="text/javascript" src="http://www.google.com/jsapi"></script>
   <script type="text/javascript">
     google.load("visualization", "1");
   </script>
   <script type="text/javascript">
     function drawChart() {
       var data = new google.visualization.DataTable();
       data.addRows(/%TotalRows%/);
       data.addColumn('string', 'Label');
       data.addColumn('number', 'Value');
/$Row
       data.setCell(/%RowNbr%/, 0, '/%RowTitle%/');
       data.setCell(/%RowNbr%/, 1, /%RowValue%/, '/%RowValueLabel%/');
/$OptionsBegin

     var options = {
/$Option
     '/%OptionTitle%/': /%OptionValue%/
/$OptionsEnd
                 };

/$Footer
       var chartDiv = document.getElementById('chartdiv');
```

Continued

```
        var chart = new PilesOfMoney(chartDiv);
        chart.draw(data, options);
      }

      google.setOnLoadCallback(drawChart);
    </script>
  </head>
  <body>
    <div id="chartdiv"></div>
  </body>
</html>
```

As you can see, the structure of the "piles of money" chart is an almost exact copy of the "bars of stuff," with some changes in the Header and Footer sections. This led to the creation of a procedure similar to *GenBOSChart*, named *GenPOMChart*. All I've written about *GenBOSChart* directly applies to this new procedure. The result, however, is very different.

Figure 8.20 is the chart produced by the sample program *TSTGENPOM1*. You can display one of two currencies here. The sample program uses U.S. dollars, which is the chart's default, but you can also use euros. Be sure to read this API's documentation (*http://visapi-gadgets.googlecode.com/svn/trunk/pilesofmoney/doc.html*), because there are a few more options to customize.

Figure 8.20: That's a lot of money!

You won't find samples for these charts on Google's Code Playground, but you can still test them there. Here's how to do it: go to the chart's documentation page and copy the sample you'll find there. Next, go to the Code Playground (*http://code.google.com/apis/ajax/playground/?type=visualization*), choose any chart type, click the "Edit HTML" button, and delete all the code. Paste the sample code in the code window of the Playground. If everything appears on a single line, delete it and paste it in Notepad; then, select everything from Notepad and copy it again. Paste it in the code window, and *voilá!*

The Table API and Chart Interactions

Usually, a well-chosen and properly formatted chart is all it takes to get your message across. There are times, however, when you also want to include the original data. You'd do this to provide the level of detail that some charts lack (the intensity map a few pages back, for instance). This can be achieved by using two APIs simultaneously; you'll need to add the Table API (*http://code.google.com/apis/chart/interactive/docs/gallery/table.html*) to whichever chart you want to show. In this section, I'll use the Combo API side by side with the Table API to achieve the results in Figure 8.21.

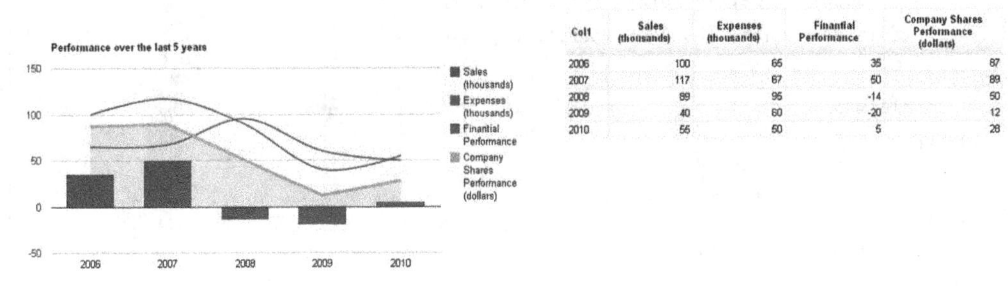

Col1	Sales (thousands)	Expenses (thousands)	Finantial Performance	Company Shares Performance (dollars)
2006	100	65	35	87
2007	117	67	50	89
2008	89	96	-14	50
2009	40	60	-20	12
2010	55	50	5	28

Figure 8.21: This chart and table combination is produced by the TSTGENCPT2 sample program.

I'll also explain step by step how you can customize the existing templates and procedures from previous sections to achieve this effect. Let's start with Google's example:

```
<html>
  <head>
    <scripttype='text/javascript'src='https://www.google.com/jsapi'></script>
    <scripttype='text/javascript'>
      google.load('visualization','1',{packages:['table']});
      google.setOnLoadCallback(drawTable);
      function drawTable(){
        var data =new google.visualization.DataTable();
        data.addColumn('string','Name');
        data.addColumn('number','Salary');
        data.addColumn('boolean','Full Time Employee');
        data.addRows([
          ['Mike',  {v:10000, f:'$10,000'}, true],
          ['Jim',   {v:8000,  f:'$8,000'},  false],
          ['Alice', {v:12500, f:'$12,500'}, true],
          ['Bob',   {v:7000,  f:'$7,000'},  true]
        ]);

        var table =new google.visualization.Table(
            document.getElementById('table_div'));
        table.draw(data,{showRowNumber:true});
      }
    </script>
  </head>

  <body>
    <divid='table_div'></div>
  </body>
</html>
```

This piece of code shows a simple table with the salaries of four employees. By itself, it's really nothing special. It becomes interesting when combined with a graphical representation of the data by its side. The Combo Chart API should be fresh in your mind from a previous section. Let's analyze a modified combo template, *ComboTbl.tmpl*, with a table next to it:

```
/$Header1
<!DOCTYPE html PUBLIC "-//W3C//DTD XHTML 1.0 Strict//EN" "http://www.w3.org/TR/
xhtml1/DTD/xhtml1-strict.dtd">
<html xmlns="http://www.w3.org/1999/xhtml">
<head>
   <meta http-equiv="content-type" content="text/html; charset=utf-8"/>
   <title>
     /%PageTitle%/
   </title>
   <script type="text/javascript" src="http://www.google.com/jsapi"></script>
   <script type="text/javascript">
     google.load('visualization', '1', {packages: ['corechart']});
   </script>
/$TableHeader
   <script type="text/javascript">
     google.load('visualization', '1', {packages: ['table']});
   </script>
/$Header2
   <script type="text/javascript">
     function drawVisualization() {
       // Create and populate the data table.
       var data = new google.visualization.DataTable();
       data.addRows(/%TotalRows%/);
       data.addColumn('string', 'Col1');
/$Column
       data.addColumn('number', '/%ColumnTitle%/');
/$FirstRow
       data.setValue(/%RowNbr%/, 0, '/%RowTitle%/');
/$Row
       data.setValue(/%RowNbr%/, /%ColNbr%/, /%CellValue%/);
/$OptionsBegin

     var options = {
/$Option
     '/%OptionTitle%/': /%OptionLongValue%/
/$OptionsEnd
                 };
```

Continued

```
/$ChartDraw
        // Create and draw the visualization.
        var chart = new google.visualization.ComboChart(
            document.getElementById('chart_div'));
        chart.draw(data, options);
/$TableDraw
       // Then the Table
        var table = new google.visualization.Table(
            document.getElementById('table_div'));
        table.draw(data, null);
        // Link the chart and table together to allow interaction
        google.visualization.events.addListener(chart, 'select',
        function() { table.setSelection(chart.getSelection()); });
        google.visualization.events.addListener(table, 'select',
        function() { chart.setSelection(table.getSelection()); });
/$Footer1
      }

      google.setOnLoadCallback(drawVisualization);
    </script>
</head>
<body style="font-family: Arial;border: 0 none;">
    <table>
      <tr valign="top">
        <td><div id="chart_div" style="width:/%ChartWidth%/px"></div></td>
/$TableFooter
        <td width="30"></td>
        <td><div id="table_div" style="width:/%TableWidth%/px"></div></td>
/$Footer2
      </tr>
    </table>
</body>
</html>
```

I used the *Combo.tmpl* template as a starting point and changed it a bit to include the call to the Table API. I wanted this new template to replace the old one, even if you don't want to show a table. To make that possible, all the table-related code was segregated into separate sections. Let's go over them one by one.

The Header section was split in two to accommodate a new section named TableHeader. This new section is used to load the table package; think of it as a prototype declaration in RPG:

```
/$TableHeader
  <script type="text/javascript">
    google.load('visualization', '1', {packages: ['table']});
  </script>
```

The rest of the Header was moved to Header2:

```
/$Header2
  <script type="text/javascript">
    function drawVisualization() {
      // Create and populate the data table.
      var data = new google.visualization.DataTable();
      data.addRows(/%TotalRows%/);
      data.addColumn('string', 'Col1');
```

Everything between the Column and OptionsEnd sections remained untouched. The Footer section, however, had to be totally redesigned. To understand why, you need to understand how the link between the chart API and the HTML page works.

The chart needs to be shown somewhere, right? Well, Google indicates that a *<div>* HTML section should support the display of an API invocation result. In this case, I have two APIs (a chart and a table), which means I need two *<div>* sections. Because I want to show the chart and table side by side, I need to control the formatting of the HTML. The best way to do this is by using an HTML *<table>* section. In my template, this translates into the ChartDraw, TableDraw, Footer1, TableFooter, and Footer2 sections. ChartDraw invokes the chart API (the ComboChart, in this case) and links it to the HTML *<div>* section named *'chart_div':*

```
/$ChartDraw
      // Create and draw the visualization.
      var chart = new google.visualization.ComboChart(
          document.getElementById('chart_div'));
      chart.draw(data, options);
```

The next section is TableDraw, which does a nice little trick. This section creates the table and indicates that the HTML *<div>* section named *'table_div'* will support the table display. More importantly, it creates a link between the table and the chart, bringing some additional interactivity to the final HTML file. This link is achieved with the following bolded lines of code:

```
/$TableDraw
      // Then the Table
       var table = new google.visualization.Table(
           document.getElementById('table_div'));
       table.draw(data, null);
       // Link the chart and table together to allow interaction
       google.visualization.events.addListener(chart, 'select',
       function() { table.setSelection(chart.getSelection()); });
       google.visualization.events.addListener(table, 'select',
       function() { chart.setSelection(table.getSelection()); });
```

Basically, I'm telling the browser to "listen" for a click on a point of the chart and, when that happens, to act as if the corresponding row of data on the table had been clicked, and vice versa. (If that's not clear, run the sample programs and try it yourself.)

The Footer1 section tells the browser to call the *drawVisualization* function. This function holds all the JavaScript code required to draw the charts. It then builds the first part of the *<table>* HTML section:

```
/$Footer1
     }

     google.setOnLoadCallback(drawVisualization);
   </script>
</head>
<body style="font-family: Arial;border: 0 none;">
   <table>
     <tr valign="top">
       <td><div id="chart_div" style="width:/%ChartWidth%/px"></div></td>
```

Then, the TableFooter section handles the *<div>* HTML section that's used by the Table API:

```
/$TableFooter
        <td width="30"></td>
        <td><div id="table_div" style="width:/%TableWidth%/px"></div></td>
```

Finally, the Footer2 section simply closes the open HTML tags:

```
/$Footer2
      </tr>
    </table>
</body>
</html>
```

Naturally, a new template requires a new procedure. I've created *GenComboTblChart* based on *GenComboChart* and added a few new entry parameters to allow you to decide whether the table should be displayed or not (the *P_ShowTable* parameter) and to choose the width of the chart and the table (the *P_ChartWidth* and *P_TableWidth* parameters):

```
 *-------------------------------------------------------------------------*
 *   Generate Combo + Table Chart                                          *
 *-------------------------------------------------------------------------*
P GenComboTblChart...
P                  B                   EXPORT
D                  PI                N
 * Input Parms
DP_PageTitle                           Like(t_PageTitle)  Value
DP_ComboColumnDS...
D                                      LikeDS(ComboColumnDS)
D                                      Dim(C_ComboMaxColumns) Value
DP_ComboRowDS                          LikeDS(ComboRowDS)
D                                      Dim(C_ComboMaxRows) Value
DP_LongOptionDS                        LikeDS(LongOptionDS)
D                                      Dim(C_MaxOptions) Value
```

Continued

```
DP_ShowTable                              Like(t_YesNo)     Value
DP_ChartWidth                             Like(t_Width)     Value
DP_TableWidth                             Like(t_Width)     Value
DP_FileName                               Like(t_FileName) Value
 * Output Parms
DP_ErrorDesc                              Like(t_ErrorDesc)
```

The *Init* routine does the usual parameter checks, and the *Proc* routine handles the writing of the Table*xxx* sections according to the value of the *P_ShowTable* parameter. If it contains a *Y* then the sections will be written in the output HTML file, as shown in the bolded lines:

```
//-------------------------------------------------------------------*
// Process input parms and generate the proper xml file             *
//-------------------------------------------------------------------*
  BegSr  Proc;


   SetNoDebug(*OFF);
   getHtmlIfsMult(C_ComboTblTmpl);

   // Header1 Section
   // Update the Header1 variables
   updHtmlVar('PageTitle' : %Trim(P_PageTitle));
   // Write the Header1 section
   WrtSection('Header1');

   // TableHeader Section
   // The Table sections are only written if P_ShowTable = 'Y'
   If P_ShowTable = 'Y';
      WrtSection('TableHeader');
   EndIf;

   // Header2 Section
   // Update the Header2 variables
   updHtmlVar('PageTitle' : %Trim(P_PageTitle));
```

Continued

```
// Find out how many rows have data
For W_RowIdx = 1 to C_ComboMaxRows;
  If P_ComboRowDS(W_RowIdx).RowTitle = *Blanks;
    Leave;
  Else;
    // If this was not the last row containing data, keep the row number
    W_TotalRows = W_RowIdx;
  EndIf;
EndFor;
// Update the TotalRows variable
updHtmlVar('TotalRows' : %Char(W_TotalRows));
// Write the Header2 section
WrtSection('Header2');

// Column Section
For W_ColIdx = 1 to C_ComboMaxColumns;
  If P_ComboColumnDS(W_ColIdx).ColumnTitle = *Blanks;
    Leave;
  EndIf;
  updHtmlVar('ColumnTitle' :
             %Trim(P_ComboColumnDS(W_ColIdx).ColumnTitle));
  // Write the Column section
  WrtSection('Column');
EndFor;

// FirstRow And Row Sections
For W_RowIdx = 1 to C_ComboMaxRows;
  If P_ComboRowDS(W_RowIdx).RowTitle = *Blanks;
    Leave;
  EndIf;
  // Update the Row variables
  updHtmlVar('RowNbr'   : %Char(W_RowIdx-1));
  updHtmlVar('RowTitle' :
             %Trim(P_ComboRowDS(W_RowIdx).RowTitle));
  // Write the FirstRow section
  WrtSection('FirstRow');
```

Continued

```
    For W_ColIdx = 1 to C_ComboMaxColumns;
      If P_ComboRowDS(W_RowIdx).Cell(W_ColIdx).CellValue= *Zeros;
        Leave;
      EndIf;
      updHtmlVar('ColNbr' : %Char(W_ColIdx));
      updHtmlVar('CellValue' :
            %Char(P_ComboRowDS(W_RowIdx).Cell(W_ColIdx).CellValue));
      // Write the Row section
      WrtSection('Row');
    EndFor;
  EndFor;

  // Options Section
  // Define the Options variable
    WrtSection('OptionsBegin');
  // Write each option on a separate line
  For W_Idx = 1 to C_MaxOptions;
    If P_LongOptionDS(W_Idx).OptionTitle = *Blanks;
      Leave;
    EndIf;
    // Update the Option variables
    updHtmlVar('OptionTitle' :
              %Trim(P_LongOptionDS(W_Idx).OptionTitle));
    // If this is not the last option of the array and the next
    // option was filled in, add a comma after the value
    If (((W_Idx + 1) < C_MaxOptions) And
        (P_LongOptionDs(W_Idx + 1).OptionTitle <> *Blanks));
      P_LongOptionDS(W_Idx).OptionLongValue =
       %Trim(P_LongOptionDS(W_Idx).OptionLongValue) + ',';
    EndIf;
    updHtmlVar('OptionLongValue' :
              %Trim(P_LongOptionDS(W_Idx).OptionLongValue));
    // Write the Option section
    WrtSection('Option');
  EndFor;
```

Continued

```
// Close the Options definition
  WrtSection('OptionsEnd');

// ChartDraw Section
// There are no variables in this section, just write it
WrtSection('ChartDraw');

// TableDraw Section
// The Table sections are only written if P_ShowTable = 'Y'
If P_ShowTable = 'Y';
   WrtSection('TableDraw');
EndIf;

// Footer1 Section
// Update the Footer1 section variables
updHtmlVar('ChartWidth' : %Char(P_ChartWidth));
// Write the Footer1 section
WrtSection('Footer1');

// TableFooter Section
// The Table sections are only written if P_ShowTable = 'Y'
If P_ShowTable = 'Y';
   updHtmlVar('TableWidth' : %Char(P_TableWidth));
   WrtSection('TableFooter');
EndIf;

// Footer2 Section
// There are no variables in this section, just write it
WrtSection('Footer2');

// Set the appropriate file name and path
W_FileName = %Trim(C_OutputPath) + '/' + %Trim(P_FileName);

// Write the html file to disk
WrtHtmlToStmf(%Trim(W_FileName): 819);

EndSr;
```

In short, if you set *P_ShowTable* parameter to *N*, you still get a combo chart, just like before. This translates into the writing of the following sections of the template:

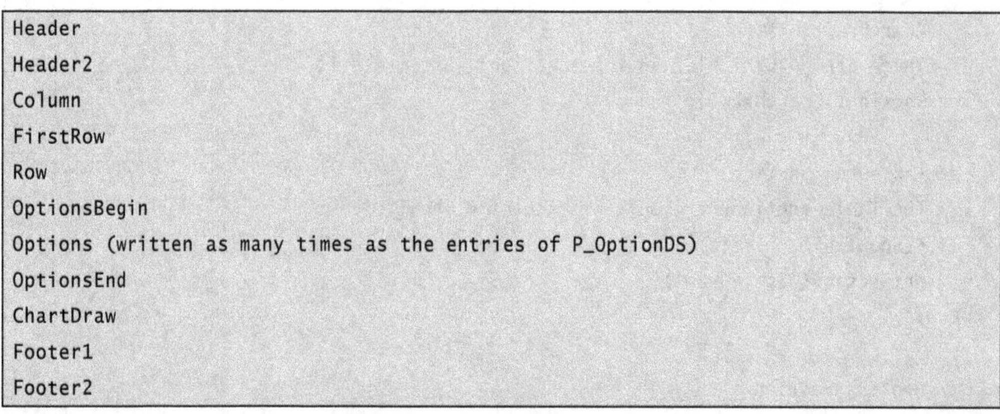

```
Header
Header2
Column
FirstRow
Row
OptionsBegin
Options (written as many times as the entries of P_OptionDS)
OptionsEnd
ChartDraw
Footer1
Footer2
```

If the parameter is set to *Y* instead, then a few more sections are written (bolded for your convenience):

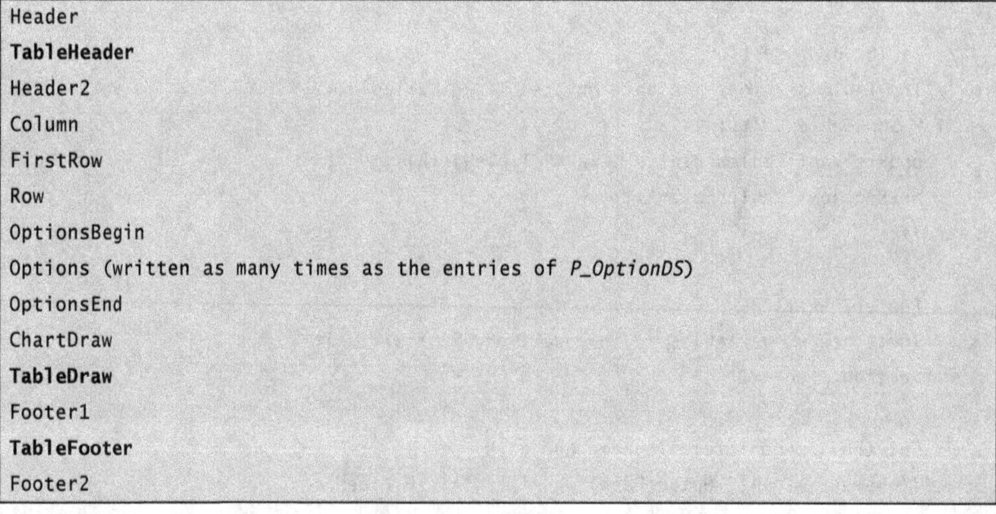

```
Header
TableHeader
Header2
Column
FirstRow
Row
OptionsBegin
Options (written as many times as the entries of P_OptionDS)
OptionsEnd
ChartDraw
TableDraw
Footer1
TableFooter
Footer2
```

Well, what does this tells us? If you want to complement any other chart presented on this chapter with a table by its side, all you have to do is the following:

- Split the Header section into two.
- In between the split Header, create the TableHeader section. If you haven't changed the names of the variables in the JavaScript code, you can actually copy and paste the TableHeader section presented here.
- Redesign the Footer section. Start by adapting the ChartDraw section shown here to the chart you're working on. For instance, if you're including a table on the bar chart template, just replace this:

```
var chart = new google.visualization.ComboChart(document.getElementById('chart_div'));
```

with this:

```
var chart = new google.visualization.BarChart(document.getElementById('chart_div'));
```

- Include the TableDraw section. Again, it should be a straight copy and paste from the one presented here, just like the TableHeader section.
- Copy Footer1 and Footer2 from here, or adapt it to include the HTML *<table>* required to display the chart and the table side by side.

Regarding the RPG code, I hope that analyzing the changes made to the *Proc* routine carefully is enough for you to adapt the other procedures the same way I've changed the Combo Chart procedure. Finally, new sample programs were also created. They were based on the sample programs in the "Combo Chart" section of this chapter. The only differences are the name of the procedure that is called and the three new parameters, so it makes no sense to include them here.

Just a note of caution: don't use the *width* keyword on the *options* parameter (*P_OptionDS*) or, if you do, be sure to use the same value on *P_ChartWidth*. It's a bit hard to explain the possible effects. If you're curious, just change the *TSTGENCPT1* or *TSTGENCPT2* sample programs, and see for yourself!

The Tree Map Chart

This chapter has covered a wide range of charts, from the simplest (bar and line charts) to the most complex (such as the geo chart), with some exotic ones (like "piles of money") in between. It's now time to discuss the tree map chart, a unique way of representing huge quantities of data in a condensed and structured way.

A tree map is, according to Wikipedia at *http://en.wikipedia.org/wiki/Treemapping*, a way to display hierarchical (tree-structured) data as a set of nested rectangles:

> *Each branch of the tree is given a rectangle, which is then tiled with smaller rectangles representing sub-branches. A leaf node's rectangle has an area proportional to a specified dimension on the data. Often, the leaf nodes are colored to show a separate dimension of the data.*
>
> *When the color and size dimensions are correlated in some way with the tree structure, one can often easily see patterns that would be difficult to spot in other ways, such as if a certain color is particularly relevant. A second advantage of tree maps is that, by construction, they make efficient use of space. As a result, they can legibly display thousands of items on the screen simultaneously.*

Google's TreeMap API is quite simple. Let's have a quick look at the sample provided in the API's documentation:

```
<head>
  <scripttype="text/javascript"src="https://www.google.com/jsapi"></script>
  <scripttype="text/javascript">
    google.load("visualization","1",{packages:["treemap"]});
    google.setOnLoadCallback(drawChart);
    function drawChart(){
      // Create and populate the data table.
      var data = google.visualization.arrayToDataTable([
        ['Location','Parent','Market trade volume (size)',
         'Market increase/decrease (color)'],
        ['Global',     null,                0,                 0],
        ['America',   'Global',             0,                 0],
        ['Europe',    'Global',             0,                 0],
        ['Asia',      'Global',             0,                 0],
        ['Australia', 'Global',             0,                 0],
        ['Africa',    'Global',             0,                 0],
        ['Brazil',    'America',           11,                10],
        ['USA',       'America',           52,                31],
                                                       Continued
```

```
      ['Mexico',    'America',            24,                         12],
      ['Canada',    'America',            16,                        -23],
      ['France',    'Europe',             42,                        -11],
      ['Germany',   'Europe',             31,                         -2],
      ['Sweden',    'Europe',             22,                        -13],
      ['Italy',     'Europe',             17,                          4],
      ['UK',        'Europe',             21,                         -5],
      ['China',     'Asia',               36,                          4],
      ['Japan',     'Asia',               20,                        -12],
      ['India',     'Asia',               40,                         63],
      ['Laos',      'Asia',               4,                          34],
      ['Mongolia',  'Asia',               1,                          -5],
      ['Israel',    'Asia',               12,                         24],
      ['Iran',      'Asia',               18,                         13],
      ['Pakistan',  'Asia',               11,                        -52],
      ['Egypt',     'Africa',             21,                          0],
      ['S. Africa', 'Africa',             30,                         43],
      ['Sudan',     'Africa',             12,                          2],
      ['Congo',     'Africa',             10,                         12],
      ['Zaire',     'Africa',             8,                          10]
    ]);

    // Create and draw the visualization.
    var tree =new google.visualization.TreeMap(
        document.getElementById('chart_div'));
    tree.draw(data,{
      minColor:'#f00',
      midColor:'#ddd',
      maxColor:'#0d0',
      headerHeight:15,
      fontColor:'black',
      showScale:true});
    }
  </script>
</head>
```

Continued

```
  <body>
    <divid="chart_div"style="width:900px;height:500px;"></div>
  </body>
</html>
```

You provide a data set with three or four columns and as many rows as you want, and it will generate a nice-looking tree map. You can customize it quite extensively via the Options section. The number of columns is related to the data dimensions the tree map is able to represent. The third column determines the area of the node's rectangle, while the fourth (if specified) determines its color. (I'll explain the columns' format in greater detail later.)

Figure 8.22 shows a tree map with two layers, although only the top layer is visible. The top row of the data table is presented as the first layer (or level) of the chart. When the user clicks on one of the rectangles that form the layer, the corresponding sub-layer is then displayed. On the example produced by the program *TSTTREMAP1*, clicking on the "America" rectangle drills down into the "America" sub-layer, showing rectangles for USA, Mexico, Canada, and Brazil. Right-clicking any of the rectangles takes the user back to the previous level ("Global" in this example). We're using only two levels, but you can add as many as you want.

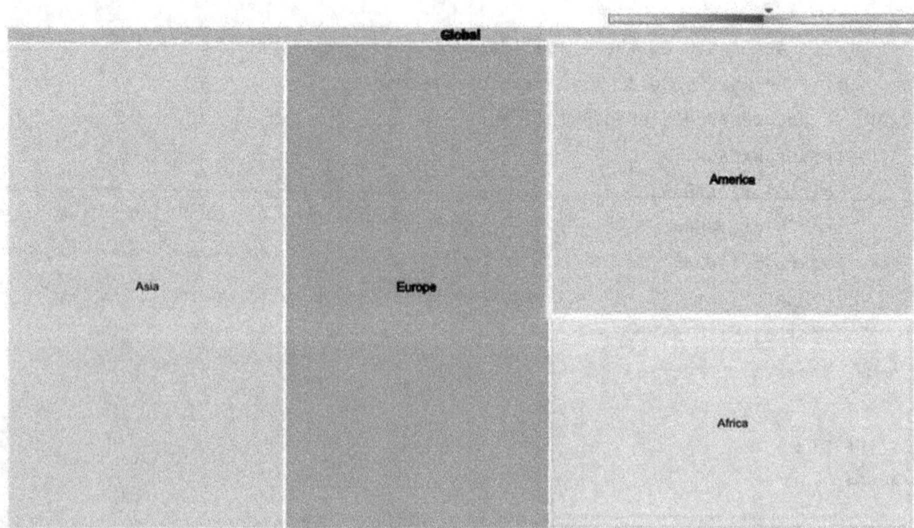

Figure 8.22: This tree map chart has two levels, produced by the sample code.

To implement this API, I've created the usual structure: a function (*GenTreeMapChart*) to which you pass a set of parameters that include the data table and the chart's options. This function will then merge your parameters with a template (*TreeMap.Tmpl*, shown below) to create an HTML file that will be rendered by Google's Tree Map API into an interactive tree map:

```
/$Header
<!DOCTYPE html PUBLIC "-//W3C//DTD XHTML 1.0 Strict//EN" "http://www.w3.org/TR/
xhtml1/DTD/xhtml1-strict.dtd">
<html xmlns="http://www.w3.org/1999/xhtml">
<head>
  <meta http-equiv="content-type" content="text/html; charset=utf-8"/>
  <title>
    /%PageTitle%/
  </title>
  <script type="text/javascript" src="http://www.google.com/jsapi"></script>
  <script type="text/javascript">
    google.load('visualization', '1', {packages: ['treemap']});
  </script>
  <script type="text/javascript">
    function drawChart() {
      // Create and populate the data table.
      var data = new google.visualization.DataTable();
/$Columns
      data.addColumn('string', "/%ColumnTitle1%/");
      data.addColumn('string', "/%ColumnTitle2%/");
      data.addColumn('number', "/%ColumnTitle3%/");
      data.addColumn('number', "/%ColumnTitle4%/");
      data.addRows(/%TotalRows%/);

/$Row
      data.setValue(/%RowNbr%/, 0, "/%CellValue1%/");
      data.setValue(/%RowNbr%/, 1, /%CellValue2%/);
      data.setValue(/%RowNbr%/, 2, /%CellValue3%/);
      data.setValue(/%RowNbr%/, 3, /%CellValue4%/);
```

Continued

```
/$OptionsBegin
         var options = {
/$Option
                        '/%OptionTitle%/': /%OptionLongValue%/
/$OptionsEnd
                        };


/$Footer
       // Create and draw the visualization.
       var chart = new google.visualization.TreeMap(
           document.getElementById('chart_div'));
       chart.draw(data, options);
     }


     google.setOnLoadCallback(drawChart);
   </script>
</head>
<body style="font-family: Arial;border: 0 none;">
   <div id="chart_div" style="width: /%Width%/px; height: /%Height%/px;"></div>
</body>
</html>
```

The template is somewhat similar to the combo chart template. Here, however, there are four columns (two alphanumeric and two numeric), which means the rows will have four cells. This allows you to simultaneously present two values for each row on your data table, or, in other words, two dimensions of your data.

Sound familiar? It should; the first dimension will determine the size of the rectangle, and the second, if specified, will determine the color of the rectangle, as mentioned earlier. Each row describes one node (a rectangle in the graph). Each node (except the root node) has one or more parent nodes. Each node is sized and colored according to its values relative to the other nodes currently shown.

The remainder of the template is very similar to those previously presented, with the usual Header, Options, and Footer sections.

As I've mentioned before, the API expects the data table to have up to four columns (the fourth is optional). These columns should have the following format:

- Column 0 (string)—An ID for this node. This can be any valid JavaScript string, including spaces, and any length that a string can hold. This value is displayed as the node header.
- Column 1 (string)—The ID of the parent node. If this is a root node, leave this blank. Only one root is allowed per tree map.
- Column 2 (number)—The size of the node. Any positive value is allowed. This value determines the size of the node, computed relative to all other nodes currently shown. This value is ignored for non-leaf nodes. (It's actually calculated from the size of all its children.)
- Column 3 (optional, number)—An optional value used to calculate a color for this node. Any value, positive or negative, is allowed. The color value is first recomputed on a scale from *minColorValue* to *maxColorValue*, and then the node is assigned a color from the gradient between *minColor* and *maxColor*.

You can find more details about *minColorValue*, *maxColorValue*, *minColor*, and *maxColor* in the API's documentation.

As a side note, if you look at the *TSTTREMAP1* source code, you'll see that the first row has a null value in column two:

```
P_TreeMapRowDS(1).Cell1 = 'Global';
P_TreeMapRowDS(1).Cell2 = 'null';
P_TreeMapRowDS(1).Cell3 = 0;
P_TreeMapRowDS(1).Cell4 = 0;
```

This is the way to indicate the top row of data. Originally, I had the top row as a separate parameter of the function that creates the tree map chart, but I decided to simplify the source code (and the template) by using this solution. Keep in mind that you'll always need a row that represents the top layer of your chart. For clarity, I've used the first row of data, but the API uses the information on columns 0 and 1 to create the tree structure.

Since I've mentioned the *TSTTREMAP1* sample program more than once, let's analyze it briefly. It starts by retrieving your system's name from a data area. Be sure to fill it in, because without it, the chart's HTML file won't be launched at the end of the program. Or, feel free to change it to use the system API from other sample programs to retrieve the system name instead.

The next step is to set up the chart's title, size, and file names by assigning values to the *P_PageTitle*, *P_Width*/*P_Height*, and *P_FileName* parameters, respectively. After that, the program fills the data structures used to hold the chart information itself—first the columns (*P_TreeMapColumnDS*), and then the rows (*P_TreeMapRowDS*), layer by layer.

There's just one step to go: configuring the options. For that, I've used the *P_LongOptionDS* introduced a few sections ago. I won't discuss the options in detail here, but I recommend that you read the respective documentation carefully (*https://developers.google.com/chart/interactive/docs/gallery/treemap#Configuration_Options%20*). Finally, the function that generates the chart is called, and the tree map is displayed on your browser. If it's not, go to the GCHARTS IFS folder and open the file *MarketTreeMap.HTML* in your browser.

Final Thoughts on Google's Chart APIs

Well, it's been a long journey, but it's not quite finished. Google keeps introducing new configuration options into the existing APIs, creating new charts and finding new and exciting ways to show data. In this chapter, I tried to cover the most relevant, but some were naturally left out. I challenge you, dear reader, to invest some time in reading Google's documentation about the charts I haven't mentioned and, based on what you've learned in this chapter, come up with your own functions to create those charts with your data.

There's a quite sizable community of developers working on ways to take these APIs to their limits. You can find it here:

https://groups.google.com/forum/#!forum/google-visualization-api

If you get stuck, there's always someone there to help you. You'll have a ton of fun doing it. I know I did!

9

BLOBs Keep PDF, XLS, and Other Reports Safe in DB2

This chapter explains what a BLOB is and how it can be used to store a binary object (any "PC file," actually) inside a DB2 table. It also provides two procedures to facilitate and automate that task. It ends with a few examples of how to use the procedures.

This chapter tells you all you need to know about the BLOB. No, we're not talking about the 1958 Steve McQueen movie or the Marvel villain. We're going to revisit a fairly old concept, with a new twist: the *Binary Large OBject*. I'll explain how and why you can use it in the context of IBM i-generated PDFs, spreadsheets, and charts.

What's a BLOB and What Can You Use It For?

A BLOB is, basically, a way to store a non-native object in a DB2 database. By non-native object, I mean a file, such as a PDF, a spreadsheet, or a Web page. This can be especially useful when your application generates reports in these (or other) formats and you need to retrieve them quickly, without having to produce the report all over again. In fact, if your report is a "snapshot" of a certain moment (like the end of the month or quarter, for instance), it might be hard to produce the exact same report. If you read the previous two chapters, I'm guessing you are already thinking that you can store the MS Excel files and HTML pages that those chapters describe in a BLOB. That's exactly what I'll show you how to do!

The DB2 implementation of the BLOB concept consists of a kind of column in a database table. I say "kind of" because you cannot actually query this column; if you do, all you'll see is a pointer reference. To access the content, you need to extract it to the IFS. That means that a DB2 table with a single column (the BLOB itself) is not going to be very useful, since you cannot "see" what's inside—you need something more. Additional columns like a record identifier and a description are a good practice, because they'll help you identify the file stored in the BLOB column. Having said that, let's start by creating a table with some information to help us identify what's inside each BLOB:

```
CREATE TABLE RPTARCHIVE/REPORTS
(RPT_ID DECIMAL (7 , 0)
, RPT_TYPE CHAR (10 )
, RPT_TIME TIMESTAMP
, RPT_RMK CHAR (200 )
, RPT_FILE1 BLOB (500K )
, CONSTRAINT PK_RPT_ID UNIQUE (RPT_ID))
```

Rpt_Id is the unique identifier of the stored file. *Rpt_Time* is just a timestamp, which can be used to limit the search for a particular set of records, otherwise unrelated. Imagine, for instance, that you are looking for all the files that were stored in this table around the last end-of-month run, and that set of files has nothing in common except the timestamp. This column can help you limit the search.

Rpt_Type and *Rpt_Rmk* (short for "remark") help you identify the content without having to extract it to the IFS. Finally, I've created the BLOB itself (*Rpt_File1*) at a size of 500K. This is something you need to handle with care, because the BLOB size is not dynamic or dependent on the content size. In other words, each line of this table will occupy a little more than 500K of disk space, regardless of the file size contained within the BLOB. Another detail that might be important for the development management of this table is that it cannot be created with a DDS. Currently, there's no way to create a BLOB-type column using DDS keywords.

Now that we have our "report archive," it's time to store something in it. To do that, you need to use a special data structure, *SQLTYPE(BLOB_FILE)*, which is implicitly composed of the following fields:

- File Name Length (*10u 0*)—The size of the complete file and path name in characters
- Data Length (*10u 0*)—The size of the file (an optional parameter)
- File Option (*10u 0*)—The operation you want to execute (explained later)
- File Name (*255A*)—The complete path and file name

The *Blob_In* sample program stores the PDF file */Reports/Test.PDF* into the *REPORTS* table:

```
D Rpt_ID            S              7  0 Inz(*Zeros)
D Rpt_Type          S             10    Inz(*Blanks)
D Rpt_Rmk           S            255    Inz(*Blanks)

D File_In           s                   SQLTYPE(BLOB_FILE)

 * The SQLTYPE(BLOB_FILE) definition will be converted by the compiler
 * into the following data structure:
D*File_In           DS
D*File_In_NL                      10U 0
D*File_In_DL                      10U 0
D*File_In_FO                      10U 0
D*File_In_NAME                   255A

 // Store an object into the blob table
 /FREE
  Rpt_ID = 1;
  Rpt_Type = 'PDF';
  Rpt_Rmk = 'Just a PDF test report';
  File_In_FO    = SQFRD;
  File_In_NAME = '/Reports/Test.PDF';
  File_In_NL    = %len(%trimr(File_In_NAME));
```

Continued

```
  EXEC SQL   Insert Into RptArchive/Reports
                    Values (:Rpt_ID, :Rpt_Type, NOW(),
                            :Rpt_Rmk , :File_In);

  *InLr = *On;
 /END-FREE
```

Here, I'm passing three pieces of information into the special data structure: the operation to execute (more on that later), the path and name of the IFS file, and the length of that string. Then I'm executing a simple *INSERT* statement. Note that I didn't actually define the *File_In* data structure; I defined a *SQLTYPE(BLOB_File)* field, which the compiler converts into the special data structure. I added the definition to the source code as a comment, so you have an idea of the implicit definition the system is doing. Keep in mind that this BLOB-storing operation doesn't delete the file from the IFS; it just saves a copy of it in the table.

If you run this program and then query the *REPORTS* table, you'll see the newly inserted record. As I mentioned before, you can't actually *see* the file inside the BLOB; you will see a pointer instead. That's why I added the *Rpt_Type* and *Rpt_Rmk* columns to the table.

Now, let's retrieve the file from the archive, with the *BLOB_OUT* sample program:

```
D Rpt_ID          S              7  0 Inz(*Zeros)

D File_Out        s                   SQLTYPE(BLOB_FILE)

 * The SQLTYPE(BLOB_FILE) definition will be converted by the compiler
 * into the following data structure:
D*File_Out       DS
D*File_Out_NL                  10U 0
D*File_Out_DL                  10U 0
D*File_Out_FO                  10U 0
D*File_Out_NAME               255A

 // Retrieve an object from the blob table

                                                          Continued
```

```
/FREE
 Rpt_ID = 1;
 File_Out_FO   = SQFOVR;
 File_Out_NAME = '/Reports/Test_Out.PDF';
 File_Out_NL   = %Len(%TrimR(File_Out_NAME));

 EXEC SQL   Select Rpt_File1
              Into :File_Out
              From RptArchive/Reports
              Where Rpt_Id = :Rpt_Id;


 *InLr = *On;

/END-FREE
```

Again, I'm passing all the relevant information to the special data structure in order to retrieve the file with a *SELECT* statement. Other than the SQL statement used, the big difference between the two programs is the file option (the . . . _*FO* field of the special data structure). In the first program, it was *SQFRD*, which tells the program I'm using the file in "read mode." In the second program, I wanted to write the file to the IFS, overwriting it if it existed. For that, I chose *SQFOVR*. Here's the complete list of file options available:

- *SQFRD*—Open the IFS file for reading only.
- *SQFCRT*—Create the IFS file if it doesn't exist, and open for writing.
- *SQFOVR*—Create the IFS file if it doesn't exist, overwrite it if it does exist, and open for writing.
- *SQFAPP*—Append data to the end of an existing IFS file.

Now That You Know What It Is, Here's How to Use It!

I'll start with the archiving operation. The *BLOB_IN* sample program expects an ID, a file type, a comment and, of course, the file's full name and path in order to store it in a DB2 table (called *REPORTS*, in this case). The *Snd_File_To_Archive* procedure expects the same input parameters, except for the ID, which will be the procedure's output. This way, the calling program doesn't have to generate a unique ID; the procedure takes care of that and returns the ID to the calling program, thus providing a simpler-to-use tool. If the returned ID is zero, it means the operation was not successful. It's a quick and easy way of having some control over the whole process without complicating things. Here's the procedure's complete source code:

```
PSnd_File_To_Archive...
P                 B                   EXPORT
DSnd_File_To_Archive...
D                 PI             7 0
 * Input Parms
D P_FileName                   255A   Value
D P_Type                        10A   Value
D P_Comments                   255A   Value

D W_ID            S              7 0 Inz(*Zeros)

D W_File_In       S                   SQLTYPE(BLOB_FILE)

  // Store an object into the blob table
 /FREE
  EXEC SQL   Select Max(Rpt_Id) + 1
             Into :W_Id
             From RptArchive/Reports;
  If W_Id = *Zeros;
    W_Id = 1;
  EndIf;
  W_File_In_FO   = SQFRD;
  W_File_In_NAME = %Trim(P_FileName);
  W_File_In_NL   = %len(%trimr(W_File_In_NAME));

  EXEC SQL   Insert Into RptArchive/Reports
                  Values (:W_ID, :P_Type, NOW(),
                          :P_Comments, :W_File_In);

  // If the insert operation was successful, return the ID
  If SQLCod = *Zeros;
    Return W_Id;
```

Continued

```
  Else;
  // otherwise, return zeros to indicate something went wrong
    Return *Zeros;
  EndIf;
 /END-FREE
PSnd_File_To_Archive...
P                  E
```

Most of the code should be familiar because this procedure is heavily based on the *BLOB_IN* sample program. The only part that is really new is the SQL statement used to generate the unique ID:

```
EXEC SQL   Select Max(Rpt_Id) + 1
            Into :W_Id
            From RptArchive/Reports;
If W_Id = *Zeros;
  W_Id = 1;
EndIf;
```

Here, I'm looking for the last ID generated, *Max(RPT_ID)*, to figure out the next one, which will be used for the remainder of the procedure. However, if the table is empty, the SQL select response is not exactly what would be expected. It returns zero, ignoring the *+1* bit of the statement. To circumvent that problem, I'm checking and correcting, if necessary, the *W_Id* variable after the statement's execution.

This ID is what the procedure returns if the "archiving" operation is successful. If it fails, then a zero is returned, so that the calling program can proceed accordingly:

```
  // If the insert operation was successful, return the ID
  If SQLCod = *Zeros;
    Return W_Id;
  Else;
// otherwise, return zeros to indicate something went wrong
    Return *Zeros;
  EndIf;
```

The rest of the code is similar to the *Blob_In* sample program. To retrieve the file from the *REPORTS* table, I've created the *Rtv_File_From_Archive* procedure. Here's the procedure's complete source code:

```
*****************************************************************************
 * Retrieve a file from the BLOB table, using the unique ID as key
*****************************************************************************
PRtv_File_From_Archive...
P                 B                   EXPORT
DRtv_File_From_Archive...
D                 PI             1A
  * Input Parms
D P_Id                           7 0 Value
D P_FileName                   255A   Value

D W_File_Out      S                   SQLTYPE(BLOB_FILE)
D W_Success       S              1A

  // Retrieve an object from the BLOB table

 /FREE
  W_Sucess = '1';
  W_File_Out_FO   = SQFOVR;
  W_File_Out_NAME = %Trim(P_FileName);
  W_File_Out_NL   = %Len(%TrimR(P_FileName));

  EXEC SQL   Select Rpt_File1
              Into :W_File_Out
              From RptArchive/Reports
             Where Rpt_Id = :P_Id;

  If SQLCod <> *Zeros;
    W_Success = '0';
  EndIf;

  Return W_Success;
```

Continued

```
 /END-FREE
PRtv_File_From_Archive...
P                 E
```

The code should look familiar from the first section of this chapter because this procedure is based on the *BLOB_OUT* sample program. It receives the unique ID of the file to be retrieved, writes it to the IFS path and file name indicated by the *P_FileName* parameter, and returns a success (or failure) indicator, based on the *SQLCod* variable. Anything other than zero means that something went wrong with the "extraction" operation. Naturally, you can enhance this procedure to handle the *SQLCod* errors and/or provide a more meaningful error message to the user. These are just basic procedures that I invite you, dear reader, to improve and adapt in your own applications.

So, with these two procedures, you should be able to archive and retrieve files from the *REPORTS* DB2 table. Cool, isn't it? But every piece of code is easier to understand with an example. Let's review three very simple examples of these procedures in action, beginning with archiving a file using sample program *TST_SND*:

```
 *
 * This is a simple test program to demonstrate how to use the
 * Snd_File_To_Archive procedure
 *
 * Prototype definition
 /Copy QCPYLESRC,DBMBLOB_PR
 *
 * Function Parms
D P_FileName      S            255A   Inz
D P_Type          S             10A   Inz
D P_Comments      S            255A   Inz

 * Work variables
D W_ID            S              7 0 Inz

                                                   Continued
```

```
 /FREE
   P_FileName = '/Reports/Test.PDF';
   P_Type     = 'PDF';
   P_Comments = 'Just a PDF test report';

  W_ID = Snd_File_To_Archive(P_FileName : P_Type : P_Comments);

  Dsply %Char(W_ID);

  *InLr = *On;
 /END-FREE
```

There's not much to it, really. The program prepares the procedure's parameters and invokes it, storing the returned ID in the *W_ID* variable. In a real-life situation, you'd store this ID somewhere (and use more meaningful comments) to be able to find the archived file later.

Sample program *TST_RTV* provides an example of how the file can be retrieved:

```
 *
 * This is a simple test program to demonstrate how to use the
 * Rtv_File_From_Archive procedure
 *
 * Prototype definition
 /Copy QCPYLESRC,DBMBLOB_PR
 *
 * Function Parms
D P_ID            S              7 0 Inz
D P_FileName      S            255A   Inz

 * Work variables
D W_OK            S              1A   Inz

 /FREE
  P_Id = 1;
  P_FileName = '/Reports/Test_Retrieved.PDF';

                                                      Continued
```

```
  W_OK = Rtv_File_From_Archive(P_Id : P_FileName);

  If W_OK = '1';
    Dsply 'File Successfully retrieved';
  Else;
    Dsply 'An error occurred';
  EndIf;

  *InLr = *On;
 /END-FREE
```

Just like in the previous example, all that's required is to fill in the procedure's parameters, invoke it, and do something with the return code. In this case, if the procedure returns one, then everything went according to plan and a success message is shown to the user. The file still exists in the *REPORTS* table, but a copy of it is created in the path specified by the *P_FileName* parameter.

A slightly more "real-life" example would be generating a chart. Let's say we're representing the end-of-quarter sales as a chart, showing it to the user, and then storing it in the *REPORTS* table for safekeeping:

```
H DECEDIT(',') DATEDIT(*DMY.)

 * Generate Charts using Google Chart APIs Procedures
 /Copy QCPYLESRC,GENCHRT_PR
 * Misc Procedures
 /Copy QCPYLESRC,MISC_PR
 * Blob operations Procedures
 /Copy QCPYLESRC,DBMBLOB_PR

 *'Data Areas
D Da_SystemName    S                    Like(W_SysName) DtaAra(DaSysName)

DW_PCCmd           S            200A    Inz(*Blanks)
DW_SysName         S             20A    Inz(*Blanks)
DW_Response        S             52A    Inz(*Blanks)
```

Continued

```
DW_ErrorDS        DS                  LikeDS(ApiError) Inz

 *
 * Snd_File_To_Archive Function Parameters
D  P_FileNameP     S            255A   Inz
D  P_TypeP         S             10A   Inz
D  P_CommentsP     S            255A   Inz

 * Work variables
D  W_ID            S              7  0 Inz

 /FREE
     // Retrieve system name
     In Da_SystemName;
     W_SysName = %Trim(Da_SystemName);
   // First, I'll set up the page and chart titles and the html file name
         P_PageTitle = 'Quarterly Sales Report';
         P_ChartTitle = 'Q3 Sales';
         P_FileName = 'Q3_Sales.HTML';
   // Then the Rows
         Clear P_RowDS;
         P_RowDS(1).RowTitle = 'South';
         P_RowDS(1).RowValue = 60;
         P_RowDS(2).RowTitle = 'East';
         P_RowDS(2).RowValue = 45;
         P_RowDS(3).RowTitle = 'North';
         P_RowDS(3).RowValue = 27;
         P_RowDS(4).RowTitle = 'West';
         P_RowDS(4).RowValue = 110;
         P_RowDS(5).RowTitle = 'Overseas';
         P_RowDS(5).RowValue = 98;
   // Finally, the Chart size
         P_Width = 600;
         P_Height = 400;
```

Continued

```
   // Generate the Chart
         If GenPieChart(P_PageTitle : P_ChartTitle : P_RowDS :
                        P_Width     : P_Height    :
                        P_FileName  : P_ErrorDesc  ) = *Off;
           // Display the Chart
           W_PCCmd = '\\' + %Trim(W_SysName) + '\GCHARTS\OUTPUT\'
                    + %Trim(P_FileName);
           P_CmdLin = 'STRPCCMD PCCMD(''' + %Trim(W_PCCmd) +
                     ''') PAUSE(*NO)';
           W_ErrorDs = ExecCmd(%Trim(P_CmdLin));
         Else;
           // Error occurred in the GenPieChart procedure
           W_Response = 'Error = ' +
                         %Trim(P_ErrorDesc);
           Dsply W_Response;
         EndIf;

   // Store the Chart in the REPORTS table
         P_FileNameP = '/GCHARTS/OUTPUT/' + %Trim(P_FileName);
         P_TypeP     = 'HTML';
         P_CommentsP = 'Quarterly Sales report';

         W_ID = Snd_File_To_Archive(P_FileNameP : P_TypeP : P_CommentsP);

         Dsply %Char(W_ID);

   *InLr = *On;
 /END-FREE
```

In this program, the Quarter Sales pie chart is generated, shown to the user, and then stored in the *REPORTS* table. For this to be closer to a "real-life" situation, the chart labels and values would come from a table or an SQL statement, and there would be more code. I just wanted to show you that it's possible—simple, actually—to get the procedures from different chapters of this book working together.

Final Thoughts

Note that the file and library names of the table with the BLOB column (*RPTARCHIVE/REPORTS*) are hardcoded in the SQL statements of both procedures. There are ways to circumvent this limitation, but I prefer to keep things simple! If you want to integrate this into your application, to use your application's library and/or adjust the file name to follow your company's naming convention, remember to modify the SQL statements of the procedures to reflect those changes.

PART 3:

GOING GLOBAL

10

GPS-Enable Your Database!

This chapter describes how to retrieve the GPS coordinates of an address, using a Yahoo!® Web service. This REST Web service is invoked using Scott Klement's HTTP API tool and the opcode *XML-INTO*. Even if GPS-enabling your addresses doesn't sound appealing, you should read the chapter and understand the mechanics of invoking a REST Web service because the same method will be used, but not explained, in the next chapter.

All of our applications' databases hold hundreds if not thousands of addresses—from our clients, suppliers, stores, warehouses, branches, and so on. This chapter explains how to GPS-enable, or *geocode*, that precious information to expand the horizons of what you can do with your data: improve your logistics processes, locate areas where your network (of clients, stores, or suppliers) is poor or non-existent, and develop many other business-specific uses for the GPS coordinates.

Almost daily, any given call center receives phone calls from clients asking questions like this one: "I'm in the *x* area; what's your closest store to my location?" Unless the operator knows the area the client is in, this is a tough question to answer . . . unless the operator has a little help from an online maps service (Google, Bing®, Yahoo!) or another application. Of course, this requires that the store locations are geocoded—that is, the stores' addresses are translated into GPS coordinates. This is what we're going to do here.

The process has three parts:

1. Receive the address and compose a proper request to the Web service.
2. Invoke the Web service.
3. Process the response (receive and parse the XML) and extract the latitude and longitude coordinates from the response.

So, let's get started!

There are a few things we'll need to set up first. We'll be using the Yahoo! PlaceFinder API, which is a relatively cheap Web service, and on the IBM i side, we'll use a great free utility library created by Scott Klement called HTTP API:

http://www.scottklement.com/httpapi/httpapi.savf

Then, we'll need to process the Web service's response. For that, we'll use the opcode *XML-INTO*. Lastly, your IBM i system must have an Internet connection. This usually means going through a firewall to get to the Internet. Since we're going to connect to Yahoo!'s servers, you'll need to set up a firewall rule or two to be able to get through.

Keep in mind that even though Yahoo! PlaceFinder Web service is publicly available, there are a few rules to abide by. Please read the terms and conditions (*http://info.yahoo.com/legal/us/yahoo/search/bosstos/bosstos-2317.html*) and the API documentation (*http://developer.yahoo.com/boss/geo/docs/requests-pf.html*) carefully. I'll be going through some parts of it, but a complete read is advised.

To use the Web service, you must create an Application ID at *https://login.yahoo.com/config/login_verify2?.src=devnet&.done=http%3A%2F%2Fdeveloper.apps.yahoo.com%2Fdashboard%2FcreateKey.html*. You're required to create a Yahoo! account if you don't already have one. After you sign in, something similar to the application form in Figure 10.1 will pop up.

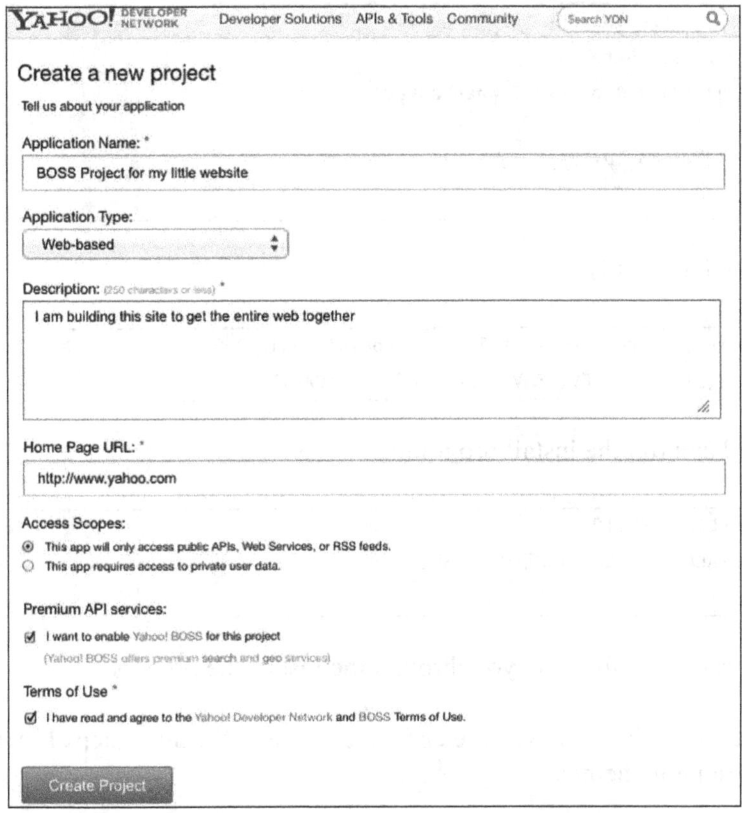

Figure 10.1: Fill in the form to access the Web service.

It's important to fill this in properly, because you might not be able to use the Web service otherwise. Enter your application name, choose client/desktop in the "kind of application" box, and briefly describe its purpose. If you choose "Web-based," you must also fill in the application and icon URLs. Finally, in the Access Scopes section, choose "This app will only access public APIs, Web Services, or RSS feeds." Check the "Terms of Use" checkbox. Click the "Get API Key" button, and make a note of your Application ID. You will need it later. Just follow the online guide at *http://developer.yahoo.com/boss/geo/BOSS_Signup.pdf*, and you should be fine.

The next step is installing the HTTP API library. This is a fairly simple process. Log onto your IBM i system, and create a save file to store the downloaded file in. To do this, type ***CRTSAVF QGPL/HTTPAPI***. Next, use FTP to transfer the save file to your IBM i system by opening an MS-DOS prompt and typing the following:

```
cd \<directory where you put the save file>
ftp your-IBM i-name-here
(enter your username & password when asked)
binary
put httpapi.savf QGPL/HTTPAPI
quit
```

Back on IBM i, type this:

```
DLTLIB LIBHTTP (ignore errors if library doesn't exist)
RSTLIB SAVLIB(LIBHTTP) DEV(*SAVF) SAVF(QGPL/HTTPAPI)
```

Finally, build and run the install program:

```
CHGCURLIB CURLIB(LIBHTTP)
CRTCLPGM INSTALL SRCFILE(LIBHTTP/QCLSRC)
CALL INSTALL
```

The install program will guide you through the rest of the process.

You're all set! Now let's analyze the code and see how the three steps I mentioned previously are implemented.

Implementing the Steps

In order to implement the steps, some context is needed. I've created a function that accepts the postal address (street name and house number, city, zip code, and country—or any combination of these) and returns the GPS coordinates (latitude and longitude) closest to that address. It's important to note that the result is not always accurate. If the house number is not found, the Web service will return the closest it finds. If the street name is a partial match to some other street name and the original is not found by the Web service in its database, you'll get the partial match. The quality of the response is also passed back by the function. (I'll explain this in detail later.) There's an additional parameter named *Error Code* that is mainly to help the application support team track down and resolve any issue that arises. (I'll also cover that in depth later.)

Here's how to invoke the Web service:

```
CallP RtvGpsFrmAddr(P_Address : P_Quality : P_Latitude : P_Longitude : P_ErrorCode);
```

The function itself returns an indicator in which **OFF* means success and **ON* means error, so the best way to use it is like this:

```
If RtvGpsFrmAddr(P_Address :
                 P_Quality :
                 P_Latitude :
                 P_Longitude :
                 P_ErrorCode) = *Off;
      // Use the P_Latitude and P_Longitude for something
Else;
      // Oops! Something went wrong! Use the P_ErrorCode to react accordingly
EndIf;
```

Finally, let's go over step 1, receiving the address and composing a proper request to the Web service. The Web service is expecting two things in the request: a properly formatted address and a valid Yahoo! Developer Network Application ID (*YDN App ID*). By "properly formatted," I mean that the address cannot have blank spaces, and any special characters (ö, for instance) have to be encoded in UTF-8. I explained earlier how to obtain a YDN App ID, so the only thing missing is where to use these two: the base URL of the Web service. Since Yahoo! is continually working on improving its tools, the base URL might change sometime in the future (to include the version number or change the name, for instance), so I've stored it in a data area referred to as *DAApiBaseUrl* in the code. The real name is shorter (*DAAPIURL*) due to the 10-character limitation on object names.

Analyzing the code below, you'll find the retrieval and check of the YDN App ID and the base URL in (1) and (2), respectively:

```
// (1)
// Retrieve Yahoo Developers Network Application ID
In DAAppID;
W_AppID = DAAppId;
// Check If the YDN App ID is filled in
                                                    Continued
```

```
If W_AppID = *Blanks;
  P_ErrorCode = 300; //Invalid YDN App ID
  W_Return = *ON;
  ExSr End_And_Return;
EndIf;

// (2)
// Retrieve Yahoo PlaceFinder API base url
In DAApiBaseUrl;
W_ApiBaseUrl = DAApiBaseUrl;
// Check If the Yahoo PlaceFinder API base url is filled in
If W_ApiBaseUrl = *Blanks;
  P_ErrorCode = 350; //Invalid Yahoo PlaceFinder API base url
  W_Return = *ON;
  ExSr End_And_Return;
EndIf;
```

The next step is formatting the input address to the Web service's requirements. The built-in function *%XLATE* is used to replace the blank spaces in the address with plus signs (+). Since the address doesn't usually take up the entire size of the variable, *%Trim* is used to ensure that the trailing blanks are not converted to plus signs:

```
// Prepare the address, by replacing blanks with the plus sign
W_Address = %Xlate(' ' : '+' : %Trim(P_Address));
```

After this, there's only one thing left to do: encode your request. For this task, I use a little something from the HTTP API library called a Web form. Basically, it encodes whatever variables you include, composing a string in UTF-8:

```
// Compose the WebService URL with the address and your YDN App ID
W_Form = WEBFORM_open();
WEBFORM_setVar(W_Form : 'q'     : %Trim(W_Address) );
WEBFORM_setVar(W_Form : 'appid' : %Trim(W_AppID)   );

W_Url = %Trim(W_ApiBaseUrl) + WEBFORM_getData(W_Form);

// Close form
WEBFORM_Close(W_Form);
```

Here's an example to make it clearer. Suppose your address is "701 First Ave., Sunnyvale, CA 94089" and your YDN APP ID is "A234fW9." After the code above runs, the *W_Url* variable will contain the following URL:

```
http://yboss.yahooapis.com/geo/placefinder?q=701%2BFirst%2BAve.%2C%2BSunnyvale%2C%2BC
A%2B94089&appid=A234fW9
```

Here, *http://yboss.yahooapis.com/geo/placefinder?* is the API base URL, stored in the data area I previously mentioned. The string *701%2BFirst%2BAve.%2C%2BSunnyvale%2C%2BCA%2B94089* is the address, after it has been transformed (blanks to pluses) and encoded (since there are no special characters in this address, the only change was turning pluses into *%2B*). Note that the base URL might be changed by Yahoo! at any time, so be sure to update the API URL data area, as mentioned before.

The YDN App ID remained untouched. The *q* and *appid* are parameters of the Web service and correspond to your query (the address) and your YDN App ID, respectively. The encoder provides this double function of translating to UTF-8 and adding the necessary parameter separators (ampersands) to make composing a proper URL very easy.

Step 2 is invoking the Web service. For that, I'll use another HTTP API function, *http_get_url*. This function accepts as an input parameter a URL and saves the corresponding Web page to a file in the IFS. The name of the IFS file is indicated as a second parameter. The function itself returns a status code where one mean success, and anything else is an error. (Check Scott Klement's documentation for details.)

To use this function, you must create an IFS file first. Since this is only temporary storage for our Web service response, I'll use another function, *http_tempfile*, to create it. Here's the complete code for step 2:

```
// Create a temp file to receive the WebService response
W_FileName = http_tempfile() + '.xml';


// Invoke the WebService
W_RetCode = http_url_get(W_url : W_FileName);
```

Continued

```
// In case of error, return *ON
If (W_RetCode <> 1);
  P_ErrorCode = 400; //Problems invoking the Web Service
  W_Return = *ON;
  ExSr End_And_Return;
EndIf;
```

I'll explain what is done in case of error later. The important thing is that after this piece of code runs, I have the Web service's response, in XML format, stored in an IFS file. The file name is saved in variable *W_FileName* for the next step, which is to process the response (receive and parse the XML) and extract the latitude and longitude coordinates from it.

There are a few ways to process an XML file in RPG. My favorite is to use the opcode *XML-INTO*. Even if you have used it before, read on, because you might find something new.

The opcode *XML-INTO* itself is very simple to use. Just provide an XML file, a data structure to receive the parsed contents, and some options that define how the parsing should occur. I'll start with this last bit. You might not need the whole content of the XML document; it's normal to use only a sub-tree (a smaller set of data) or even only a few elements (fields) within that sub-tree. By specifying the correct options, you indicate how the parser should behave and what is acceptable in terms of validation.

In the code, I don't care about the case (lowercase or uppercase is irrelevant to me) or the complete XML structure of the file. (This is done to ensure that the *RtvGpsFrmAddr* function will continue to work even if Yahoo! adds new elements to the XML of the Web service.) With this in mind, here's how I set up the options for *XML-INTO*:

```
// Prepare parameters for XML-INTO
W_Options = 'doc=file +
        path=RESULTSET +
        case=any +
        allowextra=yes +
        allowmissing=yes';
```

From top to bottom, here's what the options mean:

- *Doc=file* means that we'll be parsing XML coming from a file.
- *Path=RESULTSET* tells the parser which sub-tree we're interested in. (I'll get back to the XML structure later.)
- *Case=any* refers to the uppercase or lowercase of the element names themselves. (As mentioned, it's really irrelevant here.)
- *Allowextra=yes* and *allowmissing=yes* ensure that the parsing will still occur if the XML structure is (slightly) changed.

Now the parser knows how to act and what to act upon. *W_FileName* contains the name and path of the XML file. The only thing missing is where to store the result of the parsing. *XML-INTO* expects a data structure that "clones" the XML structure it's parsing. In other words, the data structure field names must match the XML element names so that the parser finds the proper match and stores the content of element '<street>' in the data structure field 'street'. Because I specified *case=any* in the options, the field and element names can be either 'street' or 'STREET'; I really don't care.

To build the data structure, we need to analyze the XML structure. Specifically, we need to find the latitude, longitude, quality of the match, and error code; these are the output parameters of *RtvGpsFrmAddr*. However, I've tried to leave the code as flexible as possible, so I've created a data structure that covers the whole XML structure. Still, if Yahoo! changes the XML structure, be sure to update the data structure's field names.

Going back to the example from the first step, the URL *http://yboss.yahooapis.com/geo/placefinder?q=701%2BFirst%2BAve.%2C%2BSunnyvale%2C%2BCA%2B94089&appid=A234fW9* will return the following XML:

```
<ResultSet version="1.0">
<Error>0</Error>
<ErrorMessage>No error</ErrorMessage>
<Locale>us_US</Locale>
<Quality>87</Quality>
<Found>1</Found>
                                                    Continued
```

```
<Result>
<quality>87</quality>
<latitude>37.416275</latitude>
<longitude>-122.025092</longitude>
<offsetlat>37.416397</offsetlat>
<offsetlon>-122.025055</offsetlon>
<radius>500</radius>
<name/>
<line1>701 1st Ave</line1>
<line2>Sunnyvale, CA  94089-1019</line2>
<line3/>
<line4>United States</line4>
<house>701</house>
<street>1st Ave</street>
<xstreet/>
<unittype/>
<unit/>
<postal>94089-1019</postal>
<neighborhood/>
<city>Sunnyvale</city>
<county>Santa Clara County</county>
<state>California</state>
<country>United States</country>
<countrycode>US</countrycode>
<statecode>CA</statecode>
<countycode/>
<uzip>94089</uzip>
<hash>DDAD1896CC0CDC41</hash>
<woeid>12797150</woeid>
<woetype>11</woetype>
</Result>
</ResultSet>
```


The Web service documentation explains each element in depth at *http://developer.yahoo.com/boss/geo/docs/supported_responses.html*, so I'll just cover the structure itself and the relevant elements. The structure only has one tree, called *ResultSet*. Within it there are six elements; five are simple and one is complex. This last one, named *Result*, is what we're interested in. In a situation such as this, where there's only one match, the <Result> element exists only once. I have decided to keep things simple and expect only one <Result> element.

I'll briefly explain how to change the *RtvGpsFrmAddr* function to handle more than one <Result> later. However, keep in mind that this might also mean that you need some logic in your program to decide which GPS coordinates to use. Our data structure has to match this duality of simple and complex elements. The terminology *complex element* basically means that the element has sub-elements. In the <Result> case, there are a lot of them! To match this structure, we need a data structure that contains five fields, with names that match the five simple elements, and another data structure that, in turn, has fields whose names match the sub-element names. I know it's a mind twister, so let's look at the data structure, and it might start to make sense:

```
 *-----------------------------------------------------------------*
 *   Data Structures                                               *
 *-----------------------------------------------------------------*
D ResultSet       DS                  Qualified
D   Error                             Like(t_Error)
D   ErrorMessage                      Like(t_ErrorMessage)
D   Locale                            Like(t_Locale)
D   Quality                           Like(t_Quality)
D   Found                             Like(t_Found)
D   Result                            LikeDS(t_Result)
D                                     Dim(10)

D t_Error         S              4  0
D t_ErrorMessage  S             50A
D t_Locale        S              5A
D t_Quality       S              2  0
D t_Found         S              3  0

D t_Result        DS                  Qualified
D                                     Based(Template)
D   quality                           Like(t_Quality)
D   latitude                    15A
```

Continued

```
D   longitude            15A
D   offsetlat            15A
D   offsetlon            15A
D   radius                4 0
D   name                100A
D   line1               100A
D   line2               100A
D   line3               100A
D   line4               100A
D   house                10A
D   street              100A
D   xstreet             100A
D   unittype            100A
D   unit                100A
D   postal               10A
D   neighborhood        100A
D   city                100A
D   county               50A
D   state                50A
D   country              50A
D   countrycode           5A
D   statecode             5A
D   countycode            5A
D   uzip                 10A
D   hash                 20A
D   woeid                10A
D   woetype               5A
```

The *ResultSet* data structure is qualified, just to make it easier to read in the code. Similarly, the *t_Result* data structure, which is the definition used for the sixth "field" of the *ResultSet* data structure, is also qualified. The "field" *Result* is an array that can contain up to 10 elements, just to prevent *XML-INTO* from returning an error if there's more than one <RESULT> element in the XML.

It's now time to put everything together—the XML file, the options, and the data structure:

```
// Receive xml file into data structure
Monitor;
  Xml-Into ResultSet %xml(W_FileName : W_Options);
On-Error;
P_ErrorCode = 500; //Malformed xml
  W_Return = *ON;
  ExSr End_And_Return;
EndMon;
```

I'm using *Monitor* just to make sure that the function aborts gracefully if something is not as it should be. If everything goes well, the XML contents are now in the *ResultSet* data structure. If the Web service returns a valid response (in other words, a single address match), we can extract the GPS coordinates from it:

```
// Check for API errors before processing
// In case of API error, return the error code and leave
If ResultSet.Error <> 0;
  P_ErrorCode = ResultSet.Error;
  W_Return = *ON;
  ExSr End_And_Return;
EndIf;

// If an exact match was found (only 1 result returned),
// pass the coordinates to the output parms
If ResultSet.Found = 1;
  P_Quality   = ResultSet.Result(1).quality;
  P_Latitude  = ResultSet.Result(1).latitude;
  P_Longitude = ResultSet.Result(1).longitude;
  P_ErrorCode = 0; // Sucess!
  W_Return = *Off;
  ExSr End_And_Return;
Else;
  P_ErrorCode = 600; // No exact match (none or more than 1 found)
  W_Return = *ON;
  ExSr End_And_Return;
EndIf;
```

In the *If ResultSet.Found = 1* block, you can see the beauty of the *Qualified* keyword. The *P_Quality* parameter is receiving the "quality" field of the first element of the data structure *Result*, which in turn, is part of the *ResultSet* data structure. This ends the third step.

It's now time to explain all of those *ExSr End_And_Return* calls. Each anomalous situation in the code is handled by a set of three lines:

```
P_ErrorCode = 600; // No exact match (none or more than 1 found)
W_Return = *ON;
ExSr End_And_Return;
```

You've seen this over and over again, right? *P_ErrorCode* returns a predetermined error code telling the caller program what went wrong. The error code itself is hardcoded, except in this situation:

```
// Check for API errors before processing
// In case of API error, return the error code and leave
If ResultSet.Error <> 0;
  P_ErrorCode = ResultSet.Error;
  W_Return = *ON;
  ExSr End_And_Return;
EndIf;
```

In this case, I return the error code of the Web service. (You can find the meaning of these error codes at *http://developer.yahoo.com/boss/geo/docs/pf-errorcodes.html*.) *W_Return* contains the success or failure indicator for the *RtvGpsFrmAddr* function. You might have noticed that is always set to **ON*, except when I extract the latitude and longitude from the data structure. The error code and the return indicator are used in routine *End_And_Return*:

```
//-------------------------------------------------------------------*
//  End and Return                                                   *
//-------------------------------------------------------------------*
  BegSr End_And_Return;

    // Log status (useful for debuging)
    ExSr Log_Status;

    // Delete temp file
    unlink(W_FileName);

    // End and return the indicator (*on = error / *off = success)
    Return W_Return;

  EndSr;

//-------------------------------------------------------------------*
//  Log status                                                       *
//-------------------------------------------------------------------*
  BegSr Log_Status;

    // Log request
    Open Log;
    Log_TypeReq = 'RtvGpsFrmAddr';
    Log_StsCode = P_ErrorCode;
    Log_InpParm = %Trim(P_Address);
    Log_OutParm = 'Quality=' + %Char(P_Quality)
                + '|Latitude=' + %Trim(P_Latitude)
                + '|Longitude=' + %Trim(P_Longitude);
    Log_DateTim = %TimeStamp;
    Write LogR;
    Close Log;

  EndSr;
```

End_And_Return is a very simple routine that logs the request to a file (I'll explain routine *Log_Status* next), deletes the temporary file using another function from the HTTP API library, and returns **ON* or **OFF*, indicating error or success, respectively.

The Log_Status routine will be useful in the early days of the implementation, because it saves all the input and output parameters in a record per invocation of the *RtvGpsFrmAddr* function. You might want to disable it later on, but I strongly recommend keeping it; it might be of use in the future.

Here's the complete source code of the *RtvGpsFrmAddr* function:

```
HDatEdit(*YMD)  NoMain   ExprOpts(*MaxDigits) BndDir('HTTPAPI':'RTVGPS')
 ***************************************************************************
 *                                                                         *
 *   Program .... : RTVGPS_PR                                              *
 *   Description  : Retrieve GPS Info Procedures                           *
 *   Author ..... : Rafael Victoria-Pereira                                *
 *   Date ....... : January 2011                                           *
 *   Changes .... :                                                        *
 *=========================================================================*

 ***************************************************************************

 *-------------------------------------------------------------------------*
 *   File Descriptions                                                     *
 *-------------------------------------------------------------------------*
FLog       O    E           K Disk    Prefix(Log_) UsrOpn

 *-------------------------------------------------------------------------
 *   Data Areas
 *-------------------------------------------------------------------------
 * YDN App ID
D DAAppID         S             10A   DTAARA(DAAppID)
 * YDN API base URL
D DAApiBaseUrl    S             50A   DTAARA(DAAPIURL)

 *-------------------------------------------------------------------------*
 *   Variables                                                             *
 *-------------------------------------------------------------------------*
 * Work Fields
```

Continued

```
 /define WEBFORMS
D W_FileName      S             45A   Varying
D W_Options       S            100A   Varying
D W_RetCode       S             10I 0
D W_AppID         S             10A   Inz
D W_ApiBaseUrl    S             50A   Inz
D W_URL           S          32767A   Varying
D W_Address       S            100A   Inz
D W_Form          S                   Like(WEBFORM)
D W_Return        S              1N   Inz

 *-------------------------------------------------------------------------*
 *   Prototypes                                                            *
 *-------------------------------------------------------------------------*
 * Prototype definition for HTTP API Procedures
 /Copy QRPGLESRC,HTTPAPI_H
 /Copy QRPGLESRC,IFSIO_H
 * Prototype definition for Retrieve GPS Info Procedures
 /Copy QCPYLESRC,RTVGPS_PR

 *-------------------------------------------------------------------------*
 *   Retrieve GPS Info from address                                        *
 *-------------------------------------------------------------------------*
PRtvGpsFrmAddr    B                   EXPORT
D                 PI             N
 * Input Parms
DP_Address                            Like(t_Result.line1) Value
 * Output Parms
DP_Quality                            Like(t_Quality)
DP_Latitude                           Like(t_Result.latitude)
DP_Longitude                          Like(t_Result.longitude)
DP_ErrorCode                          Like(t_Error)

 /FREE
```

Continued

```
    ExSr Init;

    ExSr Process;

  //  Sub Routines

  //----------------------------------------------------------------------*
  //  Initialization                                                      *
  //----------------------------------------------------------------------*
     BegSr  Init;

       // Initialize output parameters
       P_Quality    = *Zeros;
       P_Latitude  = *Blanks;
       P_Longitude = *Blanks;
       P_ErrorCode = *Zeros;

       // Retrieve Yahoo Developers Network Application ID
       In DAAppID;
       W_AppID = DAAppId;
       // Check If the YDN App ID is filled in
       If W_AppID = *Blanks;
         P_ErrorCode = 300; //Invalid YDN App ID
         W_Return = *ON;
         ExSr End_And_Return;
       EndIf;

       // Retrieve Yahoo PlaceFinder API base url
       In DAApiBaseUrl;
       W_ApiBaseUrl = DAApiBaseUrl;
       // Check If the Yahoo PlaceFinder API base url is filled in
       If W_ApiBaseUrl = *Blanks;
         P_ErrorCode = 350; //Invalid Yahoo PlaceFinder API base url
         W_Return = *ON;
         ExSr End_And_Return;
       EndIf;
```

Continued

```
    // Prepare parameters for XML-INTO
    W_Options = 'doc=file +
           path=RESULTSET +
           case=any +
           allowextra=yes +
           allowmissing=yes';

    // Prepare the address, by replacing blanks with the plus sign
    W_Address = %Xlate(' ' : '+' : %Trim(P_Address));

    // Compose the WebService URL with the address and your YDN App ID
    W_Form = WEBFORM_open();
    WEBFORM_setVar(W_Form : 'q'     : %Trim(W_Address) );
    WEBFORM_setVar(W_Form : 'appid' : %Trim(W_AppID)   );

    W_Url = %Trim(W_ApiBaseUrl) + WEBFORM_getData(W_Form);

    // Close form
    WEBFORM_Close(W_Form);

    // Create a temp file to receive the WebService response
    W_FileName = http_tempfile() + '.xml';

    // Initialize the ResultSet array to avoid error on unused fields
    Clear ResultSet;

   EndSr;

//-------------------------------------------------------------------*
// Invoke Web Service and return GPS Coordinates                     *
//-------------------------------------------------------------------*
  BegSr  Process;

    // Invoke the WebService
    W_RetCode = http_url_get(W_url : W_FileName);
```

Continued

```
// In case of error,  return *ON
If (W_RetCode <> 1);
  P_ErrorCode = 400; //Problems invoking the Web Service
  W_Return = *ON;
  ExSr End_And_Return;
EndIf;

// Receive xml file into data structure
Monitor;
  Xml-Into ResultSet %xml(W_FileName : W_Options);
On-Error;
  P_ErrorCode = 500; //Malformed xml
  W_Return = *ON;
  ExSr End_And_Return;
EndMon;

// Check for API errors before processing
// In case of API error, return the error code and leave
If ResultSet.Error <> 0;
  P_ErrorCode = ResultSet.Error;
  W_Return = *ON;
  ExSr End_And_Return;
EndIf;

// If an exact match was found (only 1 result returned),
// pass the coordinates to the output parms
If ResultSet.Found = 1;
  P_Quality   = ResultSet.Result(1).quality;
  P_Latitude  = ResultSet.Result(1).latitude;
  P_Longitude = ResultSet.Result(1).longitude;
  P_ErrorCode = 0; // Sucess!
  W_Return = *Off;
  ExSr End_And_Return;
Else;
  P_ErrorCode = 600; // No exact match (none or more than 1 found)
  W_Return = *ON;
```

Continued

```
      ExSr End_And_Return;
    EndIf;

  EndSr;

//-----------------------------------------------------------------*
//  End and Return                                                  *
//-----------------------------------------------------------------*
  BegSr End_And_Return;

    // Log status (useful for debuging)
    ExSr Log_Status;

    // Delete temp file
    unlink(W_FileName);

    // End and return the indicator (*on = error / *off = success)
    Return W_Return;

  EndSr;

//-----------------------------------------------------------------*
//  Log status                                                      *
//-----------------------------------------------------------------*
  BegSr Log_Status;

    // Log request
    Open Log;
    Log_TypeReq = 'RtvGpsFrmAddr';
    Log_StsCode = P_ErrorCode;
    Log_InpParm = %Trim(P_Address);
    Log_OutParm = 'Quality=' + %Char(P_Quality)
                + '|Latitude=' + %Trim(P_Latitude)
                + '|Longitude=' + %Trim(P_Longitude);
    Log_DateTim = %TimeStamp;
    Write LogR;
```

Continued

```
        Close Log;

      EndSr;
 /END-FREE

PRtvGpsFrmAddr     E
```

Now let's consolidate all of this with an example:

```
 * Retrieve GPS Info Procedures
 /Copy QCPYLESRC,RTVGPS_PR

DW_Response       S              52A   Inz(*Blanks)

 /FREE
    P_Address = '701 First Ave., Sunnyvale, CA 94089'; // Full address w/ door nbr
    If RtvGpsFrmAddr(P_Address :
                     P_Quality :
                     P_Latitude :
                     P_Longitude :
                     P_ErrorCode) = *Off;
       W_Response = 'Latitude=' + %Trim(P_Latitude) +
                    ' Longitude=' + %Trim(P_Longitude);
      Dsply W_Response;
    Else;
      W_Response = 'Error Code=' + %Char(P_ErrorCode);
      Dsply W_Response;
    EndIf;

    *InLr = *On;
 /END-FREE
```

Here, I'm calling the function from an *IF* statement and displaying the GPS coordinates of the address passed as a parameter. In case something doesn't work as expected, I'm displaying the error code. Note that the copy member *RTVGPS_PR* contains all the necessary variable definitions for the parameters, so be careful with the names of the variables in the caller program, to avoid duplications (and consequent compilation errors). I've included source member *TST_GPSADD*, which has other addresses ready for testing. There, you'll find incomplete addresses, airport codes instead of addresses (*LAX* for instance), and an invalid address (which will cause *ResultSet.Found = 0*). Try all of these to get a feel for the way the function works before using it on your data. By the way, if your address is from a country that has a different structure (for instance, the house number appears after the street name), you might have some problems because it will return the GPS coordinates for the street, but not for the house number you specified.

A Quality Issue

One of the output parameters of the function is the quality of the response. If you look closely at the XML, you'll see that there are two elements named "quality"; one belongs to <RESULTSET> (with an uppercase *Q*) and the other to <RESULT> (with a lowercase *q*). The Web service documentation explains why:

> *The response contains two Address Quality elements:*
>
> *Quality: Child element of ResultSet. This element defines the best possible quality of the address specified by the input parameter.*
>
> *quality: Child element of Result. This element defines the quality of the address data for this result. If a response has multiple Result elements, each will contain a quality element.*
>
> *If the result quality is less than the best possible Quality, then the accuracy of the result is less than requested. For example, suppose the input parameter is "1000 1st Ave Sunnyvale CA," but the result is "998 1st Ave Sunnyvale CA." In the response, the best possible Quality for the input parameter is 87. However, the result quality is 86 because closest street number found does not match the requested street number.*

You'll find additional information and the list of quality codes here:

http://developer.yahoo.com/boss/geo/docs/supported_responses.html#address-quality

The *RtvGpsFrmAddr* function returns the one from the <RESULT>, and it's up to you to decide if the quality level is acceptable or not. Ideally, if the address is accurate, you should always (or almost always) get 87 in the *P_Quality* parameter. Read the documentation carefully, and decide what you consider acceptable.

Multiple Results

I mentioned that the function would handle only an exact match (one element in the *Result* array) to keep things simple. Here's what you have to do to handle multiple results:

1. Transform the output parameters into arrays with the same number of elements as the *Result* array.
2. Change the *If ResultSet.Found = 1;* into a *For* loop that cycles through the whole *Result* array and assigns each element of the *Result(index).fieldname* to the respective *parametername(index)*. It should look something like this:

```
P_Quality(W_Index) = ResultSet.Result(W_Index).quality;
```

3. In the caller program, build logic to handle the multiple responses. I won't make any suggestions here, because it will have to be on a case-by-case decision.

Final Thoughts

The Yahoo! BOSS PlaceFinder Web Service is a very powerful tool, and I've only scratched the surface here. Bear in mind that this Web service is frequently updated by Yahoo!. This means that part of the code presented here might suddenly start malfunctioning and require a little tweaking to "bring it back to life." The documentation and support forums will definitely provide valuable help and ideas for new functions. The *RtvGpsFrmAddr* function is a basic implementation of the Web service, with a few limitations. It uses only a small, yet important, part of the data provided by the Web service. I urge you to adapt it to your specific needs!

The next logical step is to use the newly found richness of information. A lot can be done with GPS coordinates, once you have them—from calculating the ideal route between stores and warehouses to analyzing and reporting on geographical coverage of stores, resellers, or clients. Instead of building something from scratch, have a look at the Geographic Information System (GIS) applications out there (Google it up!), and see how they can help your business.

11

Using GeoNames Web Services to Collect Geo-Related Data

> This chapter explores the useful yet simple Web services of GeoNames. It explains how to use these free Web services to accomplish tasks that can help your business in innovative ways. The method used to communicate with the REST Web services is the same as in the previous chapter. It won't be explained in depth here, so it's a good idea to read that chapter carefully first.

GeoNames is an extremely large geographical database. It covers all countries and contains over eight million place names that are available for download free of charge. It provides multiple free Web services to access that huge dataset, each specialized on a certain type of information. Currently, there are over 30 Web services that cover almost all types of geographical information you can imagine, ranging from simple country information to weather forecast data and Wikipedia-related data. A complete list of the Web services is available here:

http://www.geonames.org/export/ws-overview.html

Most of these are REST Web services, like the Yahoo! PlaceFinder REST Web service covered in the previous chapter. For that reason, I'll be using the same methodology and structure used there. I recommend that you read that whole chapter carefully, because I won't go into much detail about the way things are done here. I'll just cover the highlights of these Web services.

In case you are unfamiliar with REST Web services, I'll give a quick explanation here. In a typical SOAP Web service (the most common and complete type), you need to formulate your "question" in XML, using a predefined structure and inserting your parameters in the respective XML tags. In a REST Web service, you ask your "question" by composing a URL, with predefined keywords and your parameters. You can find out more about REST Web services at *http://en.wikipedia.org/wiki/REST#Applied_to_web_services*.

To access the Web services, you need to create and activate a user in the GeoNames Web site. The user name for your application can be registered here:

http://www.geonames.org/login

You will receive an email with a confirmation link. After you have confirmed the email, you have to enable your account for the Web services on your account page, at *http://www.geonames.org/manageaccount*.

We are now ready to begin, starting with the Time Zone Web service.

The Time Zone Web Service

We live in a global village; there's no way to deny it. Long gone are the days of countries standing alone, or companies staying within the boundaries of their nations. In today's busy world, it's common to find an American company with branches in Japan, India, and France; a Japanese company with branches in America, Portugal, and Sweden; and so on. Sometimes, this global presence causes serious headaches, simply because it's not the same time everywhere.

That's where this first Web service comes in. It provides information about the time zone of a set of GPS coordinates (latitude and longitude), along with some other possibly useful details, such as the time zone's name and the country's name. These pieces of data can be used to obtain other sets of data, which is referred to as *Web services orchestration*. I'll go over that later in this chapter.

The time zone REST Web service expects you to provide the latitude and longitude. Here's how it works. First, you provide a URL, like this:

```
http://api.geonames.org/timezone?lat=47.01&lng=10.2&username=demo
```

This URL is composed of the Web service location (*http://api.geonames.org/timezone?*) and parameters (*lat=47.01&lng=10.2&username=demo*). In return, you get an XML document with all the time zone–related information (or an error, discussed later):

```
<geonames>
  <timezone>
    <countryCode>AT</countryCode>
    <countryName>Austria</countryName>
    <lat>47.01</lat>
    <lng>10.2</lng>
    <timezoneId>Europe/Vienna</timezoneId>
    <dstOffset>2.0</dstOffset>
    <gmtOffset>1.0</gmtOffset>
    <rawOffset>1.0</rawOffset>
    <time>2011-07-08 22:42</time>
    <sunrise>2011-07-08 05:32</sunrise>
    <sunset>2011-07-08 21:15</sunset>
  </timezone>
</geonames>
```

The time zone information is expressed in the hour difference to the Greenwich Mean Time, or GMT (–12 to +13 hours). I'll be using only the portion bolded in the code above, but feel free to modify it to use the additional information provided. It's simply a matter of adjusting the procedure's parameters and filling the variables with the data structure fields.

In this example, the *dstOffset* element tells us that there's a +2 hour difference from GMT for this location, while the *gmtOffset* has a value of +1. The *dstOffset* element indicates the time difference according to Daylight Saving Time (hence, "dst"), while the *gmtOffset* element shows the actual hour difference to GMT, unaffected by DST. Finally, *rawOffset* is the amount of time in hours to add to GMT to get standard time in this time zone. Because this value is not affected by Daylight Saving Time, it is called the *raw offset*. You can find this Web service's documentation here:

http://www.geonames.org/export/web-services.html#timezone

For ease of use, I've created a function that you can invoke in an *IF* statement:

```
If RtvTmzFrmGPS(P_Lat: P_Lng: P_CountryCode:
        P_CountryName: P_TimeZoneID:
        P_dstOffset : P_gmtOffset : P_rawOffset :
        P_ErrCode : P_ErrMsg ) = *Off;
  // Do something with the parameters
EndIf;
```

In order for this procedure to work (and using last chapter's *RtvGPSFrmAddr* procedure as a base), I've started by changing the data structure used on the *XML-INTO* to match the XML document returned by the Web service. That means creating the following data structure (part of the *QCPYLESRC/RTVTMZ_PR* copy member):

```
 *-----------------------------------------------------------------------*
 *   Data Structures                                                     *
 *-----------------------------------------------------------------------*
D GeoNames        DS                    Qualified
D   TimeZone                            LikeDS(t_TimeZone)
D   Status                              LikeDS(t_Status)

D t_TimeZone      DS                    Qualified
D   CountryCode                         Like(t_CountryCode)
D   CountryName                         Like(t_CountryName)
D   TimeZoneID                          Like(t_TimeZoneID)
D   dstOffset                           Like(t_dstOffset)
D   gmtOffset                           Like(t_gmtOffset)
D   rawOffset                           Like(t_rawOffset)

                                                          Continued
```

```
D t_Status        DS                   Qualified
D   Message                   50A
D   Value                      3A

D t_Lat           S           15A
D t_Lng           S           15A
D t_CountryCode   S            2A
D t_CountryName   S           20A
D t_TimeZoneID    S           20A
D t_dstOffset     S            2  0
D t_gmtOffset     S            2  0
D t_rawOffset     S            2  0
D t_ErrCode       S            4  0
D t_ErrMsg        S           50A
```

Next, I've adjusted the procedure's parameters to return the time zone information and fill them in the *Process* subroutine with the data structure fields. Here is the new procedure interface:

```
 *------------------------------------------------------------------*
 *   Retrieve TimeZone Info from GPS coordinates                    *
 *------------------------------------------------------------------*
PRtvTmZFrmGPS     B                    EXPORT
D                 PI             N
 * Input Parms
DP_Lat                                 Like(t_lat) Value
DP_Lng                                 Like(t_lng) Value
 * Output Parms
DP_CountryCode                         Like(t_CountryCode)
DP_CountryName                         Like(t_CountryName)
DP_TimeZoneID                          Like(t_TimeZoneID)
DP_dstOffset                           Like(t_dstOffset)
DP_gmtOffset                           Like(t_gmtOffset)
DP_rawOffset                           Like(t_rawOffset)
DP_ErrCode                             Like(t_ErrCode)
DP_ErrMsg                              Like(t_ErrMsg)
```

Note that I'm using the same *t_ . . .* variables, which were used to define the data structure that handles the XML. This way, no conversions will occur, limiting the possibility of data loss or corruption during the whole process. The *Process* routine is adjusted similarly:

```
(...)
// Otherwise, pass the results to the output parms
  P_CountryCode = Geonames.TimeZone.CountryCode;
  P_CountryName = Geonames.TimeZone.CountryName;
  P_TimeZoneID  = Geonames.TimeZone.TimeZoneID;
  P_dstOffset   = Geonames.TimeZone.dstOffset;
  P_gmtOffset   = Geonames.TimeZone.gmtOffset;
  P_rawOffset   = Geonames.TimeZone.rawOffset;
  P_ErrCode   = *Zeros;
  P_ErrMsg    = *Blanks;
(...)
```

There's one more detail worth mentioning. The data structure is now called *Geonames*. So, all the references to it had to be adjusted, as you can see from the lines above. This will become more clear in the procedure's complete source code, presented later.

Finally, I have to adjust the response in case of error. This is necessary because this Web service uses a different structure to return errors:

```
<geonames>
  <status message="invalid lat/lng" value="12"/>
</geonames>
```

This error structure is common to other GeoNames Web services, so you'll see more of it later. I've noticed that in some versions of i5/OS™, the fact that the closing of the status tag is "/>" instead of "</status>" causes some problems, so a real error message might be misinterpreted as malformed XML. There are different PTFs to solve this problem, depending your system's version.

As promised, here's the procedure's complete source code:

```
HDatEdit(*YMD)  NoMain   ExprOpts(*MaxDigits) BndDir('HTTPAPI':'RTVTMZ')
 ***************************************************************************
 *                                                                         *
 *   Program .... : RTVTMZ                                                 *
 *   Description  : Retrieve TimeZone Info Procedures                      *
 *   Author ..... : Rafael Victoria-Pereira                                *
 *   Date ....... : July 2011                                              *
 *   Changes .... :                                                        *
 *=========================================================================*

 ***************************************************************************

 *-------------------------------------------------------------------------*
 *   File Descriptions                                                     *
 *-------------------------------------------------------------------------*
FLog       O    E             K Disk    Prefix(Log_) UsrOpn

 *-------------------------------------------------------------------------
 *   Data Areas
 *-------------------------------------------------------------------------
 * GeoNames ID
D DAGeoNamesID    S             10A   DTAARA(DAGeoNID)
 * GeoNames TimeZone API base URL
D DATZApiBaseUrl  S             50A   DTAARA(DAGeoTZURL)

 *-------------------------------------------------------------------------*
 *   Variables                                                             *
 *-------------------------------------------------------------------------*
 * Work Fields
 /define WEBFORMS
D W_FileName      S             45A   Varying
D W_Options       S            100A   Varying
D W_RetCode       S             10I 0
D W_GeoNamesID    S             10A   Inz
```

Continued

```
D W_ApiBaseUrl    S            50A   Inz
D W_URL           S         32767A   Varying
D W_Form          S                  Like(WEBFORM)
D W_Return        S             1N   Inz

 *-------------------------------------------------------------------------*
 *   Prototypes                                                            *
 *-------------------------------------------------------------------------*
 * Prototype definition for HTTP API Procedures
 /Copy QRPGLESRC,HTTPAPI_H
 /Copy QRPGLESRC,IFSIO_H
 * Prototype definition for Retrieve TimeZone Info Procedures
 /Copy QCPYLESRC,RTVTMZ_PR

 *-------------------------------------------------------------------------*
 *   Retrieve TimeZone Info from GPS coordinates                           *
 *-------------------------------------------------------------------------*
PRtvTmZFrmGPS     B                  EXPORT
D                 PI             N
 * Input Parms
DP_Lat                               Like(t_lat) Value
DP_Lng                               Like(t_lng) Value
 * Output Parms
DP_CountryCode                       Like(t_CountryCode)
DP_CountryName                       Like(t_CountryName)
DP_TimeZoneID                        Like(t_TimeZoneID)
DP_dstOffset                         Like(t_dstOffset)
DP_gmtOffset                         Like(t_gmtOffset)
DP_rawOffset                         Like(t_rawOffset)
DP_ErrCode                           Like(t_ErrCode)
DP_ErrMsg                            Like(t_ErrMsg)

 /FREE

    ExSr Init;
```

Continued

```
   ExSr Process;

  //  Sub Routines

  //-----------------------------------------------------------------*
  //  Initialization                                                *
  //-----------------------------------------------------------------*
    BegSr  Init;

      // Initialize output parameters
      P_CountryCode  = *Blanks;
      P_CountryName  = *Blanks;
      P_TimeZoneID   = *Blanks;
      P_dstOffset    = *Zeros;
      P_gmtOffset    = *Zeros;
      P_rawOffset    = *Zeros;
      P_ErrCode      = *Zeros;
      P_ErrMsg       = *Blanks;

      // Retrieve GeoNames ID
      In DAGeoNamesID;
      W_GeoNamesID = DAGeoNamesID;
      // Check If the GeoNames ID is filled in
      If W_GeoNamesID = *Blanks;
        P_ErrCode = 300; //Invalid GeoNames ID
        W_Return = *ON;
        ExSr End_And_Return;
      EndIf;

      // Retrieve GeoNames TimeZone API base url
      In DATZApiBaseUrl;
      W_ApiBaseUrl = DATZApiBaseUrl;
      // Check If the GeoNames TimeZone API base url is filled in
      If W_ApiBaseUrl = *Blanks;
        P_ErrCode = 350; //Invalid GeoNames TimeZone API base url
        W_Return = *ON;
```

Continued

```
      ExSr End_And_Return;
    EndIf;

    // Prepare parameters for XML-INTO
    W_Options = 'doc=file +
           path=GEONAMES +
           case=any +
           allowextra=yes +
           allowmissing=yes';

    // Compose the WebService URL with the address and your GeoNames ID
    W_Form = WEBFORM_open();
    WEBFORM_setVar(W_Form : 'lat'    : %Trim(P_Lat)  );
    WEBFORM_setVar(W_Form : 'lng'    : %Trim(P_Lng) );
    WEBFORM_setVar(W_Form : 'username' : %Trim(W_GeoNamesID) );

    W_Url = %Trim(W_ApiBaseUrl) + WEBFORM_getData(W_Form);

    // Close form
    WEBFORM_Close(W_Form);

    // Create a temp file to receive the WebService response
    W_FileName = http_tempfile() + '.xml';

    // Initialize the TimeZone array to avoid error on unused fields
    Clear GeoNames;

  EndSr;

//-------------------------------------------------------------------*
// Invoke Web Service and return TimeZone                            *
//-------------------------------------------------------------------*
  BegSr  Process;

    // Invoke the WebService
    W_RetCode = http_url_get(W_url : W_FileName);
```

Continued

```
// In case of error, return *ON
If (W_RetCode <> 1);
  P_ErrCode = 400; //Problems invoking the Web Service
  W_Return = *ON;
  ExSr End_And_Return;
EndIf;

// Receive xml file into data structure
Monitor;
  Xml-Into GeoNames %xml(W_FileName : W_Options);
On-Error;
  P_ErrCode = 500; //Malformed xml
  W_Return = *ON;
  ExSr End_And_Return;
EndMon;

// Check for API errors before processing
// In case of API error, return the error message and leave
If Geonames.status.message <> *Blanks;
  P_ErrMsg = GeoNames.status.message;
  P_ErrCode = 600; //API error, check the error message
  W_Return = *ON;
  ExSr End_And_Return;
Else;

// Otherwise, pass the results to the output parms
  P_CountryCode = Geonames.TimeZone.CountryCode;
  P_CountryName = Geonames.TimeZone.CountryName;
  P_TimeZoneID  = Geonames.TimeZone.TimeZoneID;
  P_dstOffset   = Geonames.TimeZone.dstOffset;
  P_gmtOffset   = Geonames.TimeZone.gmtOffset;
  P_rawOffset   = Geonames.TimeZone.rawOffset;
  P_ErrCode   = *Zeros;
  P_ErrMsg    = *Blanks;
  W_Return = *Off;
```

Continued

```
        ExSr End_And_Return;
      EndIf;

    EndSr;

  //--------------------------------------------------------------------*
  //  End and Return                                                     *
  //--------------------------------------------------------------------*
    BegSr End_And_Return;

      // Log status (useful for debuging)
      ExSr Log_Status;

      // Delete temp file
      unlink(W_FileName);

      // End and return the indicator (*on = error / *off = success)
      Return W_Return;

    EndSr;

  //--------------------------------------------------------------------*
  //  Log status                                                         *
  //--------------------------------------------------------------------*
    BegSr Log_Status;

      // Log request
      Open Log;
      Log_TypeReq = 'RtvTmZFrmGPS';
      Log_StsCode = P_ErrCode;
      Log_InpParm = 'Latitude=' + %Trim(P_Lat) +
                    '|Longitude=' + %Trim(P_Lng);
      Log_OutParm = 'CountryCode=' + %Trim(P_CountryCode)
                    + '|CountryName=' + %Trim(P_CountryName)
                    + '|TimeZoneID=' + %Trim(P_TimeZoneID)
                    + '|dstOffset=' + %Trim(%Char(P_dstOffset))
```

Continued

```
                    + '|gmtOffset=' + %Trim(%Char(P_gmtOffset))
                    + '|rawOffset=' + %Trim(%Char(P_rawOffset))
                    + '|ErrCode=' + %Trim(%Char(P_ErrCode))
                    + '|ErrMsg=' + %Trim(P_ErrMsg);
      Log_DateTim = %TimeStamp;
      Write LogR;
      Close Log;

    EndSr;
 /END-FREE

PRtvTmZFrmGPS      E
```

Other than the details already mentioned and some other minor variable name adjustments, this procedure is very similar to last chapter's *RtvGpsFrmAddr*. Speaking of this, in the example provided in *QRPGLESRC/TST_TMZADD* (reproduced below), you'll find an orchestration of Web services. The previously mentioned *RtvGPSFrmAddr* is being used to retrieve the GPS coordinates of an address, and then *RtvTmzFrmGPS* uses those coordinates to retrieve the time zone information:

```
H DECEDIT(',') DATEDIT(*DMY.)

 * Retrieve GPS Info Procedures
 /Copy QCPYLESRC,RTVGPS_PR
 * Retrieve TimeZone Info Procedures
 /Copy QCPYLESRC,RTVTMZ_PR

DW_Response       S              52A   Inz(*Blanks)

 /FREE
   // Here I'll retrieve the timezone for the address mentioned in the
   // P_Address variable, in a two-step process:
   // First, retrieve the GPS coordinates of the address
   P_Address = '701 First Ave., Sunnyvale, CA 94089'; // Full address w/ door nbr
   If RtvGpsFrmAddr(P_Address :
                                                                    Continued
```

```
                  P_Quality :
                  P_Latitude :
                  P_Longitude :
                  P_ErrorCode) = *Off;
   // Second, use the coordinates to retrieve the timezone
      If RtvTmzFrmGPS(P_Latitude :
                    P_Longitude :
                    P_CountryCode:
                    P_CountryName:
                    P_TimeZoneID:
                    P_dstOffset :
                    P_gmtOffset :
                    P_rawOffset :
                    P_ErrCode :
                    P_ErrMsg ) = *Off;
        W_Response = 'TimeZoneID=' + %Trim(P_TimeZoneID) +
                    ' dstOffset=' + %Trim(%char(P_dstOffset)) +
                    ' gmtOffset=' + %Trim(%char(P_gmtOffset)) +
                    ' rawOffset=' + %Trim(%char(P_rawOffset));
        Dsply W_Response;
      Else;
        // Error occurred in the RtvTmzFrmGPS procedure
        W_Response = 'RtvTmZ Error Code=' + %Char(P_ErrCode);
        Dsply W_Response;
      EndIf;
   Else;
      // Error occurred in the RtvGPSFrmAddr procedure
      W_Response = 'RtvGPS Error Code=' + %Char(P_ErrorCode);
      Dsply W_Response;
   EndIf;

   *InLr = *On;
/END-FREE
```

Note that both procedures are invoked in *IF* statements, and each of them uses the *W_Response* variable to compose a "proper" error message to send to the user. Naturally, this is a rather simple example, but the fact that the procedure returns an indicator and an error code can (and should) be used programmatically to do some "damage control."

The way the orchestration of the Web services is done is important. The second Web service, which uses data obtained from the first one, can only be invoked if the data was successfully retrieved. By building your procedures with this fail-safe mechanism, you ensure that the final result is correct, or at least, it's as correct as possible given the fact that multiple Web services are being used, and each of them may or may not be working at the time you invoke it.

The Country Code and Country Info Web Services

Now that you know how to find a time zone (given an address or set of GPS coordinates), let's find out more about the country! For that, I'll use the Country Info REST Web service. This Web service requires a slightly different approach, because you need to know the country code to invoke it. If you only have an address, this might be a problem. One way to solve this problem is to use several Web services sequentially, using the output of the first as the input of the second and so on—in other words, orchestrating the Web services to get the data you need. Sounds great, right?

So, what do we need? Starting with an address, you need to figure out its GPS coordinates. The *RtvGpsFrmAddr* procedure from the previous chapter takes care of that. With the GPS coordinates, you can use the Country Code Web service to get the piece of information needed to invoke the Country Info Web service. That's why this section explains two Web services instead of one.

Let's start with the GeoNames Country Code Web service (*http://www.geonames.org/export/web-services.html#countrycode*). It's quite simple; invoke it like this:

```
http://api.geonames.org/countryCode?lat=47.03&lng=10.2&type=XML&username=demo
```

The URL is composed of the Web service location (*http://api.geonames.org/countryCode?*), its parameters (*lat=47.03&lng=10.2&type=XML&username=demo*, latitude and longitude), type of reply (*XML* in this case), and user. By the way, the *demo* user has a per-day limit of 30,000 requests and shouldn't be used in an application.

The Web service's response is also very simple:

```
<geonames>
  <country>
    <countryCode>AT</countryCode>
    <countryName>Austria</countryName>
    <languages>de-AT,hr,hu,sl</languages>
    <distance>0.0</distance>
  </country>
</geonames>
```

Notice the bolded lines; the XML structure is similar to the Country Info Web service, which I'll explain later. I was able to use the same data structure for both Web services (see *QCPYLESRC/RTVCIN_PR* for the complete source):

```
 *-------------------------------------------------------------------*
 *    Data Structures                                                 *
 *-------------------------------------------------------------------*
D GeoNames        DS                  Qualified
D   Country                           LikeDS(t_Country)
D   Status                            LikeDS(t_Status)

D t_Country       DS                  Qualified
D   CountryCode                       Like(t_CountryCode)
D   CountryName                       Like(t_CountryName)
D   IsoNumeric                        Like(t_IsoNumeric)
D   IsoAlpha3                         Like(t_IsoAlpha3)
D   FipsCode                          Like(t_FipsCode)
D   Continent                         Like(t_Continent)
D   ContinentName...
D                                     Like(t_ContinentName)
D   Capital                           Like(t_Capital)
D   AreaInSqKm                        Like(t_AreaInSqKm)
D   Population                        Like(t_Population)
D   CurrencyCode                      Like(t_CurrencyCode)
D   Languages                         Like(t_Languages)
                                                            Continued
```

```
D   GeoNameId                           Like(t_GeoNameId)
D   bBoxWest                            Like(t_bBoxWest)
D   bBoxNorth                           Like(t_bBoxNorth)
D   bBoxEast                            Like(t_bBoxEast)
D   bBoxSouth                           Like(t_bBoxSouth)

D t_Status        DS                    Qualified
D   Message                      50A
D   Value                         3A

D t_Lat           S              15A
D t_Lng           S              15A
D t_CountryCode   S               2A
D t_CountryName   S              20A
D t_IsoNumeric    S               3  0
D t_IsoAlpha3     S               3A
D t_FipsCode      S               2A
D t_Continent     S               5A
D t_ContinentName...
D                 S              20A
D t_Capital       S              20A
D t_AreaInSqKm    S              10  0
D t_Population    S              12  0
D t_CurrencyCode  S               3A
D t_Languages     S              20A
D t_GeoNameId     S              10  0
D t_bBoxWest      S                     Like(t_Lat)
D t_bBoxNorth     S                     Like(t_Lat)
D t_bBoxEast      S                     Like(t_Lat)
D t_bBoxSouth     S                     Like(t_Lat)
D t_ErrCode       S               4  0
D t_ErrMsg        S              50A
```

This was possible because of the *XML-INTO* options *allowextra=yes* and *allowmissing=yes*, which allow the data structure used with the opcode to contain elements that don't match the XML structure, and vice versa.

The next step was to build a procedure to invoke this Web service. As you might have guessed, it was based on the procedure in the previous section. It was a matter of removing all the lines of code related to *RtvTmZFrmGPS*'s long list of parameters, leaving only the *P_CountryCode* and adapting the variable names to the Web service's name for clarity. Here's the complete source code for procedure *RtvCntrCodeFrmGPS*:

```
HDatEdit(*YMD)  NoMain   ExprOpts(*MaxDigits) BndDir('HTTPAPI':'RTVCIN')
 ***************************************************************************
 *                                                                         *
 *   Program .... : RTVCIN                                                 *
 *   Description  : Retrieve Country Info Procedures                       *
 *   Author ..... : Rafael Victoria-Pereira                                *
 *   Date ....... : July 2011                                              *
 *   Changes .... :                                                        *
 *=========================================================================*

 ***************************************************************************

 *-------------------------------------------------------------------------*
 *   File Descriptions                                                     *
 *-------------------------------------------------------------------------*
FLog       O    E           K Disk    Prefix(Log_) UsrOpn

 *--------------------------------------------------------------------------
 *   Data Areas
 *--------------------------------------------------------------------------
 * GeoNames ID
D DAGeoNamesID    S             10A   DTAARA(DAGeoNID)
 * GeoNames Country Code API base URL
D DACCApiBaseUrl  S             50A   DTAARA(DAGeoCCURL)
 * GeoNames Country Info API base URL
D DACIApiBaseUrl  S             50A   DTAARA(DAGeoCIURL)

 *-------------------------------------------------------------------------*
 *   Variables                                                             *
 *-------------------------------------------------------------------------*
```

Continued

```
 * Work Fields
 /define WEBFORMS
D W_FileName      S             45A   Varying
D W_Options       S            100A   Varying
D W_RetCode       S             10I 0
D W_GeoNamesID    S             10A   Inz
D W_ApiBaseUrl    S             50A   Inz
D W_URL           S          32767A   Varying
D W_Form          S                   Like(WEBFORM)
D W_Return        S              1N   Inz

 *-------------------------------------------------------------------------*
 *   Prototypes                                                            *
 *-------------------------------------------------------------------------*
 * Prototype definition for HTTP API Procedures
 /Copy QRPGLESRC,HTTPAPI_H
 /Copy QRPGLESRC,IFSIO_H
 * Prototype definition for Retrieve Country Info Procedures
 /Copy QCPYLESRC,RTVCIN_PR

 *-------------------------------------------------------------------------*
 *   Retrieve Country Code from GPS coordinates                            *
 *-------------------------------------------------------------------------*
PRtvCntrCodeFrmGPS...
P                 B                   EXPORT
D                 PI              N
 * Input Parms
DP_Lat                                Like(t_lat) Value
DP_Lng                                Like(t_lng) Value
 * Output Parms
DP_CountryCode                        Like(t_CountryCode)
DP_ErrCode                            Like(t_ErrCode)
DP_ErrMsg                             Like(t_ErrMsg)

 /FREE

    ExSr Init;
```

Continued

```
 ExSr Process;

// Sub Routines

//-----------------------------------------------------------------------*
// Initialization                                                        *
//-----------------------------------------------------------------------*
  BegSr Init;

    // Initialize output parameters
    P_CountryCode  = *Blanks;
    P_ErrCode      = *Zeros;
    P_ErrMsg       = *Blanks;

    // Retrieve GeoNames ID
    In DAGeoNamesID;
    W_GeoNamesID = DAGeoNamesID;
    // Check If the GeoNames ID is filled in
    If W_GeoNamesID = *Blanks;
      P_ErrCode = 300; //Invalid GeoNames ID
      W_Return = *ON;
      ExSr End_And_Return;
    EndIf;

    // Retrieve GeoNames Country Code API base url
    In DACCApiBaseUrl;
    W_ApiBaseUrl = DACCApiBaseUrl;
    // Check If the GeoNames Country Code API base url is filled in
    If W_ApiBaseUrl = *Blanks;
      P_ErrCode = 350; //Invalid GeoNames Country Code API base url
      W_Return = *ON;
      ExSr End_And_Return;
    EndIf;

    // Prepare parameters for XML-INTO
```

Continued

```
    W_Options = 'doc=file +
           path=GEONAMES +
           case=any +
           allowextra=yes +
           allowmissing=yes';

    // Compose the WebService URL with the address and your GeoNames ID
    W_Form = WEBFORM_open();
    WEBFORM_setVar(W_Form : 'lat'    : %Trim(P_Lat)  );
    WEBFORM_setVar(W_Form : 'lng'    : %Trim(P_Lng) );
    WEBFORM_setVar(W_Form : 'type'   : 'xml'        );
    WEBFORM_setVar(W_Form : 'username' : %Trim(W_GeoNamesID) );

    W_Url = %Trim(W_ApiBaseUrl) + WEBFORM_getData(W_Form);

    // Close form
    WEBFORM_Close(W_Form);

    // Create a temp file to receive the WebService response
    W_FileName = http_tempfile() + '.xml';

    // Initialize the GeoNames array to avoid errors in unused fields
    Clear GeoNames;

  EndSr;

//---------------------------------------------------------------------*
// Invoke Web Service and return Country Code                          *
//---------------------------------------------------------------------*
  BegSr  Process;

    // Invoke the Web Service
    W_RetCode = http_url_get(W_url : W_FileName);

    // In case of error,  return *ON
    If (W_RetCode <> 1);
```

Continued

```
      P_ErrCode = 400; //Problems invoking the Web Service
      W_Return = *ON;
      ExSr End_And_Return;
    EndIf;

    // Receive xml file into data structure
    Monitor;
      Xml-Into GeoNames %xml(W_FileName : W_Options);
    On-Error;
      P_ErrCode = 500; //Malformed xml
      W_Return = *ON;
      ExSr End_And_Return;
    EndMon;

    // Check for API errors before processing
    // In case of API error, return the error message and leave
    If Geonames.status.message <> *Blanks;
      P_ErrMsg = GeoNames.status.message;
      P_ErrCode = 600; //API error, check the error message
      W_Return = *ON;
      ExSr End_And_Return;
    Else;

    // Otherwise, pass the results to the output parms
      P_CountryCode = Geonames.Country.CountryCode;
      P_ErrCode   = *Zeros;
      P_ErrMsg    = *Blanks;
      W_Return = *Off;
      ExSr End_And_Return;
    EndIf;

  EndSr;

//----------------------------------------------------------------------*
//  End and Return                                                      *
//----------------------------------------------------------------------*
```

Continued

```
     BegSr End_And_Return;

       // Log status (useful for debuging)
       ExSr Log_Status;

       // Delete temp file
       unlink(W_FileName);

       // End and return the indicator (*on = error / *off = success)
       Return W_Return;

     EndSr;

   //-----------------------------------------------------------------*
   //  Log status                                                     *
   //-----------------------------------------------------------------*
     BegSr Log_Status;

       // Log request
       Open Log;
       Log_TypeReq = 'RtvCntrCodeFrmGPS';
       Log_StsCode = P_ErrCode;
       Log_InpParm = 'Latitude=' + %Trim(P_Lat) +
                     '|Longitude=' + %Trim(P_Lng);
       Log_OutParm = 'CountryCode=' + %Trim(P_CountryCode)
                     + '|ErrCode=' + %Trim(%Char(P_ErrCode))
                     + '|ErrMsg=' + %Trim(P_ErrMsg);
       Log_DateTim = %TimeStamp;
       Write LogR;
       Close Log;

     EndSr;
 /END-FREE

PRtvCntrCodeFrmGPS...
P                 E
```

By invoking this procedure, the second step of our three-step solution is complete. Finally, let's analyze the third and final Web service. For a simple example, let's invoke the Web service, using the USA country code (*US*):

```
http://api.geonames.org/countryInfo?country=US&lang=en&username=demo
```

This is what you get in return:


```
<geonames>
  <country>
    <countryCode>US</countryCode>
    <countryName>United States</countryName>
    <isoNumeric>840</isoNumeric>
    <isoAlpha3>USA</isoAlpha3>
    <fipsCode>US</fipsCode>
    <continent>NA</continent>
    <continentName>North America</continentName>
    <capital>Washington</capital>
    <areaInSqKm>9629091.0</areaInSqKm>
    <population>310232863</population>
    <currencyCode>USD</currencyCode>
    <languages>en-US,es-US,haw,fr</languages>
    <geonameId>6252001</geonameId>
    <bBoxWest>-124.733253</bBoxWest>
    <bBoxNorth>49.388611</bBoxNorth>
    <bBoxEast>-66.954811</bBoxEast>
    <bBoxSouth>24.544245</bBoxSouth>
  </country>
</geonames>
```


In this case, I'll use all of the information made available by the Web service, but feel free to discard the data that you don't consider relevant. Here's a rundown of the XML, with a little help from Wikipedia:

- *<countryCode>*—This is the ISO 3166-1 alpha-2 code for the country. ISO 3166-1 alpha-2 codes are two-letter country codes defined in ISO 3166-1, part of the ISO 3166 standard published by the International Organization for

Standardization (ISO) to represent countries, dependent territories, and special areas of geographical interest. They are the most widely used of the country codes published by ISO (the others being alpha-3 and numeric), and are used most prominently for the Internet's country code top-level domains (with a few exceptions). They were first included as part of the ISO 3166 standard in its first edition in 1974. A complete list of the current codes and their meanings is available here:

http://en.wikipedia.org/wiki/ISO_3166-1_alpha-2#Current_codes

- *<countryName>*—This should be self-explanatory, but there's an important detail that's worth mentioning. The names of the country, capital, and continent are returned in the language indicated on the *lang* parameter of the URL. By default, the information is returned in English.
- *<isoNumeric>*—This is the ISO 3166-1 numeric (or numeric-3) code for the country. ISO 3166-1 numeric (or numeric-3) codes are three-digit country codes defined in ISO 3166-1. They are identical to the three-digit country codes developed and maintained by the United Nations Statistics Division, from which they originate in its UN M.49 standard. They were first included as part of the ISO 3166 standard in its second edition in 1981, but they have been released by the United Nations Statistics Division since as early as 1970.

  An advantage of numeric codes over alphabetic codes is script (writing system) independence. The ISO 3166-1 alphabetic codes (alpha-2 and alpha-3) use letters from the English alphabet and are suitable for languages based on the Latin alphabet. For people and systems using non-Latin scripts (such as Arabic, Chinese, Cyrillic, and Hebrew), the English alphabet may be unavailable or difficult to use, understand, or correctly interpret. While numeric codes overcome the problems of script dependence, this independence comes at the loss of mnemonic convenience. A complete list of the current codes and their meanings is available here:

  http://en.wikipedia.org/wiki/ISO_3166-1_numeric#Current_codes

- *<isoAlpha3>*—This is a three-letter code for the country, similar to *countryCode*. A complete list of the current codes and their meanings is available here:

  http://en.wikipedia.org/wiki/ISO_3166-1_alpha-3#Current_codes

- *<fipsCode>*—This is a two-letter country code, used by the US government for geographical data processing in many publications, such as the CIA World

Factbook. The FIPS standard includes both the codes for independent countries (similar but sometimes incompatible with the ISO 3166-1 alpha-2 standard) and the codes for top-level subdivision of the countries (similar to but usually incompatible with the ISO 3166-2 standard). The ISO 3166 codes are used by the United Nations and for Internet top-level country code domains. A complete list of the current codes and their meanings is available here:

http://en.wikipedia.org/wiki/List_of_FIPS_country_codes

- *<continent>*—This is a two-letter code for the continents. A complete list of the current codes and their meanings is available here:

  http://en.wikipedia.org/wiki/List_of_sovereign_states_and_dependent_territories_by_continent_%28data_file%29

- *<continentName>*—Just like *countryName*, this one should be self-explanatory.
- *<capital>*—This too should be self-explanatory. The note about the *lang* parameter is also applicable here.
- *<areaInSqKms>*—This is the area of the country. Please note that the data is in square kilometers, not miles.
- *<population>*—This one is self-explanatory.
- *<currencyCode>*—This is the ISO 4217 code for the country's currency. The codes are used in banking and business globally. In many countries, the ISO codes for the more common currencies are so well known publicly that exchange rates published in newspapers or posted in banks use only these to delineate the different currencies, instead of translated currency names or ambiguous currency symbols. ISO 4217 codes are also used on airline tickets and international train tickets to remove any ambiguity about the price. A complete list of the current codes and their meanings is available here:
  http://en.wikipedia.org/wiki/ISO_4217#Active_codes

- *<languages>*—This is the list of languages spoken in the country, using the IETF language tag, which is an abbreviated language code (for example, *en* for English, *pt-BR* for Brazilian Portuguese). A complete list and their meanings is available here:
  http://en.wikipedia.org/wiki/IETF_language_tag

- *<geoNameID>*—This is GeoNames' internal ID for the country. Don't discard this one, because it can be used as a parameter to invoke other Web services.
- *<bBoxWest>*, *<bBoxNorth>*, *<bBoxEast>*, and *<bBoxSouth>*—Each of these parameters contains a coordinate (latitude or longitude), and the intersection

of these four "lines" forms a rectangle with roughly the area of the country. GeoNames' complete documentation for this Web service can be found here:

http://www.geonames.org/export/web-services.html#countryInfo

As mentioned earlier, the *GeoNames* data structure from *QCPYLESRC/RTVCIN_PR* is used for the two Web services presented in this section, but a separate procedure is required for this Web service. Again based on *RtvTmZFrmGPS*, I've created procedure *RtvCntrInfoFrmCode*. This procedure has the country code as input parameter and returns all the data the Country Info Web Service does. Here's the procedure's complete source code:

```
 *----------------------------------------------------------------------*
 *   Retrieve Country Info from Country Code                            *
 *----------------------------------------------------------------------*
PRtvCntrInfoFrmCode...
P                B                   EXPORT
D                PI             N
 * Input Parms
DP_CountryCode                       Like(t_CountryCode)
 * Output Parms
DP_CountryName                       Like(t_CountryName)
DP_IsoNumeric                        Like(t_IsoNumeric)
DP_IsoAlpha3                         Like(t_IsoAlpha3)
DP_FipsCode                          Like(t_FipsCode)
DP_Continent                         Like(t_Continent)
DP_ContinentName                     Like(t_ContinentName)
DP_Capital                           Like(t_Capital)
DP_AreaInSqKm                        Like(t_AreaInSqKm)
DP_Population                        Like(t_Population)
DP_CurrencyCode                      Like(t_CurrencyCode)
DP_Languages                         Like(t_Languages)
DP_GeoNameId                         Like(t_GeoNameId)
DP_bBoxWest                          Like(t_bBoxWest)
DP_bBoxNorth                         Like(t_bBoxNorth)
DP_bBoxEast                          Like(t_bBoxEast)
DP_bBoxSouth                         Like(t_bBoxSouth)
```

Continued

```
DP_ErrCode                              Like(t_ErrCode)
DP_ErrMsg                               Like(t_ErrMsg)

 /FREE

    ExSr Init;

    ExSr Process;

   //  Sub Routines

   //-------------------------------------------------------------------*
   //  Initialization                                                   *
   //-------------------------------------------------------------------*
     BegSr  Init;

       // Initialize output parameters
       P_CountryName   = *Blanks;
       P_IsoNumeric    = *Zeros;
       P_IsoAlpha3     = *Blanks;
       P_FipsCode      = *Blanks;
       P_Continent     = *Blanks;
       P_ContinentName = *Blanks;
       P_Capital       = *Blanks;
       P_AreaInSqKm    = *Zeros;
       P_Population    = *Zeros;
       P_CurrencyCode  = *Blanks;
       P_Languages     = *Blanks;
       P_GeoNameId     = *Zeros;
       P_bBoxWest      = *Blanks;
       P_bBoxNorth     = *Blanks;
       P_bBoxEast      = *Blanks;
       P_bBoxSouth     = *Blanks;
       P_ErrCode       = *Zeros;
       P_ErrMsg        = *Blanks;
```

Continued

```
// Retrieve GeoNames ID
In DAGeoNamesID;
W_GeoNamesID = DAGeoNamesID;
// Check If the GeoNames ID is filled in
If W_GeoNamesID = *Blanks;
  P_ErrCode = 300; //Invalid GeoNames ID
  W_Return = *ON;
  ExSr End_And_Return;
EndIf;

// Retrieve GeoNames Country Info API base url
In DACIApiBaseUrl;
W_ApiBaseUrl = DACIApiBaseUrl;
// Check If the GeoNames Country Info API base url is filled in
If W_ApiBaseUrl = *Blanks;
  P_ErrCode = 350; //Invalid GeoNames Country Info API base url
  W_Return = *ON;
  ExSr End_And_Return;
EndIf;

// Prepare parameters for XML-INTO
W_Options = 'doc=file +
       path=GEONAMES +
       case=any +
       allowextra=yes +
       allowmissing=yes';

// Compose the WebService URL with the address and your GeoNames ID
// The lang parameter is used to return the country, capital and
// continent names in the appropriate language. English as default
W_Form = WEBFORM_open();
WEBFORM_setVar(W_Form : 'country'  : %Trim(P_CountryCode) );
WEBFORM_setVar(W_Form : 'lang'     : 'en'                 );
WEBFORM_setVar(W_Form : 'username' : %Trim(W_GeoNamesID)  );
W_Url = %Trim(W_ApiBaseUrl) + WEBFORM_getData(W_Form);
```

Continued

```
    // Close form
     WEBFORM_Close(W_Form);

    // Create a temp file to receive the WebService response
    W_FileName = http_tempfile() + '.xml';

    // Initialize the GeoNames array to avoid errors in unused fields
    Clear GeoNames;

  EndSr;

//------------------------------------------------------------------------*
// Invoke Web Service and return Country Information                      *
//------------------------------------------------------------------------*
  BegSr  Process;

    // Invoke the WebService
    W_RetCode = http_url_get(W_url : W_FileName);

    // In case of error,  return *ON
    If (W_RetCode <> 1);
      P_ErrCode = 400; //Problems invoking the Web Service
      W_Return = *ON;
      ExSr End_And_Return;
    EndIf;

    // Receive xml file into data structure
    Monitor;
      Xml-Into GeoNames %xml(W_FileName : W_Options);
    On-Error;
      P_ErrCode = 500; //Malformed xml
      W_Return = *ON;
      ExSr End_And_Return;
    EndMon;

    // Check for API errors before processing
```

Continued

```
    // In case of API error, return the error message and leave
    If Geonames.status.message <> *Blanks;
      P_ErrMsg = GeoNames.status.message;
      P_ErrCode = 600; //API error, check the error message
      W_Return = *ON;
      ExSr End_And_Return;
    Else;

    // Otherwise, pass the results to the output parms
      P_CountryName   = Geonames.Country.CountryName;
      P_IsoNumeric    = Geonames.Country.IsoNumeric;
      P_IsoAlpha3     = Geonames.Country.IsoAlpha3;
      P_FipsCode      = Geonames.Country.FipsCode;
      P_Continent     = Geonames.Country.Continent;
      P_ContinentName = Geonames.Country.ContinentName;
      P_Capital       = Geonames.Country.Capital;
      P_AreaInSqKm    = Geonames.Country.AreaInSqKm;
      P_Population    = Geonames.Country.Population;
      P_CurrencyCode  = Geonames.Country.CurrencyCode;
      P_Languages     = Geonames.Country.Languages;
      P_GeoNameId     = Geonames.Country.GeoNameId;
      P_bBoxWest      = Geonames.Country.bBoxWest;
      P_bBoxNorth     = Geonames.Country.bBoxNorth;
      P_bBoxEast      = Geonames.Country.bBoxEast;
      P_bBoxSouth     = Geonames.Country.bBoxSouth;
      P_ErrCode       = *Zeros;
      P_ErrMsg        = *Blanks;
      W_Return = *Off;
      ExSr End_And_Return;
    EndIf;

  EndSr;

//--------------------------------------------------------------------*
//  End and Return                                                     *
//--------------------------------------------------------------------*
```

Continued

```
  BegSr End_And_Return;

    // Log status (useful for debuging)
    ExSr Log_Status;

    // Delete temp file
    //unlink(W_FileName);

    // End and return the indicator (*on = error / *off = success)
    Return W_Return;

  EndSr;

//-----------------------------------------------------------------------*
//  Log status                                                            *
//-----------------------------------------------------------------------*
  BegSr Log_Status;

    // Log request
    Open Log;
    Log_TypeReq = 'RtvCntrInfoFrmCode';
    Log_StsCode = P_ErrCode;
    Log_InpParm = 'CountryCode=' + %Trim(P_CountryCode);
    Log_OutParm = 'CountryName=' + %Trim(P_CountryName)
                + '|IsoNumeric='    + %Trim(%Char(P_IsoNumeric))
                + '|IsoAlpha3='     + %Trim(P_IsoAlpha3)
                + '|FipsCode='      + %Trim(P_FipsCode)
                + '|Continent='     + %Trim(P_Continent)
                + '|ContinentName=' + %Trim(P_ContinentName)
                + '|Capital='       + %Trim(P_Capital)
                + '|AreaInSqKm='    + %Trim(%Char(P_AreaInSqKm))
                + '|Population='    + %Trim(%Char(P_Population))
                + '|CurrencyCode='  + %Trim(P_CurrencyCode)
                + '|Languages='     + %Trim(P_Languages)
                + '|GeoNameId='     + %Trim(%Char(P_GeoNameId))
                + '|bBoxWest='      + %Trim(P_bBoxWest)
```

Continued

```
                        + '|bBoxNorth='       + %Trim(P_bBoxNorth)
                        + '|bBoxEast='        + %Trim(P_bBoxEast)
                        + '|bBoxSouth='       + %Trim(P_bBoxSouth)
                        + '|ErrCode='         + %Trim(%Char(P_ErrCode))
                        + '|ErrMsg='          + %Trim(P_ErrMsg);
         Log_DateTim = %TimeStamp;
         Write LogR;
         Close Log;

       EndSr;
 /END-FREE

PRtvCntrInfoFrmCode...
P                 E
```

Since the procedure's structure should be familiar by now, let me just mention a particularly important detail of it. Notice the *Log_Status* routine, at the end of the procedure. You might have noticed it in earlier procedures, but I didn't explain it then. This routine is good for troubleshooting Web service issues because it writes a record to a log file (actually called *LOG*. . .) containing all the input and output parameters of the Web service invocation. Since this Web service might be used in conjunction with two others, if your starting point is an address, it might be good to have something to show exactly what happened. The *Log_Status* routine exists in all the procedures (actually, it should be a procedure itself!), so that you can easily follow the Web service calls and determine where things went wrong.

Finally, to consolidate all of this and illustrate the use of the *LOG* file, let's analyze an example. It's the *QRPGLESRC/TST_CINADD* source member:

```
H DECEDIT(',') DATEDIT(*DMY.)

 * Retrieve GPS Info Procedures
 /Copy QCPYLESRC,RTVGPS_PR
 * Retrieve Country Info Procedures
 /Copy QCPYLESRC,RTVCIN_PR

                                                                  Continued
```

```
DW_Response       S              52A   Inz(*Blanks)

 /FREE
   // Here I'll retrieve the Country Information for the country to
   // which the address stored in the P_Address variable belongs,
   // in a three step process:
   // First, retrieve the GPS coordinates of the address
   P_Address = '701 First Ave., Sunnyvale, CA 94089'; // Full address w/ door nbr
   If RtvGpsFrmAddr(P_Address :
                    P_Quality :
                    P_Latitude :
                    P_Longitude :
                    P_ErrorCode) = *Off;
   // Second, use the coordinates to retrieve the country code
      If RtvCntrCodeFrmGPS(P_Latitude :
                           P_Longitude :
                           P_CountryCode:
                           P_ErrCode :
                           P_ErrMsg ) = *Off;
   // Third, use the country code to retrieve the country information
         If RtvCntrInfoFrmCode(P_CountryCode:
                               P_CountryName:
                               P_IsoNumeric:
                               P_IsoAlpha3:
                               P_FipsCode:
                               P_Continent:
                               P_ContinentName:
                               P_Capital:
                               P_AreaInSqKm:
                               P_Population:
                               P_CurrencyCode:
                               P_Languages:
                               P_GeoNameId:
                               P_bBoxWest:
                               P_bBoxNorth:
                               P_bBoxEast:
```

Continued

```
                        P_bBoxSouth:
                        P_ErrCode :
                        P_ErrMsg ) = *Off;
            W_Response = 'CountryName = ' + %Trim(P_CountryName);
            Dsply W_Response;
          Else;
            // Error occurred in the RtvCntrInfoFrmCode procedure
            W_Response = 'RtvCntrInfoFrmCode Error Code = ' +
                         %Char(P_ErrCode);
            Dsply W_Response;
          EndIf;
        Else;
          // Error occurred in the RtvCntrCodeFrmGPS Procedure
          W_Response = 'RtvCntrCodeFrmGPS Error Code = ' +
                       %Char(P_ErrCode);
          Dsply W_Response;
        EndIf;
      Else;
        // Error occurred in the RtvGPSFrmAddr procedure
        W_Response = 'RtvGPS Error Code = ' + %Char(P_ErrorCode);
        Dsply W_Response;
      EndIf;

      *InLr = *On;
    /END-FREE
```

Here, I'm using an orchestration of Web services to retrieve the country information, using an address as a starting point. Procedure *RtvGpsFrmAddr*, which was described in the previous chapter, is used to obtain the GPS coordinates of an address, stored in the *P_Address* variable. Then, *RtvCntrCodeFrmGPS* invokes the Country Code Web service to obtain the country code that matches the address, using the *P_Latitude* and *P_Longitude* parameters returned by the first Web service. Finally, *RtvCntrInfoFrmCode* is called to retrieve the country information, via the Country Info Web service and using the country code returned by the *RtvCntrCodeFrmGPS* Web service. Run this example (the program name is *TST_CINADD*), and check the *LOG* file. What I tried to explain earlier about it should be clear after that.

The Find Nearby Points of Interest Web Service

While the previous sections of this chapter have focused on retrieving information relevant to your company, this time it'll be a bit different: this one is for your clients.

Knowing beforehand that there's a nice restaurant or bar near your car dealership is useful when you go in for a small repair that won't take long. You can either find out for yourself or, if your dealership has a really nice service, its Web site or customer support line will be able to tell you. From a company's point of view, having additional information available about its locations (stores, offices, or branches) might provide an edge over the competition.

This section explains the Find Nearby POIs Web service in order to achieve that goal. Even though the Web service is provided by GeoNames, the data actually comes from OpenStreetMap (*http://www.openstreetmap.org*). I recommend that you learn more about OpenStreetMap and read the copyright and license information at their site. It's a great open-source project.

Let's start by looking at the Find Nearby POIs Web service:

http://www.geonames.org/maps/osm-reverse-geocoder.html#findNearbyPOIsOSM

Since it is a REST Web service, it is invoked by composing a URL in which you include the GPS coordinates of the location, such as the one below:

```
http://api.geonames.org/findNearbyPOIsOSM?lat=37.451&lng=-122.18&username=demo
```

This will return an XML document with the POIs that are near the coordinates indicated:

```
<geonames>
  <poi>
    <name>Cook's Seafood</name>
    <typeClass>amenity</typeClass>
    <typeName>restaurant</typeName>
    <lng>-122.1795529</lng>
    <lat>37.4516093</lat>
                                                    Continued
```

```
    <distance>0.08</distance>
  </poi>
  <poi>
    <name>Starbucks</name>
    <typeClass>amenity</typeClass>
    <typeName>cafe</typeName>
    <lng>-122.1803386</lng>
    <lat>37.452055</lat>
    <distance>0.12</distance>
  </poi>
  <poi>
    <name>Safeway</name>
    <typeClass>shop</typeClass>
    <typeName>supermarket</typeName>
    <lng>-122.1787081</lng>
    <lat>37.4507461</lat>
    <distance>0.12</distance>
  </poi>
  <poi>
    <name>Akasaka</name>
    <typeClass>amenity</typeClass>
    <typeName>restaurant</typeName>
    <lng>-122.1809239</lng>
    <lat>37.4524367</lat>
    <distance>0.18</distance>
  </poi>
</geonames>
```

The *<poi>* element is composed of the following sub-elements:

- *<name>*—The name of the point of interest (POI)
- *<typeClass>*—The class of the POI, according to the OpenStreetMap Map Features classification at *http://wiki.openstreetmap.org/wiki/Map_Features*
- *<typeName>*—The type (or sub-class) of POI, again according to the OpenStreetMap Map Features classification at *http://wiki.openstreetmap.org/wiki/Map_Features*
- *<lng>*—The longitude coordinate of the POI

- *<lat>*—The latitude coordinate of the POI
- *<distance>*—The distance between the POI's coordinates and the ones indicated on the Web service invocation

Now, let's examine the XML. This time, there's a new type of reply. Instead of having only one set of similar data in the response XML (*<timezone>* on the first section and *<country>* in the second), we have multiple sets. The *<poi>* element repeats multiple times. To handle this, a slightly different approach is required in both the procedure's parameters and the data structure used on the *XML-INTO* opcode; they must have the ability to store multiple instances of the same type of data. In other words, they must be arrays.

In the *QCPYLESRC/RTVFNP_PR* source member, I've defined a new data structure, *t_poi*, with a structure similar to the *<poi>* element and used it to define the *XML-INTO* data structure:

```
 *-----------------------------------------------------------------------*
 *   Data Structures                                                     *
 *-----------------------------------------------------------------------*
D GeoNames        DS                  Qualified
D   Poi                               LikeDS(t_Poi) Dim(C_MaxElems)
D   Status                            LikeDS(t_Status)

D t_Poi           DS                  Qualified
D   Name                              Like(t_Name)
D   TypeClass                         Like(t_TypeClass)
D   TypeName                          Like(t_TypeName)
D   Lng                               Like(t_Lng)
D   Lat                               Like(t_Lat)
D   Distance                          Like(t_Distance)

D t_Status        DS                  Qualified
D   Message                     50A
D   Value                        3A

D t_Name          S             50A
```

Continued

```
D t_TypeClass       S                50A
D t_TypeName        S                50A
D t_Distance        S                 4  2
D t_Lng             S                15A
D t_Lat             S                15A
D t_ErrCode         S                 4  0
D t_ErrMsg          S                50A
D t_NbrElems        S                 2  0
```

Naturally, I also had to include it in the new procedure's parameters:

```
PRtvPOIFrmGPS       B                        EXPORT
D                   PI              N
 * Input Parms
DP_Lat                                       Like(t_Lat) Value
DP_Lng                                       Like(t_Lng) Value
 * Output Parms
DP_Poi_DS                                    LikeDS(t_Poi) Dim(C_MaxElems)
DP_NbrElems                                  Like(t_NbrElems)
DP_ErrCode                                   Like(t_ErrCode)
DP_ErrMsg                                    Like(t_ErrMsg)
```

I'll explain the rest of the procedure's parameters later. For now, notice the *Dim(C_MaxElems)*. This turns the data structure into an array, which fits our needs, but it requires additional coding when passing the values from the *GeoNames.Poi* data structure to the *P_Poi_DS* parameter:

```
For W_Idx = 1 to C_MaxElems;
  If Geonames.Poi(W_Idx).TypeClass <> *Blanks;
    P_Poi_DS(W_Idx).Name = Geonames.Poi(W_Idx).Name;
    P_Poi_DS(W_Idx).TypeClass = Geonames.Poi(W_Idx).TypeClass;
    P_Poi_DS(W_Idx).TypeName = Geonames.Poi(W_Idx).TypeName;
    P_Poi_DS(W_Idx).Lng = Geonames.Poi(W_Idx).Lng;
    P_Poi_DS(W_Idx).Lat = Geonames.Poi(W_Idx).Lat;
    P_Poi_DS(W_Idx).Distance = Geonames.Poi(W_Idx).Distance;
    P_NbrElems += 1;
                                                          Continued
```

```
  Else;
    Leave;
  EndIf;
EndFor;
```

Here, I'm looping through the *GeoNames.Poi* array until one of two things happens: either the last element in the array is reached, or the current element of the array doesn't contain a POI. *C_MaxElems* is a numeric constant, set to 20 in *QCPYLESRC/RTVFNP_PR*. During my tests, I never got more than 10 POIs from the Web service, regardless of the GPS coordinates.

Now for the procedure itself. As usual, you'll be able to call it from an *IF* statement, because it returns **ON* if something goes wrong. Here's an example:

```
If RtvPOIFrmGPS(P_Latitude : P_Longitude :
                P_Poi_DS: P_NbrElems:
                P_ErrCode : P_ErrMsg ) = *Off;
  // Do something with P_Poi_DS and P_NbrElems
EndIf;
```

The procedure's parameters include the same *P_Latitude*, *P_Longitude*, *P_ErrCode*, and *P_ErrMsg* as the first two procedures in this chapter. The specifics here are the *P_Poi_DS* and *P_NbrElems*. This last parameter contains the number of elements of the *P_Poi_DS* array that contain data. Even though the maximum number of elements of the array is set to 20 (*C_MaxElems*), that doesn't mean you'll always get 20 POIs. Actually, depending on how precise your GPS coordinates are (i.e., how many "decimal places" your coordinates have), you might receive an empty array, in the worst-case scenario. As I said before, the maximum I got during my tests was 10 POIs, but I couldn't get feedback from GeoNames or OpenStreetMap about the maximum number of POIs the Web service returns.

The rest of the procedure follows the same format as the previous procedures in this chapter. However, since *P_Poi_DS* is an array, some special handling was required. I've already mentioned how the values are passed from the *GeoNames.Poi* array to *P_Poi_DS*, but there's more. For your convenience, I've bolded those lines in the procedure's complete source code:

```
HDatEdit(*YMD)  NoMain   ExprOpts(*MaxDigits) BndDir('HTTPAPI':'RTVFNP')

 ***************************************************************************
 *                                                                         *
 *   Program .... : RTVFNP                                                 *
 *   Description  : Find Nearby POIs Procedures                           *
 *   Author ..... : Rafael Victoria-Pereira                                *
 *   Date ....... : July 2011                                              *
 *   Changes .... :                                                        *
 *=========================================================================*

 ***************************************************************************

 *-------------------------------------------------------------------------*
 *   File Descriptions                                                     *
 *-------------------------------------------------------------------------*
FLog       O    E           K Disk    Prefix(Log_) UsrOpn

 *--------------------------------------------------------------------------
 *   Data Areas
 *--------------------------------------------------------------------------
 * GeoNames ID
D DAGeoNamesID    S             10A   DTAARA(DAGeoNID)
 * GeoNames Find Nearby POIs API base URL
D DAFPApiBaseUrl  S             50A   DTAARA(DAGeoFPURL)

 *-------------------------------------------------------------------------*
 *   Variables                                                             *
 *-------------------------------------------------------------------------*
 * Work Fields
 /define WEBFORMS
D W_FileName      S             45A   Varying
D W_Options       S            100A   Varying
D W_RetCode       S             10I 0
D W_GeoNamesID    S             10A   Inz
D W_ApiBaseUrl    S             50A   Inz
```

Continued

```
D W_URL          S          32767A   Varying
D W_Form         S                   Like(WEBFORM)
D W_Return       S              1N   Inz
D W_Idx          S              2  0 Inz

 *-------------------------------------------------------------------------*
 *   Prototypes                                                            *
 *-------------------------------------------------------------------------*
 * Prototype definition for HTTP API Procedures
 /Copy QRPGLESRC,HTTPAPI_H
 /Copy QRPGLESRC,IFSIO_H
 * Prototype definition for Find Nearby POIs Procedures
 /Copy QCPYLESRC,RTVFNP_PR

 *-------------------------------------------------------------------------*
 *   Retrieve POIs from GPS coordinates (Find Nearby POIs)               *
 *-------------------------------------------------------------------------*
PRtvPOIFrmGPS    B                   EXPORT
D                PI             N
 * Input Parms
DP_Lat                               Like(t_Lat) Value
DP_Lng                               Like(t_Lng) Value
 * Output Parms
DP_Poi_DS                            LikeDS(t_Poi) Dim(C_MaxElems)
DP_NbrElems                          Like(t_NbrElems)
DP_ErrCode                           Like(t_ErrCode)
DP_ErrMsg                            Like(t_ErrMsg)

 /FREE

     ExSr Init;

     ExSr Process;

    //  Sub Routines
```

Continued

```
//--------------------------------------------------------------------*
// Initialization                                                     *
//--------------------------------------------------------------------*
 BegSr  Init;

   // Initialize output parameters
   Clear P_Poi_DS;
   P_NbrElems      = *Zeros;
   P_ErrCode       = *Zeros;
   P_ErrMsg        = *Blanks;

   // Retrieve GeoNames ID
   In DAGeoNamesID;
   W_GeoNamesID = DAGeoNamesID;
   // Check If the GeoNames ID is filled in
   If W_GeoNamesID = *Blanks;
     P_ErrCode = 300; //Invalid GeoNames ID
     W_Return = *ON;
     ExSr End_And_Return;
   EndIf;

   // Retrieve GeoNames Find Nearby POIs API base url
   In DAFPApiBaseUrl;
   W_ApiBaseUrl = DAFPApiBaseUrl;
   // Check If the GeoNames Find Nearby POIs API base url is filled in
   If W_ApiBaseUrl = *Blanks;
     P_ErrCode = 350; //Invalid GeoNames Find Nearby POIs API base url
     W_Return = *ON;
     ExSr End_And_Return;
   EndIf;

   // Prepare parameters for XML-INTO
   W_Options = 'doc=file +
          path=GEONAMES +
         case=any +
          allowextra=yes +
```

Continued

```
        allowmissing=yes';

    // Compose the WebService URL with the address and your GeoNames ID
    W_Form = WEBFORM_open();
    WEBFORM_setVar(W_Form : 'lat'    : %Trim(P_Lat)  );
    WEBFORM_setVar(W_Form : 'lng'    : %Trim(P_Lng) );
    WEBFORM_setVar(W_Form : 'username' : %Trim(W_GeoNamesID) );

    W_Url = %Trim(W_ApiBaseUrl) + WEBFORM_getData(W_Form);

    // Close form
    WEBFORM_Close(W_Form);

    // Create a temp file to receive the WebService response
    W_FileName = http_tempfile() + '.xml';

    // Initialize the GeoNames array to avoid errors in unused fields
    Clear GeoNames;

  EndSr;

//-------------------------------------------------------------------*
// Invoke Web Service and return POIs                                *
//-------------------------------------------------------------------*
  BegSr  Process;

    // Invoke the WebService
    W_RetCode = http_url_get(W_url : W_FileName);

    // In case of error,  return *ON
    If (W_RetCode <> 1);
      P_ErrCode = 400; //Problems invoking the Web Service
      W_Return = *ON;
      ExSr End_And_Return;
    EndIf;
```

Continued

```
// Receive xml file into data structure
Monitor;
  Xml-Into GeoNames %xml(W_FileName : W_Options);
On-Error;
  P_ErrCode = 500; //Malformed xml
  W_Return = *ON;
  ExSr End_And_Return;
EndMon;

// Check for API errors before processing
// In case of API error, return the error message and leave
If Geonames.status.message <> *Blanks;
  P_ErrMsg = GeoNames.status.message;
  P_ErrCode = 600; //API error, check the error message
  W_Return = *ON;
  ExSr End_And_Return;
Else;

// Otherwise, pass the results to the output parms
For W_Idx = 1 to C_MaxElems;
  If Geonames.Poi(W_Idx).TypeClass <> *Blanks;
    P_Poi_DS(W_Idx).Name = Geonames.Poi(W_Idx).Name;
    P_Poi_DS(W_Idx).TypeClass = Geonames.Poi(W_Idx).TypeClass;
    P_Poi_DS(W_Idx).TypeName = Geonames.Poi(W_Idx).TypeName;
    P_Poi_DS(W_Idx).Lng = Geonames.Poi(W_Idx).Lng;
    P_Poi_DS(W_Idx).Lat = Geonames.Poi(W_Idx).Lat;
    P_Poi_DS(W_Idx).Distance = Geonames.Poi(W_Idx).Distance;
    P_NbrElems += 1;
  Else;
    Leave;
  EndIf;
EndFor;
P_ErrCode   = *Zeros;
P_ErrMsg    = *Blanks;
W_Return = *Off;
ExSr End_And_Return;
```

Continued

```
    EndIf;

  EndSr;

//-----------------------------------------------------------------------*
//  End and Return                                                       *
//-----------------------------------------------------------------------*
  BegSr End_And_Return;

    // Log status (useful for debuging)
    ExSr Log_Status;

    // Delete temp file
    unlink(W_FileName);

    // End and return the indicator (*on = error / *off = success)
    Return W_Return;

  EndSr;

//-----------------------------------------------------------------------*
//  Log status                                                           *
//-----------------------------------------------------------------------*
  BegSr Log_Status;

    // Log request
    Open Log;
    Log_TypeReq = 'RtvPOIFrmGPS';
    Log_StsCode = P_ErrCode;
    Log_InpParm = 'Latitude=' + %Trim(P_Lat) +
                  '|Longitude=' + %Trim(P_Lng);
    Log_OutParm = 'Elems=' + %Trim(%Char(P_NbrElems))
                   + '|Name(1)=' + %Trim(P_Poi_DS(1).Name)
                   + '|TypeClass(1)=' + %Trim(P_Poi_DS(1).TypeClass)
                   + '|TypeName(1)=' + %Trim(P_Poi_DS(1).TypeName)
                   + '|Latitude(1)=' + %Trim(P_Poi_DS(1).Lat)
```

Continued

```
                        + '|Longitude(1)=' + %Trim(P_Poi_DS(1).Lng)
                        + '|Distance(1)='
                        + %Trim(%Char(P_Poi_DS(1).Distance));
       Log_DateTim = %TimeStamp;
       Write LogR;
       Close Log;

     EndSr;
 /END-FREE

PRtvPOIFrmGPS      E
```

In the previous section, I demonstrated the usefulness of the *Log_Status* routine. I'd like to add a little something to that, specific to this procedure. As I said before, we don't know how many POIs the Web service will return; it depends on the GPS coordinates you provide. However, if 10 POIs are returned (the maximum I got during my tests), the *OutParm* field of the *LOG* file is not able to store the complete set of data. For that reason, I'm just writing the total number of elements returned (*P_NbrElems*) and the first element of the *P_Poi_DS*. It's not a perfect solution, but it's still enough to determine if a problem occurred. If you really want to store the complete *P_Poi_DS* array in the *LOG* file, just do the math and extend *OutParm* accordingly.

Finally, let's review the example provided in the *QRPGLESRC/TST_FNPADD* source member:

```
H DECEDIT(',') DATEDIT(*DMY.)

 * Retrieve GPS Info Procedures
 /Copy QCPYLESRC,RTVGPS_PR
 * Retrieve Find Nearby POIs Procedures
 /Copy QCPYLESRC,RTVFNP_PR

DW_Response       S             52A   Inz(*Blanks)

 /FREE
```
Continued

```
   // Here I'll retrieve the Points of Interest near an address
   // in a two-step process:
   // First, retrieve the GPS coordinates of the address
   // (US largest mall, according to the Wikipedia...)
   P_Address = 'King Of Prussia, Pennsylvania';
   If RtvGpsFrmAddr(P_Address :
                    P_Quality :
                    P_Latitude :
                    P_Longitude :
                    P_ErrorCode) = *Off;
   // Second, use the coordinates to retrieve the POIs near those coordinates
      If RtvPOIFrmGPS(P_Latitude :
                      P_Longitude :
                      P_Poi_DS:
                      P_NbrElems:
                      P_ErrCode :
                      P_ErrMsg ) = *Off;
        W_Response = 'NbrElems = ' + %Trim(%Char(P_NbrElems)) +
                     '|First POI Name = ' + %Trim(P_Poi_DS(1).Name);
      Else;
        // Error occurred in the RtvPOIFrmGPS Procedure
        W_Response = 'RtvPOIFrmGPS Error Code = ' +
                      %Char(P_ErrCode);
        Dsply W_Response;
      EndIf;
   Else;
      // Error occurred in the RtvGPSFrmAddr procedure
      W_Response = 'RtvGPS Error Code = ' + %Char(P_ErrorCode);
      Dsply W_Response;
   EndIf;

   *InLr = *On;
/END-FREE
```

It shows the usual orchestration of Web services, starting with an address (in this case, of the biggest mall in the United States, according to Wikipedia). For simplicity's sake, the example lists the name of only the first POI found, but you should be clear enough now on how to use the *P_Poi_DS* array.

Even though this is a simple example, it illustrates how you can integrate this Web service into your application. I foresee this procedure being called from your customer-support applications, thus providing that "special something" that keeps you a step or two ahead of the competition.

The Find Nearby Wikipedia Entries Web Service

As a follow-up to the previous section, this one provides the means to complement the Points of Interest (POI) data with geo-referenced Wikipedia articles. GeoNames has a Web service called Find Nearby Wikipedia Entries that works like Find Nearby POIs, but returns Wikipedia entries related to a location's coordinates. It's available here:

http://www.geonames.org/wikipedia/wikipedia_features.html

Wikipedia is used by millions of people as the reference for . . . well, nearly everything! You can add your own articles to Wikipedia, providing information about your company, shop, subsidiary, office, or whatever. Tasteful articles paint your company in a favorable light, like this example: *http://en.wikipedia.org/wiki/Nordstrom*. Just be sure not to exaggerate.

The Web service has the usual simplicity of GeoNames' REST Web services: you provide the latitude and longitude coordinates, and it returns the basic information about the Wikipedia entry, along with a link to the complete article. For example, the King of Prussia Mall GPS coordinates (latitude 40.090803 and longitude ‑75.384999) from the previous section were used to compose this URL:

```
http://api.geonames.org/findNearbyWikipedia?lat=40.090803&lng=-75.384999&username=demo
```

That returns something similar to this (I removed all entries but one, in order to keep the example simple):

```
<geonames>
<entry>
<lang>en</lang>
<title>King of Prussia Mall</title>
```

Continued

```
<summary>The King of Prussia Mall is the largest shopping mall on the East Coast of
the United States, and largest shopping mall in the United States of America in terms
of leasable retail space. (...)</summary>
<feature>landmark</feature>
<countryCode>US</countryCode>
<elevation>59</elevation>
<lat>40.0883</lat>
<lng>-75.3914</lng>
<wikipediaUrl>http://en.wikipedia.org/wiki/King_of_Prussia_Mall</wikipediaUrl>
<thumbnailImg/>
<rank>94</rank>
<distance>0.609</distance>
</entry>
</geonames>
```

The *<entry>* element is composed of the following sub-elements:

- *<lang>*—This is the language in which the data will be presented. The default is English, but there are other options. I'll discuss the language later.
- *<title>*—This is the title of the Wikipedia entry.
- *<summary>*—This holds a summary of the entry, with a 300-character maximum.
- *<feature>*—This is the type of entry. It's "landmark" in this small example, but it could be anything from a railway station to a mountain or a city. See this list on the GeoNames Web site for more details:

  http://www.geonames.org/wikipedia/wikipedia_features.html

- *<countryCode>*—This is the two-character code for the country. More information is available here:

  http://en.wikipedia.org/wiki/List_of_FIPS_country_codes

- *<elevation>*—This is more or less self-explanatory.
- *<lat>* and *<lng>*—These are the GPS coordinates of the Wikipedia entry. Please note that these are not the input coordinates.
- *<wikipediaUrl>*—This is the link to the full Wikipedia entry.
- *<thumbnailImg>*—This is the link to the thumbnail image related with the article, if one is available. (Good luck finding one; I couldn't.)
- *<rank>*—This is the rank of the Wikipedia entry, ranging from zero (worst) to 100 (best).

- *<distance>*—This is the distance between the input coordinates and the ones related to the Wikipedia entry

As in previous sections, I've created a procedure that can be easily called from your program:

```
If RtvWEFrmGPS(P_Latitude :
               P_Longitude :
               P_WE_DS :
               P_NbrElems:
               P_ErrCode :
               P_ErrMsg ) = *Off;
// Use the P_WE_DS array data
Else;
// something went wrong, check the P_ErrCode and P_ErrMsg to know what
EndIf;
```

P_Latitude and *P_Longitude* are the input parameters, while *P_WE_DS*, *P_NbrElems*, *P_ErrCode*, and *P_ErrMsg* compose the procedure's response.

Let's focus on the last four parameters. As a quick glance at the sample code above hints, *P_ErrCode* and *P_ErrMsg* are the error code and message, used in case something goes wrong when the procedure is invoked. By "goes wrong," I mean a Web service error, failure to access the server (usually caused by a firewall issue), or any other issue. There are a few likely errors handled in the source code, as well as a kind of "catch-all" error.

Finally, *P_WE_DS* is an array composed of most of the Web service response sub-elements. Why not all, you might ask? Well, I found little use for *<thumbnailImg>*. It's almost always empty, and this poses a problem: the XML notation used is not fully compatible with *XML-INTO* (at least not the V5R4M0 version of *XML-INTO*). The empty tag appears as "*<thumbnailImg/>* ", and this notation causes *XML-INTO* to fail. I took a shortcut here by deciding to leave the thumbnail URL out of the *P_WE_DS* array. However, there are PTFs available for V5R4M0 and more recent i5/OS versions to correct this error.

By the way, here's a good way to "debug" a failing *XML-INTO*: remove an element at a time of the data structure that will be receiving the XML. Since the file containing the XML resides in the IFS, you can manipulate it in a text editor to determine which tag is causing the problem. (Any text editor will do, but be careful to keep the XML structure, or you'll end up with an invalid XML document.)

As you probably noticed, *P_WE_DS* is conceptually similar to the previous section's *P_Poi_DS*. This was a huge help when creating the *RtvWEFrmGPS* procedure. Naturally, some adaptations were required. Check out the complete source code below, and see if you can spot those differences. Have a little fun, playing "Where's Wally" with a source (OK, you can call me a nerd . . . .):

```
HDatEdit(*YMD)  NoMain   ExprOpts(*MaxDigits) BndDir('HTTPAPI':'RTVFNW')
 *************************************************************************
 *                                                                       *
 *   Program .... : RTVFNW                                               *
 *   Description  : Find Nearby Wikipedia Entries Procedures             *
 *   Author ..... : Rafael Victoria-Pereira                              *
 *   Date ....... : September 2011                                       *
 *   Changes .... :                                                      *
 *=======================================================================*

 *************************************************************************

 *-----------------------------------------------------------------------*
 *   File Descriptions                                                   *
 *-----------------------------------------------------------------------*
FLog       O   E           K Disk    Prefix(Log_) UsrOpn

 *-----------------------------------------------------------------------
 *   Data Areas
 *-----------------------------------------------------------------------
 * GeoNames ID
D DAGeoNamesID    S             10A   DTAARA(DAGeoNID)
 * GeoNames Find Nearby Wikipedia Entries API base URL
D DAFWApiBaseUrl  S             50A   DTAARA(DAGeoFWURL)

                                                              Continued
```

```
 *-----------------------------------------------------------------------*
 *   Variables                                                           *
 *-----------------------------------------------------------------------*
 * Work Fields
 /define WEBFORMS
D W_FileName      S             45A   Varying
D W_Options       S            100A   Varying
D W_RetCode       S             10I 0
D W_GeoNamesID    S             10A   Inz
D W_ApiBaseUrl    S             50A   Inz
D W_URL           S          32767A   Varying
D W_Form          S                   Like(WEBFORM)
D W_Return        S              1N   Inz
D W_Idx           S              2  0 Inz

 *-----------------------------------------------------------------------*
 *   Prototypes                                                          *
 *-----------------------------------------------------------------------*
 * Prototype definition for HTTP API Procedures
 /Copy QRPGLESRC,HTTPAPI_H
 /Copy QRPGLESRC,IFSIO_H
 * Prototype definition for Find NearBy Wikipedia Entries Procedures
 /Copy QCPYLESRC,RTVFNW_PR

 *-----------------------------------------------------------------------*
 *   Retrieve Wikipedia Entries from GPS coordinates (Find NearBy Wikis) *
 *-----------------------------------------------------------------------*
PRtvWEFrmGPS      B                   EXPORT
D                 PI              N
 * Input Parms
DP_Lat                                Like(t_Lat) Value
DP_Lng                                Like(t_Lng) Value
 * Output Parms
DP_WE_DS                              LikeDS(t_WE) Dim(C_MaxElems)
DP_NbrElems                           Like(t_NbrElems)
```

Continued

```
DP_ErrCode                                   Like(t_ErrCode)
DP_ErrMsg                                    Like(t_ErrMsg)

 /FREE

     ExSr Init;

     ExSr Process;

   //  Sub Routines

   //-----------------------------------------------------------------*
   //  Initialization                                                 *
   //-----------------------------------------------------------------*
      BegSr  Init;

        // Initialize output parameters
        Clear P_WE_DS;
        P_NbrElems     = *Zeros;
        P_ErrCode      = *Zeros;
        P_ErrMsg       = *Blanks;

        // Retrieve GeoNames ID
        In DAGeoNamesID;
        W_GeoNamesID = DAGeoNamesID;
        // Check If the GeoNames ID is filled in
        If W_GeoNamesID = *Blanks;
          P_ErrCode = 300; //Invalid GeoNames ID
          W_Return = *ON;
          ExSr End_And_Return;
        EndIf;

        // Retrieve GeoNames Find Nearby Wikis API base url
        In DAFWApiBaseUrl;
        W_ApiBaseUrl = DAFWApiBaseUrl;
        // Check If the GeoNames Find Nearby Wikis API base url is filled in
```

Continued

```
    If W_ApiBaseUrl = *Blanks;
      P_ErrCode = 350; //Invalid GeoNames Find Nearby Wikis API base url
      W_Return = *ON;
      ExSr End_And_Return;
    EndIf;

    // Prepare parameters for XML-INTO
    W_Options = 'doc=file +
           path=GEONAMES +
           case=any +
           allowextra=yes +
           allowmissing=yes';

    // Compose the WebService URL with the address and your GeoNames ID
    W_Form = WEBFORM_open();
    WEBFORM_setVar(W_Form : 'lat'    : %Trim(P_Lat)  );
    WEBFORM_setVar(W_Form : 'lng'    : %Trim(P_Lng) );
    WEBFORM_setVar(W_Form : 'username' : %Trim(W_GeoNamesID) );

    W_Url = %Trim(W_ApiBaseUrl) + WEBFORM_getData(W_Form);

    // Close form
    WEBFORM_Close(W_Form);

    // Create a temp file to receive the WebService response
    W_FileName = http_tempfile() + '.xml';

    // Initialize the GeoNames array to avoid errors in unused fields
    Clear GeoNames;

  EndSr;

//-----------------------------------------------------------------*
// Invoke Web Service and return POIs                              *
//-----------------------------------------------------------------*
  BegSr  Process;
```

Continued

```
// Invoke the WebService
W_RetCode = http_url_get(W_url : W_FileName);

// In case of error, return *ON
If (W_RetCode <> 1);
  P_ErrCode = 400; //Problems invoking the Web Service
  W_Return = *ON;
  ExSr End_And_Return;
EndIf;

// Receive xml file into data structure
Monitor;
  Xml-Into GeoNames %xml(W_FileName : W_Options);
On-Error;
  P_ErrCode = 500; //Malformed xml
  W_Return = *ON;
  ExSr End_And_Return;
EndMon;

// Check for API errors before processing
// In case of API error, return the error message and leave
If Geonames.status.message <> *Blanks;
  P_ErrMsg = GeoNames.status.message;
  P_ErrCode = 600; //API error, check the error message
  W_Return = *ON;
  ExSr End_And_Return;
Else;

// Otherwise, pass the results to the output parms
  For W_Idx = 1 to C_MaxElems;
    If Geonames.Entry(W_Idx).Title <> *Blanks;
      P_WE_DS(W_Idx).Lang = Geonames.Entry(W_Idx).Lang;
      P_WE_DS(W_Idx).Title = Geonames.Entry(W_Idx).Title;
      P_WE_DS(W_Idx).Summary = Geonames.Entry(W_Idx).Summary;
      P_WE_DS(W_Idx).Feature = Geonames.Entry(W_Idx).Feature;
```

Continued

```
          P_WE_DS(W_Idx).CountryCode =
                                     Geonames.Entry(W_Idx).CountryCode;
          P_WE_DS(W_Idx).Elevation = Geonames.Entry(W_Idx).Elevation;
          P_WE_DS(W_Idx).Lng = Geonames.Entry(W_Idx).Lng;
          P_WE_DS(W_Idx).Lat = Geonames.Entry(W_Idx).Lat;
          P_WE_DS(W_Idx).WikipediaURL =
                                    Geonames.Entry(W_Idx).WikipediaURL;
          P_WE_DS(W_Idx).Rank = Geonames.Entry(W_Idx).Rank;
          P_WE_DS(W_Idx).Distance = Geonames.Entry(W_Idx).Distance;
          P_NbrElems += 1;
        Else;
          Leave;
        EndIf;
      EndFor;
      P_ErrCode   = *Zeros;
      P_ErrMsg    = *Blanks;
      W_Return = *Off;
      ExSr End_And_Return;
    EndIf;

  EndSr;

//-----------------------------------------------------------------*
//  End and Return                                                 *
//-----------------------------------------------------------------*
  BegSr End_And_Return;

    // Log status (useful for debuging)
    ExSr Log_Status;

    // Delete temp file
    unlink(W_FileName);

    // End and return the indicator (*on = error / *off = success)
    Return W_Return;
```

Continued

```
      EndSr;
    //------------------------------------------------------------------*
    //  Log status                                                      *
    //------------------------------------------------------------------*
      BegSr Log_Status;

        // Log request
        Open Log;
        Log_TypeReq = 'RtvWEFrmGPS';
        Log_StsCode = P_ErrCode;
        Log_InpParm = 'Latitude=' + %Trim(P_Lat) +
                      '|Longitude=' + %Trim(P_Lng);
        Log_OutParm = 'Elems=' + %Trim(%Char(P_NbrElems))
                      + '|Title(1)=' + %Trim(P_WE_DS(1).Title)
                      + '|Feature(1)=' + %Trim(P_WE_DS(1).Feature)
                      + '|Latitude(1)=' + %Trim(P_WE_DS(1).Lat)
                      + '|Longitude(1)=' + %Trim(P_WE_DS(1).Lng)
                      + '|Distance(1)='
                      + %Trim(%Char(P_WE_DS(1).Distance));
        Log_DateTim = %TimeStamp;
        Write LogR;
        Close Log;

      EndSr;
  /END-FREE

PRtvWEFrmGPS      E
```

That's about all regarding this procedure, because its inner workings are similar to the procedure explained in the previous section. Instead, let's discuss possible enhancements to it. Wikipedia contains articles written in 240 languages, and the GeoNames database has geo-referenced articles in about 230 of those. This Web service offers an additional input parameter: the language code. To use it, you just have to add *&lang=<languagecode>* to the invocation of the Web service. If you don't specify it, the results will be presented in English. Truth be told, a vast majority of the Wikipedia articles are in English, but there are also significant quantities of articles in Dutch, French, German, Italian, and Portuguese.

So, how can you include this extra parameter in the procedure? It's quite simple, actually. Look for the *WEBFORM_setVar . . .* lines in the *QRPGLESRC/RTVFNW* member, and simply add a new *WEBFORM_setVar . . .* line with *'lang'* and whichever language code you want, such as *'pt'* (Portuguese) for instance:

```
W_Lang = 'pt';
WEBFORM_setVar(W_Form : 'lang' : %Trim(W_Lang) );
```

You can also use the postal code instead of the latitude/longitude as an input parameter. In this case, be sure to also add the country code as an input parameter, as well, since you might get results from multiple countries.

Let's finish with an example, which you can find in the *QRPGLESRC/TST_FNWADD* source member:

```
H DECEDIT(',') DATEDIT(*DMY.)

 * Retrieve GPS Info Procedures
 /Copy QCPYLESRC,RTVGPS_PR
 * Retrieve Find Nearby Wikipedia Entries Procedures
 /Copy QCPYLESRC,RTVFNW_PR

DW_Response       S              52A   Inz(*Blanks)

 /FREE
   // Here I'll retrieve the Wikipedia Entries near an address
   // in a two-step process:
   // First, retrieve the GPS coordinates of the address
   // (US largest mall, according to the Wikipedia...)
   P_Address = 'King Of Prussia, Pennsylvania';
   If RtvGpsFrmAddr(P_Address :
                    P_Quality :
                    P_Latitude :
                    P_Longitude :
                    P_ErrorCode) = *Off;
```

Continued

```
    // Second, use the coordinates to retrieve the Wikipedia Entries
    // near those coordinates
       If RtvWEFrmGPS(P_Latitude :
                      P_Longitude :
                      P_WE_DS:
                      P_NbrElems:
                      P_ErrCode :
                      P_ErrMsg ) = *Off;
         W_Response = 'NbrElems = ' + %Trim(%Char(P_NbrElems)) +
                    '|First Wiki Entry Title= ' + %Trim(P_WE_DS(1).Title);
       Else;
         // Error occurred in the RtvWEFrmGPS Procedure
         W_Response = 'RtvWEFrmGPS Error Code = ' +
                      %Char(P_ErrCode);
         Dsply W_Response;
       EndIf;
    Else;
       // Error occurred in the RtvGPSFrmAddr procedure
       W_Response = 'RtvGPS Error Code = ' + %Char(P_ErrorCode);
       Dsply W_Response;
    EndIf;

    *InLr = *On;
 /END-FREE
```

This is very similar to last section's *TST_FNPADD*. It takes an address, determines its GPS coordinates, and retrieves the Wikipedia entries close to those coordinates. Even though it's simple, it serves the purpose of showing the possibilities this Web service brings: creating goodwill for your company, presenting subliminal advertising for one of your products . . . you name it! The sky's the limit!

Final Thoughts

This chapter presented only a few of the great Web services that GeoNames provides freely, but I think it's enough to give you some great ideas of how to build your own procedures. If you read the whole chapter, you should have a good handle on the mechanics of creating a procedure to invoke a GeoNames Web service and process its results.

Keep in mind that some of the Web services require orchestration with other Web services to work, as their input parameters are GPS coordinates or some sort of code. I'd recommend that you go over GeoNames' complete list of Web services at *http://www.geonames.org/export/ws-overview.html*. You'll probably find that a lot of them can be useful for your business.

Index

A

D

E

H

Q

R

X

Y